***Dedication:

I dedicate this book to:

- My only one daughter Hannah Sarah Razban and my wife Dana Razban. They were patient and understanding to let me spend a lot of time and effort needed for writing of this book. They encouraged me throughout the eight years that it took to complete this book. My love for them is forever.
- Loving memory of my father, Dr. Eshagh (Isaac) Razban, one of the best and most compassionate MDs, and my mother Maliheh (Miriam) who was one of the most active humanitarians in our community. In addition to being loving parents, they also were teachers, and friends to me.
- My great grandfather, Ezra. He pioneered international business. My mother told me many stories about this exceptionally intelligent, daring, well-educated and humanitarian man. Indeed, he is a pioneering Executive and CEO that I have known of since childhood.
- My only one brother, Dr. Bob Razban, and only one sister Aria Razban.
- My uncles, aunts, and extended family and friends living all around the world.

***PROLOG:

I am a Senior Program and Technology Consultant in Silicon Valley, California, and I am a first time author. I spent eight years writing this book. It started the moment that I was angry enough to put my feelings and my management experience in writing. I am confident that my experiences will benefit others. It is my sincere hope that my 32 years of management experience in the often-volatile high-tech industry, will help others better cope with such painful events as layoffs and unemployment. The economic crisis of 2009 has proven to me that there is a better way. I have personally suffered through the disruptive boom and bust of industry economic cycles. I have had to lay off valuable employees and have witnessed the devastation Sudden Job Loss (SJL) has on those individuals and their families. I have personally experienced layoffs and SJL. I remember the shame, remorse, helplessness, loss of self-worth, and anger directed at myself and directed at my former employer. Their seemingly betrayal and lack of appreciation for the hard work that performed for them made me angry.

My passion for being a top notch and people oriented manager, and many years of study and hundreds of books and discussions, has lead me to believe that all of us deserve better than:

- Wasting $2.4 Trillion each year in US alone,
- Having 50 million people without jobs on a global basis,
- Having 40% or more of us unhappy with our jobs!

Following my great grandfather Ezra's lead, I have dared to take the human pain and financial waste resulting from the way things are now, and propose a blueprint for:

- 107.8% employment,
- SOX-based SOAR self-governess,
- Human Capital and Information amendments to Capitalism,
- Multiple best practices on how to prevent or at least minimize layoffs,
- Many other alternatives to revolving door "At Will" hire, fire practice.

I have chosen these by using the most recent state-of-the-art management technology such as Six Sigma Root Cause Analysis, HP Way, and Agile Management. Yet, to make this reading interesting, it is a factual storytelling. It is entertaining description of what is wrong. It also tells us how we with teamwork, we can fix these problems in a practical way. It is like a novel, with me, my career, and my experience as the characters in this fiction-like story telling that is indeed pure facts.

The real message of this book is hope and inspiration for a practical, better, and win-win work place in spite all the hardships.

I like all of us to have a song in our hearts as life is much too short and too precious to waste on fussing and fighting in the work place. I share with you some of my best and worst work place experiences to build understanding on how good things can be and how practical it is to fix problems.

This book is unique from other books on this difficult subject of unemployment and unhappy employment. This is because it does take into account and deals in the most humanly possible with our feelings. However, business and economic analysis of these normal human feelings empowers and motivates us. I have come to realize that while such feelings are normal and natural, they can be counterproductive. In this book, I have addressed practical methods I have found based on my own and many other people's experience. These practical methods almost guarantee success in coming to terms with Sudden Job Loss (SJL).

I will provide you with helpful techniques that I have found to be helpful in combating feelings of depression, anger and guilt. In addition, I will offer advice and inspiration for making a better work life for ourselves.

Copyright © 2008 - 2009 Razban Internet International, Inc. All rights reserved, File:20091022, P a g e | **2**

Table of Contents:

Copyright © 2008 - 2009 Razban Internet International, Inc. All rights reserved, File:20091022, P a g e | **3**

Copyright © 2008 - 2009 Razban Internet International, Inc. All rights reserved, File:20091022, P a g e | **4**

INTRODUCTION:

I tell my honest first-hand story of layoffs, management crisis, and badly needed re-invention of Capitalism that makes work places toxic and dysfunctional. Each year $2.4 Trillion is wasted. Fifty million are joblessness and hopeless around the world. My story is of a laid off employee and as a senior manager who had to hand out pink slips. After almost thirty years of management, I prove that layoff pain is too much for everyone. The present work place is bad for the company management, employees, customers, and the economy in general. This uplifting book offers help, and inspires us to prepare for the work life of the future.

However, there is plenty of hope, inspiration, and solutions offered in this book on how to cope and even prosper from this foolishness, madness, and dysfunctional situation. The employee goes thru a crushing, depressing, and demoralizing experience. The company also goes thru similar experience, which adversely affects business and revenue. Considering the painful human impact and negative long-term company loss, I am sure that there must be a better way.

This book was written to reduce the pain of the working-class audience that is either afraid of layoffs or affected by it. By analyzing layoffs, we can better understand them and lower the pain and negative impact to companies. I found "Fear of Sudden Job Loss (SJL)" and the associated Pink Shock as the main culprit. Fear of Sudden Job Loss Syndrome, is one of the fundamental causes of serious dysfunctional companies, unhappy employees and management. I describe how you can recognize it, and how to proactively cope, recover and even grow in spite of it.

In addition, since this book was partially written during my four hours commute, I decided to make it commuter friendly be having shorter chapters that can be read during your commute (of course assuming you are not driving.) This way you will not lose your place in the book either. Moreover, for those who driver, there are plans to generate an audio book soon after publication of this.

This book is divided into four sections.

Section 1:

First, I share with you my best job ever and how great it was. I will point out a few things that I experienced in this best job. Then I will share how, when employees felt the same things and experienced elsewhere, they caused a great deal of job satisfaction. Increased job security created much higher productivity for the company that made it a win-win situation for all. These are all based on more than thirty years of experience.

Next, I will give you a tour of what typically happens in many of the layoffs in general and those that I was either affected by or those I had to do myself as a manager. I even try to inject a little sense of humor to reduce the pain. My experience is that layoffs cost companies, communities, employees, as well as customers, a great deal in the long term. Nevertheless, unfortunately the shortsighted justification is that this is a cost-saving measure. In addition, there might be some illusive short-term savings. However, they are more than completely negated in the long term. The Fear of Sudden Job Loss Syndrome is introduced here and compared to the well-known Fear of Flying Syndrome.

What if there was a better way that cost a lot less and was a lot less painful? After all, we are all in business to make money. What if layoff avoidance resulted in substantial

Copyright © 2008 - 2009 Razban Internet International, Inc. All rights reserved, File:20091022, P a g e | **6**

savings too?

Section 2:

A new concept of Mutual Trust and Loyalty (MTL) is introduced. MTL explains the importance of employees and management mutual trust and loyalty and how it exudes into creating customer loyalty. This usually translates into higher profits. Several examples of best practices by companies such as HP, Plantronics, and PG&E are cited for better understanding.

Fear of Sudden Job Loss results in Mutual Trust and Loyalty degradation and erosion that is directly linked to layoffs. This affects branding name recognition, employee and management morale, product and service quality, and customer experience. It results in heavy cost to all parties involved and it is not worth the long-term damage. It is critical to note that we are making a transition from an asset-based to a human- and knowledge-based economy. The same human feelings of despair, anger, and frustration that result in clinical human depression are induced by layoffs. This joblessness and hopelessness will totally permeate in company culture, and become ingrained in it. This is very similar to depression in the organization, and the company, its markets, and revenue will suffer in the long term. In addition, this is responsible for much higher levels of damage in a knowledge-based economy than in asset-based one.

Section 3:

As negative as the first two sections were, Section 3 is the beginning positive side of the discussion of alternative and better solutions: There are many better ways and alternatives to layoffs, work place depression, and fear of sudden job loss! This section offers ways to cope and even benefit from a layoff for employees, proactive ways to prevent layoffs or even completely manage avoidance of layoffs. It also suggests ways consumers can exert more power to make sure companies adhere to some basic practices the same way Sarbanes-Oxley Act of 2002 (SOX) takes care of clean financial transactions in companies.

The book challenges readers, government, and corporate executives to dare to imagine a 107.8% employment as a way not to waste $2.4 Trillion each year in productivity loss and resulting human suffering. In addition, in this section, some proactive and hopefully helpful hints are directed at those employees who are already affected by layoffs, or they are suffering from Fear of Sudden Job Loss and associated Pink Shock.

As much I personally understand the pains involved for this group, I challenge myself and others to cope with the situation, recover, regroup, and even benefit from it. This truly is a major challenge, but *we can overcome this*.

Let us go do this!

Section 4:

A blueprint for the next generation of management and leadership is presented for

Copyright © 2008 - 2009 Razban Internet International, Inc. All rights reserved, File:20091022, P a g e | **7**

maximum profitability. By understanding the new era of the Human- and Knowledge-Based Economy, as opposed to the old Asset-Based economy, a better way is shown that really works for all. The understanding that it is not your fault, that the work place is dysfunctional, and that you were laid off or the company went Chapter 11, will greatly help you to not internalize it. Instead, it helps you to plan and, in fact, get out there and get out of dead-end jobs and use your human potential!

Humans, be aware, this is our era!

In the process, a few amendments to Asset-Based Capitalism are offered that focus on Human and Knowledge power. This section also rejects the illusion that since we live in a Capitalistic society and that, at the end of the day, we are here to make money at any price. This section also refuses to accept that if a company is not making money it should let go of some employees. The author provides convincing arguments that Capitalism, for the lack of a better word as Michael Douglas put it in the movie *Wall Street*, is based on greed. In addition, if greed is a good thing, then let us put it to better use. The better way to use greed to make money, and a lot of it, is to take care of people. People as employees, customers, and management, are the most important part of any company. As evident in many formerly Communist and Socialist countries' efforts in copying Western Capitalism, it seems that the best implementation of Communism and Socialism is in the imperfect and fragile Capitalism that exists. However, it could be much better. In addition, a major revolution has taken place. Most of the old Capitalism that was asset-based now needs to be transformed to being human and knowledge based. I like to call this "Blackberry Revolution." Knowledge is instantly available everywhere, and this empowers people and frees human potential to be a lot more effective. The Executive Summary in this section will help give you a very high-level view of things discussed in this book. At the time of first writing of this book, Wall Street dropped 500 points in one day, Foreclosures are rampant, even in my neighborhood, banks are going out of business, and companies are announcing mass layoffs. I know what these things mean; I have lived in the dysfunctional work place that causes all these and more. Yet I have survived and, along the way, I have learned a few lessons that I want to share with you. This book is meant to inspire you to cope with difficult times and never give up hope in spite all of these awful things around us. Let us have a song in our hearts, plan and work on the future, and we will make it. We will survive, just as the song says, "I will survive!"

Copyright © 2008 - 2009 Razban Internet International, Inc. All rights reserved, File:20091022, P a g e | **8**

ACNOWELDGEMENTS:

I want to sincerely thank many people who have helped me make my life meaningful and productive.

Soraya, a family friend of more than forty-five years, has always been there to help support and encourage me. She was there for me from that first day that I arrived at New York JFK Airport on a KLM flight from Amsterdam at the age of seventeen to start college, and has continued to this day. She has always been there to help, encourage, and provide really effective help for more than forty years. She has been an inspiration to my family and me. She has a law degree and she is extremely positive about life. She has been a great role model regarding the importance of education and the power of empowerment. Every discussion with her, and her family for that matter, has persistently given me hope and inspired me never to give up.

John, who helped me move to California's Silicon Valley and who has been a great friend for more than thirty years. We were classmates in college and took a lot of computer Sciences classes together. He was instrumental in my move to California and working in Silicon Valley. He never, ever refused to talk to me even when the subject concerned most complicated technology or management. John is one of my heroes who, in spite of giant medical challenges, refused to give up hope and literally walked every day to gradually recover from potentially devastating health problems. Also, he is one of the few ex-Californian Oregonians I know who does not complain. He goes for his walks no matter if it rains, and it rains most of the time.

Adam, who helped me find an excellent "Humanist" Venture Capitalist. Adam is a trusted friend and colleague who is always there for our family in the good times and bad. His extensive experience in one of the most famous corporations inspired me to learn and learn, even when I was tired, since my career depended on it!

Hope read one of the very first drafts of my "crazy book" and came up with great suggestions and encouragement that helped me immensely. She is an outstanding technology and management professional with many years of consulting experience.

Susanne was the encouragement that I desperately needed at one of the lowest points in writing this book. Susanne is one of the best Psychotherapists I have known. She told me not to give up since creative work such as writing a book is a great accomplishment.

Dan Crandall, former VP at IICON Corporation and a friend and colleague of more than 25 years provided extremely helpful business and management insight during the entire writing of this book.

Bob Steinberg provided a great deal of encouragement. He reviewed and helped editing two manuscripts. His ability to look beyond the words and comprehend the total picture was needed at the time and that several approaches were being discussed.

Dr. Gil Amelio, the former CEO of National Semiconductor, is forever my hero and mentor in technology and management. He had the courage and insight to transform National Semiconductor from a struggling company into one of the leaders in teaching us Leading Change Leadership and to show us how Teamwork really worked in practice. We gained pride in our company, and job satisfaction went up exponentially. I am forever grateful to him for discussing my product and management ideas at Apple Computer Board of Directors, ideas that might have given Apple the first early signs to think outside the box and think something like iPod. His book, *One Hundred Days on the Firing Line*, again refers to the writings on the doorsteps of a very old church in Europe that says, "Never Give Up!" Our last meeting in the San Jose Executive Airport was monumental to me. He spent a lot of time reviewing my Business Plan. For the first time in my life, I felt like I too had a chance to do great things. For the first time, I was told by someone very important in my career that there is lot more to this life than just career success at any price and the importance of ethics in day-to-day business. He always had time for any of us. I never

Copyright © 2008 - 2009 Razban Internet International, Inc. All rights reserved, File:20091022, P a g e | **9**

forget that he was wrapping Christmas presents, and I asked him if he had five minutes to discuss a "Management Challenge." He agreed, and that particular discussion in the lobby of Building 16 of National Semiconductor, which took more than forty-five minutes, prepared me for a major accomplishment in my career. I am forever grateful to this futurist that I had the honor of knowing.

Shauna, from BookSurge.com, which is a subsidiary of Amazon.com was instrumental in helping me finish this book. On one day I had voicemails and e-mails that were really the incentive to finally put the last touches in the book and get it ready for publications. She was instrumental in helping me make the right decisions regarding the publication of this book. The editing team including Sandy, Lindsey, and Justin were superb in working and working with me to get this done. Special thanks to Ron for editing the final manuscript with infinite patience to read each and every word and sentence.

I also owe a great deal to O'Reilly Publishing house in Sebastopol, California, for their frank and helpful discussion about how to go about publishing a book.

Howard Schultz, the CEO of Starbucks and his book really inspired me to write this book, as well, and really write from my heart. His e-mail in response to my e-mail made me feel like a CEO of a major corporation since he, the CEO of a major corporation, took time himself to respond.

Stanford University Business School continuing education course helped me decide to totally change my career and have the courage to work with the best of the best and go for my passion. University of Wisconsin-Madison that has been my most valued teacher for more than nine years. Not just in classrooms, but also in a grand campus that provides extremely high-quality learning for life.

And to my loves in music, Aretha Franklin, ABBA, Petula Clark, and Cousin Brucie who have helped me put a song in my heart even during the darkest times in my life and career.

Jerry, who was my management and life coach for a very long time, helped immensely during good times and bad times. His timely advice still echoes in my ears. He helped me understand that we are not what we do and to be an excellent manager, you need to know the technical aspects of the job better than anyone else. He taught me about realities of day to day survival and even success in the work place. He was there to listen to my complaints, frustrations, and textbook management solutions. He would listen carefully, but usually he was able to help by providing a practical solution that was time tested, and a solution that one could not find in management books. Many times, he would challenge my thinking and add a new twist that was much better than anything that I had ever imagined before. It was his encouragement that helped me keep up with the latest technology as well as management. He had predicted people losing their homes to foreclosures long before the October of 2008. He was the one who made me actively learn new computer languages and to be at the leading edge. Jerry is my mentor, friend, coach, and life coach. He was a life coach before that term was in common use.

A friend of more than thirty years, Al, has always been a mentor, friend, and a rescuer. He helped me learn the discipline of going to the Memorial Library at the University of Wisconsin campus and study each night. He helped me immensely during one of my darkest days in my education. It was Al who drove me to the Emergency Room and stayed there to make sure I was OK. He would explain the most difficult engineering concepts in easy-to-understand terms. He never gave up on my graduation with Honors, even after I had given up many times. He and our mutual friend, Kam, will always remain as role models. They helped me recover from the near probation situation for taking the most difficult computer sciences class in my first semester, to rejoicing my first time being on the Dean's Honor list.

Very special thanks to Rabbi Wolfe of Australia whose lectures in Meditation helped me re-learn to meditate.

My friend Jamshid, who plans to become a Hajji soon, helped me get my very first "real job" in industry in California. This helped a great deal, just about the time that I had given up my first job

Copyright © 2008 - 2009 Razban Internet International, Inc. All rights reserved, File:20091022. P a g e | 10

search ordeal after graduation and was planning to give up. I was staying in a motel in Santa Cruz, thinking that I would not get the job, when I called him to thank him and say farewell. He was cheerful and encouraged me to wait a few days, as he was optimistic that I should get a job offer. He also took it upon himself to guide me through some very difficult situations at work and at life.

My friend, Ron who is a devout Catholic, taught me that forgiveness and love are foundations of recovery. He too never refused to take my phone calls during the good times or bad.

I will always remember my Dost (Hindi for friend) BN, who gave me a deep understanding of Hinduism basics. My conversations with him regarding Karma and other concepts during our BART commute helped me understand why meditations have been so critical to my spiritual survival in a fast-paced work place.

I would like to give my sincere thanks to my many Persian Sufism Practitioners, Zoroastrian, Shinto, and Baha'i friends and colleagues who enlightened my life and my career.

I owe a great deal of gratitude to Google.com. Google.com is within walking distance from where I live. And their website has provided me great assistance in research and writing of this book. All lyrics in this book and a lot of statistics were found at Google.com. Without Google.com, this book might have been impossible to write! Many music lyrics and basic research was done using their awesome site.

And most importantly the love of my family that is the dearest thing in my life.

I was inspired to write this book by several people. One is the real life hero Santiago that Ernest Hemingway had used to write his book "The Old Man and the Sea." The story of this old man encourages me to work for as long as I am capable of working, no matter how old!

The second source of inspiration for me is Prof. Robert Hutton of Stanford University. One of his management books validated my thoughts that there are a lot of unhappy workers in America and how serious this is.

The third source is Vint (Vinton) Cerf of Goolge.com. As a scientist, he presented so many facts that led me to decide my previous thoughts were all correct. There has been a knowledge revolution just as big as the industrial revolution and we must adapt it in our free-market system. The last is Dr. Gachet who hired a then desperate, half crazed, unknown painter, namely Vincent Van Gogh, and empowered him to do his portrait. This type of compassion is what we need to have more of in our employers. Of course, at the time, Dr. Gachet had no idea that his humanitarian investment in a worker would someday bring an $82.5 million reward. Also, Theo, Vincent's brother who supported him throughout his entire life.

***Section 1:

- Best Managers, and Best Places to Work
- Worst Managers, and Worst Places to Work
- Fear of Sudden Job Loss (SJL)

Copyright © 2008 - 2009 Razban Internet International, Inc. All rights reserved, File:20091022, P a g e | **12**

CHAPTER 1:   Chain of Fools That Wastes as Much as a Stack of $1,000 Bills from Wall Street Building in NYC, to US Capital in Washington D.C.

"Chain of Fools" was one of Aretha Franklin's most successful songs. This song reminds me of the fact that many things are going wrong in the work place today. The result is that 40%, or more of the American and European employees are unhappy with their work. In addition, 50 million people will be unemployed around the world. The chain of fools sounds a good way of describing our present double bind. We have enslaved ourselves with this chain. The very same chain that has enslaved us, also symbolizes global connectivity of everything to everything else. The Internet global connectivity of global markets is chain of interconnectivity. In a way, both meanings of a chain apply to what is happening in the work place: A chain that enslaves us, and a chain that connects all of us together on a global basis. Due to factors discussed in this book, this chain is at a breaking point just like the lyrics of Aretha Franklin song. The daily work place difficulties for the unhappily employed and the unemployed are surpassing our emotional and economic tolerances. In a way, we need to reinvent Capitalism as a way of fixing our work life problems.

This enslaving and interlinking chain causes a $2.4 Trillion waste, which would be a stack of $1,000 bills from Wall Street Building in NYC to the US Capital in Washington D.C. It is that bad! It is ironic that this stack of $1,000 bills goes from the heart of the Capital of Capitalism right to the center of US government. This $2.4 Trillion loss is the productivity loss directly related to "ideal" 4% unemployment.

In order to show you how grave this matter is, I did the following calculation. A Google search shows that According to the U.S. Treasury, a Dollar bill is .0043 inches thick. Therefore, a stack a mile high will be as much as $14 million. Furthermore, according to Google, the driving distance between Washington DC and New York City is about 225 Miles. Then, it does not take a rocket scientist to calculate that a stack of Dollar bills from Wall Street Building in New York City to Building of Congress represents $3.15 Trillion.

As you will see later in this book, unless we change some of our thinking about global economy, we will continue to have the Global Financial Crises like the one that started in May of 2009. Do not get me wrong, I am not blaming government, small businesses, employees, management, unions, or Capitalism. We need to rethink and act, and act quickly to bring in the "Post Internet Global Economic Revolution." The abbreviation for this turns out to be PIGER! As for Capitalism, itself, I think that it is alive and well. However, it needs two badly needed amendments. The root cause in a serious six sigma analysis will prove that the Global Financial Crisis was caused by business and economy leasers and companies and consumers which is all of us, acting like Klots (Yiddish for Clumsy and slow witted.)

The rampant work place violence and employee low morale and work related depression caused by massive layoffs force us to find a better way. This book does just that, it formulates a better way. Otherwise, we will continue our foolish ways that do not work. Revolving door hire fire practices, short-sided Wall Street, CEOs, and companies that are fixated with short term profits, lack of sensitivity for the human sufferings caused by layoffs, and persistent management crises in the work place have contributed to the economic Armageddon or the Tsunami waves of disastrous company and bank failures. This makes it imperative that we understand what is wrong and formulate a solution,

Copyright © 2008 - 2009 Razban Internet International, Inc. All rights reserved, File:20091022, P a g e | **13**

now!

To understand these human suffering problems, and solutions, I have written this unique book in that it expresses human feelings in the context of economy and business. After all, a good manager has to empathize the human side of things as much the economic part. In Aretha Franklin's Chain of Fools song, it says:

<

> "One of these mornings
> That chain is going to break
> But up until then
> I'm going (to) take all I can take, oh yeah"

>

"Chain of fools" captures the idea of foolishness in the workplace. It points out that it is not just one thing but it is a chain of fools. As a professional management consultant, I accept that some of the things I have done as a manager are just plain foolish. I also vividly talk about a breaking point that has been due for quite some time. It makes a mental image of the things that can be so bad that we might feel we are in chains. Unfortunately, as of this writing, the breaking point that I described in this book has become a global reality. I started writing this book in 1976 when I first arrived in California's Silicon Valley. Some thirty-two years later, it seems like most of my nightmares as a manager and an employee are coming true. The sad thing is that it does not have to be this way. Aretha and others, who made this song, really poured their hearts into it. It transmits a painful, high-energy sensation to listeners that can remind them how dysfunctional our work lives have become. The intensive love and care that went into this poetic expression, transfers a sad reality to the listener, and it sets his or her soul on fire. This song is about a chain of fools, with the singer, and therefore all of management stiffs, and us work-a-day workers which we can painfully identify with.

It expresses pain, hurt, sorrow, feelings that we all come across through the suffering that we might feel in a work day, in a typical workplace. The pain is just too much to be blamed on managers or work, or corporations or whatever. Yet this pain is there it is real and it is foolish.

Just as it says in this song, "Someday something is going to happen". I want that "Someday" to be a happy day for all of us. I would like us to have a song in your heart on that very special someday, when you remove these ominous chains. We can remove not just your chains, but also the entire work place chains, one person at a time.

That *someday* that I wrote about in the first writing of this chapter about three years ago, came sooner that I thought. For example, a typical layoff announcement and report from AT&T broke the ominous news in early December that 12,000 jobs, or four percent of the employees, would be without jobs. In a succession of such layoffs, DuPont announced plans to lay off 2,500 employees; Credit Suisse Group slashed 5,300 jobs, and others did similar layoffs.

Before the end of December 2008, Toyota announced that they had lost money. This situation for Toyota, which is a well-run company, is a first since 1941!

On my business trips to Japan, I tried to understand the Japanese monumental success in the economic fronts. Japan was defeated in the World War II, and they had a shattered infrastructure to repair. They overcame and became an example for all other nations. Japanese almost never experienced layoffs prior to 1990s. In fact, I had difficulty to translate or even explain it to Japanese managers that I had met in a Tokyo. In one occasion, a Japanese bank manager and I discussed layoffs during our long San Francisco to Tokyo flight. Of course his English and my Japanese were not so advanced for me to make things clear. After several attempts, he finally started to get the Idea. His reaction, in a combination of surprise and anger was "That American way. Not work in Japan!" I could read in his polite, yet pronounced facial expression that he was deeply against these layoffs. That was in the mid 1980s.

Then the lost decade of 1990s came. Japan's economy prior to 1990s was based on exports benefiting from a favorable exchange rate. High overseas demand for Japanese products such as cars and electronics, old industries, chemicals, steel, cars, and consumer electronics created astonishing windfall wealth.

The introduction of layoff culture, which is as foreign to Japanese as anything, might have resulted Toyota lose money in 2008 for the first time since 1941. Along with exporting McDonalds, we seem to have exported to them the concept of layoffs in and around 1990s. The layoffs side tracked their original human capital based economy to pure asset based. Their denial of knowledge as fundamental enablers of the economy, which is understandable and similar to US, caused serious trouble for the second strongest global economy. The Mutual Trust and Loyalty (MTL) that was embedded and reinforced by the ancient Japanese culture, pride, and community got hurt in the processes.

As horrible as layoffs are in US, they are much more difficult in Japan. The Japanese tradition of one job per life, and the shame related to not having a job is overwhelmingly unbearable. Even if that individual is part of the entire group is laid off, it is personally devastating to a Japanese worker. It is interesting to note that it is equally painful for a Japanese executive as well as an individual contributor. It is well know that a laid off Japanese does the best he or she can to hide the fact that they do not have a job. They even pick up their briefcase and pretend to go to work each day as they had done for ever. Although, there is no job to go to. This has created a surge of suicides in this hard working nation that breaks my heart. A layoff in Japan is like a person losing his or her "Mokato" which is Japanese for dignity, reputation, and humanity. It is a form of dishonor. Dishonor that not only affects the individual, but the entire family.

As for our belief that 4% presents ideal US unemployment, I would like to site Jefferson Airplane's song "Somebody to Love" that says:

<

When the truth is found to be lies
and all the joys within you dies
don't you want somebody to love

>

By challenging this, I like to establish that 4% ideal unemployment is a lie that we have fed ourselves for ever. With the vast US resources, I like to point out that we can do better than this. It just does not have to be this painful way.

Please let me make something clear about McDonalds in Japan. In 1980, when I was in Tokyo, and as much as I love Japanese food, I started to feel homesick for the Big Macs and the Quarter Pounder Burgers. There were no McDonald's in Japan at that time. So, when I got back to San Francisco on my United Airlines flight, I had to stop at the nearest airport and get my fill of the Big Mac, French fries and a large Coke. Of course, this is not the food, especially compared to that previous two weeks that I had very healthy Japanese food that is naturally low in fats. But, I guess this is part of the American experience.

On the positive side, I like to give credit to McDonald's management for creating those $1.00 menu items. This shows that they are in tune with the market and agile enough to realize that they need to something to help so many families that are financially hurting. Their 36 Cents Senior Coffee somehow tastes better than the usual coffee to many seniors that I have seen cherish it. McDonald's is in tune with customers! In my opinion they are a lot more knowledge based than other companies in their rampant use of computers as controllers and dashboard indicators in many of their stores.

McDonalds has also employed retired, older senior, student summer workers, and even disabled workers. McDonald's hired them as if to proudly tell their customers and employees that they cared for the human capital not just things capital.

I got an excellent service and attitude from a disabled worker at McDonald's that I called the 800 number to say thanks and tell the McDonald's Corporation how great this hiring practice was. The reaction from the proud 800 number operator who answered my call was that this particular employee has had several similar good comments about her excellent work! This goes to prove that when a company cares for its employees, the employees also take good care of the customer. Of course, better customer care usually translates into better profits.

To my knowledge, McDonald's is one of the few companies that has done OK in this awful economic times. Needless to say, I do not agree with everything that McDonalds does. But as a senior management consultant and the CEO of a real tiny company, I admire them for these things.

When companies, big and small do not manage themselves well, they end up losing money or not making as much of it as they did before. Then, they routinely have to lay off and fire employees, to balance their books. Consequently, after layoffs they have fewer employees to do the job needed to regain the market they lost in the first place. At the same time, a layoff or firings, has a costly impact on morale. This loss of morale then does make the company produce inferior products and services and lose good employees. In the long term, these all result in even less sales and profits.

In a heated discussion with a reader of my book at a Starbucks Coffee shop, someone told me, "I do not understand all this bellyaching. You might be a management maven (unknown to him, maven has Yiddish meaning too. It means an expert.) They hire us, and then they fire us. Do not talk to me about Mutual Trust and Loyalty. They have none, and I have none. Who cares?" My response was a baffling, "Exactly!"

The annual waste resulting from dysfunctional work places, management crises, layoffs, and general unhappiness amounts to a $2.4 trillion. Statistics show that 40%, or more of the American and European employees are unhappy with their jobs. And, the total number of unemployed people might well reach 50 Million.

If you stacked $1,000,000 of brand new $1,000 bills, it would be only six inches high. As you will see in this book, the present workplace dysfunctional situation resulting in unemployment, underemployment, layoffs, firings, and general unhappiness in the workplace do result in a $2.4 Trillion loss annually. To show how much money this waste is, it would be a stack of $1,000 bills that would start on Wall Street and go the entire 222 or more miles to US Congress. It is that bad.

Copyright © 2008 - 2009 Razban Internet International, Inc. All rights reserved, File:20091022, P a g e | **16**

This book will show that it does not have to be this way. But, since it is the way it is, this book is intended to give you hope and insight, as well as practical advice, on how to cope and/or recover.

CNN reported on May, 8, 2009 that there is 83% higher chance of illness for a laid off employee compared to the one that was not. This study sites heart attacks, strokes, depression and other serious health problems. CNN added that even when a laid off employee finds a job, he or she will still much higher chances of serious illnesses than those who were not laid off.

HP for example refused to lay off a single employee for fifty years. This proves that a company can do as well as HP did and not have to lay off employees. Also, it is a fact that a well-managed company does not really need to resort to layoffs and firings.

In CBS Evening News on August 8,2009, Several companies were mentioned as companies who did everything they could not to lay off any employees during this Global Financial Crisis. These companies were:

- Aflac. According to their CEO Dan Amos, he did "Whatever it took to keep his employees!". One the CEO heroics was that he decided not to get his own bonuses and cancelled his own golden parachute that amounted to $16,000,000. These types of heroics done by management of the company saved 500 jobs. In an interview with an employee, Susan Ough who is one of the 4700 employees, she said that "If they had to lay me off, I would have known that they did everything they could to prevent it". This type of loyalty shown by management is what keeps mutual trust and loyalty alive that creates superior products and services and happy employees that in turn creates high profits.
- Container Store. Tip Kindell, the CEO of Container Store said that "In many companies layoffs are the first thing that a CEO does, just like a knee jerk reaction, instead of being the very last thing after all alternatives are tried".
- Devon Energy Corporation.
- Publix.
- Scottrade.
- NuStar.
- QT (Quick Trip).
- Nugget Markets.
- Stew Leonard's.

I am positive that there are other companies that did the very best they could to preserve jobs. Again, I like to caution you here. I also believe in the same idea as the CEO of Aflac did. He said that while he did everything he could to keep good employees, he "Will let unproductive employee go in a minute." In other words, it all depends on performance. No company can put up with bad employees and survive.

Intel, the world's biggest semiconductor company, the same company that makes the brains for your laptop and other computers, at one point decided to ask everyone to work ten percent harder—without additional pay—since the times were tough. They did this to cope with a down market, and it paid off.

A textile East Coast company that was managed by a bible-quoting CEO caught fire and burned to the ground. The CEO decided to keep paying salaries and quickly rebuilt the company. Employees are human beings. They become more loyal and trust more when the company does the same for them. This will positively increase productivity, reduce costs, and make the company innovative. These are gradients needed for success.

I have to boast about my dentist of many years, Dr. Eggers. He is extremely comfortable with Knowledge and Technology. He was one the early users of TV sets that showed your teeth. You could see the crack that he was talking about, or the decay that had been building for a decade or more.

In one case, he asked me if I wanted to use the latest technology in teeth crowns at the time that I needed one. Without undue pressure, he explained that he will be using a computerized robotic computer controlled device. This latest technology will take a 3D picture of the teeth and will then enable a machine to design a mold and then the new material will be made on the spot. What was amazing was that he himself did all the work instead of having his assistant do it. He was able to explain each and every step to all of us about the magic of the latest technology. It worked and worked extremely well. As I was happily getting ready to get off his chair, he said, "Oh by the way, I know that you do not have dental insurance, I have given you a 20% discount this time since you are a good patient of many years!"

Another trademark of his success is that he and his staff work like a well choreographed dance team. This was particularly important in his last office that space was of a premium. But, the staff would learn from each other to be the best of the best and to do the best of the best. With my Senior Management Consultant eye, I could see that as proud as he might have been of the latest technology, including the ergonomic patient chair, he was even prouder of his staff, the Human Capital.

In one visit, a staff member was doing a procedure for the first time. Other two staff members were waiting in the wing to help, cheer, and support her to do the best that she humanly could do. Of course, there is a very high standard of quality in that office. But the teamwork makes even a first timer to so it right the first time. This is how he continues to build expertise and for a team of the best of the best.

During my most recent visit, he was proudly explaining things to me, and his staff would also chime in to add details step by step. It occurred to me that this was their passion. The work was the same as having fun! And their sense of humor made a two hour very difficult appointment go by very fast.

It does not really look like a boring or painful dentist appoint when I go there. He always has a story to tell to break the ice. He, of course unknowingly, uses the HP Way that includes respect for all.

Let me tell you about another one. As I was writing this, I got a call from a Bank of America employee regarding the fact that my Credit Card payment is now late. They refer to this as a reminder. They apologized saying they know that people are busy. They pointed out that there is a number that I can call to make arrangements directly with them for a lower payment. The tone of voice, the respect they offered me, the helpfulness, and the efficiency of the call encouraged me to ask to talk to the supervisor to put a good word for "Tonia"! Whether everything is perfect at all Bank of America branches everywhere is not analyzed or scientifically investigated by this Management and Technology Consultant. But, let me tell you that I have written at least three thank you letters to them. I have seen the same fantastic Human Capital and Knowledge based treatment in their Palo Alto, Oakland, Sunnyvale, Los Altos Hills, San Francisco South of Market, and other branches. These thank you letters were sent when times were good and they encouraged me to take those home equity loans, and in the bad times when almost

Copyright © 2008 - 2009 Razban Internet International, Inc. All rights reserved, File:20091022, P a g e | **18**

no loans were given by any bank.

In a Time Magazine article in Time, the Bank of America founder A. P. Giannini, is referred to as Builders & Titans. The article starts by "Consumer banking owes a big debt to a produce seller who refused to say no". So is the humble start of Bank of America with assets of more than half Trillion Dollars. He gave more to customers. He figured a way to help the "Little Guy". He jumped out of his bed after 1906 San Francisco earthquake to safe guard his customer's assets and started providing them with badly needed cash the day after earthquake in a make-shift outdoor bank that consisted of two barrels and a piece of wood on top of that to make a table.

The service has been consistently good all around. At the risk of being sued by every major corporation in America, I want to discuss something that is very dear to my heart. I had previously shared with you that my dream had been to be the CEO of a major corporation such as Bank of America, or Virgin Atlantic, or The American Express. At 59 years old, that dream might be impossible. So, sometimes I dream, remember to dream and dream big that I am one of these CEOs. Then I ask myself what I should do. In the dream of being the CEO of Bank of America, I dream about mounting an advertising campaign that "Declares War on Recession and Unemployment". This is a fantastic time to do this. Bank of America did this with paperless loans concept when times were good. This time, when a "reminder" call (which according to my call center experience says costs more than $100) is to be made, I will automatically suggest some alternatives to help out the customer who is suffering due to unemployment or Fear of Sudden Job Loss (SJL).

With what I have seen, the Bank of America employees are empowered enough and equipped with enough customer assistance training and experience to pull this off with great success.

If I was a ... and so goes the song in the Jewish Musical hit called "Fiddler on the Roof" , If I was the Bank of America CEO for one day, I will take this opportunity to build Mutual Trust and Loyalty (MTL) with customers who are the life blood of any company. Maybe, I will "forgive" one Credit Card payment, without interest or Credit Rating penalties.

The first printing of my book in 3/21/2009, I predicted that nature of American Work Place will change and it will change forever after the Global Financial Crisis. About six months after that, while I was working on the second printing of the book, Time Magazine of 9/21/2009 had a cover story of "Out of Work in America" which validated all my predictions. Now even the Daily Journal of San Mateo County in their 10/20/2009 say the same thing I had been saying on their cover page. They say, "High Unemployment May be The New Norm! Sadly, I have been saying the same things for eight years! I had predicted a lot of this. Unfortunately, I too had not predicted the magnitude of this awful Tsunami. Greenspan did not either! Let us use the last one third of the book to empower, inspire, and prepare ourselves for the work place of the future! We can do this. Let us get to work!

In my not so humble opinion, the present Credit Rating Scores will be the first victims of this recession, or even depression. They were once the meaningful standard and I had a near perfect then. They are meaningless now too. I did make my payments, but I was a few weeks late each time. They took this as an occasion to keep slashing my credit rating. Also, let me repeat again that I do not think highly of everything Bank of America does.

For example they spent a lot of money to change their logo. I am not sure that this is a great thing to do at this time of financial crisis. It is interesting that Bank of America chose to use dark red colors. To any accountant, dark red is an awful color as it indicates loss. So, much for me being a CEO one day, I would probably get fired after that one day. Keep on reading. Later, I will refer to another song from another singer that will hopefully set your soul on a happy fire and help you sing!

Copyright © 2008 - 2009 Razban Internet International, Inc. All rights reserved, File:20091022. P a g e | **20**

CHAPTER 2:   Do Not Ever Just Sit There!

Dr. James Dobson**,** in his book, *Coming Home: Timeless Wisdom for Families*, has the following chapter titled "Chippie the Parakeet":
<

> "Author Max Lucado reported a delightful story about a parakeet named Chippie, who had a very bad day. It began when the bird's owner decided to clean his cage with a vacuum cleaner. She was almost finished when the phone rang, so she turned around to answer it. Before she knew it, Chippie was gone. In a panic, she unsnapped the top of the vacuum and ripped open the bag. There was Chippie, covered in dirt and gasping for air. She carried him to the bathroom and rinsed him off under the faucet. Then, realizing that Chippie was cold and wet, she reached for the hair dryer. Chippie never knew what hit him.
> The owner was asked a few days later, how he was recovering.
> "Well," she replied, "Chippie doesn't sing much anymore. He just sits and stares."
> Have you ever felt like that? One minute you're whistling through life, and the next you're caught up in whirlwind of stress. You are running frantically through the airport and arrive at the gate just in time to see your plane take off. The table is set for guests when you see smoke curling out of the kitchen. These annoyances of life strike when you least expect them, and they always leave us dazed and disappointed.
> The next time life sucks you into the vortex, hang on and make the best of it. But unlike the experience of Chippie, don't ever let the song go out of your life."
>

Never give up! Keep on keeping busing. Make phone calls, go visit different businesses. Do not wait for the "Hiring" sign to go up before you approach a business. That will be too late. Just tell anyone, anywhere, and any time that you are looking for a job. Ask for advice, send resumes, advertize. In other words, keep moving.

Writing of this book was a true labor of love. On top of that, it was using all my lifetime savings, all my meager resources, and I did everything on my own. It was tough because I was a shoestring and strict budget. Having said all of this, this book saved me from going insane (or more insane since she thinks that was insane to start with, as my wife would say.) Every night at eight O'clock, it was my time for myself to write. I would do this after a difficult, or even after a fun day. Writing was therapy and rejuvenating for me. This was my time for me!

This book started about eight years ago, right at the beginning of the dot-com bust. I had no intention of writing a book. In fact, I had never in the wildest of my imagination ever thought that I could write a book. Writing was simply not "My cup of tea!" As a senior manager, I had learned how to write for presentations, lectures, and technical and management documents.

The first few pages were written while I was being burned alive with rage! My feeling was not just anger; it was 100% pure rage. While it is true, that I have always been peaceful and at peace with others, that day was an exception. That evening, I remembered one of my most loved fifth grade teachers. She had made a convincing case to us. She had told us that if we were angry, that in itself was not bad. However, if we did something stupid as a way of reacting to it, then that was awful and most of the time we will regret our actions forever. Her solution was simple and powerful. Powerful enough to convince me as a 51 year old man to channel my negative anger into positive and build something nice and beautiful. Actually, she had made this even more attractive by saying that the angrier, the more negative energy, the better. Because when that huge negative energy is channeled to positive, then you have a huge success. She was actually saying that we needed to choose love instead of hate, since anger is the evil twin brother, of hate. I had about 4,000 words, when I decided to send it for publication. Then I gave up. Some few months later, I started to add to it. I became 15,000 words quickly. Then, I ran out of things to say. Then each day, I would think of something and go home for the eight O'clock appointment with myself and for myself to write.

When it was roughly, 50,000 words, I took it to the FedEx shop near where I worked in Oakland. Ray took pride in making this "bookletized" and for the first time, it looked like something that resembled a book. That gave me the badly needed confidence and empowerment that maybe, just maybe, I too can write a book. Ray being an excellent employee who himself took pride in his work, decided to help beyond his call of duty. He asked if he could read a few chapters before I came to pick the "book" up after he was done with the printing.

He waved at me before I even entered the store on my way to pick it up. He enthusiastically told me "This is really nice work" and added, "You need to continue". "I am interested in reading the rest of it. What you have here helps and it is from heart from someone who has walked the talk". That meant a great deal to me. It had just taken my effort to the next level.

I still had worries about what I was doing. A first time writer always goes through these thoughts and anxieties. Therefore, I gave the first manuscript to several people to read and comment. I got mostly good remarks. It seemed like they all were ready to forgive my poor writing since the subject of layoffs had resonated with them. Coming from my heart, it soothed their feelings that were deep in their hearts! They no longer felt alone with these painful feelings about their careers, work life, and layoffs.

What I am trying to say here is that once you start doing something that you never thought you could do, then you find courage and energy that you never previously had thought you had. I had found so much hidden talent, passion, courage and desire that I could not stop even if I wanted to. My original promise to the publishers was that the book would be around 50,000 words. Even at 92,000 words, I was not ready to submit the final copy for the first edition. The Second Extended Edition ballooned to 125,000 words. I was a different man after writing this book. I had found a mission in life because of a 32-year career. I was a changed man. In one of my biggest mentor's book, "What Color is Your Parachute" he points out that we need meaning and purpose to our work and labor. Conveying an uplifting message of hope to 100% of people was my new mission. The reason why I say 100% is that many of us are unemployed and those who are employed are seriously scared about losing their jobs to layoffs. Therefore, this book talks to all of us in all levels of organization from an individual contributor to executives. Again, speaking of mission, I would like to share with you a powerful idea. Richard Bolles, the author of "What Color is Your Parachute" who has been my hero, guide, mentor, and source of inspiration for many, many years, makes this clear by asking a few questions. He asks, what is our mission in life? His book, the authoritative book in this

Copyright © 2008 - 2009 Razban Internet International, Inc. All rights reserved, File:20091022,

field tells us that there is something beyond getting a job and making money. In fact, in my opinion there has to be otherwise work life becomes miserably boring.

My mission is now defined as helping individuals affected by layoffs to realize that it is not their fault and help inspire them to find their mission and next career move. It is also equally my mission to tell executives that there are better alternatives to layoffs. I am hoping that my book convinces them that this "Revolving Hire Fire 'At Will' Door" in the work place is causing a $2.4 Trillion loss.

Remember when smoking cigarettes were cool and everyone did it? Or the time that X-Rays were done each time you had any medical problems? Later on we found out that they were not! I am hoping that soon I find some big CEO to decide to understand that 107.8% employment is possible, and we should not resign to accepting 4% unemployment as "ideal." This is similar to the thinking that human beings could not run faster than 3 or 4 miles per hour that once we firmly believed. Interestingly, that record was shattered repeatedly. Even 4% unemployment is not acceptable as it is wasteful and seriously damaging to the American Free Market based Capitalism.

I have gotten a lot of flack regarding 107.8% employment as a proactive way of avoiding the 4% unemployment. The idea is very similar to National Guard Reserves. These people do have a full time job. Yet one weekend once a month, they go to "work" and "Train." In the sixties there was some interesting TV advertizing for this. A group of men was asked what they did the previous weekend. One person said I did some chores and sat by the pool drinking beer. The other man standing near him explained his weekend as "I drove a multi-million Dollar tank in simulated battle field" Describing his one-week a month volunteer work for the National Guard Reserves. Wow, that is what a real man or a real woman can do in a weekend! Imagined that some of the 107.8% workers saying. They would be saying, I learned and did reinvent Capitalism. I saved my country's free market system.

Look at the vicious cycle our high school kid's experience. They have no idea what fields will be in demand by the time they graduate from high school. The same hit and miss, random guesswork happens in college and graduation from college. We are flying blind. As for the first job selection, it is a lot of time another Russian Rolette. In many cases, there are two problems:

- Colleges and Universities are not really training students to have marketable skill sets that are in demand. Of course, a college education in an area of exciting and interesting specialization is great if you are independently rich. It is also true that college training and higher education is for us to live a richer (richer in intellectual sense), but are we able to support ourselves and dependents with at least part of the education that we got?

- In my case, when I started college in 1967, a degree in Electrical Engineering almost guaranteed a good paying job! In 1971, when I graduated with Honors from one of the finest institutions, I was greeted by picture of a graduate, in graduation gown, pumping gas in a gas station. Surprise! No jobs!

Please do not get me wrong. It is nobody's fault. There is no conspiracy here. No other "ism" has figured this out either. Except for we have let "Stupidism" to do a hostile takeover of the free market Capitalism during the last thirty years or more! We had this coming. The Global Financial Crisis is nothing but a hostile takeover of free market Capitalism by stupidity and foolishness on all our parts! We did this to ourselves, and we can solve this too!

Unfortunately, for our free market democracy, it is a shame that so much is left to random and non-productive foolish and stupid choices. We must manage this better.

Please let me introduce some ideas at this point and then I will expand on them later in the book. Imagine:

- Each first grader's future career was respected and treated just like a corporation. In Chicago Commodities Exchange Market, we trade futures for pork bellies. Why do we not pay same amount of attention to our kid's futures?
- Why not companies, especially those who have been adversely affected by the hit and miss of the schools and Universities offer practical classes along with credits that will be honored later on in college and work selection/search?
- Nobody is forced to study, or spend time in anything that they do not want. Just like the fact that the honorable Coast Guard is formed of 100% volunteers.
- Free market is alive and well, and it will be. Let us compare free market to Open (free) skies! Any airline passenger plane from any country can fly to any other place in the open skies in the free world! Yet, we have had to have some self-governing regulations that are internationally recognized and followed. Starting with English language as being the standard language of the Air Traffic Controllers who make sure these thousands of flights each day in open and free skies do not crash into each other.
- The Air Traffic Controllers carefully watch everything to make sure no accidents are happening, or in the case of a crash, they are the first to notify authorities and to start a rescue mission.
- There are World Health Organizations, which quickly detect spread of the diseases and are able to detect and quickly prevent epidemics.
- Civil Defense teams in many countries are watching forest fires, earthquakes, and other natural disaster and they can re-act quickly to prevent spread of destruction, death and injuries.

Let me tell you one of my more interesting findings. Financial down times (Recessions) are like any other natural disaster. For example, let us think of San Francisco earthquake of 1903. The earthquake did not nearly cause as much damage as the fire that followed. Had we had the 8.7% of work force to be deployed with an hour notice, then the damage would have not been anywhere as bad. This is something that was proved in the earthquake of 1998. We were able to fix the damage quickly and prevent bigger trouble. One way that the world could have proactively prevented the Global Financial Crisis of the 2009, would have been to have an international watch group that helped self-regulate financial transactions on a global basis. We do have Sarbanes Oxley Act (Sox) as an excellent start for cleaner financial transactions inside a company. Why not expand this to make employee rights violations, unneeded layoffs, and other company mismanagement to focus as an added measure of transparency? As you might have guessed by now I have a big ego. So, why not let me propose SOaR (as in Sarbanes Oxley with Amendments from Razban)? For one thing, that can put a stop to companies practicing Hire Fire Revolving Door policy. It will have enticements for companies to manage their employees and cash better.

Remember that because of the Internet Revolution, human capital, that of intellectual

Copyright © 2008 - 2009 Razban Internet International, Inc. All rights reserved, File:20091022, P a g e | **24**

property is becoming more and more important than things capital. The best way for the greed to work, and since Mike Douglas in Wall Street movie put it is not a bad for the lack of a better word, and for companies and people to make more and more money, is to just take better care of human capital. Human capital consists of employees, customers, and shareholders!

As in Simon and Garfrankle "The sound of Silence", which "Like a cancer grows" we let some of the first signs of Stock Market potential disaster to be ignored. The root cause stayed with us and then came to hunt us later on in the form of Global Financial Crisis. In May of 2009, Swine Flu is a hot news items. The world is proactively preventing its spread. The same can be done by early detection and quick recovery by these 8.7% reserves. Layoffs permeate from one company to another just like Swine Flu virus. While, I am a 1005 advocate of free market, I am cannot accept a free fall market that causes so much job loss.

Just like Doctors have a self-policing policy, we can extend the SOX regulations to integrate integrity and honesty into the day-to-day operation of a company processes, procedures, and operation. Let us call this SOAR (as in Sarbanes Oxley, Amended by Razban) regulation for free market. Before a company or industry segment has to lay off employees, let us send the Cavalry of these 7.8% trained workers to diagnose, detect, and formulate proactive solutions. The Cancer like spread of a company's misfortune can be cured before it will destroy an industry segment, or even an economy or the global economy as it did in 2009!

No company is forced to use this option if they do not want. This is there to help. Their help can be crucial in preventing a company to go deeper into financial problem that can spell its demise.

Many companies seem to use layoffs, and lack of good management practices, as an addiction that is based on some bad assumptions. Then, they go into this vicious cycle of layoffs to bring expenses in line, and then more layoffs to deal with moral and customer loss. Seldom, if ever have they really done a root cause analysis to find out what happened and how they can prevent it the next time. I have seen many companies lay off and then lay off again, and again without solving the root cause problems that caused the first layoff!

General Patten is quoted as saying "When you see your buddy's brain looking like goo in what used to be his helmet a few minutes ago" then you will instinctively know how to fight. Fight we must! When I heard a smart and well-educated professional had intentionally driven her tiny car in front of an eighteen-wheeler, I was convinced that layoffs are not right. They do not work in the long term, and the human cost in suffering is awful. This particular woman had finally given up working in her career, which was high tech and work in Department Store, lost all hope when Department Store let her go. She would have been back on her feet with something as little as $800 in training and effective job searches. Yet a young and productive life was forever lost. This educated woman was from a highly respected family in her original country therefore she had her Mokato, or dignity. Unfortunately, this dignity was destroyed by several layoffs in Florida and California. She had to work additional hours each week just to make ends meet. She was one of the three angles who took care of my mother on my mother's last days. What made me feel so bad was that she would have been an excellent employee for some company. She had accepted much lower level jobs just to work and she was always

Copyright © 2008 - 2009 Razban Internet International, Inc. All rights reserved, File:20091022, P a g e | **25**

making sure that everything was done well.

There are reports of other developments:

- In China, the Chinese government has decided to pay for damages done to an employee who took his life after several of his fellow employees had harassed him in that factory's toxic work environment. The company's name is FoxCon and this sets precedence that even governments are accepting responsibility for damage that can be done to employees in a toxic work place.
- In Korea, a car manufacturing division took over several building threatening to blow up the place. One of these building is full of flammable paint!
- In France agricultural workers blocked highways.

We know what to do. We will make our own job security by constantly improving our market valued skill set and constantly look for that next job.

I hope this book helps you do just that. Do not ever let the song go out of your life! In addition, let us slightly modify the title of this book to *do not just sit there, sing, sing!* Keep your spirits up. Prepare for the next up market. It is always feast or famine. You do not want to waste your time during famine time and be caught empty handed when feast comes around. Remember that this foolishness in the way we are literally conducting our business and economy manifests itself in either famine or feast, never enough to keep everyone happy on a continuous and on-going basis.

CHAPTER 3:   But, How Can You Avoid Being a Chippie Parakeet in Your Dismal
               Work Life?

First, let me tell you that I am a "nobody" with thirty-two years of bittersweet experience in the workplace. As a human being I, too, have feelings just like you. I try to hang on to my job, put food on the table, keep my FICA score up, avoid collection agencies, and make sure that my house is not foreclosed.

Even though I have a CEO title and am a Senior Manager, I am not much better off than the average American. I live in a tiny town house and have $100,000 or more balance on my Credit Cards. This balance is accumulating at twenty-four percent interest. I have given up on my dream of having a nice, big house someday. I have also forgotten the dream of flying in my own executive jet some day. As of this writing, I am struggling to make ends meet. I have been an American, Middle-class, and Unemployed (AMU) since December of 2008.

I am not blaming anybody or anything, including myself. Yet, with the thirty-two years' worth of experience, I now have a better dream now. This dream is not just for me, it is for all of us.

I consider myself a work-a-day stiff. I work as hard and the best I can every day. I love my family, friends, and colleagues. I cherish my co-workers and admire them. After all, they are doing the very same admirable, honorable thing of earning a living the best they can.

I do not have a Ph.D. although I did most of the work. Unfortunately, instead of getting that degree, I would give a lecture to Graduate Students. I guess I revolted and the faculty did not appreciate it. I was showing leadership. I had the entire graduate students backing me. I had formulated and proposed a better Ph. D. program in one of the most prestigious universities, like the University of Wisconsin. Many graduate students were in favor of my better solution, but they did not dare to speak. I had to be the student activist that I was used to be. Years of lecturing in front of many students, had made me a powerful speaker. Standing in front of many people and talking is easy and natural for me. Almost the entire Graduate student body in that department attended my lecture and almost everyone agreed with me. We were not blaming the students or professors or the academics, but we were showing a better way. This same pattern repeated itself again in my career when I stood up to upper management. I made a point that firing the employees would not teach a lesson. I have been an evangelist proposing that layoffs do not improve the company's revenue. The upper management hated my guts, and they almost fired me. Yet amazingly, they started to have respect for me when my better idea helped them.

That was my goodbye to a University that I still admire and love. It is true that I did not get the degree. I could have finished it later. Yet, I decided against that since my first actual job in the real world proved to me to that, that was my prime ambition and passion. Then, when I was one of the youngest Directors in a major corporation in California at the age of thirty-four, I learned a great lesson. Call it Baptism by fire, or on the job training. I soon realized that management, employees, and even corporations were all losing their song in their hearts. They all sat there just like Chippie.

I have used my thirty-two years of experience as a manager, to determine how we can all do things better. Further, on in this book, I will describe the best and worst jobs I ever had. I try to explain why this was so. Then, I use that comparison as a foundation to come up with better way. Then I talk about the best managers that I have been lucky to work with and tell you what they had in common, and why they were the best.

In this process, I will explain my feelings as an employee and as a manager. We will journey through the valley of Sudden Job Loss (SJL) and to the peak so you too sing a song of happiness in your work life. Pete Seeger, on his ninetieth birthday in August of 2009, said, "There is no such a thing as a wrong note so long as you are singing".

We will do our best to not act like fools and become yet another chain in the present toxic work place. As employees, managers, executives, customers, and stakeholders we will refuse to act like Zombies in our work life! As in Aretha Franklin's song, this is the day to break this chain. Most importantly, by learning, unlearning, and relearning new things we will try not to just sit there as Chippie did.

CHAPTER 4:   My Best Jobs—Ever!

In 1999, Renaissance World Wide hired me to work at Hewlett Packard (HP) as a Senior Management and Technology Consultant. My job was to work with the HPshopping.com division responsible for online sales of HP computers and products. I did have prior work experience with HP. However, then I was working for another company.

The interview process was nice, even though they asked many questions. The interviewers had the highest respect for me as an individual, my time, and my experience. They tried to discuss hypothetical situations with me. Then, they asked what my reactions to them would be. These questions tested my ability to work for HP. They also tested to see if I would be happy working for HP. Indeed, they were interested in a win-win situation. They made sure to explain to me all details of the job and make sure that I understood all the good and bad aspects of the job.

My co-workers all seemed to be excellent team players who were also the best in their jobs. Every day it seemed that we had discovered something new and creative. In fact, some of the advanced knowledge that I got from that job continued to help me for many years afterwards.

People did their jobs and did them well.

Those days, I was so excited that I could not wait to go to work in the morning, and then look at the clock to notice that almost all the day was gone and I was not tired, eager to put in more hours.

This particular building was a temporary building in Cupertino that looked toward the main HP Campus. In fact, the work was so smooth that I did not see much difference between work and coffee breaks. My managers were all very interested in my work and made sure I got everything I needed to do my job.

As a new team member, sometimes I did make a mistake or had questions. In those cases, several people came to help. More importantly, to assure me that it was OK and together we would fix it. Their focus was on how to make a working relationship and create teamwork. They knew that it might take a bit more time to learn to do it right the first time. However, this extra investment at the beginning will pay handsomely in employee morale, productivity, and pride of being the best of the best and producing amazing results.

Of course, I also know that no company or individual can be perfect all the time. HP is no different in that regard.

However, the fact remains that I learned a great deal. One particular lesson I learned was that it takes less effort and aggravation to be the best of the best. It is more fun to be a hero than an employee or manager who just tries to get by with minimum effort. I learned that teamwork and consensus building might take a bit more effort at the beginning, but as a worthwhile investment, it always pays big in the long term. The pride of having worked for one of the so-called "Gold Standard" companies has great rewards in itself.

Even coffee breaks were interesting. At first, I was not much interested in going on a fifteen-minute break at 10:00 AM and 3:00 PM. Soon I found out that almost everybody else did, and I noticed how refreshing these breaks were when they came back. It seemed just like a bunch of friends had gone to have coffee and carry interesting conversation. There was a lot less friction among these people and other HP employees compared to other places that I had worked.

There is joy in the company and your team telling me "Bruce, you are in charge, we respect you, and we are all in this together to help each other. We will make this work well." This is empowerment of the first type and helps a great deal in productivity and innovation.

Later in the book, you see the very same attitude practiced by Sir Richard Branson of Virgin Group. Attitudes like these make a company complete success.

The Mutual Trust and Loyalty (MTL) that existed among teams made sure that we discovered mistakes and corrected them right at the beginning. There was no fixing of blame, there was no cover up, there was no "us against them," there was just the honest desire to figure what had gone wrong and to correct it as a team.

On that consulting assignment, I am convinced that I what I earned in lessons and the associated pride of a job well done was equal to ten times the salary I was paid. The joy and lack of stress and life-long professional connections were just golden.

I had a similar experience at other places as well. In PG&E, everyone respected and was ready to work with me. Considering the fact that some employees had worked there their entire career of twenty or more years, they were not willing to risk that long-term relationship. One of best Executive Administrators that I have ever seen was my mentor, colleague and friend. Her office had a window with a beautiful view of Bay Bridge. In the few minutes that it took for her to make appointments and arrange for catered lunches, we would talk about stock market, sports, and she will help me with my questions about the people that I needed to find or work with.

National is where I practically learned how to become a "world-Class" manager. I worked with and travelled to many parts of the world. Many of the old co-workers are still friends. We have kept in touch after all these years.

CHAPTER 5:   My Best Managers

I was very lucky to work for some of the best of the best managers in the industry. These were superb human beings with outstanding training and intrinsic talent to master the art and science of management.

My first superb manager was Jim. He had worked at HP for some time, and he was a respected manager. His technical skills were also very strong. He was very good with people and he knew how to motivate them.

There was also Bob. He was not my direct manager, but I learned a great deal from him. On one occasion, there seemed to be a conflict between several managers and engineers. Being an excellent ping-pong player, he invited us to his house. He and his wife lived in a beautiful house in Santa Cruz Mountains overlooking the Pacific Ocean. They served us a delicious lunch, and then we watched a few sports updates on the TV. After that, there was tournament time before "Conflict Resolution." Well, by the time the tournament was over, the conflict had subsided and we quickly resolved it with some give and take. Driving home that day on the gorgeous and picturesque Highway 17 in California, I could not believe that we had fussed so much on that so called "Conflict" that Bob and his wife resolved so easily.

My second outstanding manager was Jerry. He had a very strong technical background, and we were colleagues and friends for several years before he actually became my manager. He was able to always attract top talent and keep them challenged so they worked for him, and learned from him for a very long time. He had completed General Electric School of Management and, to this day, I have a great deal respect for his training and skills. The most important thing about him was that he knew what was real and what was not. He always delivered his commitments on time and within budget and exceeded quality expectations. For the last 26 years, we have kept in touch. He is a superb career and life coach. He is one of the reviewers who gave my book a five star rating. In the review he said, "Bravo Bruce". This is the best complement I have ever gotten from a coach.

Then, I worked for a woman who had started her career in the medical field and had obtained an MBA. The company had promoted her to a Senior Manager. She was extremely capable and she was a caring person. She would make sure that I learned all that I needed to learn on the new job. She was also there for me any time I was stuck and she was always ready to help.

We had to work on several high-visibility and demanding tasks. She was always ready to constructively review my work and help me understand what could make the job better. She would explain and explain things. In fact, she had a saying that she repeated many times. "Let's learn together." This says it all. She had by far a lot more experience than I had, yet she made sure that I did not feel stupid. She was also very quick to say, "Hey, look, this one is not your fault! In fact, it does not matter whose fault it is. Let's do our share to fix this."

Rih's Pyro Company has created fireworks for the world-known Oshkosh Air show. He and his team, literary, work with explosives and fires in that show. In an interview he said, "Things do not go wrong unless somebody does something stupid!" He should know. He risks his life and that of others each year. The most stupid thing to do is to lose that MTL. Layoffs do precisely that, they destroy MTL.

Of course, being a consultant, I am used to working some place for some time and then finding another task (or gig) and go somewhere else. When the end of my contract time came, she made sure that they all recognized me for the good job that I had done. We had delivered impressive results on time and within 3% of the original budget. She arranged a surprise going away party and announced it as a "staff meeting." It included real tea and the most delicious almond cookies. The real tea was her symbolism that what is real is good. By the way, real tea brewed, beats teabags any time. I worked until the last minute of the last hour I was at that company. She was there to give me a personal send off, and a hug.

She had helped me accomplish a great deal for the company. The new technology that we embedded in the product is still in use many years later. Our original budget was only three percent below the final actual budget. Her MBA knowledge and my efforts and Stanford University Continuing Education on how companies work, made this possible. She truly believed that her job as a manager was to remove hurdles and to help her employees get a chance to do a great job.

On another job, which was extremely demanding and had to do with the operations of a major corporation, I worked for another woman who was indeed one of the best executives I have ever seen and worked with. She had considerable experience working for startups and major corporations. She would make sure to talk to all her direct reporters every day. We always felt comfortable to have a fearless conversation with her about how things were. She was always able to quickly figure out the real symptoms (one of the best in the application of Six Sigma management technique) and build teamwork and consensus to solve the problem. She practiced what I had learned many years ago. This management technique says that there is no such thing as insubordination. If the employee is trusted, respected, and listened to, then he or she will come up with the best ideas to solve any problem. We must accept that those closest to the actual problem, can be the best source of solutions. However, the employee must feel comfortable to air his or her opinions and not be afraid of negative consequences. So many companies try to hide fire under the carpet for so long that it is overwhelming.

One of the most devastating effects of the Global Financial Crisis of 2009 is that fear of Sudden Job Loss (SJL) is almost everywhere. Employees, managers, executives, and stakeholders are afraid of saying and/or doing the right thing. Their focus is on keeping their job for one more day, week, month, or more. They are willing to do this at any price to themselves and/or company. Therefore, everyone is afraid to communicate, or to be innovative. This creates humongous future problems.

Nevertheless, what they and many other excellent managers know is that a manager has to be good in working with other people. They also know that management is the art and science of getting things done by other people. They know communication can be the problem, and they know that communication is also a solution. One of my managers had a sign in his office. It said, "Communicate, Communicate, and then Communicate SOME MORE."

CHAPTER 6:   "Building 7 of a Start-up in Sunnyvale"

One day after a long day of work and the four-hour commute, I got home in time to watch in shock the local news. It was a devastating story. An Ex-Employee had returned with a gun and murdered, actually murdered in cold blood three managers, including the CEO. I had seen "employee rage" as in well-known road rage before. I had seen it in some companies and in the form of shouting matches. I had also seen it in the form of deliberate sabotage to get revenge by employees for what they believed was the company wrong doing to them. For example, in 2009 it was a well known fact that some of the hacking and the breaking in that happened to company secure systems were done by disgruntled former or present employees. I was also well familiar with the serious problems that US Post Office had had with angry and sometimes unstable employees taking a gun on a rampage killing other employees, or managers. Media and management consultants invented the expression "Going Postal" to describe this.
When I read Robert Hutton's book from Stanford University, I realized how common and serious this epidemic of work place potentially violent toxicity rage had become. My management experience and six sigma rout-cause analysis lingering in my mind for thirty years, has come up with Fear of Sudden Job Loss (SJL) with its associated pink shock of layoffs as the main culprits in this.
Here is a description as it appeared in *San Jose Mercury*:
<

Suspected gunman arrested in 3 deaths at Santa Clara chip startup

By Brandon Bailey, Sandra Gonzales and Scott Duke Harris *Mercury News*
Posted: 11/15/2008 03:01:32 PM PST

There was no indication that Jing Hua Wu posed any danger when he walked into the offices of his Santa Clara employer Friday, a few hours after he'd been fired. So there was no reason for three top company officials to refuse his request for a meeting.

But some time after Wu and the three executives went into a room to talk, police say, the 47-year-old engineer pulled a 9 mm handgun and shot all three dead.

Nineteen hours later, a Bay Area manhunt ended when police cars swooped into the parking lot of a shopping center at El Camino Real and Grant Road in Mountain View. Wu was unarmed and made no attempt to struggle, police said, when officers piled out of the cars at 10:45 a.m. Saturday and handcuffed him in front of the Home Consignment Center store.

The shootings caused "genuine fear in the community," said Santa Clara police Chief Stephen Lodge at a news conference Saturday afternoon, adding that it was a relief "to be able to take him into custody."

Authorities said Wu would be booked on suspicion of three counts of homicide for the Friday afternoon slayings at SiPort, a small semiconductor company at 3255 Scott Blvd.

Police identified the victims as Marilyn Lewis, 67, of San Jose, who was the company's head of human resources; Brian Pugh, 47, of Los Altos, who was vice president for operations, and Sid Agrawal, 56, of Fremont, who was the company's co-founder and chief executive.

"These were truly three innocent victims, just doing their jobs," Lodge said. "That's what makes it such a tragic event."

Wu, a test engineer who worked at SiPort less than two years, was "let go" Friday morning because of his performance, a company spokeswoman said. Early police reports indicated he was laid off, but the spokeswoman said that was not the case.

Later in the day, sometime after 3 p.m. Friday, Wu returned to the business and asked to speak with the three executives, according to Lodge. Citing statements from other employees who were in the offices at the time, police said Wu was dressed casually and gave the executives no reason to be concerned.

"He must not have been acting too strangely for them to agree to the meeting," Lodge said.

Only Wu knows what was said during the meeting, the chief added, because only he and the victims were in the room. But other employees heard the shots and saw Wu leave the offices and drive away in a silver sport-utility vehicle. They called police at 3:53 p.m. Officers arrived within minutes and found several workers cowering in fear. The three executives were dead.

Wu had no history of violence or mental illness, as far as police know, Lodge said

>

This hit me like a ton of bricks. I had been getting ready to contact their CEO and a Board member to present my business plan to see if their company could co-operate with my tiny company to start a new venture. The first news casts would only refer to Building 7 of a Sunnyvale Startup. I was already feeling awful about this, but when they mentioned the names, it hit near home to me.I was sick to my stomach for a few days. One of my most respected colleagues called me to tell me about what had happened. He was most sad about this since the CEO had been his next door neighbor and friend for many years.

This triggered some painful and suppressed memories for me. I remembered when I had first moved to Mountain View, I had looked at several different apartments and houses to buy. At that time, one of my biggest concerns was that I wanted to be in a safe neighborhood. We had to look at several different properties and finally I picked one that we thought was the safest. One night, I went to the local grocery store to buy food. After making my purchases, I went to the cashier stand, but right at that time, a thin guy showed me a pack of cigarettes, which was the only thing that he was going to buy, and asked if it was OK for him to go in front of me. Considering the fact that my shopping cart was full, I nodded OK with a smile. He got in front of me and, when it was his time to pay, he pulled a gun out of his pocket and pointed it at the cashier. The cashier, while keeping her cool, handed bundles of cash to the gunman. I do not know what made me get very angry at the gunman, and I decided to do a John Wayne act and grab the gun from him. I wanted to be a hero and stand up to injustice. I think that I am alive today to tell you this, because the gunman was an experienced one. Without any hesitation, he pointed the gun at me, and said, "one move and you will be dead!"

I will never forget that eerie feeling of looking into a gun through its barrel.

In such cases, one starts to sweat, a warm sweat that comes down our foreheads and goes into our eyes with a burning sensation. There is another type of sweat too. This one is a cold and heavy one that goes down one's spine. A feeling that all the things that I worked for, all the things that were dear to me, are all going to be wasted in one instant, in one pulling of the trigger. Dead! Gone! Finished!

Copyright © 2008 - 2009 Razban Internet International, Inc. All rights reserved, File:20091022, P a g e | **34**

I had a similar experience one night in Madison, Wisconsin, during the height of the Vietnam War. This was during the Nixon presidency and, right after the Tet Offensive. I was coming back from the Memorial Library after a night of studying to go to my dorm. As I turned the corner on the University Avenue to go to the Johnson Street, I suddenly found the barrel of a gun near my face. It was only a few inches away, and the National Guard Soldier shouted, "STOP!" Then he asked me if I did not know that there had been a curfew.

I had gone to Memorial Library as soon as it had opened in the morning to study for final exams. I had noticed that there were not the usual crowds that gathered during the final exam times to study. I studied until early evening, when the library officials came to tell us that they were closing the library earlier than usual that night. So, I picked up my books and headed toward the exit door. As I stepped out, there was the smell of tear gas everywhere. There was a lot of noise, and one or two helicopters in the sky with search lights. The streets were deserted, except for a few students and waves of National Guardsmen.

Without paying much attention to the fact that I was going directly towards the Guards, I noticed that one of the helicopters focused his search light on me. I was near a bookstore window and I could see the light reflected back on me from the window as well. "Stop!" was the cry as I turned. "Put the brick down!" My mind had gone into overdrive. This was the stuff of action movies in Hollywood! "I said put the brick down." OK, but what brick? I had no brick. I looked down my hand and suddenly realized that my Control System Engineering book is what they must have thought was a brick. I raised it a bit to tell him it was not a brick and show it to him. "Drop it on the floor! Drop it on the floor, I said! NOW!" I realized at that moment that he was even more scared as I was. I dropped my book on the floor. From the sound of it, the Guard was convinced it was a book. He continued his talking with his gun still pointing at me. In a much less frenzied and lower voice, asked, "This is a book, isn't it?"

"Yes sir, it is!" I said. A few codes and words went back and forth between this relatively young National Guard and his commander. I could catch the part that said, "He ain't a rioter, he is a student cramming for his exams, just like I would have been doing if it was not for this. I will let him go!" OK. The search light that was frozen on my head turned into something like an usher's light to light up the street in front me, which was full of broken glass and debris.

Even though this was scary, I cannot blame that National Guardsman. In that dark night, he was doing his duty and he did not want to be killed! Yet the horror of a gun being pointed at me, comes back to me even now, thirty or more years later.

I have my private opinion that all wars are hell!

There was also a nasty explosion at the University of Wisconsin during the summertime that took the life of a research scientist working late that night before his planned vacation to Hawaii with his family.

And it took the death of four students at Kent University during riots to jolt all America to find a better way than war. In my uneducated opinion, again, I think that this shooting was a turning point in the Vietnam War!

I am grateful to University of Wisconsin for having given me an excellent education in one of the top ten, big ten schools in America. Classroom education was not the only education. I learned a great deal from more than eighty-seven nationalities that were studying in that huge campus. At that time and perhaps much more now the campus was home to a diverse cultural, religious, and ethnical number of students. I learned a great deal from all those protests. They taught me a great deal as well, even though I am not political. When I finally made it back to my dorm, Witte Hall, I found the basement converted into a makeshift military style gas-mask factory. Students were using paper cups as gas masks against their noses with a string. In the bottom of those cups cotton balls that were saturated with a solution of vinegar and salt to fend against the heavy pepper gas that was used that night. I think that this crude formulation must have come from some Chemical Engineering student. At that time, Wisconsin was number one in the nation in this area.

I used to joke that tear gas was used so much in those days that I had gained immunity to it. Pepper gas is a lot worse. Tiny fragments of hot pepper lodges itself in your skin and cloths and gives you a choking sensation in your throat. Drinking water or washing with it usually make things worse as the pepper fragments dissolve in the water and burn even worse. When I got to my room, I found my room on the tenth floor, was saturated with this obnoxious gas since the gas goes up in the air and hits top floors. I took my pillow and blanket and went downstairs to sleep in a dining room right next to the makeshift gas-mask factory.

The other time that I found a gun pointed at me, was when I had gone to Israel on a business trip, and heard that my father had passed away. I made my way back to the Tel Aviv Airport only to discover that all flights departing from Tel Aviv were full. The operations manager of several airlines tried to help. But to no avail. The El AL manager, after a few hours, told me that I could not be too choosey and I should hop on the first flight that had one empty seat. About an hour later, there was a tap on my shoulder from him to tell me that my only chance was with the El Al flight to Vienna. While I had always loved to visit Vienna, I quickly realized that I was not interested in visiting Vienna under such circumstances. Yet, I did not have a choice.

I was sitting in the middle seat. On my right, a soldier that had just finished his mandatory three-year service in the army. He was going to Vienna to "enjoy calm and quiet and live and breathe classical music since his grandfather was from Austria."

On the left, there was a Yeshiva (Jewish school for Rabbis) from Brooklyn. He introduced himself to me and apologized from overhearing that my father had passed away. He told me that while they do not recommend grieving people to travel, he might have done the same. Then he read the Caddish, the Jewish prayer for me. Then sort of amazed, he realized that I did not know much Hebrew. Of course, this is difficult for a very religious Jew to understand. But, the fact remains, that I considered myself a reformed Jew. For the Shabbat Services, I would go to the Hillel Foundation at Stanford University Campus. And in those days, Rabbi Kartoon, a reformed Jew himself, conducted the entire service in English. That gave me a deep understanding of different Jewish concepts.

Then, I had to run from one side of the airport in Vienna to the other to catch an Austrian Airline's flight from Vienna to London. Once in London, I would be almost half way home, since British Airways and United Airlines would have frequent flights to San Francisco and New York, as well as other American cities. I got to London Heathrow Airport about twenty minutes after the last United Airlines flight of the day had taken off! Over the last 30 years or so, I have developed a love hate relation with Heathrow. I will

Copyright © 2008 - 2009 Razban Internet International, Inc. All rights reserved, File:20091022, P a g e | **36**

tell you more about that later.

I was disappointed and depressed, so I found a comfortable chair. Then I put my bags near my feet, and decided to take a nap. That nap must have lasted more than an hour. I felt something wet touching my knee. This was the watery nose of a German Sheppard. To my disbelief, as I looked more carefully, I saw a strong dog barely held back by his handler and growling while showing me his teeth. And similar to the previous two cases, there was a gun, in this case an Israeli made Uzi machine gun pointed at me! What! "Am I a gun magnet? I asked myself." A very thick Scottish accent, ordered me, "Do Not Move! This is MI5 and Heathrow Airport Police." I complied. "How did you get to this secure area?" I said, "Sir, I did not know this was a secure area." "Well it bloody well is!" They must have asked me about ten questions, before they decided that I was OK. During that questioning period, my heart was racing just like it did when I had a heart attack.

I decided to write about these nightmares so you get a taste of what it is like to look into a gun barrel, and from the wrong end! Definitely, my sympathy goes to the victims of the SiPort massacre.

One of my heroes in life is Mohandas (A title that means engineer) Mahatma Ghandi. He condemned any type of violence. Based on my own brutal experience, I can imagine what the victims must have gone through. I survived, but they did not.

Then I could not help but remember three other friends that also had a tragic fate.

One, let us call her Robin, was an outstanding Director in a major corporation. She has just begun a startup in a traditional garage in Silicon Valley in her apartment. Just like me, she had put all her life-long savings into her startup company; she had big dreams of striking it rich. She had all the credentials and all the experience to make it happen. She invited me to her "Home Office" and we had a great discussion about the business and potential partnerships. She and a long-term friend of mine were working very hard in making a web site that was a showcase with their invention. As it is customary, she asked for some technical and management help, and I was more than glad to give that to her company. We do a lot of this as a small company to small company, with the hope of benefitting from each other in case there was success. A few months later, I heard that she had passed away suddenly. I had tears in my eyes. In general, startups in Silicon Valley have about a ten percent chance of success, but she had ninety percent. Her business plan, approach, and everything else was superb. Just like the CEO in the above story, she also had children and her colleagues and friends all admired her.

Another friend was a mastermind of several huge industrial shows all over the US, including one of the biggest in Las Vegas. He started to have difficulties at work. This, in turn, made his marriage even more difficult, and then an ugly divorce followed with a layoff or job termination. One day, I got an e-mail from his daughter telling me that he too had suddenly passed away.

Another heart breaker is the story of an engineer who used to work for me. We had hired him from a small town in Canada. He was passionate about his job, and he just could not believe the amount of money that our startup had to spend and to recruit him. To him, money seemed to be everywhere! He was elated with this fact. Of course, that was during the height of Dotcom. He had just been lucky to have had graduated at the right time and with the right major from college. His career had been on a steep and very successful path. Every year he had gotten double-digit raises and received many fringes as well. He

Copyright © 2008 - 2009 Razban Internet International, Inc. All rights reserved, File:20091022, P a g e | **37**

was grateful, happy, and proud. He had not seen the other side of this business during an ugly downturn. He was one of the last ones to be let go shortly before the company, startup called Exp.com, had to close down. One day, I got a call from a colleague that our mutual colleague had had a hard time with depression and drugs and that he was shot dead in a parking lot. Details are very sketchy. Unfortunately, I have seen a similar decline and destruction in others as well, resulting from Sudden Job Loss (SJL). Media defined an expression to reflect the repeated number of employee revenge killings that had happened in the US Post Office. The term was "Going Postal." This term ties closely with the first chapter in this book that says, someday, somehow, something is going to give.

While I have zero sympathy for these cold-blooded murderers in the workplace, I would like to emphasize that we have to change and improve our management and work practices in the workplace to stop this awful trend! I am not blaming any one in particular. As HP Way says, we are in this as a team. Let's use teamwork to resolve this! In Jewish Religion and Tradition, we light a candle and say a special prayer when someone close to us passes away. Somehow when this prayer, which blesses God, is said, it soothes the feeling a bit. The candle is symbolic for fighting darkness with light and sadness with hope and light.

These last two things happened around mid 1990s, when I had finally had gotten enough courage to write this book. Yet after seeing these things, I took the manuscript as it existed and dumped it in the trashcan. I told myself that it was worthless, so why even bother? The management crisis was so deep and devastating that no one would ever listen to me! No one would listen, even if I had solutions and could offer a better solution. What is described in this chapter, of course is a monumental tragedy. Yet, this is just the tip of the iceberg if we realize how much of human potential is wasted all the time.

Newspapers reported another CalTrain "accident" as follows:

<

> "The No. 274 train hit the person around 6:15 p.m., temporarily stopping trains in both directions, said district spokeswoman Christine Dunn.
> The train engineer reported to investigators that the pedestrian was standing on the tracks as the train approached. The engineer reported deploying the emergency brakes, but was unable to stop in time. No other information was available about the victim.
> Within 30 minutes, officials were able to reopen the northbound tracks and allowed trains through alternating directions. Caltrain restored service southbound at about 8 p.m.
> Caltrain officials reported continued delays along the lines.
> The incident was the 16th Caltrain fatality on the tracks this year. Last year there were seven and the year before 17."

>

There are no definite confirmed reports saying that this was a work-related situation. Yet, what really hurts me is that I had taken this particular train for many years, and Castro Street is where I get off the train to go home at night. I cannot help but wonder how many of these "incident" victims are doing this, at least partially as a result of Sudden Job Loss (SJL). I wonder how many of these were workers who took the very same train to work each working day. After all, one needs to be intimately familiar with the train schedules and know where and when to jump so they are not detected.

Over these many years, I have made a practice of not just asking fellow train riders about how they feel about their workplace, but I have also learned to observe the workplace-related frustration, rage, and anger that is obvious in a lot of faces. The same is also true at BART too. When I opened a discussion about how things were going at work with my fellow riders, I got the same two-thirds majority telling me that they were not happy with their workplace. What is also true is that they did not blame a particular function or group, such as management, or the CEOs, or the other workers, or a shortsighted stock market. However, if they were to point to one issue, they would all point to everything as in the chain of fools song by Aretha Franklin as the source of their rage!

In one particular case, a banker with a box containing his "personal belongings" after a layoff told me that he had served them very well. Each day, he had gotten up at 5:00 AM to catch the CalTrain to San Francisco to be at his desk by 9:00 AM. He had almost never been late. He really cared for the bank and they had his one-hundred-percent trust, loyalty, and commitment. Then, one day, after more than fifteen years of this, he was told that that day was his last day. They did give him six weeks' severance pay, but he thought that he would need six months at least to get another job! He told me that the worst part was to let go of three long-term employees that he had personally hired for the bank. One of them who had just been diagnosed with cancer and needed Chemo treatment, which she would not go through so she could pay for groceries.

By the way, I do have outmost respect for both BART and CalTrain. These companies are run by professional and even first-class management and excellent workers. Go to any BART station, and you will see that the station is spic and span clean. The same also holds for CalTrain.

CitiBank had announced a layoff of more than 50,000 employees. Some of this would come back to hurt the bank. Remember, some employees are also customers, who now without a job, would not be able to make deposits any more. The loss was a one in the morale among the surviving employees, which would be translated into inferior services to customers. And stress was added among the surviving employees who now had to work even harder than ever before.

Lower Customer service and lower productivity then would manifest in further market loss and then, if history is any indicator, there would be less revenue. Less revenue then would trigger a short-sighted Wall Street mentality to push even more layoffs.

And thus, the vicious cycle repeats itself.

Companies that have employee layoffs cannot have innovations. They cannot have caring employees. As one credit card company employee told me, "Why should I care that you are not happy with my service? You can complain to my manager, but he does not hear. You can stop using our card. But I am on notice and soon I will be out of this job too. So, you see, nobody cares! Why should I?"

The credit company was charging me twenty-four percent on top of late fees and "punishment" for being with them for a long, long time.

As the song says, there indeed is a chain of fools. One thing leads into another thing and soon, employees do not care, and sales go down the drain. In the meantime, the acute management crisis continues while CEOs of big corporations fly executive jets and collect multimillion dollar salary and benefits checks.

All these gun stories here are intended to help us all realize what a dreadful and scary experience it is to face a gun that is pointed at someone. I also, want to make it crystal clear that our work place has become so toxic that these things are happening.

A little earlier I referred to my love hate relationship with London's Heathrow airport. In my professional management opinion, this is one of the best run airports in the world and it is the hub and gateway to the world. It is run very efficiently even though it occupies less square feet than many other smaller airports in the world that do not have anywhere near as much departures and arrivals per hour.

On my collage days, I would pass thru Heathrow on the way to Tehran. Also, after graduation, I would pass thru Heathrow on many business trips. I never lost any luggage; never saw a tactical mistake from many thousands of the people who worked there.

I also had learned my way around that airport. It is intimidating and confusing on the first glance, but it does follow a pattern and it grows on you. I loved arranging my flights such that I spend some time at **Harrods** department store and other Tax Free Shops. I would also arrange to visit friends and family that live in London at the airport for a dinner or coffee. The Terminal 3 was my usual preferred place for this. Of course, this was before the 9/11 security restrictions.

I am not in love with Heathrow airport, not for anything wrong that they did to me, but because I got stuck there for some fourteen hours after my father had passed away. I had a lot of great and happy memories and one real heart breaker.

There is another romantic side to my Heathrow stories. It is a film called Last Chance Harvey. The acting is superb and it was filmed partially at the Heathrow. My guess is that it is around Terminal 5, which is the latest. Dustin Huffman, who always wanted to be a Jazz pianist, is giving himself a chance at living life after he decides that his lucrative ad jingle composition job is just not good enough. He finally finds courage to fall in love again, after an ugly divorce, and quits his toxic previous job.

It also turns out that I had the most interesting career lesson of my life right there in the Heathrow airport. As I was just trying to get myself comfortable in the upstairs deck of British Airways 747 flight back, I just realized how devastating my father's passing away has been to my feelings. As tears started to come down my face, I suddenly realized that I do not have the "forever" that I always thought I had for the things that I wanted to do. My father's passing away had forced me to understand that life is very fragile and finite.

As anyone who goes through a layoff finds, sooner or later we are forced to walk a tight rope with feelings on one end and "Makoto" on the other. "Makoto" in Japanese means sincerity, genuineness which is one of the highest values according to Daniel Crump Buchanan's 1987 Foreign Language Study published in **Japanese Proverbs** and Sayings - Google Books Result. He adds that "Makoto" signifies utter devotion to code of conduct. But feelings are feelings. We cannot fight them. We cannot somehow persuade a feeling to be in strict compliance with a "Makoto" directed principle.

Management is that tight rope between these two opposing ends. We want to do the honorable thing, yet we have feelings. We are human beings and we have feelings and we want to live with "Makoto."

In the most polite management term I can describe this, I feel and I know from management point of view that a layoff violates both feelings and "Makoto" ends. Worse yet, it does not help long term prosperity, survival, innovativeness, or productivity of any corporation or small company.

Vulnerable as I was, and in pain as I was, I promised right there and then and in that moment that I will someday write these feelings and principles in a book. Maybe, I will change the world after all. Maybe!

I was pondering these ideas, when a father figure like person asked if it was OK for him to join me at my table since all other tables were taken. For that moment, he kept my

Copyright © 2008 - 2009 Razban Internet International, Inc. All rights reserved, File:20091022, P a g e | **40**

father's memory alive right in front of me. After some discussion about life, "Makoto", feelings, and responsibilities, he gave me some interesting fatherly advice.

"I honor all my responsibilities, but I also, just as equally, honor my feelings!" he proudly told me in a soothing voice.

Every time I had to give somebody the layoff notice, I honored my own and their "Makoto". I always told them that it was not their fault that they got laid off. I offered to be their reference if they wanted. I offered to help them with advice. I was also honest and told them that from a feelings point of view I hated this foolish layoff concept.

In spite some very hard feelings, I am proud that I kept my promise to myself, and my father that someday I will speak against layoffs and maybe convince the world that this is wrong. It does not work and that there are better ways. I wrote the book that you see to make a point, with all its inadequacies, as I am a first time writer. My father was strongly present there and then. He was of the old school that you went to work for a company for life. He did not know anything different. He was present there at Heathrow, and he was also replaying a scene that he played when I was meeting with him and my mother and sister in Paris Orly airport. Somehow, because he spoke near fluent French, the good people of Air France had allowed him to come very near the very first exit right after passengers got off the plane. He was proud to see his son who had come to Paris from US for a visit. He was exuberant for showing me the entire Paris, his most loved city.

Maybe, I have somehow captured my "forever" by writing this book and proudly sharing my belief that layoffs are wrong and that they can be prevented with good management. Maybe, I did change the world as I had decided to do when I was seventeen years old, by writing this book even if it did not sell or even if I had made a big fool of myself by writing it.

Maybe, reading this book convinces a CEO to be the expected captain of his ship, which is the company, and use good management as an alternative to layoffs. To be the last one who leaves in an emergency just like Captain Sully.

More importantly, maybe reading this book convinces a victim of layoffs to realize that this is not his or her fault, and that his or her "Makoto" is intact. Also, that his feelings, as hurt as they might be at the point of layoffs, they will recover. I hope this convinces them that assuming guilt after a layoff by the victim is a faulty assumption.

For many years my "Makoto" kept punishing me for not writing this book. I kept remembering my decision on that corner of Heathrow in vivid colors for many years. I even kept the first chapter that was started on a piece of paper with flight schedules from Heathrow. But, then it took about 20 years and 91, 616 words to accomplish this.

Editors and others who reviewed the manuscript tell me that I wrote too much of macabre gun stories here. I do realize that this is the case and apologize in advance.

And, yet in spite all these, it is my firm belief after 32 years of experience and as a Senior Management and Technology Consultant that a lot less of these things could happen if there was more Mutual Trust and Loyalty (MTL) and less Fear of Sudden Job Loss (SJL) in the work place. It can be done by better management. There are indeed alternatives to layoffs that are a lot healthier and more economical.

CHAPTER 7 :   Important Phone Number, Just in Case

Forgive me for even writing about this. Nevertheless, writing the previous chapters convinced me that it is a good idea to write this chapter.

Sometimes, life gets to be too difficult. Sometimes, we feel so much hurt and desperation that we cannot take it anymore. Sometimes, like that Petula Clark song, Night seems never to end. All we see in front us is pitch black darkness and hopelessness. Sometimes, we find ourselves filled with rage, and sometimes we are so depressed that we cannot even remotely be functional. The daily hardships, and even daily chores, become a huge burden.

I am not talking about occasional blues. I am not talking about being mad at our spouses for one entire day and another day, or week. I am talking about those times that we just decide it is not worth it and we think that we cannot go on with our lives and continue to be functional.

If you have a feeling of wanting to hurt yourself, or someone else, then, please, please call:

National **Suicide Prevention** Lifeline 1-800-273-TALK, which is 1-800-273-8255.

On the other hand, even if you know someone that might need to get help, or at least talk those painful feelings out, ask them to call this number. The operative word here is "need to get help" and not "want to get help", because for the most part many people are very reluctant to make such a phone call. A gentle persuasion or encouragement will go a long way.

One day when I was in college, everything seemed to go the wrong way. I did not seem to be able to cope or even tolerate all of the physical and emotional pain. Stress of not getting enough sleep because of having to study hard and part time work on top of a chronic headache coupled with just plain and simple starvation and terrible junk food, when I could get it, had totally clouded my brain. There seemed to be no hope! I had only a few caring friends, but aside from them nobody seemed to care. I was so angry, hungry, frustrated, and depressed that I did not care to live. Therefore, as a person who has gone through this, I want to assure you that I understand. I can feel your pain. It is real. Those clowns who tell you to "snap out of it", or the ones who told me that I was a crybaby, do not understand. The pain is real and nobody can tell us what to feel!

I distinctly remember that right in that moment, I thought, I did not care to be alive anymore! I would think, "The hell with it all!" I had had enough!

Somehow, I had some unfinished business to take care of. That was to call my friend Al, who has been like a brother and a father to me, to say goodbye. I had almost nobody else. I dialed his number and he was there. I started to say hello, and he asked, "What is wrong?" Somehow, this Mensch of a man had figured out and he cared enough to come and pick me up and take me to the University of Wisconsin Emergency Room. The word Mensch is Yiddish Language that means, "A person of integrity and honor".

My blood sugar was way below what it should be. The doctor took care of the pain, and she asked me to promise to go see a therapist. She gave me the number of Dane County Mental Health and I found a Psychology Graduate Student who had volunteered his time to help. Mike Spirer was his name. Since as a student I only could afford $3/Session, and

Copyright © 2008 - 2009 Razban Internet International, Inc. All rights reserved, File:20091022, P a g e | **42**

even at that I had to give them IOUs several times, they had accepted me as an outpatient to see Mike once a week. That was the first time that I had seen a therapist! Mike was kind and friendly. We started to talk about how difficult life can be. He sat quietly and listened intensively. He would at times tell me that he understood what was going on in my life. After two or three sessions, I was thinking that I had made a mistake by going to see a therapist. Yet, just talking to a professional was great help. As I started to describe my feeling, my fears, I realized that there was hope for ma and others. After that, I could not wait to go see Mike each week.

I am positive that in my previous life, I must have been a very successful psychologist. This subject from childhood had fascinated me and I was reading articles about this subject in the Daneshmand Magazine when I was in high school in Iran. Finally, I took Psychology 101 in college. Our Professor was stunningly attractive half French and half German. German and French is just as an explosive compound as being Iranian and Jewish. Her accent made me fall in love with her during the first five minutes of the class. As I was thinking about her astonishing looks, I noticed a commotion in the class. The commotion rudely disrupted my fantasy and planning to make this German French Professor to fall in love with me, the Jewish Iranian Junior in college, as if I had a ghost of a chance. I was thinking about who my best man should be, when the student next to me asked me to move my seat so we can all sit in circle as per Professor's request. I started to move my chair thinking that best chance I had was to impress her with my French. It turned out that I was sitting at the end of the U-shaped seat arrangement right next to where the Professor usually stand to write on the board. My nose quickly detected a faint yet familiar scent. Those days Trojan brand condemns had this distinct lavender scent and some thick petroleum based lubricant. The scent would remain for a few hours after use. After a few class sessions, it became clear that this scent was coming from where condemn must have penetrated. I was totally convinced since my nose would be near the point of insertion of the condemn inside her body. It made sense. She was a newly married bride madly in love with a Swiss national. She told me this after I had impressed her with my Parisian accented French. That made disappointed with her. I was happy for her and the Swiss man. Nevertheless, she had destroyed my plans and my expectations that we get married and live happily ever after! I was so disappointed with her that I tried to switch places with another student. She replied, "What is the problem?", "You cannot take the heat?"

A Persian proverb says that it is always darkest before daylight. There are periods that I have hoped I was dead. One of them was when I was on a business trip from San Francisco to London, and the plane lost 4,000 feet in no time at all. I think that my thinking at that time was that I wish I was dead instantly and not suffer any pain as it is in the crash of a 747 in the Atlantic Ocean. I was especially horrified about those sharks. Yet when the plane had to turn around and land in Gander in Canada, and after landing, I somehow had all the passion to live infused in me again, and instantly. I wanted to see my mother and father again. I wanted to see my brother and kid sister again. Wow, life is beautiful in spite all the awful things that happen.

Back to that University of Wisconsin, a year prior to that Emergency Room visit, an ambulance had taken me to the University Hospital half way in between life and death on a very stormy evening. Doctors were able to tell me that it was food poisoning. Since it was Christmas Eve, I remember that the Intern is charge decided to call and talk to the

Copyright © 2008 - 2009 Razban Internet International, Inc. All rights reserved, File:20091022, P a g e | **43**

Doctor who had gone home to his family after his 16-hour tour of duty that day. The Intern had made sure that a certain medicine would fix, and fix quickly the problem. One injection and I soon ended up in comma. I was one the few among millions who have serious and life threatening reaction to this medication. I remember that while I was suffering from the killer stomach pain, I was telling the Doctors that I wish I were dead. They seemed to try to cool me down by saying the pain will go away. You will see. Doctors repeated that they know how to fix this, and told me not to worry. Well, I was saying the Heavens Gate with a beautiful white light, screaming, "God Take Me, Please, I have had enough!"

I am glad that God did not listen to me. After I came to, Doctors told me that the reaction was so unusual and so severe that they almost lost me. However, by then I was looking forward to some rest and a good meal. By the way, most of my screams were just incoherent noises that they were not able to understand. Thanks for this.

I used to think that everything that I had done in my entire life was a mistake. I used to think that everybody else had it better than I did. I used to think that I would never amount to anything. I used to compare my insides with other people's outside. Until one day, one of my friends told me that he had been very jealous of someone for many years, only to find out that he had pains much greater than he ever had. Some thirty years later, I am convinced that I am all that I can be and it is all for good. I have done my humanly best, with what I had, and what I knew then and there. I forgive myself for not being that Mr. Perfect that I had intended to be, or that agent of change that changed the entire world. However, with all my human frailties, my stupidities, and my mega mistakes, I am here and now and I try to do my humanly best for one minute, one hour, one day, one month, one year, or one life!

It is also a fact that many people who jump from Golden Gate Bridge, feel a great deal of remorse for their act right after they jump. The scientific finding is that they would not jump, if they had known what it feels like moments after they jump.

I have learned to tell myself, "Do not give up Fifteen Minutes before the Miracle!" This whole stupid life is miracle with all the ugliness, hatred, sorrow, and depression. There is also a lot of good.

This number (1-800-273-TALK, which is 1-800-273-8255), is a national hotline that is open all the time, it is free, and a caring and trained professional will talk to you.

Copyright © 2008 - 2009 Razban Internet International, Inc. All rights reserved, File:20091022, P a g e | **44**

CHAPTER 8:   Management Crisis in American Management

The technical definition of management is "The art and science of getting things done through other people."

In a CNN story regarding the "Big Three" automakers around November 14, 2008, Brian Ross had tapes of the CEOs arriving in their fancy executive jets to Washington to beg for bailout money. Moreover, there have been plenty of reports about the astronomical salaries CEOs are making. Moreover, this, on top of repeated layoffs and division shutdowns, has created a sense of distrust and anger (or rage might be a better word) towards big company CEOs. Having worked with senior management in many companies, I have convinced myself that as much as CEOs are to be blamed, there is also enough blame to go around to employees, customers, Wall Street, and the entire set up. As a previous chapter says, the entire chain is like a chain of fools.

About a year after writing most of this book, some of my worst predictions came true and they came true in a devastatingly scary form: bank failures, HP announcing a lay off 50,000 employees, banks not trusting and not lending to other banks, and even the potential collapse of the Capitalism, itself.

Later on in this book, you will read about these things. Nevertheless, in industry, we like to do a "Six Sigma" analysis of what has happened as a basis for how to fix it.

To honor my HP management experience, we start by saying, "It does not matter whose fault it is, let's find what went wrong, and how to fix it." Moreover, we always respect everyone. To fix this mess, we need to build more and mutual trust among employees, management, the finance community, and customers. It is just as simple as that.

However, to build this fragile Mutual Trust and Loyalty (MTL), we need to teach the human side of management-to-management, and we need to realize that there has been a huge revolution in the form of internet technology and now capitalism needs to focus on human capital and potential instead of assets. In addition, we all need to work with knowledge as the more powerful currency of business.

On December 22, 2008, Toyota, one of the best-managed companies in the world announced that they had a big loss. A friend of mine was telling me about what must be millions of unsold, brand new Toyotas sitting in Long Beach Harbor! This was a first for Toyota since 1941!

Let me describe my own first-hand experience with layoffs that result from the management crisis in US, Japan, and even Europe. My gut feeling is that Europe, especially UK, was hit even worse than we were. America, as a world leader, exports the good and bad, whether we like it or not. The Reverend Billy Graham in his books asks God "Why am I selected to lead? Who am I to lead?" Of course, this is a humble question from one of the most respected leaders in religion. Interestingly enough, this has a direct analogy to the US and its ability to lead the rest of the world. We have to do this whether we really want to or not. Nevertheless, we must be a good example.

This rampant management crisis has created a great deal of job dissatisfaction. This dissatisfaction is just as bad with the upper management, middle management, and first-line management. In fact, I have a fact-based discovery that the C-Level executives (For example, CEOs, CTOs, CFOs, etc.) are even more depressed and dissatisfied than the other employees.

Layoffs that are a direct and fundamental result of our management crisis are two-edged

Copyright © 2008 - 2009 Razban Internet International, Inc. All rights reserved, File:20091022, P a g e | **45**

swords that depress and disappoint management just as badly as employees. In addition, boards of directors and stockholders take it out on C-Level management when things go wrong.

Later on in this book, I refer to this as an $800 Billion, or for those of you who are gifted with Math, a $.8 Trillion waste, pain, and suffering that does not need to be there.

I have personally felt this God-awful pain as an employee and as a manager. I have a record of accomplishment of being a people-oriented manager, and I have kept up with the latest in my field. At the risk of being considered arrogant, in most cases, companies need me more than I need them. Yet, with all that I have to offer, the dysfunctional and toxic workplace was so huge that I was having rage attacks. My upbringing and my belief system is such that if we went after revenge, then we would be just as bad as those savages who did these awful things to us. Therefore, in return, I will channel all that toxic rage into productive energy such as writing this book.

Here is story of one day when, as an employee, I was so stressed and so angry that I did not know what to do. The expression is that I saw blood everywhere I looked. I had suffered so much in that particular consulting assignment that I was shouting from the top of my lungs as I drove down highway 101 to go to an unneeded meeting with no agenda. What made it worse was that I had to be in my office at 4:00 AM as a convenience to the European colleagues. The meeting was listed as critical, and there were people all over the world who had to attend. Years earlier, I had learned that one way to deal with anger was to get in my car, roll up all the windows, go park in some parking lot, check to see that nobody was watching and then SCREAM just as loud as I could. The person who had called the meeting had no special agenda (at 4:00 AM!) but just wanted to "see how things were going? My voice was hoarse for two days!

On another occasion, again as an employee, things went so badly due to lack of leadership and management that I started to feel a great pain in my left chest. I thought, maybe it would go away. In fact, I was so frustrated with my job that I did not even care if it did not go away and was a heart attack. I was told that a heart attack feels like an elephant has stepped on your chest. Well this felt like a dinosaur had stepped on my chest! It is ironic that, later in the book, I refer to some inefficient companies as dinosaurs. I went to Community Hospital in Los Gatos. Before I could complete my description of chest pain, the alert receptionist picked up the phone and called a nurse, who arrived with a wheelchair. I was whisked to the interior, kept for a three-hour observation, and connected to many wires and medical devices.

The Chief Doctor, an experienced and excellent doctor, who had taken a personal interest, did a great deal of tests and finally came back to talk to me in private. He said, "You WILL have a heart attack, but not TODAY!" He added that I had to learn to deal better with stress. He told me about stress management that the hospital was planning to have for a nominal fee as they had seen many cases of similar situations and some that indeed had led to heart attacks. His point was well taken. I knew about psychosomatic diseases. These are the type of diseases where someone has convinced himself he had it, and these diseases were sometimes just as bad as the real disease. Well, this it was similar to that, except for the fact that workplace stress had induced this near heart attack for me. I have also had other near heart attacks resulting from management of some employees who were so dysfunctional and full of hate that any attempt in their management would encounter serious opposition, rage, and sabotage. Of course, as his manager, I could fire

Copyright © 2008 - 2009 Razban Internet International, Inc. All rights reserved, File:20091022. P a g e | **46**

him, but I was doing my best to be ethical. However, that was no match for someone who hated the company and everything it stood for, that he would sabotage it and would do his best to get away with absolute minimum punishment. When confronted with lack of performance, or backstabbing resulting from his giving misinformation to another group that we had to work with, he would say: "Fire Me!" and walk away.

This is another lose-lose case that is the opposite of the HP Way that inspires, win-win.

CHAPTER 9:   My First Real Taste of Layoffs as an Employee

I saw my first layoff when I was an employee in my first professional job at Plantronics, Inc., in Santa Cruz, California. This was right after graduating from the University of Wisconsin. On a nice Thursday afternoon, my manager and mentor came around to ask me to go with him to get coffee. While drinking coffee, he quietly said that there would be a layoff the next day. He added that I was safe since I was a hard worker. He added that as an Honor Graduate of a Big Ten University, I was a high potential employee. Years later, we became good friends. However, as my management mentor, he told me that the only thing he hated, as a manager, were those awful, draconian layoffs that did nobody any good.

Those days, layoffs usually happened on Friday afternoons. The rationale was that then the employees had the weekend to recover. Even though I had not lost my job, I still felt pain in my stomach as if somebody had punched me in the belly with a boxing glove. I started to think about those affected people being unemployed and not having enough money to feed their families. I felt so sorry for them that I started to become depressed. The next day, the day of planned layoff, the stench of a pending layoff was in the air. I had promised my manager not to say anything to anybody. I had also promised to act as if I had not heard anything about it at all. Based on my manager's instructions, I had to deny it if I heard a layoff rumor. This was a company secret.

The so-called company secret lasted about ten or fifteen minutes. My colleague and my best friend at work came to my cubical. They quickly passed me a small piece of paper. This looked just like school kids cheating without being caught by the teacher. The note was simple and to the point: "Lay off Tomorrow PM. You are OK!"

This was a long-term company employee who knew how scared I was about suddenly losing my job. After being a Foreign Student for nine years while attending the University, a job was now critically important. I needed the job to get my Permanent Visa. Without it, I would be deported. I was OK according to my manager and a colleague, but I was anything but OK. My student leader previous life was pushing me to revolt. This was social injustice, and I had to stand up against it! This layoff, just like any layoff, was painful even though Plantronics was a caring company. Luckily, the job market was also good those days. Getting a generous severance package, and a good market, had even encouraged a few other employees to volunteer. I never, ever saw any of those laid off friends. This is common. One day you are good friends, and the next day, there is layoff and they are gone forever!

That very long Friday afternoon, we all tried to work as if everything was normal. As the afternoon lingered on, whenever I bumped into somebody in the hallway I could not help but worry whether they were affected or not. In other words, whether they were walking dead and did not know it. This feeling was mutual since many of the others in the hall way were also trying to avoid eye contact.

Very few things were done that Friday, or the most of the following week.

The sense of helplessness was in the air. Tempers were slightly shorter than usual. There was no enthusiasm or creativity anywhere in the workplace. Meetings tended to be without the usual jokes. We somehow pushed ourselves to do the job, or at least pretended to do the job. We were professionals after all.

Where did those happy days go? Where did the exciting days go where I was learning many new things? Where did one of my friends, an older man married to a French teacher, who used to try to teach me the difference between different wines, go? He was attending a French class in a local college and this had given us a good reason to learn together. I had told him that he was one of the very few elite who pronounced Cabernet Sauvignon correctly. He was so elated that promised to boast about that in his resume. I still remember him and his wife. They had travelled the entire world. They indeed were world class.

Next Monday, much to my sadness, suddenly I noticed the empty chair that my other colleague had occupied. She had helped me understand Operating Systems. In the turmoil of a layoff storm, she had forgotten to take her poster that said, "I am a Child of the Universe…"

CHAPTER 10:   Layoff Executioners' Activity

As if on the cue, all managers who had to lay off any employees went to their employees' desks and asked them to go to one conference room. It was unmistakable; they had fat envelopes containing the last paychecks, documentation needed for the unemployment office for unemployment insurance collections and information about where to go for food stamps and federal medical insurance.

In the conference room, I heard some managers also gave a short speech in addition to making sure that the paper work was OK. And some decided not to say anything as it was not in their pay grade and directed the employee to the personnel office (now called Human Resources or HR).The affected employees had one or two hours to collect their personal belongings and say good-bye to friends and colleagues and "leave the premises." Some affected employees were visibly upset, some objected loudly, and some were resigned and just wanted to get the process over.

Since I had not worked there long enough, I did not know most of them, yet it hurt. How could this be? In my mind, I could see someone being fired as much more rational and fair than this. You do something wrong and you get fired. However, this was not the case. As I was going in deep thoughts, anger, frustration, and feelings of loss, the phone on my desk rang. This was not a business call. It was a call from one of my colleagues telling me this was the way layoffs were, and would always be. He also added that I was lucky to be a college graduate and good in several engineering areas; therefore, my job was a lot more secure than his was.

One of the documented facts about concentration camps is the guilt that the survivors feel when they survived and their relatives did not. In fact, this survivor guilt can be extreme. A Stanford professor told me once that his father believed that he himself killed his relatives who lived in Europe. In his survivor guilt rationality, he thinks that he killed them since he did not force them to leave Europe and come live in US. Of course, my survivor guilt was not, and could not be as strong as that, yet it broke my heart.

Copyright © 2008 - 2009 Razban Internet International, Inc. All rights reserved, File:20091022, P a g e | **50**

CHAPTER 11:   The Weekend after the layoff

I was living in a one-room motel room equipped with a TV and a private bathroom in Santa Cruz, California. During those years (late seventies and even eighties), Santa Cruz as well as many other Silicon Valley, California, cities had a severe housing shortage due to high demand from technology workers. Santa Cruz, in particular, suffered from an even worse housing shortage since it was only a resort town with all the vacationer amenities including hotels and motels and a world-famous boardwalk. But at that time, it did have housing for year-long living. Many hotels and motels, during the off-season, have special rates for the so-called "permanent guests." I was at Seaway Motel just a few steps from the boardwalk and the mighty Pacific Ocean. I discovered how mighty it was as I found it icy cold even in winter with huge waves. And some nights, I could not sleep because of the ocean sound and the wind that whispered in my window facing it.

The mighty Pacific was another disappointment to me. All those nine years that I was in Wisconsin, I dreamed of moving to California and going swimming in the ocean every day. "California Dreaming," as the song went, played in my head and was a source of encouragement.

Now I had this depressing thing. I was in California to fulfill my life time dream, but the water was so cold and frigid that I could not even go in it barefoot for most of the year.

The frigid Pacific and my daydreams of swimming in it had a similarity with my feelings of depression, disillusionment, anger, fear, and emptiness from my first observation of layoffs. Seeing this first layoff shattered my concept of job security. I thought that job security was just as real as my dreams of swimming in the Pacific. But it was just empty, wishful thinking!

How could I continue as a loyal employee to a company that had so cold bloodedly affected my co-workers' livelihood?

What if it had happened to me? They could have easily laid me off due to lack of industrial experience, or some of my co-workers, who had been intimidated with my extensive college. They could have tried to put my name in the list for whatever reason.

That Friday night, I got very little sleep. And, when I managed to fall sleep, I had a nightmare that would wake me up. The nightmare revolved about my not helping a co-worker. I would explain something to him thinking that if I helped him, then he would be more useful than I. Because of this, they would lay me off instead of him the next time.

This nightmare is a real source of worry for Management Consultants, trying to encourage teamwork and cooperation among different groups. A company, no matter how big or small, cannot sustain productivity and develop value-added products and services if the employees are constantly worried about their jobs.

This painful phenomenon is something that I have observed as an employee, as a

Copyright © 2008 - 2009 Razban Internet International, Inc. All rights reserved, File:20091022, P a g e | **51**

manager, and as a consultant. Trust and loyalty between employees, at all levels, and between a company and its customers is the fabric and major *reason d'être* (reason for existence) of a company. Once this is damaged or minimized, then there is a slow and expensive recovery process to fix it. It is also important to note that the former trust will never be the same.

But my experience is deeper than that!

As an arrogant, top notch Senior Manager who thought I would always be in demand, I could never understand or feel the pain others felt, unless and until I went through it myself.

It is one thing to walk a tightrope at work and yet have that paycheck at the end of the week. It is another to have to pull your life savings and spend it on groceries. People save their retirement money in what is called a 401(k). The joke I have heard is that my 401(k) retirement is now 01(k), pronounced "Zero one k." This is so because I had to withdraw all my savings and, in effect, leave ZERO dollars there.

But, this joke is not funny to me. When my 401k became 01k, I had no, absolutely no, safety net. Six or seven weeks without a paycheck and I would have been in a bad shape.

CHAPTER 12:   The Monday After

Finally, it was Monday, and I rushed to work. I had not gotten enough sleep and I was trying to guess how things would look like on Monday. More importantly, I kept wondering if I could handle the stress and the survivor guilt.

The entire workplace in my eyes looked like the scene after an emotional hit-and-run accident. There were blank looks on the faces of the onlookers trying to figure out what happened and how to cope with it. About ten minutes after the beginning of the day, my manager called me in his office and spent some good twenty minutes talking to me to calm me down and cheer me up at the same time.

Prior to this layoff, I had arrogantly thought that, graduate management classes and many management books that I had carefully studied, would help in situations like this and I did not need a mentor. However, that day I realized how good it was to have such a nice manager and manager. I appreciated his human efforts to help me recover. He also related to me that he had felt the same when he actually witnessed the first lay off.

The rumor mill at work was hot. On the coffee break, I heard that so and so had seen this coming so he did not work too hard the last three months. He just simply did not care. Somebody was asking a co-worker, "Did you hear about the lucky woman who was only happy to get the severance pay, put it in the bank and go to the next job that she had already lined up for some time?" Everyone admired her for this; she was smart enough to look at the *San Jose Mercury* jobs section every week and go to a few interviews. There was the common guess that so and so "*got it*" because the management had confused him with someone else. In addition, there were rumors about the young person who just bought a motorcycle and started his trip on California coast to recover. The story was he was not married and had no children and he could live like a Hippy for a long, long time. Productivity was very low. We also found out that one of the affected people had some critical computer software that we needed for testing and we could not find the documentation. Panic set in. Her manager called her and she was kind enough to personally come in and help us find the documents and get the software to work. She refused payment for those hours. This dignity on the part of the employee is Mokato! Surprising to me she was not bitter about the company or the process. She told a friend "Plantronics had been very good to her from the beginning when she started as a clerk". She had gotten on-the-job-training and several promotions. She understood the layoffs since she had been observing the loss of sales in one of the product lines for some time. How could a company be good that had taken her job away, even though she had not done anything bad?

It turned out that Plantronics also was very good to me and many other employees. I learned the fine art and science of management, in practice in the "real world" in real time. All those textbooks and education were great. This was the "real thing" and it was grace in action.

Copyright © 2008 - 2009 Razban Internet International, Inc. All rights reserved, File:20091022, P a g e | **53**

CHAPTER 13:   Cousin Brucie

In 1968, I spent one of my first summers in New York City, working as a Third Shift Janitor in Thomas Bakery. I became a fan of Cousin Brucie. He is one the best of the best in the business. He would play the hottest and most popular Rock and Roll music on WABC Radio of New York. This was his passion, and it exuded from every word he uttered. His pioneering disc jockey format involved introducing the song and then giving additional information regarding its history, the artist, and lyrics. In addition, some times the show would switch to talk show as listeners called. This was quite a new format those days. I got used to listening to his program in my small room, and when I was outside, I had a very basic portable radio I carried with me.
His tone of voice had the same effect as a ten-ton truck passing through a neighborhood. His tone of voice and knowledge would shake me and would invigorate me. I could not hide from it, or I could not ignore the vibration and joy that he embedded in his voice and the music he played. The excitement would touch me and put a fire in my soul. Everyone respected and credited him for the success of that type of programming that frankly I think made WABC a phenomenon.
One day I heard that WABC had fired him. This made my blood curdle. Cousin Brucie was bigger than life. With this the music stopped! He was the lifeblood of WABC. How could they do this to him? In a *20-20* interview on ABC Television, John Stossel, argued that, "You do not own your job," so it just makes sense to be fired when you get old, or for whatever reason or for no reason at all.
While I was doing my best to accept his words for what had happened, I had a sudden realization that he did not sound like the Cousin Brucie I had known and worshiped, from my New York days. The man who could ignite a fire in my soul via the radio waves had lost the Mega Watt Energy that was his voice signature. Yet he was still the Radio Celebrity and Royalty worthy of worship and bigger than life.
I am glad to report that in a fundraiser by KTEH, a Public Television Station, which aired in September of 2008, Cousin Brucie seemed to have made a comeback. Petula Clark was also part of this great program focused on the historic "British Invasion," the time when the Beatles and other British musical bands had a strong showing in US. If even an icon as big as him is fired, then who am I to complain about my own being fired?
During the height of Cousin Brucie popularity, I was on a New York to Chicago red-eye midnight flight. It was the first week of September and I was going back to Madison after a summer job that had left me with good earnings to pay for tuition. While waiting for the flight in newly minted TWA French Hat Architected Terminal at JFK airport, I noticed an attractive woman almost my age, or a few years older. She was carefully reading and eagerly studying every sentence of New York Times the same way I liked to read mine. I started a conversation about the fabulous New York Times newspaper telling her that I had just finished reading a very similar article in French in Le Monde, and New York Times in English. I added that the same facts and figures were described totally different. Hearing an instrumental rendition of one of the most popular songs on Cousin Brucie's program, soon shifted our conversation to mutually praising Cousin Bruce's program. There was a first one hour delay "Due to weather conditions in Chicago O'Hare" followed by two others that increased the total delay to about three and half hours. Any seasoned traveler knows that this is to be expected in Midwest in September. Our

Copyright © 2008 - 2009 Razban Internet International, Inc. All rights reserved, File:20091022. P a g e | **54**

discussion was exciting and helped the time go by real fast. Final boarding call on the speakers came, and we said our goodbyes and went to sit in our pre-assigned seats. It was clear from the way we said goodbye that we both had more things to tell each other even after almost three hours. Love at the first sight had infatuated and then quickly inflicted me with love. It was as if I knew this woman all my life and I wanted to be besides her for eternity.

After the airplane was flying at cruising altitude of about 30,000 feet, I went to get something to drink. I noticed that she was sitting in her seat with a disappointed and bothered look. Just seeing her again got my heart pounding. Unfortunately, she did not seem to be happy. Being in the middle seat, she had a snoring old man in the window seat, and a French woman who spoke very little English on the aisle seat. My newly found friend asked me to translate a few words for the French woman. Actually, she was from Belgium, but spoke French. Then as soon as I told my newly found friend that there happened to be two empty seats where I was seating, she did not waste a New York minute and joined me. I was lucky being very close to front of the Coach Section which seem to have more empty seats compared to where her seat assignment was. Interestingly enough, I was only a few rows away from the FAA required curtain that separated Coach and First Class. There seemed to be slightly more light in the First Class as if to prove that grass is always greener on the other side! Talking about Cousin Brucie and some of the latest songs, started to get us in a romantic mood. I also had to boast about having been a "Movie Extra" in Goodbye Columbus with Ali McGraw of later "Love Story" fame. "So you are a movie star?" "I always wondered how those love scenes were made in the movies." Then she added, "Were there any love scenes in your movie?" I quickly said, "Yes Madam!" The truth is that having had lost a lot of weight that summer and an excellent hair cut from a stylist, I did look good. Correction, I did look handsome, but nowhere as good as Movie Star. A few drinks later, in passing, I hinted about the Mile High Club. To be a member, you had to have sex at that altitude. Most people achieved this "elite exclusive" membership with a quickie in the uncomfortable bathroom. I had dreamed about this divinely pleasurable concept and idea, but doing it in the restroom was totally appalling to me. I could only imagine and fantasize what having sex with such attractive woman would feel like, regardless of altitude. I was trying to convince myself that this will not happen in a million years, and that I will never be a member of such club, when I noticed that she had moved just half an inch towards me. I did the boldest thing I had ever done. I moved half an inch towards her to notice her Chanel Number 5 perfume enticingly blended with a hint of Scotch and Soda. A few minutes later, my shoulder was gently touching her shoulder, in a beautiful dark blue/green satin European designed blouse. Gently, I held her hand thinking that she might just put a total stop to the entire thing. The opposite happened. She gently squeezed my hand. The squeeze was poetically gentle, yet felt slightly erotic and sensual to me.

The interior lights were dimmed as we were flying at 30,000 feet and it was pitch dark outside. "Will I, and for that matter this attractive woman, be the latest members of the prestigious Mile High Club?" As the question was lingering in my mind and as I was doing my best to recall a movie that had a scene about making love in an airplane, I noticed that there was a blanket and two pillows right next to her. The blanket was brand new and in a thin clear plastic cover. I am of the firm belief that dirty blankets ruin sex. "May I?" I asked and she gave me the red maroon blanket with TWA trademark

Copyright © 2008 - 2009 Razban Internet International, Inc. All rights reserved, File:20091022, P a g e | **55**

beautifully embossed on it. "Remember the Mile High Club?" Then she started in a sexy, moaning whisper asking, "Do you want to …" I did not even let here finish. I had anticipated what she was going to tell me. Now my heart was beating faster and I was sensing a scent that was like Chanel Number 5, Johnny Walker Scotch and Soda, and strangely enough, mixed with a trace of a jarring sensation caused by my testosterone hyperactivity. After all, it was the "Age of Aquarius", and the height of the sexual revolution of the sixties. There was also this once in a lifetime chance of becoming a member of the Mile High Club.

My background kicked in! I started to hear voices in my head, "Sex, only after marriage. With the life time commitment, and after proper City Hall marriage certificate! No, No, this is not right! No! Even though you are both singles! No!" Too late, my lips were already caressing and ever so slowly kissing those sexy, plump, and beautiful lips. Very quickly, my IQ of 148 kicked in. "Well there is no City Hall at 30,000 feet and she is a great, intelligent, and beautiful woman and you are deeply in love!" So, "Consume the marriage now, and then do the paperwork later!" My self-talk in a forbidding manner jumped in to intervene. "Technically, the Captain of this 747 jumbo jet has City Hall and Law Enforcement powers during the flight for the country whose flag was painted on the fuselage." "In this case, it is an American airliner, so the country must be US." A lover's whisper from her caught my attention; Barbara was asking, "What is going on in your mind?" I kissed her on her chick and said, "You, you, and you", "Let us make love!" we both seem to say at the same time. Seeing this, the real gentleman sitting across the aisle, the only passenger awake on that side, quickly got up and left. He found a better seat further away. The remaining passenger on that side was a middle-aged man. He had been sound sleep. He was actually drunk and had passed out, for what seemed centuries. Luckily, his faint whistling snore was perfectly bearable.

It took about five minutes for us to officially become members of this fascinating, exclusive, Mile High Club. I had joined the world class club of Hugh Hefner and perhaps Howard Hughes the CEO of TWA. After all this entire multi-million Dollar jet belonged to him. I had finally joined the Jester Club. Never mind that both of us had paid for a cheap standby ticket.

By now, with pride racing at million miles a second in front of our eyes for our membership, we had been almost zipped up, when the senior flight attendant appeared from nowhere! I have a good hunch that she had quietly observed our membership initiation making sure that we did not bother others. This thought was even more probable by the fact that she had several times peeked from the opening in the curtain that separated First Class from Coach Class a few rows away. For some reason the light was dimmer in Coach than it was in First Class. Therefore, I could easily see that she was watching. I am sure she knew what was going on, she must have seen these things before. I think that she might have even gotten excited with it too. However, her look at us seemed to convey some sort of question. More than that, it was a question but combined with admiration, warning, and acceptance of our bravado. I did not give it a chance. In a quiet and carefully enunciated yet assuring voice, while Barbara was showing a slight sign of blush on her cheeks, I said, "Honeymoon, … !" "I, …, Oh, I see." A perfect facial expression of disbelief but wanting to believe, pleasant surprise that there was no scene, or other passenger complaints. As she walked away from us in slow motion, I also could read in her face "OK, consider this a gift from me to you love birds, but I do not buy that

Copyright © 2008 - 2009 Razban Internet International, Inc. All rights reserved, File:20091022, Page | 56

honeymoon excuse for a moment!" As she had barely passed our aisle, she turned back to take another look as if to silently say " You should know better, I am a professional senior attendant and I have seen it all!", "You cannot fool me, but watching it was sexy even for me. I had fun too!" Then she flashed a flirtatious loving smile on her beaming face and waved goodbye at us for the last time.

Just for the record, I did do the honorable thing. I got on my knees and proposed as the plane was getting ready to descend over "Chicago Land". Being a smart woman, she studied the marriage proposal for a good ten seconds, and then she said, "Not in a million years!" This same "Not in million years" had been what I had been telling myself about having sex with one of the most beautiful and smart women on earth. She quickly added that we are both too young, too idealistic, too naïve and on our way to change the world. "We have too much to do before we are ready to make a big commitment like this. Let us not rush."

Unfortunately we never met again, and, we never married each other either. Of course, one could argue that I owe a great deal for this to Cousin Brucie's excellent radio program. Writing about this some thirty years later, makes it feel like it was just yesterday! It does feel like it was yesterday, but now so many years, it feels also like twilight between reality of a cheap standby ticket, and golden colored fantasies. Was it just a dream? No, there is just too much reality for it being just a dream. Was this real? Yes, I still remember all the minute details. Perhaps, a more important question is that was it smart or some juvenile thrill. I still ponder about this to this day which is some forty years later.

The overwhelming reality was that I had been "fired" for the first time from my third shift sanitation job at a franchised and famous bakery working near a hot burning oven and back breaking working conditions. Being fired had dampened my spirits after a summer long time of visiting best that New York City had to offer in museums, Radio City Theater, fantastic restaurants especially my most favorite French one on Madison Ave. as well as Tel Aviv Café. I had worked hard and everyone was more than happy with my work. I was letting that grief process to take its course while, I wisely decided that life was too sweet to be ruined by one, or even more firings. Later on, my foreman at the bakery in a phone call, explained to me that they fired all the summer job workers so they could collect unemployment for a few weeks before they went back to college. Thanks, but no thanks!

CHAPTER 14:   Carley Fiorino, Hewlett Packard (HP)

Carley Fiorino was the first female CEO in the history of HP. She started working at HP at nearly the same time that I was going to HP to work on my best job. In my opinion, she was a pioneer who tried to make HP understand that, in the end, a company is there to make money. Therefore, sales were vital. HP, for many years has had a tradition of trying to be the best technology company. Do not get me wrong, the HP Sales Department has always been an excellent part of HP. Nevertheless, Carley put prime emphasis on sales. This was more than some people, especially technical people, liked or could handle.
I admired her guts for making HP more sales-oriented. I also liked her idea that, for HP to compete with Dell, they had to give *carte blanche* to the division that hired me. We were going to increase the on-line sales directly. Therefore, Carley gave us high priority.
On the other hand, I think she got too attached and too emotional on the purchase of Compaq Computers. This move really stirred up HPers to no end, and in the end, it was her downfall. I am not going to judge her on this issue alone. However, she should have reconsidered that decision when she had monumental opposition from many angles. Even the children of HP founders were opposed to this. In addition to this, there were also serious dysfunctional events happening on the HP Board. When that scandal hit the press, it caused serious damage to HP.
At any rate, I continue to admire her for "not just sitting there" like that parakeet after she was let go. She wrote a book. In addition, she was one the advisors to Senator McCain's presidential campaign. Life and careers sometime need to have a defeat or two for people to learn and become even stronger. She had her defeat. I hope that she recovers and gets even more successful. As a senior management consultant, and executive coach I have learned too well that success is a very poor teacher.
As I have mentioned in this book before, some executive search firms will not hire an executive who has had nothing but continued success. The logic is that if someone suffered defeat and recovered, then there is a much better chance that that person will not break when hit with the first defeat on the job. Unfortunately, this prediction cannot be made about someone who has never tasted defeat. You never know what they will do. I also admire Carley for making sure that HP knew that it is not just the pure engineering excellence of a product. She drilled it in that HP has to sell to be successful. If it does not sell, then all that innovation and first-class engineering is a loss.

CHAPTER 15:   Dan Rather, CBS News Anchor

Following the tradition of Walter Cronkite's success, CBS chose Dan Rather as the next Anchor for the CBS News. In my opinion, CBS is one of the best and classiest of the evening news programs on TV. Dan had gotten my attention for the first time when he stood up to President Nixon. No other news reporter had ever done that before. When Nixon asked him, in a somewhat humiliating voice, whether he was running from something, he turned the question back at Nixon. He asked if President Regan was running from something himself.

An image that I will never forget was the picture of Dan reporting from Kabul Afghanistan. He was in the location and had local clothes on, He was one of the first to really tell it like was while he was embedded among troops! Of course "tell it like it is" was a phrase that was coined by Walter Cronkite, the most trusted man in America.

Dan had done his homework. He knew what he was talking about. He had also invented embedded reporting that became famous later on during the Iraq war. Embedded reporting is when a reporter, risking his or her life, goes to the battlefield exactly like the soldiers. He or she breathes the same air, sees the same blood and gore, is subjected to the same real bullets that the soldiers are subjected to, and feels the same pain as others. But this way, the report is real. There is no sugar coding and no glorification. The reporter talks about deaths, injuries, devastation, destruction, and destitution. He or she reports about the inherent inhumanity that exists in any good or bad war whether defensive or offensive! In spite all these heroics, Dan Rather was fired!

In an interview some years later, Dan tried to explain. Unfortunately, and this is something that I am really ashamed of, he lost me in the middle of his explanation. How could this be? This was the same Dan Rather who would, with razor sharp reporting, get my attention. But it was not the same. This was a man who was hurt from the firing process. The insanity, stupidity of firing a leader, pioneer, champion, was really rough on Dan as it is on many people. Dan, if you are reading this, I hope to see you do a comeback, and a very strong one at that. Who knows, you might do what Ted Turner did and a lot more.

Dan, we are waiting!

CHAPTER 16:   Elephants

In an ironic twist of events, the same *20/20* program on ABC Television that had the interview with Cousin Brucie also had a segment about elephants. Of course, these two segments were totally independent. But this segment somehow resonated with the previous segment.

This segment was a about elephants that go into a rage and have killed people. For example, there was a circus elephant trainer who got murdered by the elephant he was training. This is awful.

In some circuses animal cruelty is reported to include the use of chains and beatings.

The *20/20* segment continued by showing an asylum built by a lady to take care of these elephants as well as baby elephants whose parents were killed by poachers.

The lady who made this asylum explained that, as part of healing process, these baby elephants are treated just like human babies. The caregiver for each of these baby elephants even lives with them, and eventually they tend to start some sort of healing, but they never recover fully.

These baby elephants seem to always remember the violence that happened to their parents by human beings.

On the other hand, those violent elephants that have gone through years of abuse start to get a bit better as well. Of course, an animal that was violent should always be carefully watched so that it won't repeat the awful behavior. But they tend to get better by being with other elephants, as if elephants can heal each other.

Given a supportive environment, company workers seem to do both of the above. Just like baby elephants, they seldom forget that their best body was let go for no reason at all in a layoff or firing. Also, in a supportive environment, employees can really take care of each other and heal themselves.

Another sad thing about elephants is that when they get old or ill, they depart from their community, even though elephants are very social animals, and go somewhere to literally die.

A colleague once described the layoff and at will firing just like sending an elephant somewhere to die. He just felt that bad about this treatment. He was still young and full of energy and ideals. This conversation with continues to bother me to this day.

In a movie titled *Elephant Man* about a badly deformed man who was kept like an animal in a cage, he would be taken to different amusement parks as a freak show; he became quite an elegant scholar once the abuse and bad treatment stopped and he was treated like a human being with trust and mutual respect and loyalty.

By the way, he was called an "elephant man," because of his awful scars that made his skin look like the skin of an elephant.

This sad and awful depiction of animal cruelty, exemplifies the power of human potential and empowerment.

Copyright © 2008 - 2009 Razban Internet International, Inc. All rights reserved, File:20091022, P a g e | **61**

CHAPTER 17:   Vicious Cycle of Layoff Cycles

In many companies, layoffs are not just a one-time thing! Since layoffs do not work in the long term, many companies are relying on frequent and massive layoffs just to operate. Unfortunately, it is the consequences of layoffs that eventually destroy companies, careers, and even lives.

In the *Kabala*, one of the holly Jewish books, it says everything is connected to everything else. Based on this and the fact that with the global markets now the entire world is connected to each other, vicious cycles resulting from layoffs can have global consequences. Consider this:

Event 1:   A company experiences low sales and/or low revenue.

Event 2:   The Company decides to cut costs. This is based on the false assumption that cutting the work force results in savings.

Event 3:   The Company decides to lay off employees.

Event 4:   Morale goes low, and resources to do the job, or to do it right, are not there anymore!

Event 5:   To cope with Event 4, the company decides to cut services and skimp in quality.

Event 6:   Customer expectations are not met. The Customer Satisfaction Index goes down.

Event 7:   Surprise, surprise, customers DO NOT BUY.

Event 8:   Customers DO NOT BUY results in low sales and/or revenue!

Event 9:   As President Regan said, here we go again! Back to Event 1!

Many companies who do repeated layoffs, end up going out of business, or are acquired by another company. The layoff thing does not work in the long term. Layoffs destroy creativity. They destroy the fragile Mutual Trust and Loyalty among employees, between the employees and management, and all of these affect the ability of a company to produce good products and services.

One devastating fact is that excellent employees decide that they do not have to put up with constant fear of the next layoff and they find another job and leave. On the other hand, those employees who are not the best get scared and start looking for a job, and they in turn leave as well.

Then, companies desperate to get things done do pile the job of two or three employees on a poor survivor. Tempers get short. Conflicts among employees become more severe, more frequent, and more damaging. To save their jobs, employees end up playing more politics and games. All of this happens at the expense of productivity and creativity.

With all this much turmoil, then customers do not get their money's worth. As we said, since everything is related to everything else, when customers are not satisfied with one company, go to the competition. The company that laid off employees loses and employees and customers lose too. In fact, everybody loses in a layoff! Then the entire company becomes victim to low morale, politics, and trying to save jobs at any price.

"At Will," which says the company can fire and the employee can quit any time, has had an awful impact on productivity, and MTL I do not care, you do not care, attitude on the side of company, employees, and customers.

Copyright © 2008 - 2009 Razban Internet International, Inc. All rights reserved, File:20091022, P a g e | **62**

CHAPTER 18:   Layoffs Can Be as Painful as an Ugly Divorce or a Death in the
Family and my Heart Attack on the Job

A layoff can be just as stressful and as painful as an ugly divorce.
Please think about these lyrics from ABBA in a song called "Knowing Me, Knowing
You," which is about the pain of divorce and separation, especially as it affects innocent
children.
<
"

No more carefree laughter
Silence ever after
Walking through an empty house, tears in my eyes
Here is where the story ends, this is goodbye"
>
And to emphasize the emptiness after a divorce, which is similar to what happens after a
layoff, somewhere else in the song it says:
<
"Memories (memories), good days (good days), bad days (bad days)
They'll be (they'll be), with me (with me) always (always)
In these old familiar rooms children would play
Now there's only emptiness, nothing to say"
>
I have felt this sudden emptiness of layoffs in my bones. My stomach-wrenching experience
of layoffs is vividly reflected in the above lyrics. I saw this in a major company's
headquarters in San Jose California. I saw after row of empty offices and rooms that someday
might have had happy employees working there. We are human beings and this hurts. I am
not blaming that company or their management. In fact, their CEO is one of the most
respected in the industry. But the effect is as painful as getting an ugly divorce. A layoff is
not unlike an ugly lingering devastating divorce. Divorce and layoffs also seem to have an
ugly inter-relationship. Unfortunately, sometimes a layoff makes a divorce happen or even
vice versa. The most painful part of this awful duo is the impact they individually or
collectively have on children.
Delkesh, a famous Persian singer, had a very old song that had these as part of its lyrics:
<
"The cheerful noises and giggles of childhood,
They will never come back!"
>
The sadness here is that a divorce robs these kids from all those giggles in the first place, so
they never will have them. It steals from them the chance to just be children and play as it
shows in ABBA's lyrics.
Of course, in some cases, divorce is the only solution to a tragic and abusive marriage, or a
company in some rare dire circumstances just has to do a layoff.
It has been my experience that when someone suddenly loses his/her job, this can be just as
painful as losing a loved one. In our American society, it seems that we are totally consumed
by our jobs. We develop a firm identification and attachment to them, and when they
disappear, we go through a grief process.
My first exposure to this was when I went to see one of my best colleagues while I was
working at Plantronics. Eric was my mentor and helper, and he had exactly the same job

Copyright © 2008 - 2009 Razban Internet International, Inc. All rights reserved, File:20091022, P a g e | **63**

function as I did. The only thing was that he was a lot more experienced at it, and great at it. He was always full of advice, insight, and help for me. One of the last things he told me was to try to help his fiancé cope. His fiancé also worked at Plantronics, and we had become friends. After Eric passed away, she told me that it was one of the most difficult things that happened in her life, yet years later, when she had to face a Sudden Job Loss (SJL), this was just as difficult as well. The basis for this is that, suddenly, what you had and thought you would always have is gone! No more! In some psychological charts, this is just as bad. This pain is something that has to be carefully considered prior to the decision to divorce. Enough time has to be given for healing process.

My parents loved Delkesh, who in her time, she was considered the Prima Singer in Iran! They cherished her voice and songs because they had a great deal of meaning for them. Delkesh was also the entertainer in my parents' wedding. They tell me that she had a golden voice. Unfortunately, I was not yet born to enjoy her great music personally. My mother used to tell me, over and over again, that Delkesh had her start by singing in Cafés that were in distant places on the roads. At first, her songs were not very good, and her voice did not have the quality that it developed later on. But she did not give up. A layoff can mute all the excitement and the "cheerful noises and giggles of childhood" that were fundamental to happy work environment full of job satisfaction.

I suffered a heart attack in 2001. It was a hot day, and it was the last day I was working for that client. I had worked very hard and generated all the results that were expected or more. Unfortunately the contract was coming to an end. I had not lined up another contract. I had tried to get another contract, but I did not seem to get anywhere.

I started to feel a lot of pain in my chest. I started to feel shortness of breath. I felt like I need to vomit, and felt a bit dizzy. My heart was racing, and I was sweating profoundly as if someone had poured water on me. I could not keep standing up. I was near a chair and I sat down. It felt like I had passed out. When I came to, there was still nobody else around since it had been the lunch hour. I did not even think that this was a heart attack that could have killed me. This was my life, yet I was somewhat absorbed in other things such as making sure that I did return my badge and final report. I could not afford any delays in my final paycheck from there. A few hours later, it suddenly occurred to me that I must have suffered a heart attack.

I had been very angry there for the previous few weeks. My manager had carefully asked me to generate several reports. When you are in this business as long as I have been you can tell that those reports were carefully orchestrated to get his competing colleague fired. Those report, although theoretically OK, were used to paint, or actually frame somebody else in a bad light. I felt used. I felt that I had violated one of the ten commandments that says you should not give false witness. The truth is that I was doing my job and I did not lie. The truth was that there was no 100% proof that this was indeed what those reports were being used for.

To my outrage, I heard the next week that the person who was the subject of those reports had been fired. He had worked diligently for that company for many years. He had three young kids, and in his culture, being fired meant losing your Mokato, or your human honor and dignity. I am sure that he must have had a hard time recovering.

A few months later, when I finally went to see our physician, he essentially said I had a heart attack and he could see it in the electrocardiogram or EKG. Which brings me to an interesting observation. We might be unemployed and not have money. Yet the fact remains that we are alive. Is a job, any job worth a heart attack? Life does go on while we are disappointed about not having a job, or the ideal career!

After I had found another job that required business travel to Europe, I decided to live life to the fullest. On my first trip to Amsterdam and on a tour bus, we were shown the Red Light District. This is where some of the most attractive prostitutes pose in front of window. I had read about this for years, and I had determined that in Netherlands, this was legal and regulated. More importantly, it was clean. I had decided not to visit these women even for once. It was exploitation. It was against my belief system.

But this time, I was sitting at London Heathrow and waiting for my flight that was about three hours later. I noticed there was an advertized special ticket from Heathrow to Schiphol Airport in Amsterdam that was 60% off. I was pulled to the special KLM counter and had my round trip tickets in less than three minutes and I was told these are hourly flights and I did not have to worry if I missed this particular flight that was taking off shortly. I ran to make sure that I caught that flight and not the later one. I was determined to get the Red Light District urge out of my system, have sex, and then be back within that three hours. I was one of the last passengers boarding this squeaky clean MD DC 9. I was in Amsterdam before, I could finish my drink on that super short flight. I got a cab from the airport and went directly to the Red Light District. About twenty steps from where I got off the taxi I noticed a red head with a whip. She was not for me. Astonishingly enough, right next to her place, there was a strawberry blonde woman in a formal airline uniform. For thousands of years, I have fantasized about having sex with flight attendants. She sensed my desire and flaming passion and motioned to me to get in. A small and clean bed with fresh sheets was waiting. "You want it with my uniform on or off?" Well to save time, we had sex with her having her uniform on. By now my three hour limit was expired. Along with that the idea of having sex once and going back to the airport had totally vanished too. I asked her name, and gave her a generous tip. She lit a cigarette and offered me one too.

"I do this mainly for my kids." "Dutch Government respects us as Sex Workers and we even have a pension." "How Many kids do you have?" "Three." "How about husband?" "He is decent man, but he cannot even support himself with his salary." Alarmed that her husband could come and kill me any moment, I asked, "Does he know?" "Of course yes!" "We have a good marriage and excellent sex!" "From your question and accent I can tell you are from America!" "Yes, and I wish America was also as enlightened to treat this right and avoid all kind of crime that surrounds the "illegal" American Sex Work. We continued talking about this for some time. She remembered to look at her watch. Then politely, she said "Sorry, I need to make more money. I will give you 50% off if you can do it again! This time, I will take my uniform off!" I had been ready for the encore performance only a few minutes after she had been fully satisfied and fulfilled me the first time. The second time was even more satisfying. It seemed like our discussion and my point of view about Sex Workers had convinced Ingrid to be more gentle and loving the second time. My heart did stop during the act. I was having sex with a professional and a sex artist that indeed wanted to show me the super sex pleasure in a clean and healthy way. As I was putting my clothes on, I seriously thought about what felt a heart stop. I asked myself "What if I had died?" I was old enough and had risk factors to die from a heart attack.

These thoughts were occupying my mind during a one hour cruise in Amsterdam canals passing the flower market, and several important historical sites.

Copyright © 2008 - 2009 Razban Internet International, Inc. All rights reserved, File:20091022, P a g e | **65**

I found Former Hotel that was right next to the airport so I can board the first flight back to Heathrow the next day. Next morning, I decided that I had go and see Ingrid one last time. It was like Marlon Brando's "Last Tango in Paris." I had memorized where Ingrid was there. To my surprise, Ingrid did not work on Tuesdays, Wednesdays, or Thursdays. I had to wait until Friday. Angelina who had been in Ingrid's window told me that she was the exact same size as Ingrid and they had many steady clients in common. "Do you want KLM, Air France, or Alitalia uniform this time?" "It does not matter that much, but I seem to try Air France this time." "Vous parlez Francise?", which is you speak French? "Bien Sur" Which is of course in English. "I speak five languages" she burst off in perfect Parisian accent French. "I used to work for KLM, but now at forty I am a bit too old for them." "I can go back and work for them if I pushed, but I like this job more. It is more pleasure and fun." "I specialize in first-timer young ones. I teach them that this is fun and healthy, but they have to be protected and careful." "I am convinced that I have saved many young men from serious trouble, by taking care of their urge the right way and the right time!"

Copyright © 2008 - 2009 Razban Internet International, Inc. All rights reserved, File:20091022, P a g e | **66**

CHAPTER 19:   Fear of Losing It All, and Fear of Sudden Job Loss (SJL)

The first time I discovered that I had a fear of heights, was during my Freshman Physical Education (PE). In that cold and freezing Wisconsin winter, I was attending my PE class that consisted of swimming. I had done relatively OK. However, that day, we had to go up on the high dive and jump.

We followed each other in a row going up the steps. After getting on the highest dive board at the end of steps, swim teacher would instruct us to jump. I started to sweat so bad that I thought that I had a fever. My only consolation was that there were many others ahead of me. Therefore, I thought that I had some time before I had to make the jump. If they could do it, I should be able to do it too. Fear of falling down and dying because of a miss-step, or even pushed by someone behind me, made me feel a level of anxiety I had never felt before. I started to look around and felt dizzy. The PE instructor calmly announced over a speaker that I did not have to "complete" the jump there and then. His sentence sounded funny to me. How could I complete a jump that I had not even started? I could come down the steps if I wanted and do it later, only if I wanted to. When I came down, he told me that, just the same very some people have allergies to certain foods, some of his students, usually one- in-fifty or so, find it too difficult to make this high jump. The University recognizes this and respects this. Therefore, it was in his jurisdiction not to ask me to jump again without any grade penalty. He thanked me having done my best. That made the day for me.

This was a few years before psychologists coined the term "fear of flying." Fear of flying affects many famous celebrities, including my most favorite football coach and sportscaster, John Madden. He would travel on a bus for days instead of flying for a few hours to get to the next sporting event across the country. Moreover, it is my opinion that this fear of flying does not reduce the people's respect for him even one iota.

My job and my career were very important to me then as they are now. In many cases, when we meet a new person, after the name, we are interested in what they do. As if their job and career is their most important identity. Moreover, the fear of losing it all, and suddenly, started being a real fear that even persists now more than thirty years later. Just the same as the fear of flying, this fear of Sudden Job Loss (SJL) is real and powerful.

The very sad part of SJL is the high emotional, business, and management costs. A layoff as a short-term band-aid, ignores many long-term impacts of layoffs are not considered. Yet, company after company, lays offs their employees in a knee jerk reaction as a short-term fix. Unfortunately, many of these short terms fixes back fire and create serious long-term problems. Interestingly enough, when I tell people about Fear of Flying, they seem to remember the erotic book about this subject first.

During my very short single life that lasted until I was forty-nice before I got married, I had a hot lover who was studying to become a psychologist. I had met her trough one of the dating clubs. I had been tired of a perpetual Monty Python single and lonely life where I would chase attractive woman and never manage to marry them. Laura was one that I really fell in love. I was infatuated, fixated, and obsessed! She was writing her Ph D thesis and she was attracted to me just as strongly as I was attracted to her even though she was super attractive and dress to kill, and I nothing. Nevertheless, I could speak French and she had studied in Sorbonne, and I would have been that envied research

Copyright © 2008 - 2009 Razban Internet International, Inc. All rights reserved, File:20091022, P a g e | **67**

subject that her Stanford Ph D heavily depended on. We became fast friends. We would spend hours talking in restaurants. We went to Carmel and many other romantic places. She was fascinated to learn about my "No beg, no push" philosophy towards sex. My argument that this is a "man thing" got her even more interested. She insisted that I need to meet her friend and Stanford Psychology friend/mentor who had happen to be a world renowned Stanford Professor teaching sexual dysfunction. In return, I introduced her to my family. My mother fell in love with her right away. My Dad who was in a nursing home a few months before the end of his life was impressed. Laura insisted on visiting my Dad almost regularly. During the winters, it does get cold in California Bay Area. Our discussion that night had taken several hours during dinner, and we decided to it was time for me to drive her home in my car. Half way driving home, I noticed that her hand was on my shoulder. It was not very comfortable. Then, I asked her if I could stop for a few minutes since I had something important to tell her. "Absolutely!" We stopped in parking lot behind a building and just as far as we could from other cars. I kissed her on the chick and I told her that I loved her. The response came in French. It was "Me too!" In a semi whispering tone, I said "But look at you and look at me!" Then I added, "I am over weight and you are perfectly ideal and attractive". She said, "No Mon Amie, it is what is inside, I fell for you in the nursing home when your Dad said that he used to be your Dad and now you are his Dad!" The neither of us could resist. We had the hottest sex that fogged up all the windows. It took almost fifteen minutes after we were done, and with all windows completely rolled down in a 45 Degree winter night to get rid of the fog. She was one of the women that I had ever met who had a permanent make up. By then I had gotten good in planning marriages. Therefore, around Thanksgiving, we decided to get married. We would have white-picket fenced home, two kids (one of each or two of the same kind did not matter to her.) The plans were finalized, as we got closer to Christmas. Then my company had a layoff across board and that got me down and depressed for a few days. Then it was my Dad's turn to get really sick and be moved to hospital. Finally, it was her thesis, which had a serious setback since some of her research turned out to be based on a "Faulty Assumption". Then there was one thing after the other and slowly we drifted apart. There is a saying that God has a sense of humor. To prove this, I drive past a white picket fence that Laura and I had intended to purchase and raise a family in it. I called her many years later to tell her that I was writing a book about psychology of layoffs. There was a lot of noise on the cell phone. She exploded and said, "What? You are writing a book about getting laid? What is there to getting laid that is about psychology? I do not understand." We had a big laugh after I had explained.

Patrick J. Carnes, in "Out of the Shadows: Understanding Sexual Addiction", puts emphasis on "Faulty Assumptions" as a powerful reason and root cause for Sexual as well as many other addictions including over eating, alcoholism, and substance abuse. Of course, over eating has been my life-long dilemma. I have found that in my own case, other colleagues, and friends that are victims of layoffs or other types of Sudden Job Loss (SJL) a powerful "Faulty Assumption" is made. This then causes many problems that are difficult to shake later on.

In addition to this, in Psychology, we know that people who are depressed often have a "Fixation" to something or someone that they hold, rightly or wrongly, as the cause of their depression that results in not being to be functional. Again, I not a Psychologist and I like to emphasize again that if you are having a difficult time coping with the aftermath of a Sudden Job Loss, you need to reach out and ask help from experts. Who knows this might have been result of a chemical imbalance and a medication that costs less than fifty cents a day might take care of it. It is important to note that just talking things out with a professional will help considerably. Of

Copyright © 2008 - 2009 Razban Internet International, Inc. All rights reserved, File:20091022, P a g e | **68**

course, going to a twelve-step program might end up being the best thing for the person and others in their lives.

Nevertheless, the fact remains that we are working with a painful fixation or faulty assumption. In my experience, this fixation or faulty assumption results from the "Pink Shock" which is a colorful way of expressing the layoff and SJL. A colleague told me that he lost his job because he drove a car that was much better than his manager and that had made his manager very jealous. Another one told me and firmly believed that at age sixty-two he was let go just because he hated his career. He had hated his career for all these years. According to him, he had become such great actor that no one ever even suspected how much he hated this career. However, he kept his dad (who had passed away a good thirteen years prior to this) responsible for this.

In both cases, these were massive layoffs affecting the entire groups. It was not their fault. They could have done nothing differently to avoid these layoffs on their own. Therefore, their assumptions were faulty and they were nothing but a well-known fixation that kept them so preoccupied that they did not do their daily functions needed by normal living.

Let us stick to Faulty Assumptions for the rest of this discussion. In a layoff, there will be twin faulty assumptions. The employee will assume that he or she is "not good enough" to be hired again, a kind of "Damaged Goods!"

Sadly enough, the company is assuming that cutting ten percent of employees will result in a ten percent reduction in operating costs. This too is a faulty assumption.

Unfortunately, they are both wrong. For example, there is nothing wrong with an employee who loses his job in company A. It did not work at company A. Remember this is the age of "At Will" firing and employee walking out! Nevertheless, the fact remains that he or she, exactly as he or she is, will make a fantastic employee for company B, C, D, and all the way up to company Z. This works, and works well if we do not give up. Learn from our experience, empower ourselves and go for even a better job. Mayor Bloomberg, one of the best mayors, who is the Mayor of New York City, fits this category. He has said that he would have never become such good mayor had he not been "fired" from his previous job!

As for the company who laid off ten percent of the work force to save ten percent, they might be in for a shock. They can lose another ten percent due to MTL erosion in the long term, or even have to close doors.

Unfortunately, so many CEOs are isolated from the harsh market realities. They do not see the toxicity that layoffs produce. I am sure that we will get out of this awful financial crisis. Then, cooler heads will prevail. CEOs decide not to act in a dazed fashion like the rest of Zombies in the work place including myself. Then we will come up with alternatives. We will find better ways to create even more profits by focusing on our most important asset that is human capital. As you see in other chapters in this book, some companies like Aflac Insurance have already discovered better ways to avoid layoffs.

On February 15, 2009, CBS sixty Minutes interviewed a company that had invented a new way of recycling steel. I think that they are the biggest recycler in US. Their management and workers talked about the disastrous economics situation in 2009. They mentioned that they laid off nobody. They all got a fifty or fifty-five percent reduction in their paychecks. They were not excited about this. However, they stuck together and did not "lose" anybody.

Now with the government plans to improve the infrastructure, we stand a chance to do well. The outcome will have to be good for the entire economy. This company stayed together as a team, and now with a fortified MTL, the company will make better profits.

On the other hand, there are consequences resulting from frequent and repeated layoffs. For example, riots are occurring in Italy, France, Korea, China, and other places protesting layoffs and economic disaster. As a part of the Disaster Recovery Plans that companies had to prepare for the Year 2000 (Y2K) impending doom and gloom, they had to plan for "Social Unrest". This referred to serious riots that would disrupt cities. These are riots similar to what we see around the world. Luckily, it turned out that the year 2000 came and computers did not do massive crashes,

Copyright © 2008 - 2009 Razban Internet International, Inc. All rights reserved, File:20091022, P a g e | **69**

airplanes did not fall from the sky, patients did not die on the operating table due to some computer malfunction. Yet corporations had foreseen the potential for social unrest in the event of even a technology induced disruption in economy.

Yet, the economic Tsunami that we are facing, and will continue to face for another few years, will have much more potential for unrest resulting to serious damage to cities and citizens. This is the sad part.

However, we need to come together on a global basis. We need to review and modify our operating processes, as any well run-company would do at a time like this. There is much need for governments, private enterprises big or small, and all of us to do teamwork and be agile enough to prevent any such outcome.

We can and must do this. Let us go do it! We shall overcome. We will survive, and even thrive if we learn our lessons.

CHAPTER 20:   Was that job "The It All" that was promised or Thought?

In interviews and job orientation meetings for new employees, companies like to think that when they give us a job, they have given us it all! I was certainly thinking that way, even if my first company, Plantronics, did not say it.

You get a base pay that is calculated for a year, so it sounds greater than life. You have fringe benefits like insurance, sick leave, vacations, life insurance, and that most important health insurance for you and your dependents. You get structure in life. You get colleagues. You get to have daily social contact with other people who are somewhat like you since you work in the same company.

I agree that a job gives you many good things. But not all!

You do not have the freedom to be productive and innovative at your own pace and your choice. This is especially true if you are the creative inventive type. You already have agreed to give your invention rights to the company. This happened in my case. It turns out that I gave the rights to the company happily. This was good for me and good for them. It established me as a world class inventor with a Patent Grant, and made the companies a lot of money. Had I had the resources to quit and start a company of my own using the rights to that invention, I would be a millionaire now.

In addition, you do not have the right to be yourself since you have to fit into that company's culture and processes even if you have a much better alternative that you can suggest. You are right, I am a super example of those classical sour losers. I love to live in the past. I always maximize the good things about a job that I have lost and minimize the bad things.

However, a critical important fact emerges here. Just the same way that the work you had or still have, was not "it all," you have not lost it all either. You still have your loved ones, family, and friends. You are still the same person that you always were and will be. Your skills and experience did not self-destruct or reset as a result of a layoff!

To borrow from Jefferson Airplane lyrics:

<
Today you'll make me say that I somehow have changed
Today you'll look into my eyes, I'm just not the same
To be anymore than all I am would be a lie
>

I have done a lot of stupid things in my life. Someone had told me to stand in front of mirror each day and say good things to yourself as opposed to this constant self verbal beating. I tried it a few times. But when he told me that I will be the same person that I was before layoff as after layoff, I had to stand in front of the mirror several times just to make sure. I assure you I too was, and am the same person!

For example, a day after a harsh layoff, you are the very same person you were the day before. Nothing has changed about you. You are who you are and who you were, and who you will always be. Let us use the negative energy produced by the layoffs and channel it to positive. A positive might be that you get a chance to find a job that is a better fit and you enjoy more. Another positive can be that you take a few classes in a close by college. And the most important positive can be that you spend more time with your loved ones, friends, colleagues, and family. Also, this might give you a chance to spend some time with yourself too.

All of these of course at the same time with job search!

Copyright © 2008 - 2009 Razban Internet International, Inc. All rights reserved, File:20091022, P a g e | **71**

CHAPTER 21:   September 15, 2008, a 500-Point Drop in Stock Market

I will never forget this day. The stock market heavy drop has alarmed me. When I started to write this book, I was working with ideas. Now those ideas are happening. These actual happening of my predictions is scary to me.

In a sad way, this rather proves my ideas presented in this book. Companies are failing because they did not develop Mutual Trust and Loyalty (MTL) with their customers and employees. As per Google, in February of 2007, CNBC Reported that:
<
"Americans hate their jobs more than ever before in the past 20 years, with fewer than half saying they are satisfied.
The trend is strongest among workers under the age of 25, less than 39 percent of who are satisfied with their jobs.
Workers age 45 to 54 have the second lowest level of satisfaction (less than 45 percent), according a survey conducted by The Conference Board, a market information company that also puts out the Consumer Confidence Index and the Leading Economic Indicators.
Again as per Google, FOX News in April of 2008 said:
"An internal survey of about 141,000 of the department's 208,000 employees found that only 58 percent were satisfied with their jobs, the same as results from a 2006 survey that measured job satisfaction across the government. The department ranked at the bottom in the 2006 poll, which was conducted by the Office of Personnel Management.
While 91 percent of the people who work at the department think the work they do is important, only 54 percent would recommend the department as a good place to work. That number is up from the 51 percent reported in 2006."
>
I will also never forget that on this same day, HP, the same HP that refused to layoff a single employee in fifty years, announced that it was laying off 25,000 employees. Fortunately, about eight months after this knee jerk massive and frequent layoffs, several companies including Aflac declared that they would not lay off until and unless they have tried everything else first.

No matter how we want to sugarcoat this, it seems that somewhere around forty percent of Americans are unhappy with their jobs. Let us just say that this job unhappiness translates into a fifteen-percent loss of productivity. There are approximately 116 Million Households in US, and the average annual income is $50,000. Then, this means that we have wasted about $870,000,000,000 each year. This is about .87 of a Trillion (One Million, Million Dollars). Borrowing from the *Trillion Dollar War* book, if you stacked $1000 Bills, this .87 Trillion would be a stack 56.5 Miles high.

Another sad fact is that unhappy employees are more prone to accidents, they file more lawsuits against their companies, and they produce lower quality products. This should sound like a great bragging point for the Europeans and the rest of the world to laugh at Americans. Just imagine how much fun they would have had blaming us about wasting paper. Nevertheless, almost one trillion dollar career, talent, and workplace productivity is wasted each year, year after year. This is sick!

I was waiting for my 6:57 AM train from Mountain View to San Francisco, when I heard several of my Banker type train riders murmur, "Bad Day for the Market." The next day I saw the title on my home-delivered paper that is usually wet from the nightly sprinkler action. I did quick calculations:

Copyright © 2008 - 2009 Razban Internet International, Inc. All rights reserved, File:20091022. P a g e | **72**

- With the limitless influx of millions of H1 visa holders,
- With 25,000 Layoffs from HP and perhaps a bigger number from other companies,
- In addition, with the fact that each month several hundred brand new employees enter the market, I was sure that finding a job now would need two or three times as much effort. If it took one-hundred resumes and twenty phone calls to find a job, now it takes 200, or 300 resumes and forty or sixty phone calls to land a job.
- The nightmare of going without a job was so overpowering that I had to take a day off just to clear my mind.

Then on the 18th, the stock market went up 400 or so points. My problems started when I had applied for a $20,000 home equity loan that seemed to be approved well ahead of all these disasters. All of a sudden, banks totally stopped any loans. I have a FICA score of about 748 or so which is almost a perfect score. Then each month that I was late each lending institution unilaterally decided to chop of several points, level brutally high interest rates, and then charge all kinds of fines. In one month, my entire bi-weekly unemployment check went into payment of about $900 minus that Bank of America had leveled against me. That hurt. That was one time when I went to bed hungry.

If there were some SOAR self-regulations, it would have prevented this. Of course, I pay my bills; I have done this for many years. I lose sleep when I am behind. However, if the penalties are so harsh as to financially killing the goose that was laying golden eggs, then the result is what we see now. A glut of foreclosed home, each of which resulting from devastation of a families nest and home, and banks that cannot "liquidate" these things capitals because their policies were so short-sighted that they ignored the human capital. As in the book "Perfect Storm", I found myself in a sea of red ink. I realized that we need to have fundamental changes in our way of doing business. My unemployment check of $1,900 each month cannot possibility cover the $2,000 to $5,000 interest only charges that were leveled against me. Several credit card companies decided that to solve this, at least in my case, is to call me every hour of day and night. A Toll-Free number will show on my BlackBerry that I knew is coming from Bill Collectors, so I will not answer. They in return did not leave a message. Every day around 8:00, I will get Bank of America calling followed by Chase, and one other one. This is nothing less than the famous "Water Torture"! This destructive, iron fisted, unilateral, action from our financial institutions made me defiant. I wanted to take a picket sign and go scream outside! Like a mad man, I would have wanted to scream stop this vicious cycle. Give Main Street Work a Day Stiffs like myself a break. Then on top of my longs shout, "Read my Book, Read my Book for God's Sake!"

However, like many others I was singing Simon and Garfrankle's "Sound of Silence" in silence! I thought if I keep my unemployment and financial situation silent, then I would have a better chance of finding a job. My financial difficulties grew exponentially. I almost lost a chance to go to an interview for a job that would have saved the bank and me because I would get an electric shock every time the phone rang. I would not pick it up. Ann, an outstanding recruiter had to call more than ten times to get hold me, right the day before the interview and prepare me for the interview.

I also am convinced that FICA Scores are a joke. I had no respect for them in the good days when bank managers would beg (that is right, the exact word is beg) to take a home equity loan. I really did not need them, but just for a rainy day! They did not even look at

Copyright © 2008 - 2009 Razban Internet International, Inc. All rights reserved, File:20091022, P a g e | **73**

the FICA 20, because they were giving loans to anybody. Therefore, at that time, FICA was irrelevant. It is even more irrelevant now. How could I get a bad score of 520 in six months? God knows how many points were taken off because one bill was consistently late each month, even though it was paid, for a year. Early in my management training, I heard the expression that a manager is like a military commander. Of course, you do know my private attitude toward wars. I do not like them unless they are in absolute self-defense! At any rate, the expression is that a manager, like a military commander, cannot send soldiers to war and in front of live bullets, and then ask them why they are bleeding! General Patton, a professional soldier that I respect along with Omar Bradley always protected their soldiers and did the best that was possible to take care of them. This is how his army won when the others lost! War is hell, but he made it tolerable!

I am hoping that soon there will be help to Main Street as well as it was for the Wall Street.

Copyright © 2008 - 2009 Razban Internet International, Inc. All rights reserved, File:20091022,

CHAPTER 22:   Unhappy America

The Economist magazine, on its cover story around the end of July 2008 had a major article about unhappy Americans. *Economist,* which is a European magazine, looks at us with a different frame of mind. Nevertheless, the article tries to point out that due to the financial downturn, the war with Iraq, and other factors America is an unhappy nation. This was a time when credit crunch had hit the worst. It was a time that many economists were giving bad indications of the future economic conditions. Unemployment statistics were heading upward. Many companies were announcing layoffs or even plant closures. I also remember that economists used to have, or they still may have, a misery index. This index takes into account the economy and other factor to indicate our well-being. The same way that a person can lose his or her job and become depressed, a group or a company can become depressed. In addition, this article indicates that an entire nation can become depressed emotionally and financially.

Frequent layoffs, firings, and mismanagement have caused eighty percent of American and European management and workers job dissatisfaction. In fact, this is one reason why they are not happy with their lives either. My experience show that job dissatisfaction frequently spills into life dissatisfaction. This overall dissatisfaction resulted in so many domestic abuse cases, divorce, and other destructive behavior that radio stations and news organizations decided to give it some badly needed attention.

A respected colleague who had a chance to work in Europe for a few years told me that work there was considerably easier than in US. For example, he told me that layoffs were not as common as they are here. He also saw many long-term employees in different companies. The American idea of working some place for a few years, or even months, and then going somewhere else is not popular in Europe as it is here.

In September of 2008, my research on Google indicated that the average American had about $15,000 in his or her retirement account as opposed to the Europeans who have much more. Having said these let me set the record straight. I am not in favor of the old government systems that kept employees on the payroll no matter what. I am also not advocating keeping nonproductive employees employed either. However, to quote what I think is from HP management, there is no such a thing as a bad employee, but there is such a thing as misplaced employee.

However, this knee jerk and random layoff practice is not helping anybody. It is hurting too.

CHAPTER 23:   Symptoms of a Dysfunctional Workplace

Humans are humans. If we are not treated well in life and the workplace, we try to find ways to cope. I hope that most of the time, we find positive and productive ways to cope and deal in a productive way with the workplace problems and difficulties.
Unfortunately, the dysfunctional workplaces have created or encouraged bad behavior. Abramson's Classical Book "How to Cope with Difficult People" has made the following classifications:

Sherman Tanks: These bullies intimidate and attack anyone rightly or wrongly. They are destructive and are used to destroying anything or anybody in their way.

Snakes: These are people who pretend to be your friends on the surface, but who will stick a knife in your back when you least expect it.

Snipers: Another type of destructive people is those who do not even try to pretend that they are your friends. Nevertheless, they hide and shoot at you. You never know what hit you.

Wolf Packs: A group of one or more co-workers who have an explicit or implied understanding that, if one of them is attacked, then the rest will go to the rescue. The rescue can be fair or unfair and it can be about a real threat or an imagined one.

These are mostly symptoms. Many experienced managers have learned to deal with the root cause as opposed to the symptoms. The real cause that management experts call the Six Sigma Analysis clearly indicates that the workplace has become sick and non-productive. The sad thing is that other countries are imitating the American dysfunctional workplace. They are copying the layoff mentality. They are copying lack of respect for the human element that consists of employees and customers. These bad practices in turn have created problems that are reflected (using some humor) in the following.
Let me add a few more examples based on my own observation,

Nowhere Men (Women):   The Beatle's "Yellow Submarine" has a song with this title. These types of people are those who never take a stand on any subject. Therefore, you never know where they stand.

Power Pointers: Power Point is Microsoft software that has worldwide use for presentations. These types of people have learned to use this tool to its limit in creating colorful presentations that practically say nothing of importance in a meeting.

Russian Village Makers: It is said that a Russian Tsar passed through a poor village in the morning and did not like what he saw. The real reason was that the village was sadly poor. Therefore, he told the mayor, "you make this look good by the end of the day, or I will kill you." The mayor, out of desperation, orders everyone to put great facades in front of their run-down and dilapidated buildings. Moreover, they almost kill themselves and succeed in making the village look good on the outside. The next day, the Tsar was very impressed, so much so that he gave the mayor a medal. A few days after that, high winds destroyed the superficial decoration and the villagers were faced with the

	same problems as before.
Data Obsessed:	These ask for more and more data and never tell you why. Even given many data, they lack the ability to analyze it in a meaningful way to produce results.
Reality Challenged:	Any employee that decides to ignore facts and stick to a rose-colored marketing or accounting picture of how things are. This is frequently in odds with realities known by just everybody in the company and in the market by customers.
Executive Cluelessness:	A high-level executive who has no clue about how his company is doing.
Turf Worriers:	These people fight and fight for what they think is their turf. They can fight even after the company has declared Chapter 11.
Fire Fighter Arsons:	These people are excellent in creating a crisis in the company that only they and their group can solve. This therefore makes them essential to a company operation, but at a very high cost.
Hot Air Balloonists:	They create many unpractical ideas but are so good at convincing others, that these ideas might even cause the demise of the company.
The Nile Rafters:	These are people who are in denial (Therefore, the Nile and they sound the same) who convince themselves and others that everything is fine.

Early in October of 2008, the following email was going around:

A sort of sick joke that became popular during the market crash of 2008. I got this joke from two or three people.

CEO:	Chief Embezzlement Officer (I want to apologize to those 90% CEOs who care and are honest and competent).
CFO:	Corporate Fraud Officer.
BULL MARKET:	A random market movement causing an investor to mistake himself for a financial genius.
BEAR MARKET:	A six to eighteen-month period when the kids get no allowance, the wife gets no jewelry, and the spouse gets to have no fun.
VALUE INVESTING:	The art of buying low and selling lower.
P/E RATIO:	The percentage of investors wetting their pants as the market keeps crashing.
BROKER:	What my broker has made me.
STANDARD & POOR:	Your life in a nutshell.
STOCK ANALYST:	Idiot who just downgraded your stock.
STOCK SPLIT:	When your ex-wife/ex-husband and her/his lawyer split your assets equally between themselves.
FINANCIAL PLANNER:	A guy whose phone has been disconnected.
MARKET CORRECTION:	The day after you buy your stocks
CASH FLOW:	The movement your money makes as it disappears down the toilet.
YAHOO:	What you yell after selling it to some poor sucker for $240 per share.
WINDOWS:	What you jump out of when you are the sucker who bought Yahoo @ $240 per share.
INSTITUTIONAL INVESTOR:	Past year investor who is now locked up in a nuthouse.
PROFIT:	An archaic word no longer in use.

Of course, this must have been written by someone who must have lost a lot of his or her money in the stock market.

Please do not get me wrong. A big majority of people in companies including CEOs and

Management and employees are hardworking and honest employees. However, two or three percent of the time we all might be guilty of doing some of these things.

In the recent situation with Captain Sully, one lesson that corporate America needs to learn, is that the CEO is like the captain of the ship. He or She is the one that is finally responsible for everything. This responsibility bestowed with the honor that the job of CEO as the best of the best in the company, makes it imperative that CEO is accountable for everything. He or she is accountable for the good things and the bad things during the good times and the bad times.

In addition, all of us are the CEOs of our lives and our career. A fact that I learned twenty-five years ago is something that applies today. We are responsible and accountable for our career. This means that we constantly need to refine our skill set and our network to find that next job. It means that our next job might very well a job that we ourselves have created, or a company that we have created.

I found creating a small company to be ten times easier and hundred times more satisfying that look for the next job was.

Copyright © 2008 - 2009 Razban Internet International, Inc. All rights reserved, File:20091022, P a g e | **78**

CHAPTER 24:   BBC Radio Report of Workplace Unhappiness

For many years, I have enjoyed listening to the BBC World News program broadcast on California Public Radio stations at 9:00 PM weekdays. Of course, I admit that I am a news junkie. I like to religiously watch BBC, TelemondeTV5, and Channel 2 on the British, French, and Israeli TV Satellite Network. As if this is not enough, I watch all American Channels such as ABC, NBC, and CBS. I fondly remember Walter Cronkite for his daily newscasts signing off with his favorite "This is Walter Cronkite, and that is the way it was…" . The CBS Evening News was a family tradition. We all sat around the TV and observed Walter Cronkite present the news. Dinner would only be served after the CBS News. I was truly sad when he passed away a few days ago. He was America's most trusted man. He had enough courage to say Vietnam was wrong, when it was politically wrong to say such things. Yet he was empowered and inspired by being the best of the best in his job, career, and profession. I was thinking about Walter Cronkite and his humble Dutch Immigrant background when I happened to come across the KLM, Dutch Airline clip in youTube.com. The Clip in several languages, emphasized KLM's corporate responsibility. The corporate responsibility to people which was employees and passengers (KLM understood Human Capital well) and making sure that they have the best equipment. At the age seventeen, way before I knew anything about management and on my first transatlantic flight from Amsterdam to New York, I could see this pride, professionalism, empowerment and passion in the entire KLM crew. As for the equipment, KLM had taken delivery of one the first and most advanced Super DC8 jets. On BBC nightly news business section, they discussed a recent survey that was done in London around the end of July of 2008. The report had found that the majority of Londoners were unhappy with their jobs, with only a few minor exceptions.
One of those minor exceptions happened to be hair dressers. Why? This was because they made people happier by helping them look better. The survey also found that even during tough economic times, men and women still did those nice things such as getting a nice haircut or hair styling. So, the hair dressers' business was not hurt as much as others. Even at these difficult economic times, customers still felt especially entitled to this minor luxury. After all there were too many other luxuries they could not afford at these hard times.
A highly respected management colleague of mine told me about her first-hand experience with stress-induced physical pain. She was seven months pregnant and was having serious back and leg pain that were so unbearable that it was preventing her from going to work. When she would persist and go to work, this excruciating pain would get worse and worse as she went into meetings with her manager. It got so bad that she tried to get maternity time off, and somehow it was denied.
She quit her job! This was a job that she could not afford to lose. But the idea of a miscarriage and/or heart attacked one day finally convinced her to quit. Her husband who had seen her suffer, was extremely supportive.
Only few weeks after she quit, she started to feel better. She was free, and she was back to being a human being. Most of the leg pain went away. The back pain was reduced to much less than she had suffered in silence for several months. A few months after the birth of a beautiful baby girl, she was able to get a better job! Her explanation was that the time off helped her feel more like a human being; empowered, motivated, and

Copyright © 2008 - 2009 Razban Internet International, Inc. All rights reserved, File:20091022, P a g e | **79**

inspired. She started to think creatively and to look at things with an open, optimistic, and happy mind . Then, she found an excellent job! Interestingly enough, the new company would have, as a matter of policy, given her the maternity leave. It also would have given paternity leave to her husband had he been their employee with no questions asked.

She described what sounded very much like Mutual Trust and Loyalty, to me as the reason for the success of the new company. She worked hard for them, and she was able to produce much better results that was impossible to be had in the previous company as a result of all the dysfunctional practices there.

The reason for her unhappiness was the uncertainty in the job market and the economy in general. This is the primary manifestation of the Fear of Sudden Job Loss (SJL), which is the root cause of much job unhappiness that exudes into our careers and lives. She quietly suffered as in the "Sound of Silence" song for many months because she had fear of sudden job loss. This is not unique to her. Almost 83% of those who are victims of layoffs get sick more than the ones that were not laid off. This vulnerability to illness persists even after they find jobs. In a CNN news in August 8, 2009, several laid off employees were interviewed who told us they never got back to the level of income they had before layoffs.

In an interview by BBC, a former Russian Company Manager was being interviewed in a street corner. He had been laid off by his company after many years and he had no marketable skills to find another job. He was standing in a street corner begging.

In another interview with a college grad in KQED, FM, a San Francisco Public Radio station, the subject of new college graduates with ninety thousands of dollars in college loans was being discussed.

They both equally break my heart.

Yet, I am stubborn! I will not give up on American way and HP Way. We will find a win-win way solution. I hope that this book has helped by showing the emotional pain associated with layoffs, and then put that pain in the economic and business context to show a $2.4 Trillion loss. A loss that can be put into productive and honorable means of 107.8% employment, SOaR, and the two amendments to Capitalism.

I wrote this book with meager resources. More than fourteen people helped me by working on things or even lending money. I used my last paycheck on the last day of my employment on December 19, 2008 to sign the contract for publication of this book. My friend Dan lend me $12,000, Bob about $1,000, Farah $300 (Cash in an Envelope given to my wife), my brother about $8,000 at a time that he had been unemployed for more than a year.

Writing of this book kept my sanity. Each day as I channeled all my anger and frustration with unemployment into positive and wrote inspiring and motivational words for the others, I had no anger left any more. I was free with a clear mind. I was somebody, not just an American, Middleclass, and Unemployed (AMU)!

At some point in my own unemployment period, we had to decide whether we pay for food or gas in the car.

Yet, I know that I was on a mission for writing this book. My mission is to convince at least one CEO not to lay off employees in a knee jerk reaction, or an employee that you are not just an AMU, but you are somebody very important! To the employee, I want to say it is not your problem, do not internalize it. I want to convince all of you that you are the CEOs of your life and your careers. Therefore, I want to empower and motivate all of us that we deserve better than being a Zombie in a toxic work place, or just sitting there in the event of a layoff! I apologize for using the word Zombie. However, it does portray the feelings involved well. The origin of Zombie word is from a West African word. It literally means, "One who moves and acts in a daze". One of the first usages for this was in Hindu text, circa, 1000 BC. I also want to challenge our great educational institutions to understand and teach Human Capital better.

If I see one job that is not lost as a result of this book, I declare my meager investment in writing and your generosity in buying this book a complete success!

CHAPTER 25:   Take this Job and Shove It!

This was a song that became very popular. At that time, I was not particularly happy or unhappy with my job. I had learned to keep my head down and put my nose to the grind stone and do the work. I was somewhat convinced that thinking was not in job description, therefore, I just did the work in front of me. Also, I would put up with whatever stupid, non-productive demands that were made. I had revolted against the powerful bosses before and found that to be lonely, dangerous, and costly. Most others did not have the guts to stand up for their rights let alone someone else's.

This song which played in my car for a long time, revived my free American thinking. It rekindled thoughts that this is only a job. It reminded me that it is not worth all the hassle. Be ready to give it up and you will feel free. By giving up, I do not mean just get up and quit. I mean that you need to prepare yourself by empowerment and find a better one waiting. Like it says, take this job, it is not worth the pain, suffering, and the anguish.

This song also resonated with a lot of people who had hard feelings about their jobs. To an unemployed person, this was poetic justice for all the firings, layoffs, demotions, and exclusions the company had done to them.

To those who were working, this was a theme song for all the outsourcing, downshifts, reduction in pay, verbal and written notices, as a prelude and justification for terminations. This song refers to all the politics, infighting, and stupidity that happens every day in the workplace.

I recently saw advertising on the side of a Goodwill truck. It said, "Give somebody else a chance to hate their Mondays too." I was moved by this. This message tells me that it is now the norm for people to hate their jobs, in fact, to hate their jobs so much that they hate Mondays since that is the time they have to go back to work.

I have also seen signs that say something to this effect: "I live for weekends." I am not criticizing this sign, or advocating that we need to drop everything and go to work and be happy with our work.

However, I hope you can see the waste this presents in our personal lives, in company productivity, and in our general well being.

If there is a direct $.8 Trillion (that is millions billions), then there is just as much waste related to heath and insurance costs resulting from this waste. There is also the same amount of waste that is lost due to destruction of families and marriages. How could you not let an awful day at work, not negatively affect your marriage? This makes this problem waste three times the $.8 Trillion, or $2.4 Trillion.

To put things in perspective, if a stack of fresh $1,000 bills is only six inches tall, this $2.4 Trillion will be as long as approximately 153.6 miles high!

It is by far easier to get out of a job that you do not like than to continue nursing a resentment that is a "lose-lose" for all.

I know this first hand. It cost me a heart attack! I had put up and accepted that that job was the most important thing at that time. I owed a lot of money and I had to do the work. Then like it says in Aretha Franklin's song, one day I just could not! Evidenced by the fact that many heart attacks happen on Monday morning, there must be many others who feel the same I felt before I got my heart attack.

I hope that by having done this book, I would prevent some of those.

CHAPTER 26:   The Invisible Man

As of this writing, the average forty-three-year-old American has no more than $45,000 in his or her IRA account. According to CNN reports, the average American has nine credit cards. So, considering that the average cost of living for an American family of three or four is somewhere between $6,000 to $8,000 per month, and assuming no unexpected events like sickness or hefty car repairs, then the average American can "retire" for just seven months.

And the average American has minimal savings. The sad thing is that, for many of us, we are only fifteen or so paychecks away from becoming homeless!

This was one cold, hard fact that I did not understand, or did not want to understand all those years that I was gainfully employed.

The invisible man, who is a homeless fellow in the Streets of San Francisco, was instrumental in my awakening to this fact. The fact was that I too was also about fifteen paychecks away from being homeless just like him. This was a shock for me to comprehend.

This explains why I talk about the subject in this book. This is dear to my heart.

When I worked for PG&E in the San Francisco Financial District, I would see several homeless people near where I worked. Some were in fact victims of some sort of mental disease, and there were some that just did not look the part of the typical homeless.

Among those, I found a college student who was reading a highly intellectual book and seemed to have fairly decent clothes. When I dropped some coins in his cup and started a conversation, he told me that he was a member of the *fresh* homeless. His mother had just kicked him out of her house and asked him to go get a job.

But the invisible man was a title he had granted himself since a lot of people ignored him when they walked passed him, as if he was indeed invisible.

The invisible man seemed to be in his twenties, and he was usually clean, and he would hold his sports cap in front of passersby and ask for money. He seemed to have a style of his own as well as considerable self-respect.

I usually saw him during the lunch hour, and I usually had a dollar bill folded to drop in his cap. he would usually say, "thanks young man" (even though I was fifty-eight at the time and looked it too), and usually, I would say thanks for the undeserved complement!

Then we would have a minute or so of conversation on many subjects including arts, careers, airlines, family life, Madonna, the Iraq War, the economy, computers, utility companies, and even psychology. He clearly was able to carry a conversation at the level of a college graduate who was reading the *San Francisco Chronicle* almost every day.

Sometimes, I wondered if he, with his wasted knowledge, could maybe make a good or at least average elected official of the government, only if he had the resources available to him.

What a waste for this man to live on $20 to $25/day on a good day and only $3 to $4 on a bad day. Rainy days in San Francisco—this most beautiful and sophisticated bride of a city—were particularly depressing.

One day he told me about an article in his paper that he was sure was from the *New York Times*. The article said that the average working American was only fifteen paychecks away from homelessness. It certainly was true about me, a senior consultant with more than thirty years of experience and in one of the most lucrative fields, high tech in Silicon

Valley, California.

By the way, I have other heroes. There is man that lost everything he had about three months after lost his job. I think that he was a pipe fitter for new buildings. Being single, he decided to take his beaten up Truck and tiny trailer and move to another area that was not so badly hit. For about two months, he "lived" in that tiny space during his off hours from working in a donut shop. And right after his shift was over in the donut shop, he would walk two blocks to work somewhere else.

He worked as hard as he could each day, and at night he would just pass out in that trailer.

I would see him every morning when I went to get my breakfast. In spite all this hardship, he was proud and one time I heard him boast to another worker that he had saved about three hundred.

Just like this man, we have a great number of invisible unemployed or underemployed people whose talents and productivity is wasted, yet they are not part of our statistics. That is the sad part. But if some CEO or Venture Capitalist gives my blueprint a chance, I can prove that we can avoid this waste and put it to a good use. We are doing something like this in Hybrid cars. When you press on the break, that energy that used to go waste can now be stored to be used next time that you press on the gas pedal. Let's use the same concept with a 107.8% employment. Let's help our workers stay globally competitive, let's do what old Personnel Offices or Human Resources used to do and cannot do. Let's be greedy capitalists who want to make money, and lots of it!

To do this, we need to focus and empower our human capital. This is so easy and simple that it defies imagination since we are brain washed to think that 4% Unemployment is ideal. Yet this 4% unemployment is responsible for a $2.4 Trillion productivity loss each year.

Let's stop our addiction to layoffs!

Copyright © 2008 - 2009 Razban Internet International, Inc. All rights reserved, File:20091022. P a g e | **84**

Bob did not look the part of the typical homeless at all. He had a good college education. He was smart, alert, and sounded every bit as good as those who worked in the financial district of San Francisco. Even though he had to have second hand cloths, still he kept them relatively clean.

His cardboard with neatly written characters introduced him as a homeless Vietnam Vet. He almost always stood right in front of the CalTrain, the commuter train that goes between San Francisco and San Jose. Like me, he had leg problems, so he had selected an area near a pole so he could lean on it. The word Vietnam somehow hit me between the eyes. In my Senior year in college, I was about to submit an application for permanent visa to be able to get a job. Also, since a permanent visa is the first step towards citizenship, I was seriously thinking about taking this step. But I never filed that application because a counselor at the University told me that I will get the visa for sure, but along with it, I will also end up in Vietnam for sure too. Yet for many years I had tried to guess and/or imagine what Vietnam would have been for me. Standing next to Bob each day and having a few minutes of conversation, would serve as a time machine that would transform me to that world of guilt. Believe me that as a Jew I know only too well about guilt, the very same guilt that is deserved or not.

It seemed like I connected with Bob from the Vietnam point of view at first. Then suddenly, and abruptly one day I seemed to strongly connect with him on the painful homelessness. I, the invincible professional who spoke four languages, I the world class manager, I who had been a Director in huge companies, I too could end up like him.

It was different with the "Invisible Man". He had a sense of humor, and he seem to have a few relatives who would take him in occasionally during the holidays, etc. But, Bob who had a striking similarity to me in the background and education, had hit home and had hit home really hard. Fifteen missing lousy paychecks and I would be in the streets too!

Bob used to be a car salesman in the Midwest. I also spent some time working for car dealers. I was not a car salesman, but I worked on the Internet car sales. Bob told me that his job was killing him a bit every day. He was by far better than his manager and he always met his quota. The anger and frustration from his job, spilled over to his personal life and eventually, his wife divorced him. He had a loving son that was admired by everybody. On many occasions he would talk about his son. He would say how much he loves to see him just one more time. How much he likes to explain to his wife what he went through on the work place. He still loved his wife, and he never blamed her for anything. He would say that "She had to take the child and rescue the two of them since she could not rescue everyone".

I repeatedly tried to find his son that he had not seen since he was seven or eight year old. I used the latest Internet companies, and made many phone calls. But there was no response. This made me sad.

My previous experience working for Lexus and Toyota, and his experience at car dealerships gave us a chance to talk shop. He truly loved "Car Business"! Had his job not had been so toxic and devastating, he still would have had his life and family. He was not an irresponsible man. He did his best, but everyday being an uphill battle with a crazy manager finally got to him.

Copyright © 2008 - 2009 Razban Internet International, Inc. All rights reserved, File:20091022, P a g e | **85**

He knew what he was talking about, and I kept encouraging him to give it one more try. He would respond that if he did not have a mailing address, companies would not hire him. Of course as a homeless man, he did not have "home" address that he could use. One day, he just disappeared!

I almost always hoped to bump into him again someday and I pray and wish that someday he would return to his life and career in the Midwest. In fact several people that I talked to in the process of finding his relatives, promised to help. They knew of some people who might know somebody who might be related to Bob. Unfortunately, I know of no such luck.

In one of our last discussions, I had shared with him my sheer horror regarding unemployment, and he had some interesting observations. Things have gotten a lot worse since then. It is so bad that in a letter to Oprah, I invented AMU as a new acronym for American Middleclass and Unemployed.

In his experience, a career is like marriage. You do the best you can as a human. Your co-workers become your temporary family, and you get a sense of usefulness, accomplishment, and importance from your work. But yet, he had seen so many people destroy their health and family for work that he had decided that he would not sacrifice those things for work again. This is if he ever got another job.

What a terrible loss! What a heart break! Why are we so stupid to discard people like this? These are people who can make our economy grow. These people can be worthwhile members of our community. Bob could have served as an excellent car salesman or manager. He could have been an excellent teacher. He could have even been an Executive Career Coach/Consultant. What a loss!

Regarding my own story, I am writing this as I am worried about electricity to cut off any moment due to non-payment. Our Cell Phone is "suspended" and our Internet access is cut off. One of our Doctors, has created a $4,000 Bill, like he had done for years, and when I needed to get urgent care, his office manager told me that unless I can pay $400 she will not arrange for an appointment. She in a condescending voice as if blaming me for the Global Financial Crisis, pointed out that there are more affordable Doctors. By the way, she added that there I need to go to the county hospital. Since that would be what I need without insurance, then it will be important that I go three hours ahead of the time.

I had a macabre feeling that someday my family and I might end up in the streets. In a sadistic way, I felt I deserved it because as a good citizen I too should have gone to Vietnam swamps and fought the enemy. My Dad did it for his country and almost died from Malaria. Looking at Bob, I felt the same survivor guilt that is known about people who did not die in concentration camps while their friends and relatives did.

Recently, I have discovered the shock of seeing a professional like myself in Bob's situation, had me jealous. Jealous about having been deprived from that journey of being a war. My father was in a forgotten one, and my wife had seen two wars in Israel. I wonder what my reaction would have been. I try to imagine if I would have been brave enough to shoot and be shot at. Right at this point in my thinking, it also becomes clear that I did not go to Vietnam. I did not go because I found a smart way out of it. I did not go because I think all wars, with a few exceptions about self-defense are wrong. Hell no, I won't go! Nevertheless, I still remember that God-awful survivor guilt about pains of hopeless homelessness that I found sadistically attracted to prospect of a deservingly similar faith as Bob's. Is this macho, foolish bravado, or even patriotic?

Copyright © 2008 - 2009 Razban Internet International, Inc. All rights reserved, File:20091022, P a g e | **86**

CHAPTER 28:   Move to Management and Zilog, Inc. and Recognition of Human Capital

In graduate school, it became clear to me that my first career love was management, even though most of my studies were in engineering and computer sciences. My introduction to management was a course called Organization Behavior. I knew there and then that this was my passion and my mission in my career. Of course, those days, I thought that this was my way to change the world for the better.

As successful as I was at Plantronics, and as happy as I was there, I started to realize that I missed the leading-edge technology and really wanted to enter management.

Fear of Sudden Job Loss (SJL) had been working on me and making me aware that if I lost my Plantronics job, there were not too many other opportunities in Santa Cruz at that time. Of course, this has changed since when I was there. The University of California in Santa Cruz has become extremely strong in computer sciences and other fields to the point that it is internationally recognized and respected. And there are a lot more companies there now.

In 1980, I applied for an engineering management job at Zilog and qualified easily for it. I was told that I was management material since I liked to work with people and that I was technically strong, too, since I had kept up with the latest developments. I owe a great of this to those mentoring on the job training that I got from Jim in Plantronics.

I was in heaven. So many best of the best Stanford, MIT, Berkeley, and other top school graduates worked there that I started to feel that I was second best.

As a manager, I had to recruit and keep top talent, which was what I did. I had an excellent group, the first that I had created from scratch, and the group had my management signature in it.

I managed somehow to never have to lay off my own employees, since I had made sure they were the best of the best, and our group was much more productive. One of our products was recognized in the entire industry as the best in its category.

I had made a major discovery. I had learned quickly that there are two types of capital. One that I call "Things Capital" is what traditionally we think of capital. The other that was by far more important was human capital. This included intellectual capital and how happy people were. People includes employees of a company, customers, and stakeholders. If the human capital is paid as much attention as there is with things capital, we will be a lot better off in productivity, and profit and the work life will be much happier too. Kevin Covey has discussed and emphasized this in his latest books.

In 1984, I was promoted to Director at the age of thirty-four. My employees as well as others were happy for me. They liked me because I was on their side and they respected my people skills.

In return for this promotion, Zilog, Inc., had my complete trust and loyalty. I had planned to retire from there. I was so dedicated that I worked late every night and was one of the first to show up to work in the morning.

I would watch their CEO carefully with the hope of someday becoming the best CEO they had ever had. I cared for every dollar of budget that was being spent as if it was my own. Twice, I got offers from other companies, and they would have paid me more, but I did not move. My loyalty was with my company.

I was proactive and extremely people-oriented, making sure that my group was the best of the best. We produced Zscan 80 and Zscan 8000 that were recognized as one of the best by the trade journals. My group had an almost zero turnover rate and almost all high talent that worked in my group was happy and excited about their jobs. We had Brown Bag University where, each time, one of us would teach our expertise to others in the group.

I introduced some of the latest technology, re-organized groups, and made sure that most, if not all of the employees, managers, and customers were happy with me.

As you will see later in the book, my dream of working for Zilog, Inc., until I retired did not happen, in spite of all my hard work and hope.

I reviewed Debra Benton's latest book called "CEO Material". She is a New York Times bestseller writer. She is what I would have always wanted to be. Also, she has been an excellent roll model and mentor. She reviewed my book and gave me a five star rating. I look up to her and I am convinced that she is one of our national heroes who has ideas regarding management. But seeing everyday what is happening to CEOs makes me feel that I do not really want this CEO job. But, the fire in my belly shouts out that I should want it and I will do good at it.

In fact as of this writing, I have heard that Zilog is in such dire financial situation that it will be sold or acquired piece by piece. This is hard for me to accept. When, I was a Director there, we had the best talent working for us. We had every chance to be the best of the best of the best.

But, I am sad to think that they are slowly and steadily going out of business. What they could have been with that fantastic human capital always hurts my feelings.

One of their products, the Z80, was so much more advanced than the competition that it was used universally and for a very long time.

I also tried to be a coach to new managers and, of course, the HP Way was discussed and practiced as much as possible.

CHAPTER 29:   My First Time Layoff

A new CEO had arrived at Zilog. The new CEO had a sales background, and the rumors were rampant that he really wanted to make Zilog more of a sales-oriented company. The previous assumptions at Zilog were that by being the best there could be in technology, sales would automatically take care of themselves.

I was the local hero, even in the eyes of the new CEO. I had delivered on some of the tightest schedules, and people in general seemed to be happy in my department.

One day, all directors were called in to a meeting, and we were told that we each had to cut about ten percent of our headcount, and each had to come up with a cost savings of about fifteen percent of our budgets. Times were difficult then for economy, and we had no choice.

I did everything within my power to try to avoid the layoff. I offered job sharing, I offered part-time jobs, etc.. I even emphasized as strongly as I could that layoffs were destructive and HP proved that companies did not really have to do layoffs. The argument that will be emphasized some years later in TV news program indicating that even in Global Financial Crisis, many companies such as Aflac, or Container Store or others decided not to lay off. There is more details about this later in the book. Interesting enough, those companies that did indeed do frequent and massive layoffs are finally seeing employee protests. Employees are asking that "You told us these layoffs will save money and later on save jobs", so, "Where did the money go? Why did you do more layoffs if the previous layoff was supposed to preserve jobs?"

HP had not had one layoff in fifty years of its history. So, it stands to reason that good and caring management can actually proactively prevent layoffs and be much more prosperous in the long term by having the full mutual trust and loyalty of its employees. That day, I went home with a chest pain, and I thought that the stress was so bad that I might have a heart attack and not make it to the next day.

The company had a list of criterion that we had to consider for each employee as part of our decision.

The employees had not done anything wrong. It was the economy, and unfortunately, I lost all my appeals to prevent the layoff even if only in my group. This is a critical point to understand. So, many victims of layoffs internalize it. So many think that there should or could have been something that they could have done not to be laid off! Let me assure that in 99% of cases there is really nothing that the employee could have done that would have changed the outcome. Unfortunately layoffs have become a knee-jerk reaction by management as the first band aid to apply to hide bad management, or to make the company look better on paper. Yet, it is this that creates a $2.4 Trillion loss each and every year in productivity loss.

Reluctantly, I made the list and checked it many times. There was another director that was a good friend of mine, and he had a lot more experience. I compared notes with him and asked for advice.

The day I had to give notice to my employees was the worst time of my career. I knew as a manager that I had failed. I had failed to plan better. I had failed to help them get ready for their next job. I seriously considered getting get totally out of management just because of this.

My experienced colleague told me that it must be very painful the first time, but it does get easier later on. I found the same pains every time. It never got any easier.

Copyright © 2008 - 2009 Razban Internet International, Inc. All rights reserved, File:20091022, P a g e | **90**

CHAPTER 30:   Finally, my Dreaded Turn to be Laid Off at Zilog

I had noticed that CEO was holding meetings for directors, and he did not invite me. I noticed that I got considerably less of a raise compared to previous year even though performance was same. Nevertheless, I had done just as good a job as ever. Somehow, it seemed that the upper management all of a sudden was not interested in me anymore. The new CEO had also curtailed some of my authority, and he was questioning my decisions. I had not changed at all but he had. I had enjoyed being the rock star for some time. It seemed like everyone liked to work for and with me before. Yet, there was a change.

The new CEO had gotten notice that one of his previous directors who had worked for him on the East Coast had shown interest in coming to California. They were also friends for quite a number of years. However, the other director was more "sales oriented" and I was too "technology oriented," therefore CEO really preferred to work with him. The rumor started to spread. I frankly did not quite know what to do with this. On the one hand, I had always maintained that my excellent record should be my best job security. On the other hand, even I knew that I did not have that much sales experience. The job title was Director of Engineering. The title clearly did not say or imply anything about Sales.

One of the most respected vice presidents in the company intervened and helped make a very nice transition for me in view of my accomplishments. I had an office, even though it was an individual contributor office as opposed to my spacious and plush director's office, and I had ninety days to find a job in or outside Zilog. This did go a long way to lower my pain. In return, I was there to help make the transition a success. In the meantime, I had a chance to get a nice job with my first startup.

On my resume, it looked OK too. I had worked for Zilog until Friday of a certain week and then, that very next Monday moved to a startup. I got this startup just because a colleague of mine was already working there. Again, connections and networking are very important. This colleague had always been great help. He had been unemployed for some time so he was well aware of the situation. His help was instrumental for me to get the next job.

In spite of it all, I felt a big loss. I had put a lot of my blood, sweat, and tears into my work at Zilog. I had hired top talent and kept them happy and creative. I had created groups and defined products. Then one day, I was gone as if I had never been there. Even though my startup job kept me very busy and occupied as we were really working on the latest technology, I was grieving inside. I missed my old friends, and I missed the chance to make one of the products as a best-seller product of the year. It took more than six month for me to deal with the grief process. I literally went through all stages that Kubbler Ross had listed in her book regarding loss. I went through step-by-step, one step at the time. Each step was just as painful as the others were. This is when I learned about meditation and relaxation music, and the soothing power of silence.

A month later, I heard that Zilog had lost one of the best architects to a competitor and that they had to stop work on the product I was sure would become a best seller. On another occasion, I heard that they were having so many problems that they did not know where to start.

Copyright © 2008 - 2009 Razban Internet International, Inc. All rights reserved, File:20091022, P a g e | **91**

CHAPTER 31:   The First Weekend after My Notice

I was feeling ashamed. I was angry and I was very scared. I kept asking myself, "What if nobody hired me after this?" "What if I lost my insurance?" "What if I could not find another job?" Ninety days notice sounds like a great deal of time. However, I had really served Zilog with all my powers for three and a half years. The company had recognized me as a key employee. They gave me additional stock options. Most importantly, I was well liked and respected. How could this happen to me?
Dr. Elizabeth Kubbler-Ross is one of the internationally famous experts in death, dying, and loss. She says that in the case of a major loss, people go through several stages of grief. Then, finally, they make peace with the aftermath of loss. There is anger, denial, bargaining, and finally, acceptance. We need to give grief and ensuing depression that comes after that some time. We cannot push or shorten this grief process all by ourselves. We need expert help. I am not a psychologist, but I do know this much: if a depressed person is told to snap out of it, he or she cannot. Sadly, he or she will hate you for suggesting such a stupid thing. With professional help and effort, one can heal and recover.
However, I never forget that sleepless weekend. Anxiety was so high that I did not have much appetite for food, and I could not sleep. Most layoffs are based on knee jerk reaction. They are usually carried out before the Six Sigma, or for that matter any other analysis, can be done. Organizations are decapitated needlessly. Product lines are left incomplete or without sufficient support. Careers are damaged. Customers are left on their own to take care of product problems. Morale is one of the first victims. Severe damage to productivity always follows. In another word, layoffs create a no-win situation for all. They also create additional long-term problems. The most effective help I got that week was in the form of a telephone call from a good friend. He reminded me of Psalm 23 and then he told me that he would be a reference. He added that he would try to find me a job in his company.
After the CEO gave my old group to the "Sales Oriented" Director of Engineering, it self-destructed in about four months after I had left. A Stanford University Ph D who worked for me then, is still a good friend and colleague. He was instrumental in helping me come up with several new inventions last year. I flew to his home in Arizona to visit with him and his wife. His thesis advisor is now the president of the Stanford University. Can you imagine how successful that company could have been? Those viscous cycles of layoffs, loss of Mutual Trust and Loyalty, low morale, and joblessness almost destroyed it. Not only it did not become all that it could, it also is now much smaller.
Around day seventy or seventy-two, I got an offer to go work for a startup that was pioneering ISDN technology. One of my colleagues was instrumental in getting me this opportunity.

CHAPTER 32: Life at My First Startup

Working in startups is considerably more difficult. Everything has to be rushed, and there is never enough money to get things done right. As a director, I reported directly to the CEO. I made some fantastic accomplishments for the startup.

In spite all these, there came a time when "I had to reluctantly be let go." It was a layoff since I got some two weeks of severance pay. Apparently, decisions had been made a few days earlier by the CEO based on pressure from venture capitalists who thought the company was a bit too "top heavy." They let me go around saying goodbye to my employees and colleagues, and someone helped me put my stuff in my car.

Bingo, it was done and I was gone. As I said before, in startups things move very fast. A few weeks later, I got a call that they wanted to give me a short contract since my departure had caused serious discontinuity. I decided to find out more details. I drove to the company, which is now one of Google's many buildings in Mountain View, California. I parked my car on another block and decided to have a moment of silence with myself to make sure if I indeed wanted to go back. The promise for that contract was only a few weeks. I decided against it! I told the CEO that they could call me any time, and I would be more than glad to help for free. They did take me up on that offer.

In less than three months, and after two layoffs in that period, the company went out of business. Even the furniture was gone in a few days after the announcement. I had worked six and a half days a week with all my might and heart and I was extremely dedicated. Poof and it was gone! Just like that!

After hearing this news, my anger and disappointment toward that company changed to guilt. I thought that I should have done more. Maybe I should have done things differently. Maybe I should have not hired the last person, whom I had hired, and a thousand other equally useless thoughts and worries.

Yet, startups are the lifeblood of American industry and economy.

Innovation, agility, flexibility, and low-cost operation, which are trademarks of many startups including mine, Razban Internet International, Inc. is crucial to creating new jobs and trends and industries. If this is stifled, then we will be in a serious situation. This serious situation might lead to even bigger bank closures, more home foreclosures, and more unemployment. We just cannot afford this. Big American business is built on and fueled by small businesses just like mine. Some statistics indicated that eighty percent of American industry is composed of small business.

The knee jerk reaction to what CEO perceived as top heavy organization had a very sad after effect. About three years later, when several of us got together, I made a simple observation regarding the elastic buffers. My group had spent a lot of time fixing problems with elastic buffers. My simple idea presented while having desert, was greeted by total surprise from another colleague. "How did you come up with this idea?" I replied "As I was driving here tonight." "Oh my God, this idea would have solved our problems and would have put us in front of Texas Instruments!" Texas Instruments, was one of the major corporations at that time. They had bet a great deal on those elastic buffers. Had I not been considered as the part of top heaviness, that tiny startup might have been another Texas Instruments today and might have made many people rich instead of jobless.

A small loan, actually a microloan since it was as small as $50, to a real tiny business in some third world companies has created awesome results. The most awesome thing is

Copyright © 2008 - 2009 Razban Internet International, Inc. All rights reserved, File:20091022, P a g e | **93**

that people regain their dignity by being productive. The pride and joy from this is monumental.

With the internet revolution, these tiny companies can compete on a global basis.

CHAPTER 33:   9:00 AM to 5:00 PM All Day Forced Coffee Breaks

After my sudden layoff, I decided that I did not want my neighbors and family to know. Every day, at the same time as before, I would get into my car with my briefcase, drive to a chain of coffee shops, and not come back before the usual 6:00 PM. I tried not to tell anyone either as I was ashamed. This is a particularly bad thing because we need our network of friends and colleagues to know we are out of a job so they can help.

I started to teach myself some of the latest technology and management developments. I would go to Stanford University, which is very close to where I live, and spend time in their bookstore or campus. I met Mr. Hewlett and Mr. Packard who were founders of HP while they were on a books signing. They afforded me the kindness of talking to me for a long time. I had read their book each and every work, and cover to cover. They were impressed and we had an excellent heart to heart talk. Also, Stanford University Bookstore almost always has a most up to date collection of Computer and business books.

At some point, I had turned into a student professional. I would purchase the same textbooks that are in Stanford Graduate School and study them as if I was a student.

One day, somebody tried to get hold of me and she did not have my phone number. The directory informed her that no such company and phone number existed. At that point, I decided to ask for help and to tell my family. I have a very good friend who is extremely healthy and has the nickname of "Greyhound Bus." He was fired from his last job. He agreed that he had made some bad mistakes, but he did not think that he deserved to be fired. Thus, I was not alone in hiding my joblessness and its shame and pain many others did too.

He started to get anxiety attacks and he could not go to his apartment. Of course, he lived alone in a tiny studio apartment in the attic of an old San Jose house. It was clean and nice, but there was a lot of noise from the teenagers living next door. Therefore, he bought a monthly bus pass, and every day at a specific time, he would go for a walk. He started with less than half a mile a day and it got to about seven miles a day. Moreover, since he kept going from place to place, his friends gave him the *Greyhound Bus* nickname.

I found out by accident that he was fired. I had called him to see if we could go to lunch and discuss the latest ideas offered by his company. The operator, in a firm and unfeeling voice, told me that Mr. so and so, was no longer with the company. Any questions I had, I should refer them to the HR. I did not even try to call HR since I knew it would be hopeless.

If you go to any coffee shop, fast order join, play ground or park you can see these 9:00 AM to 5:00 PM Business Hours People on Coffee Break.

There is an unexplained shame and hurt that hovers over our heads when fired. It is painful, unreasonable, and stupid, but it is what it is! Almost all the time a layoff is not our fault. Then why do we internalize it and feel shame that we do not deserve to feel.

CHAPTER 34:   American Fat, Sugar, Starch Shame

I am an overweight person. I have been overweight most of my life. My dream has been to lose the extra weight just for health reasons. I am talking about this here since I have found a painful similarity between being fat and suddenly losing a job (or something important or dear to us).

In 1967, you would see very few people who were 200 or 300 lbs. Since I had joined Weight Watchers many times in my life, I could safely say that maybe one in fifty or more would be over 250 in those days. The Weight Watcher scales did not go above 200 then. Now they do!

Today, I am over 200 lbs and closer to 280. There are many factors involved. The unfortunate thing about this is that I am sure I have not gotten some jobs or promotions because I am fat. I have always had to fight the "fat, therefore lazy" form of discrimination in the workplace. But much more painful than that, it has been the shameful pain that I have suffered from this condition. And, like many others with this problem, I try my best to hide the pain and the shame. When I joined the 30,000 Feet Club, I was about 180 Lbs. I wore suites that were 42 R (R for Regular.) I could always find cloths at reasonable prices. I could get dates, and women were attracted to me.

An Alcoholic or a drug addict can hide their addiction. But not so for a heavy person! To make matters worse, we have to eat three times a day, while the first two categories I mentioned do not really have to drink or use. We have to eat to stay alive and this makes food even more painful for us to handle. My sympathy goes with those who suffer from any kind of addiction.

Many Asians, or Europeans especially from the Mediterranean region, who ate healthy and nutritious food prior to coming to US are also gaining weight. The trend is scary.

Many job losses end in an undeserved shame that is similar to the same thing suffered by addicts and overweight people. After my first layoff, I was so ashamed that I did not want anyone to know. I went to the bank ATM and transferred $2,000 cash from the credit card to my checking account. It is the same undeserved shame that an overweight or addicted person feels that plagues an unemployed, underemployed, or unhappily employed. It is powerful and must be understood and dealt with.

Joblessness, and the internalized undeserved shame related to it, triggers all kinds of pain. These pains prevent us from feeling good about ourselves. It prevents us from being productive, empowered, inspired, and energetic about finding that next job!

For God sake, unemployment is not a crime!

CHAPTER 35:   Drugs, Alcohol, Damn Fat, Sugar, and Starch

I was sitting in a restaurant eating a moderate lunch after having ordered it just as right as I could. I had ordered, light Mayo, no potato salad, tomato wedges instead of that tomato salad, and on a whole wheat bread. I had courageously told them a weak no when they asked if I wanted dessert. I noticed a 450-pound woman sitting outside with two kids. Each kid was delightfully biting into a delicious apple. Both kids were in clean and nice clothes and they were both thin. The woman was not eating anything.

This reminded me of most of my childhood below the age four or five when I was really not obese.

However, the chain of foolish foods in the environment, and my just sitting there like Chippie, got me to gain weight. How could I or this wonderful woman with two kids, handle the multi-billion-dollar Madison Avenue, sleek, food advertizing? So many models are so thin that they must be sick. They are also, "air brushed" to look even thinner in pictures. This is wrong. We must correct this. The entire food industry is to do better in restaurants and supermarkets. There is foolishness at all levels when a super-thin male or female model shows up in just about any advertizing or TV program.

Interestingly enough, some of these super thin models are advertizing sugary, starchy, fatty food! This is the height of hypocrisy. I do want, or even have an urge to look like those perfect models myself. Even though I do know how much lighting, make up, and other factors go into making these people look so nice. It is not real.

How could an ordinary person win this awful battle? The powerful, subliminal, polished, glorified models entice us to be thin, or even bulimic, or alcoholic in order to enjoy the good life of the models. The shame this brings on overweight people, of which I am one, is what I have coined the phrase "Fat, Sugar, Starch Shame."

By the way, a few centuries ago, sugar was an item that only royals could use. Even then, it was just as expensive as gold to produce. People did have honey as a natural substance to get a taste of what sweet was, but not in the purified sugar that is so common these days. It is interesting to note that they did not have it and they did not even know that they did not need it. Joblessness creates the same dilemma.

That is such a contrast to what we see these days. Each soda bottle has many, many spoons of sugar, and sugar is everywhere. Just imagine a teenager watching a TV show. First, the entire TV show might revolve around glorification of being skinny. Then a commercial comes on, and it is full of images of what is considered tasty treats that, if you do not try them, you are missing the most important thing in life. To make it even worse, the advertizing companies also show many other teenagers doing the same thing just to add excessive peer pressure.

However, the truth is that not only we do not need this stuff, but also these products can damage our bodies. Studies show that addition to sugar, as well as fat and starch, makes it even more difficult to resist the snacks that are advertized on TV.

The hidden and subliminal message from this is that you should enjoy eating all this fat, sugar, and starch. Nevertheless, we expect you to look like these super-slim and most likely anorexic models. Moreover, if you do not look the part, then shame on you! This is similar to a corporation telling its employees that they need to work very hard, not look around for another job, and stay with the company. Then the corporation turns around and lays them off massively and frequently. This is a double message that CEOs need to

Copyright © 2008 - 2009 Razban Internet International, Inc. All rights reserved, File:20091022, P a g e | **97**

understand.

When I was about fifteen years old, my dad described his thesis in medical school on malnourishment in poor countries. He told me about the depressing number of children that die before they are five years old. He told me about other kids that die from some simple diseases like common colds. Malnourishment has taken away their bodies' ability to fight and recover. Sadly enough, I see malnourishment in a different form, nevertheless malnourishment, in America. We are seeing kids develop diabetes and obesity from an early age. We constantly see kids being tempted with some of the most awful, sugary food on TV. In addition, obese kids always become obese adults. I am an example and it hurts, it hurts really badly. Malnourishment is just like mismanagement related to layoffs. It is just as ugly and as painful. We have internalized it. Our song inside us is almost dead.

For joblessness recover, we can apply the same ideas and practices that the 12 steps of Alcoholics or Overeaters Anonymous uses. They are successful. They have been for many, many years. They get the victims of alcohol or drugs to come out of isolation and get help. They work with the shame and blame. They teach new tools. Most importantly, some life-long friendships evolve that no amount of money can ever buy.

My hat is off to Alcoholics Anonymous and Overeaters Anonymous for trying to help people to overcome and recover, even if it is one day at a time.

CHAPTER 36:   Empowered Weight Management (EWM)

It must be surprising to find a sort of diet chapter in a book like this. However, the basis for writing this chapter here is to emphasize that the same ideas that work in producing better results in the work place, also work in the personal improvement. This is application of Mutual Trust and Loyalty to us. This is treatment of unlimited human potential as the human capital that we all posses regardless of our weight.

I think that primary reason why many diets fail is that they do not treat us with that Mutual Trust and Loyalty, and respect that we deserve. Their success rate is the proof of the pudding (No puns intended.)

I have seen, and I have tried many diets during the last forty or more years. I have had great success with some and, I was not able to follow others. I am not a diet doctor or an expert on this subject. Evidenced by my own weight management problems, I have decided to figure out what works for me first. After I do the walk on this, then I walk the talk. The fact that it might have worked for me does not mean that it will work for you. Yet, I have used myself as a test case.

Without passing judgment, I would simply say that on Weight Watchers; I had been able to lose weight and go down to the ideal weight for me and my height. Our leader, Mrs. Smiley was excellent in creating a community feeling, and her sessions in the Dominican Hospital of Santa Cruz were great. In addition, Alyssa more recently was leading a session in Mountain View that was outstanding. Then I had to commute to Oakland each day and it did not leave time for going to meetings.

My chiropractor insisted that I must lose weight, or else those excruciating pains in my lower back would come back. He recommended the South Beach diet on the basis that it was simple to follow and many people had gotten many results. I purchased one of the many books written on this subject and started to follow it.

I did something smart (if I may say so myself!) I decided to empower myself! To empower myself, I needed to have an exact weight measurement each day. I saw a digital scale that promised up to quarter-pound accuracy. I needed this so I would not argue with the scale reading, deceiving myself that the scale was off.

Each day, I would weigh myself right before I brushed my teeth. The first time it was 307.6! This was not bad considering that I had been higher than that. Then I decided to sort of follow the South Beach Diet by eating very little bread and/or rice. I started to add more chicken and fish, and avoided sweets, as much as I could.

I do not feed myself shame, or blame others and myself for this situation; I just step on that scale as an intelligent empowered adult that needs some fact-based data to make the next smart step.

I am proud to say that today February 6, 2008, it showed 278.4 Lbs. This is a full 29.2 Lbs. weight loss in an "I do not care to even remember" period. This is my empowered weight management. I am happy with it. Each day if the scale shows that I have gained some, then for that day, I will reduce the rice, and bread intake. The beauty of this is that it empowers me to do what is right for me for that day. It helps me act like an adult and work on my weight management as an adult. This is not a diet that includes deprivation, but a way for me to empower myself.

The EWM utilizes Six Sigma Root Cause Analysis as well of Agile Management methods that have proven to be very effective. The EWM provides instant feedback

Copyright © 2008 - 2009 Razban Internet International, Inc. All rights reserved, File:20091022, P a g e | **99**

regarding how well we are doing. If I go to a restaurant the serves a lot of rice, and have big dishes with a lot of starch and fat, I will most likely see it on the scale the next day, or the day after the next day.

In addition, the empowerment in EWM is very strong. It is what we need in the work place. I am treated as an adult, with the power to choose, and be responsible. There is no sophisticated process or marketing scheme in this Weight Management that puts me in a viscous cycle. A viscous cycle of feelings of induced and internalized shame, the same silent pain many unemployed or underemployed, or unhappily employed feel. This induced shame then triggers defiance, and feelings of unmanageability that drives me to overeating each and every time.

There is nothing for me, even at 292.7 Lbs, which was my weight a week after I had purchased the scale to be ashamed. I am just as good as the next person who is blessed by the fact that he will not gain weight even if he eats likes a pig and drinks bear instead of water. Of course, he will not be healthy, but our media does not show that.

I have often had the foolish idea, and yes if my book says some CEOs are foolish, or our capitalism now sounds stupid and needs amendments, then I also am entitled to foolish and indulging ideas about food! I have not been able to do a great job in this area. If we accept that any addiction is based on some faulty assumptions, then I can write another book about my faulty assumptions about weight loss. Nevertheless, as my guru, Mr. B. of "What Color is Your Parachute" advises, "Life is a process of learning, and relearning better things in place of old things."

For the record, some people who read the manuscripts felt that this chapter needs to be removed. Their argument is that this is a hell of a serious book on a painful subject of layoffs, so my invented EWM has no place here. Others thought that this in itself seems to validate the ideas presented in this book about empowerment, and management. In addition, since weight loss is something that frustrates many people, this chapter will help.

I decided to share this with you. I am not a psychologist, I am not an eating disorders expert, and for that matter I am not a layoff expert either in spite my 32 years of experience in the work place. Nevertheless, as an oversized, large, or big person, I have felt exactly the same pain, shame, and discrimination that unemployed people or addicts feel!

Each day as you step on that scale, it will precisely and clearly tell you if you had eaten the right things, and in right quantities during the last few days. Each day the gain is around ¼ or ½ Lb. Each day a fact-based incremental decision is made on what to eat the next day. Nevertheless, if you indulge in overeating, the weight can go up by 2, 3, or even 4 depending on how much fat, starch, carbohydrates, or salt intake was. I have also found that if feed myself healthy food that is available everywhere, including McDonalds, and KFC and in right proportions, then I can manage my weight problems even better. If I eat enough protein, which is meats, and diary, then I will feel fuller and there is less desire to binge. One thing that I learned in Weight Watchers was that we need to eat two medium sized fruits each day. This is also has helped me a great deal. Eating oranges, or occasionally half of a banana helps cravings for sugar go away.

I admire, worship, and have great respect for Oprah. Yet, she is a human being just like us. If this weight management is difficult for her with all the resources that she has at her disposal, then this must be difficult. In one Oprah show, there was an overweight woman

Copyright © 2008 - 2009 Razban Internet International, Inc. All rights reserved, File:20091022, P a g e | 100

who had, out of desperation, placed some electrical probes connected to battery surgically implanted in her chest to deliver a small electrical shock to her brain each time she felt hunger. I felt very sorry for her. I do not judge her. I can understand her pain and desperation that lead her to such drastic action. However, Oprah made the day for me during this program. She said that she herself would not do this.

The EWM is simple. Unlike many other sophisticated ones, we can remember all of this empowerment-based Weight Management. Do not eat Rice, Bread, sugar, and fat too much. In addition, with the level of exercise, your weight and/or loss can be measured precisely each day.

CHAPTER 37:   Princess Diana

Princess Diana is one of my heroes that I admired, worshipped, respected, and hoped for her success in all the charity work that she did. I was extremely touched by her charity work. Her work in making landmines illegal was particularly important to me. I still have nightmares about children trying to play when a landmine explodes as they step on it. These are also from very poor countries with no money for the medical treatment.

I remember her frequent trips to Africa to make sure her charities were doing the job. The tragic circumstance in which this very precious life was lost breaks my heart. This loss goes beyond belief. She could have spent many more years being a mother to her sons and continuing the charity work.

I heard the news when I was having dinner with my wife in the Italian section of San Francisco, the North Beach. It was night in San Francisco and I heard the news from another passerby who was walking with a transistor radio and repeating Diana is gone, Diana is gone. To him, and too many others, including me this was a painful loss.

She was one of the most attractive and glamorous of excellent Royalty. In spite all of that, she suffered from Bulimia, an eating disorder, that makes a person feel overweight even though they are not. This is a direct result of our society being obsessive with our appearance. I can feel her pain from this point of view since I also have an eating disorder.

As I have mentioned, I do not drink or smoke. Overeating is my demise. Overeating comfort foods and going to restaurants frequently is what does this to me each and every time! The last day that I worked at PG&E, I was about 260 pounds. This was a direct result having a fantastic job that helped me feel good enough to exercise each day. PG&E is on Market Street, San Francisco, California. In fact, their main building is a historical building. During the lunch hour, I would make sure to have about thirty minutes of walking to the lunch place. About a year after my being let go from my next job after PG&E, I had reached 312 pounds.

When I stepped on the scale in a Weight Watcher meeting, I could not believe my eyes. Overeating can be just as bad as alcoholism. Nevertheless, people do not understand this. Therefore, there is shame that the stupidity of society has put on us. In addition, we internalize it since we feel shameful about it. Then, just like anything else, this becomes a viscous cycle. We eat more because we feel shameful, angry, and frustrated. Moreover, when we eat more, we gain more weight, and then, because we become even heavier, we feel even more shame, to sooth this shame, we have to eat more, and the cycle has destroyed many people.

On Weight Watchers, I was able to stop the weight gain. Nevertheless, my daily, four-hour commute made it almost impossible for me to continue to go to those wonderful and supportive meetings. I missed going to the one that one of my biggest fans in that meeting was getting recognition for losing one-hundred pounds or more.

On the advice of my chiropractor whom I really respect, I started reading about the South Beach Diet. It is now the third week and I am at about 306 pounds.

Copyright © 2008 - 2009 Razhan Internet International, Inc. All rights reserved, File:20091022. P a g e | **102**

CHAPTER 38:   The Oprah Show

My wife and I have been fans of Oprah Show for a very long time. Many things about her program resonate with us. Recently the cast of Mary Tyler Moore had a reunion on her program and she was given the "Big M" Emblem, as in Mary in *The Mary Tyler Moore Show*. I used to watch this show, which was set in Minneapolis and is about a single working girl working in a TV Station.

Oprah's show, which is taped in Chicago, has also brought many other interesting, moving, and deeply touching subjects to our attention. Oprah, clearly being the top TV show, has earned being the best of the best programs in their class by transmitting a megawatt energy idea or concept that is so sincere that sets fire to your soul.

I can see it in her eyes. The magic power is there. You cannot avoid being touched by the profound ideas and concepts that are produced each week in this powerful program. Her sadness, when it comes to weighty issues is so captivating that it burns your heart. Here is the Titan of the TV programs. She has no limitation to what it might cost in dollars to deal, cope, and defeat her tendency to lose weight. She has one of the best Physical Trainers in the world. She gave Dr. Phil a chance to get a start in the TV as well as others.

Finally, a few weeks before this book went to print, there was an article that she had gained and now she has surpassed the 200-pound mark. Again, I am not an expert in the multi-billion dollar weight-loss industry. Nevertheless, just like Oprah, I have a problem when it comes to my weight. As if to follow the "Chain of Fools" lyrics word for word, I am also at a breaking point each day. The food and advertising industry, with their unlimited money and power, have brainwashed me, one of the most stubborn, and skeptical critics, that food is beautiful. The more sugar, fat, and starch the better. Every ad shows an attractive woman or handsome man eating sugar-saturated snacks and cereals. My mind's eye is brainwashed to agree. The empty calories in these foods will addict me to sugar, fat, and starch. I will feel hungry almost immediately after eating a lot junk food.

Unfortunately, this vicious cycle repeats itself. We all have seen the vicious cycle of layoffs, and company revenue loss before. These two are very similar. We have created a chain of fools. A chain that everybody and everything are playing the wrong role. They also seem to be continuing to play the same role in spite of awful results. This vicious cycle will keep on going, resulting in a global management and workplace crisis. Never the less, you can see the sadness in Oprah's eyes! Even for the most powerful of the powerful, when it comes to weight issues, there is this sort of unhappiness that is there from an emotional origin.

This chapter started with Mary Tyler Moore. If you contrasted Oprah's body language and facial expressions in this program to those talking about weight issues, you would agree with me that weight loss is a difficult topic even for her. Yet, she does provide a lot of hope on this subject. Moreover, she does not just sit there. She has several programs each year devoted to diet and exercise, and she organizes group walkathons and other activities for weight loss.

I have a dream of being invited on *Oprah* to discuss my book. I found that all book authors have a dream of being in Oprah Show. I would love to tell the world that America is experiencing a management crisis that is, in part, causing this so-called financial tsunami, this economic Armageddon that has manifested itself as massive layoffs, in toxic and dysfunctional workplaces. I would love to tell people that, as an employee and as a senior manager, I have lived this tough life for more than a decade. I would like to tell them not to internalize this. It is not your fault! However, you have to prepare to get out of this mess. You can be CEO of your life. You can live and work too!

Plan and prepare and you will make it! After all, one of the lyrics in *The Mary Tyler Moore Show* was, "You can make it after all!" You can indeed make it!

Oprah keep on being the best of the best, we all love you!

CHAPTER 39:   The Sound of Silence

Simon and Garfunkel have a hit of a song that has the same title as this chapter. I will never forget the time they sang this particular song in Central Park in New York City. Somewhere in the lyrics, it says that the silence grows like cancer. I have seen many people who were affected by Sudden Job Loss (SJL), who just plain disappear from the scene. They do not socialize with friends and colleagues. They stop going to churches, synagogues, and decide to hide their pain in silence! They just want the world to go away. They think that internalizing their pain will help it go away. It does not!
On an intellectual and logical level, they know that this is wrong. This is all they can do. They go into feeling sorry for themselves. They feel miserable and refuse to ask for help. My advice is to do this if you have too. Yet, I encourage you to keep it to a minimum.
A Persian proverb says that you cannot keep fire under the rug. You cannot keep this silence for too long under wraps. At some point, you need to tell others that you must get a new job and the sooner the better. You need to reach out and ask for help.
The Sound of Silence Lyrics:
<

> "Hello darkness, my old friend,
> I've come to talk with you again,
> And the vision that was planted in my brain
> Still remains
> Within the sound of silence."

>

I know a man who lost his job, and he decided to save as much as possible. He would buy a loaf of day-old bread and a jar of the cheapest jam he could find. Two slices of bread and some jam would be his dinner, and he would have one slice for breakfast and nothing for lunch. He wanted to suffer with his pain in silence. He did not want to reach out and ask friends for help or loans. He wanted his meager savings to stretch as far as possible. Because of his pain, pride, and upbringing, he wanted to do this in silence.
He would go to the unemployment office to find a job, but before entering the building, he will make sure that nobody saw him.
Delightfully enough, there is poetic justice in this world. He found a very good job. He is a proud man who not only sent his kids to college, but paid for several relatives to go to college as well. He continues to be a source of inspiration for me, even thirty years later.
In Japan, this suffering in silence is cultural and rampant. I love Japan and Japanese culture. Unfortunately, in view of the fact that some fifty million people will be jobless around the world, it makes my heart and soul break if this traditional continues. Please note: there is nothing that is really our fault in a layoff. There is nothing that we could have done different that could have changed the outcome.
In a New York Times Best of the Year movie, called "In the Bedroom", Sissy Spacek has several captivating lines. After having lost her only son, she observes that pain of this loss comes in waves, and then nothing like a "rest" in music. No sound, but so loud. "I do not know what to do. I feel so angry."
Let us talk among ourselves. Let us talk to the experts who can help us recover and even thrive after being a victim of layoffs. Professionals always keep their silence if we talk to them about our joblessness pains and suffering.

Copyright © 2008 - 2009 Razban Internet International, Inc. All rights reserved, File:20091022,

CHAPTER 40:   Let's Talk About This!

Let us break the dreaded silence taboo. Let us talk to a psychologist that you trust. Let' talk to a trusted and caring colleague or to a family member that might be in a position to help. I guarantee that you will feel great for getting this off your chest. As well, there is now a chance that you might find some help.

You have a lot more chances of getting a good job if several people are looking for you. For example, a colleague of mine went to a job interview and he was not accepted. He told me about that job, and when I went for interview, I got that job.

This is one of the things that you cannot go it alone! In addition, I have walked this talk for many years now! I know what it feels and I know what I am talking about here. Some years ago when my unemployment was affecting my marriage, my wife insisted that we needed to go see a psychologist. Is it not funny that wives usually can be the first to realize that their husbands need help before the husband himself figures it out?

This outstanding psychologist is in Menlo Park, California. Our first session was a lot less painful than I had thought it would be. My wife went to many sessions, and now she is not going any more. Fortunately, these sessions were a heaven-sent gift to me. By being able to talk things over with an unbiased and nonjudgmental professional one feels a lot better. Feelings are just as important as impressions and as important as facts and figures. A psychological hurt can be just being as painful as a real injury. The current layoffs and constant fear of sudden job loss, compounded by lack of trust and loyalty has inflicted a lot of pain and sorrow. I feel this pain, and I have thirty years of experience. Some people think that the time to go see a psychologist is when they have serious psychological problems. Nevertheless, in my experience and the experience of a lot of others, the best time to see a psychologist is when you want to prevent a moderate hurt or bad feeling from getting worse. This is like preventive medicine.

By going there every Thursday, I discovered that I needed to nourish my artistic side and go back to my beloved photography. I might even someday publish my photographic work. I love to photograph people and make abstract and colorful pictures. Later on, it was writing of this book, which has been indeed a labor of love. I am just as proud of any creative artist. Each day, I go back to my creation and add a line of a paragraph, or correct a sentence and that makes me feel great. It is an empowered stress management tool!

She was also extremely helpful when I would lose a job, and or when I needed the added encouragement to continue with this book or the inventions that I was just about to give up. In fact, I am not sure that I would have started or finished this book without her encouragement.

Talk brings solutions and good feelings that silence and shame stifle. Talk with friends and colleagues, and especially with professionals and experts, give us hope, help, and insight. Just the same way those executives have advisors that routinely help them; therapists are there to help too.

Sadly, it is an established fact that with all the Social Networking, Texting, Blogging, etc. we are even more isolated than ever before. Isolation, combined with fear, account for many ills in our community. Knowing this, Let us outsmart this potent evil and talk things out. Luckiest people are those who know how to get it out of their chests by talking to even strangers in a train, plane, or bus.

Copyright © 2008 - 2009 Razban Internet International, Inc. All rights reserved, File:20091022, P a g e | **106**

CHAPTER 41: Job Search Ordeal

I have yet to find someone who likes to look for a job! Even most experienced recruiters agree that job search is not fun. Writing resumes, after all these years, makes me want to quit the entire field. Interviews are painful.

Rejections are even more painful. Rejections are so painful that Mr. B. in "What Color is Your Parachute" devoted one chapter on how to deal with rejections. He encourages us to regroup and then continue the search.

One dreary and cold winter day, I looked outside my window and it looked like everyone was going to work except me. My old car that is in bad need of repair was the only one sitting in the carport in the entire apartment building. Why was this happening to me? While working, our life has a structure. There are meetings to go to, deadlines to meet, social interface with other co-workers, the financial independence, the pride and sense of accomplishment, rewards, and the fact that we are kept busy most of the time. When unemployment breaks that routine to pieces, we, as human beings do indeed feel discouraged, disorganized, and disappointed. Joblessness seems to put a cold blanket on our dreams, hopes, aspirations, financial well being, emotional well-being, and tends to dive us into isolation. Isolation is the Six Sigma root cause of many problems.

Immediately after a layoff, the job security (or even the previous illusion of job security) and steady paychecks evaporate as if the job never existed. Many of us feel foolish for having spent our time and life serving that company so faithfully. A bitter remorse sets in, as if all our life had all been a mistake. We feel that we made bad mistakes, and we feel that the mistake was something only "I" had made. We think it was a bad mistake, for example, for something mundane: "if only I had not gone to that coffee break for five minutes when the project deadline was looming above my head.

We also have a sense of belonging when we are employed. Many sociologists believe that the main reason a young person gets attracted to gangs is the sense of belonging, especially if they are from broken homes.

As a senior management and technology consultant, I had to look for a new job or contract almost every six months. Therefore, I am very familiar with these feelings. Someone once gave me a complement regarding job search. He told me I was a pro at it. I think it was a complement. Maybe not!

Just like layoffs, the job search did not get any easier after the first time. Nevertheless, for me at least, job search has become a full time job in itself. I keep track of companies that I have applied to. I network with my friends and colleagues. I try to create some interesting work for myself. I try many different types of jobs since my career had to be diversified some time ago. I do not let rejections be internalized. I go with the assumption that once we get out of this Global Financial crisis, hopefully the work life will be improved. In addition to doing what it takes to find a job, or at this point, any job, I am also working on business concepts that I plan to send to big companies and hope that one of them, and I only need one of them, to succeed. Then I will be home free.

In fact, it does get worse as we age. Many companies think that if they hire younger employees, they have to pay less. This too is an illusion. It is another false assumption. On the average, over the years, I have realized that it takes fifty phone calls to network with friends and colleagues, and about one-hundred resumes in addition to be sent to any potential job on line, in newspapers, and even on bulletin boards.

CHAPTER 42:   Death March

What I am about to disclose here is very painful. Like everything else in this book, I have tried to be as brutally honest as I can. Yet for this one, I have to change some of the facts to protect the innocent colleagues that got hurt.

In one of my jobs, I had to work for a ruthless Vice President who loved, in a sadistic way, to scare the hell out of his employees. He would show up at somebody's desk at 5:30 PM on Friday to tell him or her that they had to put in what amounted to twenty-two hours of work on the weekend. Now, if this was some urgency, and it happened once in awhile, people could understand. Yet, this happened repeatedly. By the way, there was no overtime pay for those routinely demanded to do overtime work. This is illegal, but some companies do this and get away with it. The workers, who were from a diverse ethnic group, had to obey and tolerate this type of treatment. In fact, in some cultures, especially when people are from countries that have totalitarian governments, they have been raised with the idea that you obey the rulers.

Management would give them almost impossible tasks with do or die deadlines. It also did not seem to concern the management that some of my colleagues in their twenties or thirties looked pale or seemed like they were in pain. The V-P would seem to shed some crocodile tears by asking them if they wanted to go home and work some other time during their weekend to be done by 8:00 AM on Monday. Nevertheless, he did not really mean it. One such person from India, who was here on a H1 Visa, seemed to be having a heart attack. Yet, instead, he went outside for five minutes to get some fresh air and then rushed back. I have been there myself too. I had a heart attack while working for an ungrateful manager. He did not even care to come and ask me how I was doing even after he saw I was very pale and somewhat unsteady.

Most of the assignments were not urgent, as much as management was trying to tell us that they were. This consolidated their near dictatorial power over the employees. What made matters worse, was that most of assignments were ill defined with an impossible deadlines. This type of management is well described in the book by the title *Death March*. We did assignment after assignment this way. Our Thanksgiving holiday was destroyed because we had to work until 8:00 PM the night before and had to respond to e-mails or cell phone calls immediately on Thanksgiving. On top of that, we had to work on the day after Thanksgiving and the weekend after. Imagine how difficult it was to work on a strict deadline on the day after Thanksgiving when most of the company had taken that day off to enjoy it with their families. None of our counter parts in other departments was available. This made it impossible to get anything done.

One colleague who was a perfect gentleman and whom I respect a great deal technically, told me that he was suffering from serious sleep deprivation. In fact, he did not have to tell me. I knew this! I was suffering the same. The unfortunate thing is that his work suffered a great deal. When people are pushed beyond their human limits, their work quality and quantity suffers.

Another one was in tears and was trying not to show it. This is a combination of being harassed and forced to work to such an extent that you are not a human being any more, you have succumbed to being a subhuman or a human robot! Zombification is the word I use to describe this.

Mistakes piled up and the vice president got impatient. He could not understand why this

Copyright © 2008 - 2009 Razban Internet International, Inc. All rights reserved, File:20091022. P a g e | **108**

was happening. At some point, it became clear to me that the entire group was looking totally spent and tired.

In spite all of these; management death marches do no favors to the company. It seems like the faith of employees who are forced to obey and go along with these death marches that companies practice are in the end similar. They both lose.

What is sad is that, repeatedly, I offered to use my programming skills to make the job easier. My manager had no interest in this and wanted me to do some ridiculous paperwork during this trial. At the end, half of the results were not usable. So all that working till 2:30 AM, doing the same tedious task three or four times, were a waste of time. Management knew it too! Yet somehow, either to impress the next level of management, or to do a cover up, or something else, the management picked the most shortsighted brute force solution and forced employees to do it.

I had been put on several of these assignments. Death marches have the effect of degrading the individual to the point that something has to suffer. There are three measures of success for any project. One is whether the deadline was met or not. The other is the quality of job. Finally, meeting specifications is another measure.

As an almost fifty-five year old manager, I went through one particularly painful death march for me. I worked several weekends and evenings, and then produced a final product that I wished I had never done. It worked, it met the specification, and the Quality Assurance Group testified that it was of acceptable quality. Nevertheless, it failed all three Razban measurement criterions of pride, robustness, and value to the customer. My manager at that time who had the nickname of "Poker Face" finally smiled (a labored and contrived half-smile). Then he said, "See you could do it." He was happy and proud that he had "Done it Again!" However, the customer was not very happy, and I and my huge ego and pride were hurt and unhappy.

A few months later, I got a frantic call from a different manager who had inherited the project, begging me to explain certain difficulties with the product. I offered to visit them at their location one evening to help. Of course, I told them that I would do it free of charge because my pride was at stake. This led to another contract to totally re-do the project! The new manager, a GE School of Management Graduate, had the good sense to realize that, although we all did our jobs, the final product was not good enough. Quality is often one of the first things to be missing in a Death March company. This is the exact opposite of the HP Win-Win management practice.

Copyright © 2008 - 2009 Razban Internet International, Inc. All rights reserved, File:20091022, P a g e | **109**

CHAPTER 43:   Others Cannot Understand

It is quite discouraging that when we are out of work, others who are working have a difficult time understanding what we are going through. They seem to be in their own world. A world that says they are busy. They just do not really want us to remind them of what it feels to be outside looking in. Of course, we as the unemployed are living in a different world too. We need the help and encouragement of those in the other world. Unfortunately, that help is slow and difficult to find.

Worse yet, some of those working will give the wrong advice, or with the best of intentions, cause serious heartache for their unemployed friends and colleagues. The fundamental wrong assumption on their part is that since they are working and we are not, then they must be doing things right. On the other hand, since we are not working, we must be wrong. There is nothing in the world that is a bigger mistake than this. I do understand that some of the working folks are under severe pressure. In fact, some of these jobs are by far more painful than not having a job! In some companies, because of this toxic and relentless stress, the employees walk around in a daze just like zombies. They work very hard. However, they are not convinced that what they were working so hard for was worth it. They had to be on the defensive all the time to prevent a colleague from causing them harm out of desperation, or fear. This fact in itself is responsible for the breakdown of Mutual Trust and Loyalty. This breakdown then undermines productivity for the company and job satisfaction for the employees. This defensiveness typically prevents employees from spending any time helping each other in the work place and leaves little chances for helping those outside.

In most of the twelve step programs, there is a saying that when someone asks for help, we are responsible to give them help. This, in fact, has religious and spiritual roots in just about any religion I have studied.

When someone calls a colleague and asks for help, that colleague must take it seriously and act upon it promptly and correctly. I have encouraged a lot of people to call their colleagues. Moreover, they do. It takes a lot of courage to do this. Furthermore, when they do this, I also make a point that they need to follow up and ask again if needed.

Look, banks stopped giving out loans all together. So many of our friends are desperate. A friend was so desperate for some cash just to prevent his electricity cut off; he finally gathered enough courage to call an old friend in Beverly Hills. An interesting thing happened. The friend in Beverly Hills who had millions and millions of dollars told him that he did not do business with friends and relatives. It was smart on the part of my friend to make a list of all his friends and call. The fourth call resulted in a distant relative who did actually lend him the money. In my own case, I have had this experience on two occasions. In one case a CEO who was a former colleague and a friend, would invite me to play gold Saturday mornings. I would save some of my unemployment, or borrow from my wife to pay golf cost and somewhat pricy lunch that we would have after wards. On all of those six times, I made sure he know that I was very qualified and capable. He had always known that I was a hard worker. On top of that his wife was a recruiter. They did not lift a figure to help. None what so ever and they were in a position to help. During the height of the Iran crisis, I know of many relatives who were financially in a secure position who did not lift a figure to help others.

In another case, I have seen friends not even sending their unemployed friends even a short email just to keep in touch. Even though a call takes less than three minutes to keep in touch with a friend, is not done wither. Calls like this can cheer those in the cold and dark outside hopeful. Remember, in this day and age, we need all the help we can get when we are unemployed. Actually, we need help in keeping our skills current even when we work. With all these layoffs, we could be working today and not tomorrow. In general, once people find a job, they tend to want to forget those who helped them. They quickly forget those times when they were both unemployed. Some people give totally unpractical advice. This is not acceptable.

Nevertheless, I do know a lot of caring people who go out of their way to help others. In my own case, my friend and colleague Sam got on his bicycle and brought me two checks. Each of the checks was for two thousand dollars. One check was from his account, and the other was from his wife's account. With a big smile, he said that the condition for this loan is twofold:

- He insisted in no interest payments. He was an Orthodox Jew, and believed that this had to be an interest-free loan,
- It had to remain confidential.

In addition, he kept calling me to make sure I was doing OK with the job search and offered to lend me another $1,000 if I needed it. He helped teach me some of the latest technology developments. He forwarded my resume to others. He cheered me up by sending me Dilbert cartoons. One day he told me why he did all these. He said that when he was down and out only two or three people genuinely helped him. He decided that he would be better than others are, and help whenever, and whatever he could. For example, he personally introduced me to another friend who worked in a company that was heavily hiring. This type of help is extremely beneficial.

Unfortunately, some working folks act as if unemployment is contiguous. They try to avoid former colleagues who have lost their jobs. They do not realize that the layoff situation is like musical chairs. In this dizzying game of musical chairs insanity, one moment it is my turn to be unemployed. However later on, it will be their turn. This is just like one giant game of musical chairs. The painful fact is that this music continues to start, then suddenly stop, and restart again, and again. Please help your former unemployed friends! The rewards are heavenly! Moreover, believe me; you will not catch the disease of unemployment from them. This type of behavior of not helping, is a "lose-lose" situation for everyone. They do not want to accept that this job loss situation is an epidemic. Today, they have a job and some illusive job security. Nevertheless, tomorrow, when our turn comes to have a job, they might be out of a job! Therefore, it is to their benefit to help since they might need help later on.

There are also those working people who think they are smart, but indeed, they are not. One of them is a man that I had known for several years. I was instrumental in helping him find a job. He was qualified, but his resume was old. Worse yet, that resume focused on another type of job all together. I spent hours helping him to re-write his resume and then I made sure that the hiring manager got it. I also spent many hours helping him at the beginning in being his tutor since he was not very familiar with the latest technology. He and I are exactly in the same profession. Therefore, I was able to help him a great deal.

With my help, he got a good in our area of specialty. We continue to be excellent friends,

Copyright © 2008 - 2009 Razban Internet International, Inc. All rights reserved, File:20091022, P a g e | **111**

but he does not anything, and I mean anything to help me. This is so, even when I ask for help since he is in a position to help. He must have his reasons, but I just cannot understand.

I remind myself that this a musical chair situation. Today, I do not have a job and he has one. Nevertheless, tomorrow, it might very well be the other way around. As a matter of principle, I will help him each and every time he needs help. I do realize that this is stupid of me! I wish I were selfish enough, remind him that he did not help. However, no can do, I cannot bring myself down to a level that is just the not helping type.

There are plenty of people, who are in a position to help somebody else find a job. Yet they chose to stick to their own work and not even call their jobless colleague even when months go by. Actually, I have seen worse. I have seen groups in a company that are desperate about recruiting a certain person with a certain skill set. What is sad is that there are people in these groups that know of some colleagues who could be a perfect fit for that job. Sadly, they do not bother to introduce their friend. Why is this so? They do not want to get involved. I find this unacceptable. By the way, there is that selfish benefit in helping others, or as we call it doping mitzvah! In this, when we help someone who is out of job several good things happen for us:

- One thing is that we realize how lucky we are to have a job, and we will not keep our job for granted.
- By seeing the thoughts, the undeserved shame, the self-damnation, the depression, the anger, the rejection, and the dejection, we will be better prepared to face these things and bounce back quicker.
- Remember it is only human to think that we should have done something better or different to avoid our lay off. However, since a sudden job loss is almost like an ugly divorce, we learn how to cope, when our turn comes around. Sadly, one thing that is common in many children of divorce is that they blame themselves for their parent's divorce. Aside from being the real victims of the divorce, it is highly unlikely that they had anything to do with it. The same unfortunate false assumption holds true for the victims of layoffs.

Remember, the best time to get back on the horse is just when we fell down!

Spouses, better halves, and living together partners, usually have to deal with much more pain than friends, and colleagues. This obviously is because they have to live under the same roof. A colleague told me that his spouse of many years gave him an ultimatum that she will take the kids and fly to her parents in Europe if he did not find a job in one month. She made life miserable for her husband for several months, until he agreed and signed the legal papers that would let his wife to take kids and go. He is still bitter over this. Unfortunately, several months later he was still unemployed. Therefore, she took the kids and left for Europe.

One of my relatives told me that her husband, who takes care of kids while she works, had to cut a lot of expenses just to help make ends meet and has gotten a part time job himself. She shared with me how they would first serve dinner to the kids, and then they wait until they finish eating, so they can go in the kitchen and eat the leftovers. This way they make sure that kids get enough to eat, even if parents have go to bed hungry.

Sadly, spouses end up carrying a big burden in this unemployment situation.

I, myself, have experienced the entire gambit. In one company, we knew that the entire group would be laid off. I sat down with my wife and we decided to finally do the dream career planning that we had wanted to do for so many years. I could not wait until I got the severance check to start the dream business partnership with my wife. She was very encouraging and supportive. We started on the plan, and even started to spend money to buy the things that were needed to start our new business. The business was less than successful and we both got disappointed. All that dreaming and effort went down the drain.

I also know about another couple, where the spouse got so angry with her husband losing his job again, that she subjected him to name calling, and really stress at home. He was totally demoralized when he needed every ounce of his self-respect and confidence to find a job. She was so angry that she would hang up on recruiters those seldom times that they called. She was angry with his loser husband and she was taking revenge.

Another colleague told me that his wife was the principle reason why he found such a great job. His wife had many golf buddies and some of them were executives of companies, or had strong connections. One these golf buddies introduced my colleague's husband to an outstanding executive recruiter that found him a job in less than a week. When, it came time to negotiate salary, my colleague wrote down what he thought his salary should be and asked his wife to get advice. His wife calls her golf buddy, and finds out that her husband had been underpaid for many years. These are the type of help that is badly needed.

The most important advice in the case of spousal anger is that we as the person with the full time job of finding a job must not let spousal issues to defocus you. I know for a fact that those who decide to spend some time in improving their marriage since they now have some extra time, soon discover that the best time to do this is after they get a job. One of my colleagues did what was a very tempting thing. He started remolding his kitchen, since he thought he had extra time on his hand. Then, since the kitchen looked so good, and the dining room so bad, it was time to remodel the dining room. Before he know it a year has gone by and they have become a full time "Home Improver" while totally ignoring job search.

Remember again, you do have a job. It is the full time job of finding a job.

Also remember that we have one primary full time job now, and that is making money to live on by finding a job. Once, we find a job, then a lot of other problems will be either less important or can be easier resolved.

Best way I know of putting this is that first and foremost, we need to realize that even when unemployed, we do indeed have a full time job of finding our next job.

Copyright © 2008 - 2009 Razban Internet International, Inc. All rights reserved, File:20091022, P a g e | **113**

CHAPTER 44:   Do not Internalize It. It is not Your Fault!

Almost all of my experience shows that even though layoffs are supposed to be "No Fault" actions. That is what a layoff is supposed to be by definition! Nevertheless, employees sometimes ask themselves whether there was something that, if they had done better, they would not have been affected by the layoff. These layoff victims mostly seem to internalize it by thinking that there must have been something that they did not do right. That nonexistent "something" is so impossible to find that even senior management and technology consultants with years and years of experience cannot find! Repeatedly, I have had to explain to people that this was not their fault. The fact most of the time remains that there never was nothing that they had done wrong. This is just the way the business is right now. When the business is tough, then these kinds of things do happen. In September issue of Time Magazine with picture of unemployed San Francisco and New York, there were several articles saying this will be the future trend in the work place.
It is not management, employee, customer, or even unions' faults. It is that we all need to realize that massive changes are happening in our work lives. We are going through a new revolution, very similar to the Industrial Revolution that will be a complete paradigm change. This is an ultra big game changer. Instead of asset management, we will be in the knowledge management age. This techno-humanization of the workplace as part of the new Capitalism is either ignored or totally pushed aside. People like Michael Moore are saying or implying that Capitalism is dead. Interestingly enough, they make lots of money from the very same Capitalism that they claim is dead. How could it be dead if it is working for them? Capitalism needs reinvention. We do reinventions of companies in Silicon Valley routinely. It is not a big deal. As Richard Bolles has said, we need to learn, unlearn, and then relearn. Reinvention, which is a Hewlett Packard logo, is even part of their logo. We need to reinvent capitalism to bring it up to speed with Internet mega revolution. We need to reinvent it to shift emphasis from material Capitalism to human Capital. As you might have noticed, this is the era of being knowledge workers. Going back to that Michael Douglass "Greed for the lack of a better word is a good" thing I like to add the following. Suppose greed is good. Everyone can be greedy and wanting to make money. Paradoxically, to make money and lots of it, we need to focus on humans and their unlimited potential. Humans are the company, the products and services that the company produces. Most importantly, they are the customers.
One of the most respected economists, Greenspan, said that this economic tragic situation was like a tsunami that he did not predict it, and it seemed to have hit suddenly, I believed him. I am just as guilty as anyone else in this is. I did not see it coming with the vengeance that it did. I somehow missed seeing it even though I was heavily involved in my book research that took most of eight years. As Steven Covey, the author of *The Seven Habits of Successful People* has indicated, we are going from capitalism that is based on things to capitalism that is based on knowledge and human power.
As sad as it might be to lose one's home to foreclosure, one *can* recover if there is enough knowledge in terms of experience, skill set, and networks with others. A home in this case is just a house. Keep in mind that knowledge is human power that is much more potent. With the power of knowledge, we can make unemployment, underemployment, and work-life rage and frustration go away. As they said in the *Six Million Dollar Man*,

Copyright © 2008 - 2009 Razban Internet International, Inc. All rights reserved, File:20091022,

"we have the technology." Now we have to harness and humanize this technology! The Global Financial Crisis was in the making for twenty or thirty years. Our wasteful ways of material based capitalism will not work anymore. It was not easy loans alone. It was not the collapse of housing alone. It will not be the collapse of commercial property alone either that is going to happen soon. Nor was it the Dot-com bubble burst alone either. The Global Financial is an earthquake that was caused by collision of the material Capitalism with humanitarian Capitalism. The catalyst was the advent of information available instantly everywhere, which is the Internet Revolution. Next remaining chapters will build on this.

Thus, the era of technology humanization has arrived, and it has arrived on a grand scale and on a global basis!

CHAPTER 45:   Toughest Commute as a Result of Job Loss

After it seemed like I could not get any jobs near where I lived due to a bad economy, I decided to look at places that are more distant. I landed a consulting job with Kaiser Permanente in Oakland, California. Driving from Mountain View to Oakland was an act of insanity due to heavy, slow traffic along the way.

Each day, I would wake up at 4:30 AM to go to the CalTrain Station and catch the Baby Bullet Train at 6:00 AM. Then I will be in San Francisco at 6:50 AM. Just in time to take Muni Light Rail and go from the train, station to Embarcadero Station to catch BART to Oakland and be at my desk around 8:20 AM. Then I would make the same two-hour commute to return home.

This commute, as difficult as it sounds, was much easier than the fifteen steps it took from my bedroom to the bathroom in the morning. I was so down and depressed (or more poetically, "Damn depressed" as was in a popular song) that this was more than an ordeal. Surprisingly enough, this is the only commute that an unemployed person has to make. Once this heroic, overbearing stage is complete, take a shower and start working from home, or the Home Office. I had learned to validate my feelings about pain before this monumental march. Then I always praise and cheer myself as a champion for having done the most difficult part of the day. The rest would be a cakewalk!

Back to my four-hour round trip commute from my home in Mountain View to Oakland. When people hear about this long commute, either they feel sorry or they think that I am some sort of crazy and/or desperate person. The truth is that this long commute, usually on top of an eight- to ten-hour stressful workday, sounds a lot worse than it really is. Humans are very agile and they can adjust to new conditions. I have integrated the small nap that I take on BART on my way to work in the morning commute, and triumphant ride back on CalTrain, in the afternoon. They do not bother me as much. This is much easier than the two-minute commute out of the bedroom when I was unemployed.

The pleasure of these rides, as tiring as they might be sometimes, is much more than those Business Class flights I had when I was director of some big corporations. All that pampering and service given to business and first class, does not compensate for the self-respect of having worked as hard as humanly possible. At the end of the day, the pleasure of taking the same train that I and several friends and colleagues take was immeasurable. Unfortunately, sometimes I feel that I was not grateful enough for the luxury of Business Class. Ironically, when that feeling hits me when I am tired, I look around the train and rejoice. I rejoice in the fact that these are hard working folks putting up with a tough commute just to put bread on the table. I am then quickly a member of this club just as much as I am proud of being a member of the 30,000 Feet Club. Cold brutal reality sets in when I get up in the morning to a less-than-kind bill collector call, instead of the wake up calls I used to get in some four-star hotel when I was on a business trip with all expenses paid by the corporation, these calls have a way of grinding at me all day long. After a while, this daily grind makes the two-minute commute from the bedroom even more difficult. Imagine you are on a mission and on a journey to better jobs and Life or a "Solder in the Poverty Army" as another popular song said it.

Copyright © 2008 - 2009 Ranban Internet International, Inc. All rights reserved, File:20091022, P a g e | 116

CHAPTER 46:   Try Once More Like You Did Before

The soothing effect of ABBA music permeates my car. I am driving from Hillsdale
Shopping Center back to my home. It is nice day on October 11, 2008. It is a nice and
sunny day, even though there is a lot of wind coming from Pacific Ocean. ABBA is a
Swedish group. I know a retired Pan American Flight Attendant by the name of Aimee
Bratt who is Swedish. She is one of the most elegant and attractive women in the entire
world. Her father was the Swedish Ambassador to Iran. I met her first in an Airline
Enthusiasts' Show that is near San Francisco Airport twice each year. I cherish her
autographed books. She recognizes me as the "Jewish Iranian who lived across the street
from the American embassy." She had travelled to Iran many times when her father was
there. We both love Iranian ancient culture, and exquisite Persian cuisine. On the cover of
"Background Player", published by Vanity Press, there is a picture of her showing those
superbly sexy legs that are just as sexy many years later. She has also had an extremely
successful filmmaking career. She has been in "The Devil's Advocate", "Presumed
Innocent", "All that Jazz" and many others. When I told her that I am from Iran, I loved
Pan American, and like her I too have been a movie star, we instantly fell in love for
having so much in common. I quickly had to confess that I was just a movie extra with
Ali McGraw in "Goodbye Columbus". My forty or fifty Swedish vocabulary made me
look like a scholar to her.
In addition to being mesmerized with her star power super attractiveness, I am equally
impressed to see someone who has done super heroics with her life. "After Pan American
was no more, I felt like sitting at home and doing nothing for the rest of my life." "Well
that lasted about forty-eight hours before I decided to focus on my second career which
was movies!"
ABBA's Gold Album is playing in my ES 250 Lexus (known affectionately as poor
man's Lexus). This car is basically a Toyota Camry but it is made to look like a luxurious
car. This happened when Lexus executives suddenly realized the potentially huge market
for their luxury car division needed a more affordable and less featured car. This car
benefits from a Lexus engine and many good Lexus parts. Mine has 185,000 miles on it
and I am extremely happy. I got my money's worth when I paid $25,700 for it in 1991.
Anyway, this car was one of the first to have a CD player in it. Moreover, after all these
years, the CD player works well. The Abba song that got my attention this time was:
Chiquitita lyrics:
<
"So the walls came tumbling down
All is gone and it seems too hard to handle
I see that you're oh so sad, so quiet"
>
The lyrics continue with, "Try once more like you did before!" A sentence
just like this got me to find one of the best jobs in my career. I had just been to an
interview for a lousy job and with a totally dishonest and incompetent hiring manager.
The job title was a fancy, glamorous director, but one of the first things I was supposed to
do was to "cut the work force in half in twenty-one days" and then "offshore the rest in
three months." I did not get this job, because the hiring manager (who did not have a clue
about how his department developed software) realized that I was a bit uncomfortable

Copyright © 2008 - 2009 Razban Internet International, Inc. All rights reserved, File:20091022, P a g e | **117**

with the cutting that the job required. This was an important job with a major company and I was hoping that, if they hired me, I would find ways to drag my feet and not "cut" or "offshore," at least not to the extent that they incompetently were thinking they could do and still survive in this tough business. I had just started to internalize this. I was asking myself "Why can't I get a job?"

This same "Why Can't I get a job?" is exactly what Olga was asking herself every minute of every hour of the day. Olga is from former Soviet Union and she sold perfume in a prestigious Department Store in Hillsdale Shopping Center. She had shiny black hair with shimmers with some gold and brown hue. One of her ancestors is from Mongolia, so she has beautiful honey/hazel eyes with extra long eyelashes. She noticed that I was uncomfortable walking by her counter. She lifted her head and said "hello" with a soft yet sexy voice with a poetic Russian accent. "Interested in a sample?" Before I could find an excuse, she invited me to do a sample test. She sprayed four different brands of perfumes on some long and narrow pieces of paper that were especially made for sampling. Of course, when a gorgeous attractive woman asked me to something, I did it. But this was way different. Since childhood I had known that some perfumes seriously bothered me. I would get headaches, and sometimes even get short of breath. She, like a Dr. said, "Allergies?!" "I guess so, but people do not buy that excuse." "Not really, allergies are just as real as anything!" She then patiently helped me take a sniff of different brands. By selecting the ones that made me feel like having a headache, she quickly described the chemical compounds and brands that I was allergic to. She was right on the dot! "Are you buying this for a girlfriend?" "No, we broke up several months ago!", "I see, sorry for this. These things happen. It happened to me" "Can I buy you a cup of coffee?" I asked. "It is against company policy. But in your case, why not!" As she was sipping her Double Espresso, I discovered a quiet sadness. "You are much too beautiful and elegant to be sad." I said. She was quick to tell me that she was a scientist before. But know her credentials are not valid in US. My engineering background helped me understand her. Soon we were intimate friends. I helped her with her school work. As she gained more self confidence, she blossomed like a beautiful white rose. I had promised her that we will celebrate her training completion by going anywhere she wanted. "Anywhere?" I assured her, anywhere. What I meant was any restaurant, theater, or movies. The day came. She was there waiting for me on her day off. We drove towards Half Moon Bay on Scenic Highway one. As I was driving, I noticed that she was undressing. "Olga what are you doing? People can see!", "Keep your eye on the road!" A mile down the road, she ordered me to make a left turn and stop. There were a few other cars there too. "Please give me a minute!" I climbed the short hill and looked down towards the Pacific. At first it looked like an ordinary beach. As I looked more closely, I noticed that no nobody had any cloths on. "Surprised? This is just a Nude Beach. Do not worry, Let us go there!" I was just too chicken to go. That ruined her graduation party and our relationship. To this day, I wonder what it would have been like. Olga gave me a call a few months later telling me that she had been working in some high-tech company and her old boyfriend is joining her in US after many years. The walls did come tumbling down on her. But, she tried several more times and soon she was OK. As for me, I still have that allergy, and I cannot remember which brands are causing it. Most importantly, I will not bother Olga and her boyfriend from Russian Army for my allergies. Since doing this can be life threatening!

Copyright © 2008 - 2009 Razban Internet International, Inc. All rights reserved, File:20091022,

I remember asking Olga about management in former Soviet Union. She told me that a manager usually was someone who had good connections in the government. "But, what about their interpersonal skills? What about their ability to manage, motivate, or inspire?" She tried not to answer that but finally gave in. "They usually were some brats from influential rich families." "As far as the rest of the stuff, it was easy. They told us what to do. We did it. Sometimes, we even got paid the full salary. We did not do it, we would be in trouble. Everybody hated it! It was not like here. Job satisfaction is an American invention, we did not have it, and we did not know any better. We were consumed to put bread on the table. Sometimes, just the bread and nothing else!"

I remember one of national TV stations had a series called Amerika. Amerika was about Soviet Union of those days taking over America. This is jolting, alarming, and scary. Nevertheless, this is educational and it is imperative that we learn from this. American freedom and free market were crushed by Russian made tanks and uprisings were prevented by patrolling Russian made Jeep equivalents. Now imagine a horrible thing has happened. Imagine that a hostile takeover of American economy by Foolism. Not Communism, but Foolism. Why? We have all been foolish to make this serious financial crisis to happen. This is not a Democratic, Republican, or Independent thing. It is all of us and has been in the works for several decades. We need to re-invent Capitalism. Maybe we take a page from re-invented Boeing Company that makes Boeing 777. As a proud American, I get goose bumps every time I see a Boeing 777 painted in the Aeroflot, the national airline of Russia. My pride is twofold:

- We are doing win-win business with our archenemy of the past,
- Capitalism, via one of its re-invented companies, has had the prowess to make this happen.

The lyrics of **Chiquitita** really hit the spot with what I felt when I heard the news that I did not get that job that required off shoring.

The lyrics continue like this:

<

"So the walls came tumbling down
And your love's a blown out candle
All is gone and it seems too hard to handle
Chiquitita, tell me the truth
There is no way you can deny it
I see that you're oh so sad, so quiet"

>

The walls did come tumbling down as a result of a job loss and I was very sad and quiet. I was in a Cupertino, California, coffee shop called Coffee Society. This coffee shop is directly across the street from DeAnza College and usually many people who are "in between jobs" or are "consultants who are waiting for their next gig" spend their time reading or writing books or study the latest technical books or just relax and read some novel. I was thinking about treating myself to a coffee and a slice of chocolate cake. I will have the coffee to wake me up and the chocolate cake to take revenge from that incompetent manager. One look at the $2.50 price of the cake quickly convinced me that that was not a good idea. In addition to that, *revenge* is not my vocabulary. Therefore, I decided to have no chocolate cake that day. The cup of coffee and the tip and several refills did just well.

Another similar coffee shop was in Mountain View. It used to be an unsuccessful art store and then decided to become a combination bookstore and coffee shop. It was called

Printer's Ink. This was also a very popular place. One day, I was sitting there at 11:00 AM, and reading my newspaper, when I noticed one of my old colleagues was buying some books. It was great to talk to him about the good old days and he told me that one of his friends was hiring managers. He gave me his friend's contact numbers and this got me back to working for a good manager and a good job. We did extremely well together. Remember, we do not want to quit fifteen minutes before the miracle. We do not want to give up and not turn the corner, where right around this particular corner there might be a chance of the lifetime.

Of course, sometimes walls do come tumbling down they did in case of Pan American, "The World's Most Experienced Airline". Yet many times, "trying once (or several times) more as you did before" can and will get you a better job. Trying once more as she did before, kept Amie young, exuberant, interesting, and even super sexy after the walls came tumbling down on Pan American and her most loved career.

Copyright © 2008 - 2009 Razban Internet International, Inc. All rights reserved, File:20091022, P a g e | **120**

CHAPTER 47:   Andy Rooney of CBS's Recession

On December 5, 2008, a TV news anchor had the following announcement: "Today, it became officially clear that the country is in recession. More importantly, it also became clear that the country has been in recession for almost a year". He made this announcement with a straight face! Unfortunately, the news room anchor was not smart enough, or those who wrote his lines were just as dumb as he, to write such a stupid line when the country had been in recession and hurting so much for a long time!

This is just as funny, in a sad way. Imagine a doctor telling his patient, "Sorry, you are dead now". More importantly, you had been dead for over a year in spite all those times that you came to my office and told me you were dying and I did not agree!"

On a CBS 60 Minutes episode in the last days of November, Andy Rooney, who has the final section and commentary, told us how he is coping with the recession.

He said, "I make a cup of coffee all by myself rather than pay $1.50 to buy one at the CBS cafeteria to save". However, from the look on his face when he was drinking it, it seemed that the coffee must have tasted worse than dishwater.

Then, he showed, in a rather clumsy way, how he brushed his shoes after he had bought the brush and polish to save money. However, he did say he missed the conversations he used to have with the shoeshine person. Then he told us that he used to wear his shirts for one day and then take them to the dry cleaners. Now, he wears them two or even three days in a row to save money. He even takes public transport to go to his favorite sports activity, which I think kills the entire spirit of a relaxing sports event.

I must confess something here. I am a devoted fan of 60 Minutes. I have watched almost all their episodes for more that last thirty or forty years and I love all of them. Ever since they went on air in 1968, I have watched their program. However, I especially enjoy Andy's section each week. He is entertaining, intellectual, and the perfect stereotype of a grandfather. My father's father (i.e., my paternal grandfather) passed away when my dad was only four years old. I never saw my father's father. This has created an empty spot that I have tried to fill with father-like images and personalities like Andy.

However, as much as I love the program and Andy in particular, I cannot help but disagree with Andy on his piece. The undeniable fact is that the American economy is dependent on jobs. In our society and culture, jobs create spending. In our economy, spending is the trigger for jobs. If Andy and the rest of us started to save and save, our economy would not benefit. While it is true that American consumer is spending more than they should, yet if people literally followed Andy's super saver method, the economy will have a hard time recovering. Remember, jobs allow reasonable spending. Reasonable spending creates jobs. The cycle completes itself and keeps economy going. On a morning new program on the radio, I heard an interesting observation. The observation was that if employees did not do their jobs we fire or lay them off. The fact is that consumers have not been doing their job of consuming. This lack of consumption had delayed recovery. Considering that it is the "Consumer's job to consume" in our economy, then should we fire or lay them off if they are not doing their job.

CHAPTER 48:   Futility of Layoffs

My grandfather, on my mother's side, was a very successful and important merchant. He was like an executive in his time. My mother used to help her father in his business. Therefore, she knows about some ideas. She was found of telling us a joke about being pound-foolish:
A company employee tells his boss, "I have saved $1.25 today. Instead of taking the bus, I just ran after the bus and saved the bus fare." His boss says impressed, "But that's not good enough. Next time, make sure you run after a Taxi Cab to save $15.00 instead of just $1.25". His boss told him. So it is with so-called savings resulting from layoffs! WE think that we save money, but that is not true.
Let us look at this more closely. Management thinks that they "saved" one person-year by laying off an employee. This will cost you the following:
- Severance payments, at least two weeks, and maybe up to sixteen,
- Loss of job-related accumulated knowledge, four to eight weeks,
- Lower morale among remaining employees, twelve to twenty-five weeks,
- Loss of productivity of ten weeks,
- Training costs for the replacement of four weeks,
- Management burden to bring life back to normal in the workplace of four weeks,
Total cost thirty-six to sixty-seven weeks of productivity loss.
In the long term, companies that rely on layoffs suffer from:
- Lack of innovation because layoffs create fear of Sudden Job Loss (SJL),
- Lack of productivity resulting from low morale, and just inadequate work force,
- Excessive politics and games people feel they have to play to keep their jobs,
- Disgruntled employee sabotage,
- Employee empathy thinking why should they care for the company when the company does not,
- Serious problems in keeping top talent since good employees are always in demand,
- Serious problems in hiring top talent due to the tarnished company reputation,
- Difficulty in executing strategic and/or tactical plans due to disruptions left behind by layoffs,
- Worker and management apathy such as, I do not care, you do not care, the company does not care, and who cares attitudes,
- Communication is muffled, distorted, or even stifled by fear of layoffs and Sudden Job Loss (SJL)
With these thoughts in mind, can anyone convince me that layoffs are good?

CHAPTER 49:   The Stupidity of Layoffs and Foreclosures

Suppose you are the CEO of a mid-sized company and you decide to cut the work force by five percent.
Well, before you go ahead with your decision, let us think about other alternatives:
- You can cut salaries by five percent across the board and get the same effect,
- You can put a freeze on all raises and promotions,
- You can cut other operating costs by five percent,
- You can pay your vendors and third parties in twenty-one days instead of twenty-one days after they invoice you,
- You can discourage executive travel in business class and ask them to fly coach.

Many times, measures like this are more than sufficient to prevent layoffs. In addition, this demonstrates that the company really cares for its people. This way employee Mutual Loyalty and Trust (MTL) stays intact. I had an interesting experience with an HR professional during one of those long train rides. She made some great points.
She asked me, what if no company ever fired anyone. Would we be better off? My answer was that, if an employee is not doing his or her job, termination, done properly and with respect is OK. Then she asked, what if we did not lay off, then there would not be room for new blood. My answer continues to be no. If companies planned and managed, then they would hire more systematically to avoid the mess we are in right now. So, there would not be as many layoffs. A well-managed company would always have room for hiring additional top talent. The normal attrition and retirement always opens up opportunities for new employees. In addition to that, a well-managed company usually expands, so there is no need to layoff. HP is an example. They did not lay off a single employee for fifty years. they kept expanding and hiring new employees all the time.
This so called revolving door "At Will" hiring and then firing or layoffs damages the fabric and culture of a company. The "At Will" clause has caused chaos for employers and worse yet employees. Otherwise, how could a corporation like HP go without a single lay off for fifty years!
As I mentioned before, the down market of 2008-2009 has created an awful financial situation for me. I, as an average American, for the first time, see myself only one or two months away from foreclosure. The irony is that I have a little equity in my house, and the bank can gain some few thousand Dollars from short sell of my property.
It is eerily ironic. When I was looking to buy a house, I did not have a lot for down payment. So, a real estate agent called me to tell me that he had great news. He had found a town house that I could buy for a song. We had to cancel our first appointment to go see the house. A second appointment was set for a few days later. The agent knocked on the door and at first there was no answer. A few minutes later a dim voice from the other informed us that she was serving breakfast to her kids and getting them ready for school. She asked us to come back next day. The agent persisted and gave the owner several reasons why tomorrow was not possible. She then, with a resigning voice said OK.
As we entered, I noticed a noticeable lack of furniture, and the furniture that existed was old and out of repair. The owner was a thirty-some year old with two surprised kids who did not know Mom was planning to move them somewhere else, and soon. The oldest

Copyright © 2008 - 2009 Razban Internet International, Inc. All rights reserved, File:20091022, P a g e | **123**

was a fourteen or so years old, who had perhaps figured out the consequence of her Mom losing her job a few months ago and not being able to get a new one. She was whispering something to the younger brother's ear to sooth his anxiety while she herself was not doing much better either.

I frankly did not exactly know what was happening. We took a quick look, I apologized, and we were on our way. The agent gladly announced that she had only thirty days to vacate. I asked him why. He said "foreclosure" and added, "This is really your lucky day since you will get this house for a song.

I mustered all the power and courage that I could have and said a very strong "Hell No!" I will not, and I repeat I will not buy a foreclosed property. I said the "Hell No" just about with the same conviction that Vietnam War Protestors were shouting when they were shouting their opposition to the war by saying, "Hell No, We Won't Go!" It is against my ethics to prosper from somebody else's misfortune. How could I sleep in those rooms? I could not live with the idea that a family had to lose their house and shelter so I could move in.

I still remember that Mom who was emotionally injured by her sudden job loss, yet as a most elegant swan spreading her wings to protect her kids while serving that meager breakfast. Where has our humanity gone? This house is like a nest. It is like a shelter. Even animals need a nest.

I ended up purchasing a much smaller unit. But, I always am proud of myself. At night when I put my head on the pillow, I am glad and proud that I was not fueling the fires of a family's misery. The image of that family is still alive in my memory. Every so often when I remember this, I say a prayer for their well being and happiness.

The responsibility that that Mom was showing towards her kids, assures me that she must have been a responsible and hard working employee. It is also possible that she was a part of some massive layoff then. I sure as hell pray that she did not blame herself for the job loss and the foreclosures. I really hope that she did not blame it on herself and that she was able to find even a better job.

When I was six year old, my folks started to build their dream house. The land was located in one of the most prestigious real estate at that time in Teheran. It was located across the American embassy, on Takht Jamshid Ave. That address sounded just like Fifth Ave in New York, City.

The very first Mohandas (Engineers) that I had ever known was a friend of my father. He was an observant Moslem who drove a Saab. In Europe and in Iran, Engineer was a title that was just as prestigious, if not more so than a Doctor. My father and would go over the details of the beautifully drafted plans line by line. They had made a great team, and the work of deciding how to build this building, was not just work, but it was work and play at the same time. They seem to like to discuss alternatives and determine pros and cons of each different approach and then decide on the "Best of the Best".

That man had made profound impact on my decision to study engineering. Interesting was that his kids did not want to be engineers like their well respected and financially better off Dad. One of them wanted to be a Doctor, like my Dad when I had decided that I wanted to be an engineer like his Dad.

My father's cousin, Solliaman, had just gotten started in a building supply business. My Dad was one of his first customers. He and the Engineer who designed the house, would only buy or build the best for my folks because they cared.

The exterior of the building had Travertine stones. This kind of stone that majestically looks nice. It has a creamy, white finish and is most suitable to Tehran's climate. The building had three floors, and balconies on both side. One was overlooking the American Embassy. The other one was on the other side of the building. This side was quieter since there was less traffic. Each of the first three floors had three bedrooms, kitchens and bathrooms. There was a basement and the top floor as well.

I had the privilege of using the top floor as an office. From my window, I could see the beautiful American Embassy ground with its nice drive way and extremely well kept green grass. There was also a driveway so official dignitaries could be driven into the compound.

American people and American things amazed Iranians. Americans were bigger than life. America was the land of gold. American was the land of rags to riches, and it did not matter who you were. Streets were paved with gold! And, of course, as the common folklore had it, there is this super precious "freedom" in American. The essence of something intangible was even more precious than the gold that paved the streets. Freedom, to them at that time meant that you could do anything that you wanted. You were free. I had to explain to many that you were free so long as you did not hurt other people's freedom.

There were double-decker British Leyland buses that stop near our house. With one change of the bus, I could go to the Mehrabad Airport, which was the capital's most beautiful and modern international airport. While in high school, I would go to Mehrabad and observe Pan American Boeing 707s or KLM DC8s for hours. It was my dream to someday board one of these planes and go to US to study Electrical Engineering at MIT. I had heard that MIT was the best of the best. At that time, this seemed like an impossible dream. Studying in US was much too expensive for my parents to afford. Yet, I kept that dream alive. When, I got the admission to study in US, I was literally on the next KLM flight.

I loved our house. We always had a relative or friend to come and visit at least once a week. I loved and now painfully miss those times. In Persian culture, you treat your guests (whom were as important as emissaries from Heaven were) with the best food and treats that you had. And of course, the best room in the house was dedicated as the guestroom. This room usually had the best furniture, and we used it only when there were guests. We also had a collection of the best Persian hand-made carpets. I might be biased, but Persian carpets are the best of the best in the world. My mother and father just like birds that make a nest for their chicks, were busy for many years building that house brick by brick, stone by stone.

I never, ever could imagine that American hostage crisis there for 444 days. Americans were cool and they were our friends when I was a child. I never, ever could also imagine that someday we will lose that magnificent house. I had dreams of going back after I had completed my studies in America. Our plans were that our folks would "rent" us, the children, each of the top floors for our residence free. That was 1967.

It does look like the chain of events, as in the "Chain of Fools" song by Aretha Franklin, has enslaved my soul all these years. And in the meanwhile, the vicious cycles have brought me full circle, to fearing the loss of my house in 2009, similar to the way my folks lost theirs in 1979!

The 2009 Global Financial Crisis along with its layoffs and rampant job losses and

Copyright © 2008 - 2009 Razban Internet International, Inc. All rights reserved, File:20091022, P a g e | **125**

foreclosures have brought me eye to eye with the pain and suffering that my folks went through when they lost their house, their careers, and their social network.

Losing "The House" hurt my folks. However, what killed my father's spirits was loss of his professional career, and friends. These cherished friends were suddenly in a blink of an eye, dispersed all over the world. His retirement, like mine, went up in smokes in what looked like one instant.

The Iranian Jewish community was an internal and interwoven part of the Persian community from the Biblical times. For generations after generations they had lived in Persia. In fact, the King Cyrus of Persia, who let the Jews go back and reconstruct their temple. This is the only king named in Torah, the Old Testament. In recent years, archeologists have found a cylinder describing historical events that reflects the King Cyrus's Declaration of Human Rights. It is also said that culture and poetry runs in Persian vain.

According to Maslow's hierarchy of human needs, food is the highest and right after that, it is the shelter. Every time, I think of our ancestors living in caves, I remind myself of how important shelter has been, and will always be, to us human beings.

Yet we have to constantly rebuild, reinvent, and re-invigorate! We cannot just sit there after a job, or shelter loss.

CHAPTER 50:   SpongeBob SquarePants Show

My ten-year-old daughter loves this program. On the other hand, I do not like it. Therefore, I decided that since I have interviewed many people about the sad situation of work in the workplace, I should also ask her. It would be interesting to see what a ten year old thinks about work life.

SpongeBob SquarePants TV program is about SpongeBob, who lives "in a pineapple under the Sea". He works as a short order cook in a fast-food joint. His work is literally his life. He likes to work even during the breaks and weekends. He always tries to do his job perfectly, no matter at what cost.

In my daughter's opinion, this program makes us laugh at the "stupidest" of people. There are two stupid ones in this show. They are SpongeBob SquarePants and Patrick who are really, stupid. However, they somehow always outsmart all others who are even less smart, or more stupid.

There is also a smart aleck one. His name is SquidWard. He has many smarts, but he thinks he is great at arts. He thinks that this job, which is being a cashier in this fast-food joint, has failed him. Therefore, he does arts every chance he gets. He is bored at his job and treats customers badly. He sometimes treats customers with a yawn because he is bored. Nevertheless, as soon as break time comes, he comes to life and joyfully plays his flute.

Mr. Crabs in this joint is the BOSS. He is a stingy slave driver who is tough on his workers.

In a way, SpongeBob and SquidWard are opposites. One is stupid and works so hard he can kill himself, and the other one who is even smarter. However, he just sits there and hates his job until break time comes around.

I asked my daughter, what do we learn from this successful TV show? She said, "When you work, you must love your job, or otherwise you will be lousy at it." She added, "Look at you, Dad, how hard you work. It is because you love your job!"

Thinking about the show and my daughter's opinion, I decided there is one thing that I cannot overlook. This fact is that, this is a toxic undersea community of strange characters. As bad as SpongeBob's irrational obsession to work is, something seems to work too. What works is the community that is there under the sea. Even under worst conditions, a team can heal and help its members. The 20/20 program mentioned in this book clearly shows how this works. When abused elephants were in a good group of elephants, they started to heal. What I am saying is that communities are so powerful at work place that they can heal. Furthermore, community and team building are crucial to company success.

In a management description of Virgin Atlantic Airlines, as you see later in the book, the founder/CEO Sir Richard Branson says, hire good talent, let them be free, build a community, and you will succeed.

A community, referred to by Sir Richard Branson, is similar to what Larry Shultz of Starbucks, describes in "Pouring Coffee One Cup at a Time". In another book titled "How Starbucks Saved my Life" a laid off executive describes how a job with Starbucks and the strong community there, literally saved his life. Unfortunately, many CEOs tend to discount the heavy impact that a toxic work environment has on employees, their work life, and even their lives and families.

CHAPTER 51:   iCarley

I also interviewed my daughter about another popular TV show for kids. "iCarley" is a TV show about Carley, who lives with his crazy older brother Spencer in Seattle. She has a successful TV show in her school. Spencer, her brother, is great at art. He makes a new work of art every day. So, this program never becomes boring.

iCarley really loves her job of being a TV producer for kids. This is because it is fun to have a website for the entire school. This makes her famous, important, and popular.

My daughter says that in this program, if there is something bad they work together to fix it. In addition, always something goes wrong each time. However, they do not give up. They work and work at it until it is fixed. And she adds, "You can fix anything if you just keep working at it until it is fixed."

If we look at it more carefully, we can clearly see that enterprising small companies can do well as iCarley does in this TV program. They do well because they produce well and they communicate effectively and freely. Their passion in making a success, and the joy of success, make them survive many disappointments. You can see how exuberant they are, and how good they chime and rhyme together. They are like a symphony that plays in harmony. They look like a dance group well choreographed and has a lot of teamwork. I am sure that HP founders would have enjoyed watching the amount of teamwork and pride of accomplishment displayed in this program.

One of the things that always bother me when I am not working is that feeling of productivity and accomplishing something. This was true during that short period in my career that I did not really need to work. I gave myself a sabbatical as companies give to their employees who had worked for them seven years. I took time off for the first time in my life, thanks to NetScape and RedHat stocks. I was rich enough that I did not really have to work for three months.

Unfortunately, I was so bored and I missed the lack of productivity that I went back to work as soon as I could.

Copyright © 2008 - 2009 Rayhan Internet International, Inc. All rights reserved, UIlc.20091022, P a g e | **128**

CHAPTER 52:   Hannah Montana

This is a very popular show for my daughter and I. This TV show is based on a real-life father and daughter who are in music. However, Hannah Montana is highly successful and she has many concerts. Her father is her songwriter in addition to being her Dad and being her best friend. People also love her and ask for her autograph all the time. Her other best friend is Lily and she is a Tomboy. She is a great help to her best friend Hannah. They live in a beach house and her manager is a five-year-old nasty person. He causes her to be embarrassed all the time.

Hannah's job is singing. Her dad is her agent. She loves her job and she is very good at it. Unfortunately, she needs to wear a wig when she is singing in public so her schoolmates know that their friend Miley is the famous Hannah and make fun of her.

As a father and daughter team, they had to overcome the tragedy of losing a wife and a mother. This can be one of the worst pains in life. Nevertheless, they seem to survive and even prosper. They overcame partly because of their work. Their work, which is singing, is their passion, and they love this job.

Here is my daughter's advice: "You must love your job. If you do not love your job, your job will make you feel bad. No job is worth feeling bad. If your job is not good, then quit and get a better one. Do not accept any job unless it is something that you love."

I remember the experience of a colleague regarding stress-induced, serious physical pain that resulted in her quitting her job. Once she had quit her job, her pain gradually went away because she was free. In fact, being free from that dysfunctional and toxic environment, she started to regain her self-confidence and even land a better job. This is a new job where her managers and co-workers respect her and allow her to bring her four-year-old son to work once a week after school. They also allow her to do work-share with other employees so she has a bit more time to spend with her son.

CHAPTER 53:   Many Alternatives to Layoffs

Suppose that you are a CEO who really cares for the people and the business. Unexpectedly, your accountants discover that the company is losing money. An analysis has concluded that your competition has gained considerable market share at your expense. Wall Street thinks that this is a no brainer and you need to do a layoff before the end of quarter. When, you talk to your Board of Directors, they tend to think the same way. Layoff, layoff cries from stockholders are everywhere. What should you do? Before you decide, let me tell you about Brenda. Brenda was a smart and sensitive Sales and Marketing senior manager. She had an MS degree from a Midwestern University and she was on high dosage (1 gram per day) of a potent anti depressant. After a long period of depression and some serious weight loss without a diet, she was encouraged to start dating again. I noticed her depression in our first date. Most of the things that she told me about herself or others usually had a sad ending. She had lost all that weight due to becoming Anorexic, which was an awful consequence of depression. This might sound like a boast, but she fell in love with me before I had any clue. Her sexy body and super ability to charm and Mensa level intelligence that meant so much to others meant nothing to her. She was a reject because her company had terminated her. Terminate, for God sake, is an awful thing to say. She had a doll collection and she read some of the most difficult books on Psychology. Before I knew it, I was in deep love with her too. We were both unemployed and neither of us had any money. However, we spent three evenings a week walking from one end of Stanford Shopping Center to the other. We could not afford gym membership, so we had chosen the best alternative, which was walking. Those beautiful glamorous shopping center windows and lights would help us forget our joblessness pains. Several dates, or what I called dates, went by before I tried to kiss her. She recoiled. I, as a gentlemen, knew when no, meant no! She came up with some excuse and went home that evening. When I got home, there were several messages from her. "Bruce I love you!" "You are a gentleman, you have feelings, and you are honest. I cannot, even if I love you dearly!" "I understand. There are no hard feelings, no harm was done. These things take time. They cannot be rushed." I slowly responded to her. There was a long pause on the line. "Let us go out for one last time and say goodbye! Let us do this right! I will give you a big hug!" I could not wait until our next "meeting". She seemed to be elated. Somehow telling me what she had to say, what she had never told another guy, had made her feel considerably better. There was a family run teashop in the back of Stanford shopping center that we loved to go to. My Darjeeling and her Jasmine White tea were served without either of us bothering to order. They knew us. "Well, I guess this will be goodbye" I said. "Yes! Sorry." A career woman like her should not be like this. This is an awful loss to everyone! In fact, she never went back to work. She had some inheritance that helped her for several years. We met many times after what we thought was our last date, or meeting. She was my soul mate, advisor, help, cheerleader, hero, confident, and my best friend. She came to my wedding and told me that she had unconditional love for me forever and she was happy that I am getting married. Fact remained that she had championship trophy from one company, and best marketing plan from another. She loved children, but she "had let her career focus neglect her urge for motherhood until it was too late!" Incidentally, along with some Ad Copies, Marketing Plans, Sales Strategies that she had given me, she also gave me a collection of her

Copyright © 2008 - 2009 Razban Internet International, Inc. All rights reserved, File:20091022, P a g e | **130**

creative writing that got me hooked forever to short stories. I shared some of these with my colleague who is a Vice President of Marketing and sales. He admitted these are brilliant. I called Brenda and left several messages to see if she wanted to meet with my friend. "Bruce, I am sorry, I cannot. Did you tell him that I was terminated?"

Here is a list of alternatives to proactively prevent layoffs:

- Form a blue ribbon committee to do an honest six sigma analysis of what was wrong. You can ask some of those that will be victims of the layoffs. They will be the best to figure out how you can avoid layoffs.
- Empower and encourage a qualified outside company to analyze what is going wrong that has caused the reduction of sales and/or revenue.
- Ask both the above to think of solutions in addition to Root Cause problems.
- Give them guarantees that they can say anything they want and there will be no negative fallout.
- Unless you figure out what was wrong and fix it, you will be a hostage to these vicious cycles of repeated layoffs.
- Also, remember that there are many effective alternatives to layoffs such as 107.8% employment, and Human Capital and Knowledge Focus. I will discuss these in detail in the next chapters.

You will be very surprised by what you might find out. It is a proven management fact that people, who are closer to the problems, understand and can fix these problems a lot better than others. As an independent consultant, I have been astonished to find out repeatedly that the problems and solutions are well known by individual contributors weeks or months before upper management get a clue. Even an outside consultant can quickly analyze and determine the problems and solutions. So many companies lay off employees and then find out that they have to lay off again. This is simply because nobody took the time to understand the Root Cause problems. Everybody was trying to put on band-aids to hide the symptoms. This is similar to that Persian proverb of trying to hide fire under the carpet.

The fundamental business, organizational, processes, and culture-related problems continue festering, smoldering, and burning. Better planning and management is usually the first step to get out of the layoff quagmire for both companies and employees.

Dr. Gil Amelio practically had to re-educate National Semiconductor management and employees, with the help of Emory University Business School, and using "Leading Change" seminars. This helped everyone communicate, plan, and manage better. We were able to fix problems at the source. We were able to put together systematic processes that proactively prevented need for frequent and massive layoffs. National did not become perfect because of these improvements, but job satisfaction, productivity, and profit picture improved considerably.

Dr. Amelio had learned the concept of "Learn, Unlearn, and Relearn" well. He had done several company transformations before. He looked at this re-education, as an important investment. This investment paid back handsomely. Not just in revenue, but the day-to-day operation and working relationship among all employees. He had a saying that I will never forget. He was fond of saying that, "I am usually reluctant to spend money. However, for a good investment, I am always ready to spend. This I will do regardless of how much spending it requires."

Dr. Amilio became National Semiconductor CEO after Charley Spork retired. Charley

Spork is the father of this company known as the grandfather of Silicon Valley companies.

Copyright © 2008 - 2009 Razban Internet International, Inc. All rights reserved, File:20091022.

CHAPTER 54:   My Multi-Million-Dollar Patent

National Semiconductor was my longest employer. I worked there for about nine years. I was lucky! I got to travel and become a world-class manager. I worked for some outstanding managers, and I also got a patent grant. Getting a patent is a difficult task. You have to prove that you are the first with the idea. You have to look at the prior art, i.e., the previous work done by others to prove that nobody else has done something like your invention. You have to prove that it works. It is a long and tedious road. Moreover, it is not just technical brilliance; it takes a great deal of legal effort too.

This patent, with its multi-million-dollar impact would have never happened had I not gotten the encouragement, support, and technical and legal resources at National Semiconductor and HP.

The fact remains that, when you get a job with a high-tech company, you waive your right to hold intellectual property while you are working for that company. Fortunately, most companies do have an incentive program. This way, you will get some money (something like $5,000 or more, and a lot of recognition) for getting a patent.

I could have quit my job right after I came up with the idea and gone unemployed for one year. Then I could have borrowed about $20,000 to pay for the legal fees, and then I could have benefitted from the rewards. These rewards could have added up to be several million Dollars. This patent was a game-changer for the In-Circuit-Emulation (ICE).

Fifty or more other patents refer to my patent. Estimates vary from $5 M to $100 M value for this patent. Most interesting thing is that I have no regrets for not quitting! National Semiconductor and HP both were fair. Without the caliber of help that only a corporation can give, I would have had a hard time getting this patent. In fact, without the encouragement of Erik, an HP Executive, I would have not even thought my idea was worth getting a patent. He treated me as if I was his equal and we trusted each other as friends. This type of teamwork is the type that highly effective executives create. This type of teamwork pays off handsomely.

This reminds me of a very famous French Singer, Edith Piaf's song "Non Je Ne Regrette Rien. " This song was very famous when I was a child. Taxi drivers in Paris would play this on their car radios and it was everywhere. The beauty of this song is that it simply says I refuse to regret the past, since past gave me all kinds of souvenirs. In addition to not having any regrets about this patent being company property as it was our employment contract, this is also proof that, when employees are empowered and recognized, the company can get a much higher return on its investment.

I have the plaque that declares me an inventor, several T-shirts that say I am an inventor. Unfortunately, these T-shirts are too small, as I have gained a lot of weight since then. This is another incentive for me to go back to my own Empowered Weight Management (EWM) plan formulated in this book in Chapter 37.

It is true there is better way. To make a lot of money, a company needs to treat its human-potential power well and the result is awesome.

***Section 2:

- Mutual Trust and Loyalty (MTL)
- Transition from Asset Based Management to Human and Capital Based Capitalism
- Psychological Depression in a Toxic Work Place
- Work Place Depression can Cause Economic Recession and Even Depression

Copyright © 2008 - 2009 Razban Internet International, Inc. All rights reserved, File:20091022, P a g e | **134**

CHAPTER 55:   Be Selfish and Do Acts of Charity

One very hot and humid summer in New York City, I was watching the *Tonight Show* with Johnny Carson. I was lucky to find a summer job and a room that only cost $14/day. This included the complimentary breakfast. During a celebrity interview, Johnny Carson asked why that famous person did charity work. She responded by saying that she did charity work because she was very selfish and she always got a lot more out of it than the effort she put in it. This idea stuck with me. I thought at that time, since I never had any hope of being a celebrity, maybe, I would act like celebrities and do the selfish thing and help others when I could. This helping of others is of course in the bible.

The most satisfying charity act for me was when I was Engineering Director at Zilog. I volunteered to be the volunteer who spoke publicly in front of several groups. I was flying on cloud nine since I had made a good contribution to the well-being of others. Furthermore, United Way Charity made me a captain.

Later on, I decided to help my friends who were affected by layoffs. Of course, I have very limited means for this. I think this works so well. When you try to lend a hand to someone else, you forget your own problems long enough and this helps you as well. I have learned to use some of my Eastern culture to augment my Western culture. In the Eastern culture, with my limited understanding, one learns that material things, as important as they might be, cannot be as important as spiritual values.

Mother Theresa had observed about the East and West when it came to poverty. She had lived and helped Indians who lived in abject poverty. Surprisingly enough, she made the point that poor's problem was not as bad. A glass of water and piece of bread could solve their most dire hunger need. However, in the West, in spite of all our material things, it will take a lot more to help us with emptiness, blind greed, and selfishness.

My father used to say that money, power, fame, and belongings all come and go. However, most importantly, acts of kindness always stay in this universe. In Jewish religion and tradition, as well as many others, this is called Misvot (Acts of Kindness.) Sponsor someone who needs guidance and help him or her get over a problem, such as unemployment. Sometimes it takes very little. Sometimes it takes a few minutes to tell a jobless former colleague about a job in your company. Moreover, this few minutes might even earn you a good referral bonus.

It is said in Alcoholics Anonymous that, at the beginning, the hospitals would not accept an alcoholic for treatment unless there was a non-alcoholic to "Sponsor" him or her. Sponsoring meant that a recovering person would get help to go through the process. This sponsoring works the same in cases of unemployment as well. To prove this, let me remind you of learning. It is a universally accepted concept that the best way to learn something is to teach it. This worked very well for me when I was a Teaching Assistant (usually the second best among some thirty Teaching Assistants according to surveys at the end of each semester.) I really mastered the concept after I had taught it several times. Strangely enough, when you help someone else get a job, you benefit a great deal too. You become better in your own job. You develop contacts that will help get jobs when you need them. Remember that this employment is similar to musical chairs. You have a job today but tomorrow the music might step when you are not near a chair. When you yourself are looking for a job, and remember finding a job is a full time job in itself, you always benefit from helping someone else. Sometimes this someone else is a person with less experience, or even worse, less hope to get back on their feet and find that ideal job for them. Helping others has helped me find out about some company that I would have otherwise not known about. Just yesterday, someone told me that he was finding good jobs at Craigslist.org. Now I check with Craigslist.org everyday.

This also helps us validate the things that work and the things that do not. It is always good to have buddies who are working on the same things, or even hubbies. In one case, a recruiter had pushed me to work on an immediate opening for a company. I had gone thru the interview, and had the personal interview and for weeks, I had thought that the job was mine. Nevertheless, a colleague told me that he had also been told the same thing about the exact same job and same company. This is very interesting information that does save a lot of time and aggravation.

As envelops from charity groups pile up in my mailbox, and I am unable to send them any money, I feel ashamed. There were several of these charities that I used to donate money regularly. In one case, we donated a car when my wife bought a new car. Never the less, at this point in time, and being "in between jobs" I just cannot justify any money for them. Therefore, I try to help with non-financial things. For example, I went to visit a friend who had been confined to home for quite some time. He called me from the lobby of the hospital to tell me that he was wondering if I could go there and keep him company until his friend comes to pick him up in three hours from there. A quick mental calculation indicated that it would cost me a mere $1.25 in gas to drive there and back. I told myself that although I was without income, I was not poor and/or cheap enough to let my friend sit in the hospital lobby for three hours, alone and bored. He has aged a great deal and he has lost a lot weight. His white beard was covering most of his face, and his white hair had a certain almost religious glow to it. "Bruce, Bruce, Bruce, Over Here!" he was almost screaming with a cheered up voice when he saw me first. It took me a few seconds for me to recognize this tall, experienced executive. I used to work for him, and we were friends since some twenty years ago.

With a smile, he was telling that he had survived four heart attacks, and two cancers. Having a Math background, his calculation shows he is far ahead of the game. To prove this, he told me that he has seven grandchildren with the eight one on the in Australia. Our discussion revolved around the company that we both worked together in the good old days. During our conversation, the subject of Chinese restaurant came up several times. We used to go to a Chinese restaurant as a team one a week every week. My friend used to love, still loves Chinese food. I noticed that the three hours has gone by while we were busy talking about things. Before we knew it, my friend's "ride" called to say that he would be late. This was our chance to go to Chef Chu's Restaurant in Los Altos, for dinner. He treated me to one of the best Lobster dinners I ever had. This long lasting friendship is a good indicator of how productive good working environments can be.

I had told my friend about my leg and back pain. I had also added that the last job with two hours of commute each way had done damage to my back even more. Right about that point in time, as if on a clue, an ambulance stopped and they pulled a badly injured person out and rushed him into the hospital. My old friend explained to me that life is very fragile. He pointed to ambulance and said that he prays to God not to send one of these for him again for as long as he is alive. That was a moment of truth that put my pains in perspective. That night, when I got home, it was easy for me to do the math. I had gotten a million dollar advice from someone that I had admired for many years for a

Copyright © 2008 - 2009 Kazban Internet International, Inc. All rights reserved, File:20091022,

$1.25 cost of the gas. What a return on investment. The question popped up in my head asking in a bossy way, "Well Mr. Razban, now who helped who? Was it your miserable $1.25 gas cost, or the advice that put things in perspective? Huh? Answer me!" "Not even considering the $60 Lobster dinner!" For the record, my back pain did not seem as bad after seeing the man in the ambulance. As a matter of fact, I was determined not to get that ambulance ride no matter how much back pain I had.

When someone is jobless for some time things can get ugly. I have been jobless for ten months at this point. On the week days, I go to the fast food places and try to have a lunch for less than $4.00. I have not had fruits for some time. I am experiencing a poverty and physical hunger that I have not have felt since college days. Our freezer is almost empty. Our storage area under the stairs is almost empty. Granted that I am spiritual and well educated, but hunger is an effective way to start feeling fear. I have tried to drive as little as possible. I go to coffee shops and sit outside without buying coffee hoping that the person I am meeting has some money. More, and more they too seem not to have money to pay for coffee. I wonder if my colleague who are working and who have some savings understand these hunger pangs. This horror of not being able to put food on the table. The admission of failure as a parent to tell a teenager child that the house could be foreclosed any day. The sleepless nights when you realize that there is no way, absolutely no way that you can be financially solvent any more. DMV sends a letter that you are at the risk of suspension. Your insurance company has cancelled your insurance, and you decide not to take your heart medicine. These are what some of the jobless colleagues of our are feeling. These feelings are suffered in silence. People can take hunger pangs and malnourishment much better than losing their dignity. So, when a jobless colleague calls, please keep these thoughts in mind. In most 12 step programs, there is a saying that when someone asks for help, I am responsible! Not only this applies to a jobless friend asking a working friend, it also applies when a jobless colleague or friend calls one who does not have a job either. Telling the other person that you understand, and you will try to help will go a long way in soothing the almost unbearable pains.

Even when you do have a job, it is good to stay in contact with those colleagues who are out of work. This will cushion your Sudden Job Loss in the event that that happens. Let me assure you that according to Time Magazine what is going on now in the job market, will become the norm.

I had a lot of trouble in math in 4th grade. Somehow, I had convinced myself that I was not good at math and that I never would be. Never mind that my entire career later on revolved around math and science. In fact, by the time I graduated from high school, I had a perfect 800 score in the math portion of the SAT.

Sadly, in the 4th grade, I had indeed internalized it that I was not good at math no matter what. My Dad tried everything to help me with math. He would give me puzzles. He would make sure that the puzzles had something to do with things that were important to me. He would make them interesting and fun at the same time. He would spend hours upon hours teaching me multiplication and division. I was making some slow progress, but I was still convinced that I was no good in math.

I remember that my Dad had always been very proud of his Parker pens. They were reliable and had some style to them. On top of that, they were reasonably priced. One day, we went shopping with the specific purpose of buying me a Parker pen of my own. He would jokingly tell me that my math score would improve a great deal if I had a better pen. Of course, I would not argue with that. We bought a navy blue Parker pen for me. The arrow, which is the trademark of Parker, would make my pocket look a lot nicer. I was one of the three proud owners of Parker pens in a class of more than twenty students. Now with this pen, I could not wait to write things down and practice on math problems. I remember that I was disappointed when my two-page essay was done. I wanted to write more with this brand new pen. Human potential is a great thing. Even a small gesture of respect or value for it goes a long way in proving that humans can do just about anything. It turns out that Parker pen headquarters is in Janesville, Wisconsin. During those nine years that I lived in Madison, Wisconsin, I passed thru Janesville several times. They used to have huge automobile assembly factories in the sixties. Unfortunately, I guess a lot of those are closed by now. I have promised myself to visit this company someday and tell them how important they were to my perfect SAT math score.

Copyright © 2008 - 2009 Razban Internet International, Inc. All rights reserved, File:20091022, P a g e | **138**

CHAPTER 57:   One of My Best Working Heroes

My friend Allen works for the State of California.

I first noticed him during those long, two-hour commutes when I was working in Oakland. My tired eyes noticed this nice man who was taking the same trains the same time I did. After several days, I finally got enough courage to say hello and start a conversation. Allen was approachable and he always had a smile ready. He mostly stayed busy reading a book during this challenging commute. His office was in a building across the street from mine, and he lived a few blocks away from where I lived. I also noticed that he always had clean and ironed clothes. This was even more impressive, in spite of his modest salary. He told me that he was extremely proud of the fact that he had been able to put two kids through college. One had graduated and already had a job with a big company in Silicon Valley. He then proudly announced that another was finally done with getting a college degree. Unfortunately, he was among those recent graduates who could not find a job.

He told me that he was no longer trying to conquer the world as he had planned to do when he was young. In a most serene way, he told me that he knew that each day he was lucky he had a job to do, and he wanted to do that job well. He made sure that he did not get involved with company politics. He had saved three years to go to a vacation with his family. Then, quite unexpectedly, some major medical expense delayed his vacation plans. Rather than being frustrated, he had accepted this and he was moving forward with his life!

He looked down on promotions as he was sure the headache was not worth the extra money. He preferred going home each day and spending time with family. He preferred going home and just taking a nap on his new sofa instead of headaches of mandatory overtime that his new job would have required after promotion. Family is very important, he would tell me. He would say that it felt like it was just yesterday that he had brought his family and young children to the US. Then he added that before he knew it, thirty years had gone by. All we do is for our family, nothing else is important. He told me that several times he had opportunities to go to another company and make an additional six percent of income. However, he decided against it. He could not leave his friends behind.

He indeed walks this talk. He has been immense influence on me. One day when I was totally disappointed in myself and my work and my company, he said, "it feels like it was just yesterday that I came to this country, and it was just yesterday that I met my wife for the first time, and it was just yesterday when my son was born, and it was yesterday when he left the house to go to college!" His argument was that life is too short and it passes just too fast. Enjoy every second of it. He remembers the joy of seeing his son for the first time after he was born. He remembers the night before he was leaving his country of birth to come to US. He remembers all the joys. Even though he had lived in some of the most difficult neighborhoods where it was dangerous to go out after dark, he remembers some of the neighbors that were kind and friendly. He proudly pointed to the tie that said, "I Love My DAD!." He told me that it seemed like it was just yesterday, when he bought a bib for his three-month-old daughter that said "I Love DAD" on it. "See, Bruce, life is sweet and it goes on!"

I could not help but admire his neatly ironed and clean clothes, yet the shirt and jacket were well worn and a touch faded. He told me that his daughter had bought two ties, but she could really afford one. Therefore, she brought both ties home and asked her dad to put them against his favorite shirt. She knew and loved her hard-working dad who commuted four hours each day! Then, with help from her Mom, his daughter and he selected one of the ties as a best fit for the shirt and jacket, and she returned the other one to the store. "I worked very hard, and I was always there for them, and they are here for me as I get old!"

I recalled a similar conversation about "being there" that I had with a colleague who was an executive. He told me that he sent his daughter to one of the best private schools in Switzerland. He hired private tutors to teach her three languages. He flew her home on private company jets during the holidays, and bought her the best things money could buy from anywhere in the world. In spite all these, his daughter is a stranger to him. "I was an absent father!" I would be on business trips sixty or more percent of my time, and I was so much into climbing the corporate ladder that I had to fly out when my daughter was only hours old. "Now, I'd give anything, and I mean anything, to go back and be there for that girl that was only hours old."

Ernest Hemmingway said, "Life is one damn thing after the other." Yet the important things in life like physical and mental health, and family cannot be ignored! Remember life is what goes on, while we are busy making other plans, or being sorry for ourselves.

CHAPTER 58:   My Other Working Heroes

My friend Hugo is about seventy years old. He looks considerably younger for his age. He just had to get a full-time job with a little more than the minimum wage. He attended community college until he got certification for Java Programming when he was over sixty. He worked as a volunteer helping Greek Churches with their internet and other things. He lives alone and he does not have family living close to him in California.

He is my hero, because, unlike me, he does not like to complain. He cherishes his library memberships and he would travel many hours on the bus to go to a couple of libraries for several events or just to read in the same day. He told me that he has a rich collection of books that he has bought from libraries at $1, $2 each since libraries sell their surplus books. He puts the books that he is interested in on hold and carefully writes down when they become available. He told me that he had never missed getting an interesting book as soon as it came back to the library.

Aside from libraries, he loves the "Little House" in Menlo Park. Every day he goes there to use their free computers to send emails to family and friends, and yes apply for jobs! Little house offers a great deal of entertainment by fellow volunteers, and he gets a chance to play his beloved bridge twice a week. He has gotten so good that he is writing a book about bridge. Using his computer skills and free computers at Little House, he has created and updates regularly several websites for churches. In addition, he is modest about his work, which is free; his website creation is quite remarkable. If you bump into him somewhere, you will sure think that he is a professor. He carries a lot of books and hates to be bored.

He tells me keeping busy all the time, is what keeps him young. I told him about my secret of remaining young. I go to Stanford University Campus, or other Universities. Moreover, these campuses are magical. For the last thirty years that I have been checking people in these campuses, I have noticed that seldom they are over 30, and they have remained that way for the 30 years that I have been running my experiment. So, if spend as much time as I can around younger people, then I will also look and act like someone less than thirty.

Similar to me, he believes that he will work until the day he dies. Of course, it is true that he has not much of a savings. Nevertheless, he would not retire and sit at home even if he could afford it because he would go crazy. Another thing that keeps him going is the Book Buyers store in downtown Mountain View. One can find quality used books at excellent prices there. He still likes to laugh at a good joke and tell a story.

My other hero is Walter. He is a limousine driver who projects a father-figure image at the age of almost sixty-three. He is very sharp, intuitive, and he has had a tough life. When he drove me to the airport the first time, I was thinking this is the man living the ideal life and he is the man who has everything going for him. He is a first-class conversationalist. In his prior life, he was a cab driver in New York City. Now he is employee number three of the limo company, and everyone respects, trusts, and loves to

Copyright © 2008 - 2009 Razban Internet International, Inc. All rights reserved, File:20091022, P a g e | **141**

be driven to and from the airport by him. After many rides, he finally opened up to me. He told me that his life, marriage, and family situation are really complex. I would have never guessed how complicated things were. He insisted that he does not like to talk about his private life, but hearing what he had to say might help me. There is a famous saying somewhere that you should not compare your inside with other people's outside. This is a complete example of that. I had thought that his life was perfect.

Yet, he does his humanly best one day at a time, and he cherishes his job as an escape from his life problems. He shared a great learning experience with me. This experience is the result of listening to hundreds of customers confiding in him during those traffic jams and races to the airport. His advice to me: "Do not let life go past when you are wasting your time with anger and frustration. Life is too short to be stuck in a dead-end job!" He quickly adds, "You must live and live well. Life is to be cherished. Having a job or not should not make you lose opportunities that you get for free in this life."

In one of those rides, we at the age of sixty and sixty-three complemented ourselves by telling ourselves that we were going through "Mid-life Crisis!" This is funny because if we were in the so-called mid-life crisis, then there was the assumption that we will live to one hundred and twenty. This, of course, is highly unlikely high life expectancy. On several occasions, he would tell me about his vacation to Europe. He still remembered all the details some thirty years later. Moreover, more importantly, he seemed to rejoice and relish it as if it had just happened yesterday. As for retirement, his idea was that he cannot afford it now, or in any foreseeable future from a financial point of view. However, even if he could afford it, he would not do it because "A person needs to have something to do to keep productive each and every day and retirement would drive him crazy!"

My other hero in this category is Mina. At the age of sixty-seven she was our counselor at the Yong Man Hebrew Association (YMHA), a Jewish sort of YMCA located at the intersection of the Lexington Avenue and 92nd street in New York City. Mina was a concentration-camp survivor. She had been a successful high school teacher and, later, a psychologist and had retired early around sixty. Her accountant had convinced her that she really did not need to work. Her lifetime hard work and wise investment had provided her the opportunity to retire, and even retire early. She told us that she retired, and retired again after three months, and then decided that, to keep her sanity, she had to go back to work. Any work. It did not matter, she had to stay active and feel needed and productive.

She found out about the 92nd Street Y and became a volunteer. She had a tiny office, a typewriter, and she would spend every Tuesday and Thursday evenings in the resident's lounge, where she talked and advised him or her on anything for which they needed a counselor's advice. During one conversation, I told her that I was bored. She said, "Bored and in New York City, well that is impossible!" She encouraged me to go to Guggenheim Museum, Radio City Theater, and a Theater that was run by amateurs. The very first visit to Guggenheim is what got me hooked on Vincent Van Gogh's work that is still alive after all these years. I was never bored again while I lived in New York City. "Bruce, we need money to live, but we need hope and arts to live a good life!"

That summer I was working in New York City. My work was in 23rd Avenue close to Madison Avenue. I would walk from the 92nd Street Y on Lexington Avenue to 86th Street to catch the IRT subway to go to work. Those summers, which were really hot and humid, Con Edison, which is New York City utility company, had to institute brownouts to conserve energy. This would cause the subway trains to get stuck in middle of a tunnel, and there was no air conditioning.

My consolation in those times was to read the *New York Times* from the front page to the last page. I really cherished this newspaper, which is known to be the best in the world. Their articles about the Middle East and anything else for that matter were accurate and superb as well as extremely informative. I had learned how to fold it in the middle the long way to read it comfortably in a crowded subway. On Fridays, I would treat myself to a bus ride instead. It would take an extra eighteen minutes or so, but it would give me a chance to have breakfast at my favorite place at that time, which was Chock Full of Nuts. This meant the good life that Mina had talked about.

Of course, on those occasions that I went to Paris with my mother and father, the Metro looked fantastic. It was very clean and luxurious and poetically beautiful. We had practically memorized their maps and we went all over Paris in style and comfortably. From street cafes near our hotel, which was a block away from the Arc de Triumph, we would go to Magazine ReUnis, to museums, theaters, and everywhere. In London, it was the Underground, or Tube, which the British called their subway. It was clean, nice, and efficient. However, to my biased opinion, it was just not as poetically beautiful as its Paris counterpart.

I have cherished her advice about the good life for more than forty years!

CHAPTER 59:   Dr. Seuss' *Green Eggs and Ham*

Dr. Seuss' children books are very famous and translated into many languages. I used to read his books to my daughter when she was three or four. *Green Eggs and Ham*, in particular, has a story about a man who does not like anything and he would not try anything new. However, once he finally gives this new and different thing a chance, he realizes that he had been missing a great thing all along.

When people lose their jobs, they get even more selective with jobs. They do not like a particular job because the company has a bad reputation. They do not even apply to another company since they have heard from other friends that this company has awful customer service. And so on and so on.

On December 23, 2008, BBC of London had a special news focus on unemployment in Africa. In an interview with a man who had been unemployed for three years, two things came out. One thing is that unemployment is rampant in Africa. In some places, unemployment is around fifty percent. Another thing was that this educated man was looking for a librarian job. He was not willing to try anything else, and he was so disappointed that he was not going to get training for something else as well.

If there was a global company that would spend, maybe $200, on this man as a loan for him to become a banker, he could be back on his feet in no time at all and pay back the loan with fifty percent interest. The reason I mention banking is that the interviewer indicated that many Nigerian banks were starting branches in this African country. Our man could definitely find a job there.

When I started my tiny company, I needed help from whoever who had an engineering background. I must have talked to more than twenty people and I had offered them equity in the company in return for their work. This would have kept them busy while they were spending full time looking for a full-time job. There were very few takers. Most preferred to do nothing, not even a full-blast, serious and intensive job search.

At some point, a good friend and I were in between contracts and neither of us could wait to go back to work. That was also the time when I was working very hard on getting a patent.

Repeatedly, I asked him for help. I told him that if he could help now, there would be equity in the company for him. Unfortunately, I did not have any money to give him. Unfortunately, he preferred to stay miserable and sit at home doing nothing.

This is very sad. Do not get me wrong, I do understand what he was going through. We must always keep on keeping on. In addition, sometimes, the best thing that can happen is that you get your batteries charged by doing something while you are waiting for the right job to show up.

Some time you have to get a "survival job" and sometimes you can afford to wait for the ideal one to happen. Just like in Green Eggs and Ham, we need to try different careers. We always need to stay busy with something or the other to avoid isolation, and ensuing depression.

Copyright © 2008 - 2009 Razhan Internet International, Inc. All rights reserved, File:20091022, P a g e | **144**

CHAPTER 60:   Trans World Airline (TWA), Howard Hughes, Playing for Change,
                and Soloist

In my opinion, Howard Hughes is an American hero. He in fact pioneered American
Civil Aviation by creating Trans World Airlines (TWA). Being an aviator himself, he
made bold decisions and orchestrated the entire airline industry, as well as military
aviation to invent and take risks.
Unfortunately, he had an isolated and tragic life toward the end. What seemed like
depression that Doctors now easily treat by many medications, including Prozac, finally
drove him to isolation and excessive fear of getting infections from others.
Pioneering needs guts. I have observed and learned this myself. You have to do things
that others think are crazy. Others are too quick to call you stupid and laugh at you.
When his experimental aircraft crashed into rooftops in Southern California, he was even
more determined to try again, and again, and again. He was even instrumental in making
aircraft companies such as Boeing, or McDonald Douglass, to make airliners according to
his specifications.
Aviation was his passion! He loved his job! He also did heroic things, including using his
own money to develop proof-of-concept for military aircraft. This was his patriotic
contribution to his country. There is also a poetic side to all his work.
Unfortunately, his disease at the end is a monumental loss to what he could have done
had he not succumbed to such a malady. Fortunately, these days, the treatment is known
and available.
Everybody scolds Americans for their wasteful ways. They tell us that we use much too
much paper, too much water, too much gasoline, etc. Sadly, management overlooks the
humongous loss that results from being unhappy at our jobs, or being underemployed, or
suffering massive layoffs, or the non-productivity in our workplace.
Larry, my friend of more than thirty years, gave me a recording of "Playing for Change"
made by the non-profit group, The Playing for Change Foundation". Street musicians
from all over the world including USA, Israel, Kenya, Russia, Tibet, India, and many
other countries were singing heart-warming songs. Any manager knows that this takes a
lot of work. Paradoxically, these were musicians that did this job for free and a lot of
them were literally playing for change. By change here, I mean coins. However, this
work and play was the same. It made them and those who heard this feel good. Of course,
the change in the title of the group refers to world peace as a change. This album is proof
positive about my concept, and Sir Richard Branson's that you find good people and
manage them well, and then the sky is the limit!
The Soloist is a story that is a good example of talent that is wasted. The book moved me.
Therefore, I wrote and published the following book review in Amazon.com:
 **A Los Angeles (LA) Times Reporter's Passion Engulfs a Homeless Musical Talent to
Create Masterpiece in Spite Mental Disease**, May 1, 2009

Human potential, being limitless, is strongly portrayed in this superb story of a reporter in search of his
ultimate work passion in a story worth telling, and a homeless musician whose love and genius of classical
music that is eclipsed and tampered by mental disease.
I was driven to read this book, just to see how this can, or cannot work. Page after page, this book is a
powerful indicator of human condition at its best. Steve Lopez, the LA times reporter would have not had a
story to tell without Nathaniel Ayres. In addition, Mr. Ayres would have been just one of those
unremarkable and undiscovered 90,000 greater LA homeless people.

Copyright © 2008 - 2009 Razban Internet International, Inc. All rights reserved, File:20091022, P a g e | **145**

The book is somewhat sad as it depicts the living condition of those living in streets. Yet it is uplifting in what we can receive if we were to do acts of charity and to come out of our own isolation. Together these two choreograph a symphonic story worth telling.

As it is reflected in my own book, the average American is between ten to twenty paychecks away from the real terror and insanity of homelessness. As I discovered in my book by interviewing the "Invisible Man", and "My Most Favorite" Homeless heroes, there is something superhuman in these people. There is an immense wasted potential that could have, and still can, nourish other human hearts and souls by teaching, or even inspiration. Yet, we decide not to get involved.

Work, indeed is much more than that paycheck. It is a badly needed expression of human creativity and talent. My own father as an experienced MD could have worked another ten years. Instead, he had to retire. He would have worked for minimum wage just to be useful. In fact having worked that extra ten years, would have added ten more years to his life. It was not the loss of his home in Iran, and all the material things that got him depressed. This depression resulted from loss of his place in the community, his friends, his colleagues of many years, and his care-giving career that he passionately loved. The good feeling that results from being productive in our jobs and our lives is something that money cannot buy.

Copyright © 2008 - 2009 Razban Internet International, Inc. All rights reserved, File:20091022, P a g e | **146**

CHAPTER 61:   Van Gogh and Potato Eaters and Picasso Blue Paintings

Van Gogh invented an entirely innovative method of impressionist paintings. Unfortunately, because his paintings were different and in fact, he himself was different, his paintings were never a success while he was alive. The world discovered his paintings too late for him to benefit. Potato eaters, was sold at an extremely high price after his death.
He made many paintings. He used his feelings and intuition as a guide to these paintings. However, because he was passionately using strong colors and pronounced brush strokes with heavy primary color oil colors that no one had ever used before, others did not understand him. Not only others did not understand him, they dismissed and rejected to the point that this pioneer could not even earn a living. He spent most of his life alone and as an outcast. His passion for his art was what that kept him alive! Therefore, he could barely support himself with the money that his brother Theo gave him. His brother was indeed his keeper!
Van Gogh's brother Theo, who was an art dealer in Paris, tried to help him sell some of his work but he could not. This created a great deal of stress for Van Gogh. This is a bitter type of stress that feeling unwanted, unappreciated, and disappointed creates. It is a heavy burden. These feelings are similar to feelings that people get after they are laid off or fired. This feeling, along with the depression of not knowing if there ever will be a job after layoff, are sometimes overwhelming.
On the contrary, Van Gogh did not give up! As if Bob Dylan's song was playing in Van Gogh's head saying, "Would you want me if I am not myself?" Van Gogh decided not to change his style, or himself. This produced a genuine style of painting that people had never seen before. I have been captivated with his art, talent, passion, and pioneering spirit and have spent hours being absorbed in his work in Van Gogh's Museum in Amsterdam and Guggenheim Museum of New York.
By keeping on keeping on, one day he painted one of his biggest masterpieces, the "Potato Eaters." The dark colors used in this painting and colors on the people's faces depicted, transmitted, and conveyed the feelings these people had. Light and dark grey colors in this painting, especially dark grey colors recklessly ignite into dark, damp, and poverty stricken feelings in the room. Furthermore, this room was is only lit with one single lamp hanging from the ceiling, invokes inescapable feelings of depression in a careful observer. And, the face of the central character who was a woman, perhaps the mother, exuded a feeling of satisfaction that at least they had something to eat that night. The hidden smile in her face speaks volumes of a partial and temporary triumph, at least for this moment over the dark evils of hunger, unleashed by poverty. Yet this hidden smile also attempts to mislead and deceive all involved that this is indeed best we can do in life. This knowing deceptive smile, hides the "What explosive creative power workers could have if and only if they could use their innate, intrinsic, and immense human intellectual powers at their work" I know this darn well.
I can rant and rave about the next story that I am about to tell you. In this case, we had a terrible situation at hand. The metal casing for the product that had to go to market in two weeks, due to some measurement problems was about 2 inches too short on the side. Not shipping on time would have been a bad solution because it would have cancelled a big

Copyright © 2008 - 2009 Razban Internet International, Inc. All rights reserved, File:20091022, P a g e | **147**

contract. One of my junior engineers walked to me and said "Bruce I owe a lot to you, so leave this to me." He fired his fire engine red Corvette and went home to come back with the old truck. Loaded up all the metal casings and he was gone for the rest of the day. He showed up the next day, tired and in a painter's uniform. His brother had a paint shop. The two of them worked all day and night and "stretched" the metal by welding it! He did this because he knew that there was mutual trust and loyalty (MTL), and teamwork among all of us in the team. More importantly, this is because he had refused to become a Zombie during the working hours, and not use his brain. For God sake, we only use three percent of our brain when we are actively thinking! What a terrible waste it is to squander the meager amount that we in fact do use.

Another example was Reba's "Crooked VuSet Assembly Tool." She had to get agreement from the Labor Union Representative, for use of such tool. This in fact was a delicate management task, even though she was not a manager. The second part was that she had to make drawings and convince the machine shop operator to do this. She persisted and got permission. Her assembly tool shaved a healthy 10 to 15% of the total assembly time. Plantronics then gave some of that saving to her in appreciation of her creativity. Reba, by the way was one of my first colleagues/supervisors. She told me one time that she had a grandson my age. She never had a chance to go to college. Yet, I am positive that she would have made an excellent scientist. She had a NASA notebook; she had a white uniform that she had bought for a "song" from one of the many Santa Cruz Flea Markets. She would dry clean it and she claimed that it gave her superwoman-like creativity power. With her strong southern accent, she told me that it is just stupid to be afraid. You have to experiment even if you know there is no chance at all to win. Yet you have to be brave and try. When and if that did not work, you try something else. When you fall down, you get up and dust yourself and go on, and go on, and on, and on until you succeed. Failures "don't count, as long as you are trying!" Reba always reminded me of a librarian friend, who would say with a big smile that her first marriage was a big mistake, and the second marriage was a big success even though both marriage "experiments" were with the same man. This librarian did not have to tell us how happy her second marriage to that very same first man was, we could see it when her husband would come to pick her up. Back to Reba, she was 67 years old, and she had no intention of retiring!

Of course, my own artistic talent is very different from Van Gogh. However, it was my fifth grade art teacher that discovered my limited talent in painting. We had our work displayed on top of our desk. Mr. Shahvagh, our revered art teacher, would take a casual look at each kid's painting, say a few mandatory complements, make a few suggestions, and go to the next so called display. That day, he was observably tired. This was the last period of the day, and he had to drive a long distance that morning to make it to the first period some eight hours prior. More importantly, having studied in one of the best art studios in Paris, he was highly respected in our school. He was bilingual in Persian and French.

He looked at my painting, and seemed to start to force himself to give me one of those vanilla complements and pass. Quite to my surprise, his eyes all of sudden opened, and lit up! He somehow unwillingly whispered, "Mon Dieu" (My God). Started to ask why I used a certain color instead of another one, and why this and why that. He then took my painting and lifted it up against the dim sun light coming into the window. Then, with a

Copyright © 2008 - 2009 Razban Internet International, Inc. All rights reserved, File:20091022, Page | 148

chuckle highly uncharacteristic of Mr. Shahvagh, the French educated master artist, he rushed to make sure he had checked everyone's homework paintings.

The principle, who was an outstanding American educated man who was fluent in three languages, then stopped me on my way to home that day. He gave me a sealed envelope to give to my parents and explained that they need to answer by the next day. I worried all the way home. In previous times, a sealed envelope take home to my parents had always meant there was trouble. I tried to think what I might have done something wrong to deserve this. I wondered if in Europe and US, the law permitted someone to do self-damaging confessions. Then why this sealed envelope? My mother opened it, and before I could say mom I had nothing to do with this, she reached and gave me a big hug and a kiss. "My Picasso, I am very proud of you!" In spit all my worries, that letter was to inform my parents that I had won the first place in art class. With their permission, my work will be on display in the regional schools' art exhibition!

My Picasso Career crumbled and failed in high school where we had to do camera-like drawings. No colors, just like a camera record shapes. I went from the best to worst in arts very quickly.

Managers must be able to detect, empower, and nourish talent. Creativity is sort of like nuclear energy. If we manage to use this human energy properly, it can light up a city. If not managed or used properly, it can and will destroy. The manager has to make it possible for the creative and innovative people to experiment. Failing, which is one of the potential consequences of any attempt to innovate, should be acceptable for the sake of progress. Without this understanding, no one can invent.

It is ironic that I live about six miles from Menlo Park, CA. Thomas Edison lived there. We all know that for each invention that succeeded, he had hundreds that had failed, and failed miserably.

I want to indulge and share one last quote from Reba. She told me that many Psalms, parts of Old, and New Testament, strongly advise us not to be afraid. In fact, my limited understanding is that the bible says do not be afraid to live!

I know this real well now. A good friend was describing a new invention that will take an image from a computer memory, and then sends that image to a projector so people can share pictures in meetings. I must have had a case of "Severe Stupidities" I told him that might work from technology point of view, but it will be expensive and nobody will buy it. Every time, I see a slide projector I feel like kicking myself. Of course, my friend John does make sure to remind me about that every time we meet.

Going back to Van Gogh, for the first time, his abstract painting did more than what a camera normally could not do. It exuded the painter's passion for transmitting his feelings to the viewer via canvas and paint.

Picasso, started painting just like a camera takes a picture. In Barcelona, in Picasso, an elegant painting shows her sister with a glamorous white and gold dress. Unfortunately, he then went through a period of depression when his best friend passed away. His art became blue, just like his mood. Most of his paintings had a heavy dose of the color blue. However, he like many others recovered from this period and started to live life again and paint with passionate colors.

Are you going to give up your efforts on your career and job fifteen minutes before a masterpiece?

Of course, you will not.

CHAPTER 62:   Petula Clark

I would like to present two of Petula Clark's songs here. I fell madly in love with her voice when I was about seventeen. This famous super start and royalty of the music is very famous for the song "My Love." The lyrics for this song, which are mesmerizing and captivating, are:

<
"My love is brighter than the brightest star
That shines every night above
And there is nothing in this world
That can ever change my love"
>

I have loved this song since the first time I heard it. It was in 1967 and I heard it while I was getting ready to go to a party with family and friends. Hearing this song that has rather simple words, made me vividly paint mental pictures of love and what it might look like. I could see pristine beaches, clear waters, and all the beautiful things that this song is all about.

It was not until many, many years later, after I had collected almost all of her albums, that I realized that she also had some sad songs. I got some of her work in French. It is perhaps not widely known that she spent a lot of time in France. She was also married to a French national. She produced a song titled, "The Night Never Ends," which I bought as I was trying to improve my French Language. Unlike the song "My Love," this one is very sad and "Dark." I could feel the depressing thoughts that emanated from this song. In addition, of course, at that point, I was more than four months into that unemployment period.

The lyrics for this beautiful song are:
La Nuit N'En Finit Plus (Needles And Pins)

<
"La nuit n'en finit plus
Et j'attends que quelque chose vienne
Mais je ne sais qui je ne sais quoi
J'ai envie d'aimer, j'ai envie de vivre"
>

This roughly says:
The night never ends,
And I expect something to happen
But I do know what
I want to love, I want to live"

One day the thought hit me. I would have never appreciated the elation of the song, "My love," with all its beauty, had I not also felt the downside that is depicted in the lyrics of this song.

Unemployment, or being trapped in a dysfunctional job, is very similar to the song, "La Nuit Ne Pas Fini," but have hope, there are also lovely peaks like "My Love" that are purely uplifting.

It may not be our fault, and it will never be our choice to have pain in this difficult world, but suffering can only befall us if we choose it.

As for today, December 1, 2008, as I am trying to put final touches on this book and send

Copyright © 2008 - 2009 Razban Internet International, Inc. All rights reserved, File:20091022, P a g e | **150**

it for review tomorrow, as my present consulting gig has only four weeks left in it and it is not even clear that it will be extended, I am hopeful and positive. I have updated my resume. I have purchased several of the latest technology and management books. I have networked with several friends in several companies that are hiring, and I have done my first screening interview.

I would like to discourage companies from layoffs. I would like to tell Citi Bank executives to delay their layoff plans as there are better ways of doing business, but that is above my pay grade at this point. I can only do my humanly best for one day. Moreover, getting this book to the reviewers that Shauna has lined up for me is the best that I can do.

However, I will not succumb to a *dark night*, and will live and hope for my love!

This is a book focused on the dark and painful subject of job loss, dysfunctional workplaces, recession, depression, and economic Armageddon. Yet it goes into detail about the good life, about happiness, about being there, about family, about life, and living. The most important reason is that, as people lose their jobs, which in a one-paycheck family can be disastrous, sadness sets in. As the painful pursuit of the next job starts and intensifies, people forget to live the good life. I have seen that their language gets darker, as if there is no hope. In addition, they forget about all the good things in life that are free and abundant. Not having that regular paycheck is hell. I agree. However, as you do your humanly best each doing the full time job of finding a new job, you must not forget to live the good life!

Remember, this is only money!

CHAPTER 63:   First Glimmer of Hope

It has been my experience that depression, revolves around a fixation. A fixation, in my limited knowledge of psychology, is being so pre-occupied with some thought or a memory that one cannot be functional. The memory could be some real trauma experienced, or totally imagined, and even a mixture of both. But this memory, as it is played like a movie in the depressed person's mind, over and over again, becomes even more real and more urgent and more painful each time that it is played.

People usually linger in this stage, until and unless at some point something happens that persuades, encourages, or even forces them to "Bottom Out." They might get tired of feeling sorry for themselves, or they just decide to try something new or different. Unfortunately, sometimes this takes a brutal form. A foreclosure, or car repossession, or just not having enough money for food, etc. In my own case, it was a day of "vacation" from feeling bad about not having a job. I drove to Belmont, CA and stopped at several nice vista points, and then off to my favorite Chinese restaurant the makes the best "Salt and Peppered Shrimp" that I have tasted. They have several awards that indicate that they were recognized as the best in the city for their category. Then just a few steps further, are the Starbucks Coffee Shop and its European style tables outside to enjoy my usual black coffee. Across the parking lot, there is a very old church and beyond that church there are many beautiful and yet simple houses and apartments on the green foothills. Each of these buildings has nice and colorful roofs and windows. This is very relaxing view to me since the entire background and colors make this view just like a nice oil color painting. Somehow a twenty-four-hour reprieve from all the anger, shame, frustration, and repeated bad thoughts, helped me gather my courage and go for an all out job search. The job search was still an ordeal, but it was an ordeal that I could tolerate for those few hours of making phone calls and sending resumes. This was my turning point.

At this turning point, we usually take a baby step. A tiny step, never the less is a step. This is like grinding two pieces of wood together and seeing on spark that is needed to start a camp fire. I have learned how important that baby step is for me. One day, I decided to just call an old colleague whom I had always admired and ask him for advice. I had thought about this for years, and years. Finally, I got his phone number from the directory and what had taken me years and years to act on, worked in seconds. The phone had not rung more than once, when my friend said hello. In fact, he said hello before I could chicken out and hang up. We talked for quite a long time on the phone, and I was amazed to realize that he had gone through very similar things and feelings that I had gone through. So, all that time that I was thinking that I was eternally unique in my problems and suffering, he too had gone through the same things, and he too had thought that it was only him who was not smart enough to find a way out.

One of my friends decided to finally use the health-spa membership card that he had paid for all those years and never used. This kind of helped him to get out of his shell. Many years ago, I was really down. I had a very bad cold that had persisted for quite some time. On my brother's insistence, I took a short walk in the Old Mill part of Mountain View. That short walk was all I needed to start my recovery from the cold and start to feel better.

Sometimes, it is that first interview that helps a great deal. My brother taught me that one should always go to one first interview after some time just to get back into shape. In his

Copyright © 2008 - 2009 Razban Internet International, Inc. All rights reserved,

thinking, that interview can even be for a job that you are not that much interested in. But, this will help immensely to prepare you for the next one that might be a serious interview for the opportunity of your career. Over the years, I have experienced this for myself, and I have seen it in the others, that a first faint glimmer of hope or that first tiny success can go a very long way to recovery and restoration of what had been lost. It is critically important to recognize this glimmer as a most important phenomenon needed for recovery, and not to dismiss it as insignificant.

When I was working at PG&E in San Francisco, there was a older woman who seemed to have suffered from a stroke. Many times, I will see her slowly and carefully, with one foot slightly ahead of another get out of the elevator. Each day she seem to be just a fraction of second faster and faster. One day, when I was admiring her courage, she seemed to nod to me and give me a smile. But, if I could read her minds at that time, she was also telling me, just with that smile, that live is sweet in spite all its ups and downs. She would also emphasize that we need to be strong to appreciate each moment of this life. Aside from the life lesson embedded in this encounter near the elevator, this is proof positive on how Mutual Trust and Loyalty (MTL) concept works in business. The company had decided to support her in spite her medical condition, and she was in return determined to get better and to help the company in return. I, as a consultant working for the company could not ever do an iota less for such a company that had this ethical Mutual Trust and Loyalty with this employee. When you see acts of goodness you cannot help but feel good too. It is super contagious.

The next story is the opposite. In one of my frequent visits, I noticed a frustrated but beautiful woman in a corner of a MacDonald's on a Sunday afternoon. I quickly remembered that we had had a conversation several weeks before. "Mr. Rayman, I hope you are doing OK!" I said, "I am impressed, you still remember me!" "Sorry, I called you Mr. Rayman; I know that your last name is something like that. To remember, I associated you with Rayman. This is because, last time, you gave a ray of hope when you told me about your book." "I like to tell my story. Do you have time?" I said, "I always love to hear other people's stories. Also regarding the last name, you are close, my last name is Razban." She added that as the salesperson of the year for a major corporation, she almost never forgets any person that she meets. I recalled that she told me that she had breast cancer. The surgery and one round of Chemo had to be rushed before the insurance coverage would run out. I asked her how things were going. "We had the worst weekend. The unemployment check was late. Unfortunately, we had to spend his entire paycheck for car insurance. We had no money left and we had to starve during most of the weekend until a friend could lend us some small money.

Ravages of hair loss resulting from Chemo had left her with not enough hair to make a pony tail in the back. Never the less she had somehow managed to barely make one. However, this required her to frequently check to make sure that the bow was still clinging in place. My mother, a strong and courageous one like this woman, had also had breast cancer. If I was a CEO and had a job to offer her, I would. This is a painful example of the $2.4 Trillion annual loss of productivity for that so called ideal 4% unemployment. We cannot afford this exorbitant waste. This woman, who had been Sales Person of the year, could have easily flourished in her career and would have created many jobs. With proper management, she might have had a much better life and career! I know another sales professional who told me, "I worked for some awful manager who

Copyright © 2008 - 2009 Razban Internet International, Inc. All rights reserved, File:20091022, P a g e | **153**

did not seem to have a clue on how to interact with people. In many cases we would lose customers because he would impose impossible processes and procedures on us." "He was incoherent, illogical, and unfair. After several years of this, I decided that it was time for me to move on. When I told manager that I had cancer and needed chemo, his response was not that helpful. Then unfortunately, my husband got transferred to East Coast. Then he was fired by the new company that had acquired his old one. I had to stay on that terrible job and suffer. This got to me. I slowly gained weight. Then, I started to neglect my life. My husband who could barely handle his own problems fell in love with a coworker that he had met in East Coast. I survived two layoffs by dedicating my life to my work. Then I kept gaining more and more weight. Then I was finally let go. I could see a lot of resentment in her face as she said, 'Then, I was finally let go!' I could identify with her. The same had happened to me and many others I knew. Suddenly, I realized that she had jumped off her chair, grabbed her empty coffee cup and was heading toward the cashier to get a refill.

She came back quickly as if to tell me the rest of the story. "I was down and out for a while." "I took some time and visited my grandmother in Milwaukee, and then visit my ex-husband in the East Coast. To my surprise, his second wife had left him and their divorce was in the works. He had turned into a complete couch potato. He would sit around his apartment and watch TV all day and subsist on junk food and off brand bear. The next day, I went to his apartment and banged on his door. "Get off your rear end, pack up your suitcase, and take a shower. You have exactly two hours!" He started to mutter something like, "You cannot do this to me," but he stopped in mid-sentence. With a mixture of amazement, surprise, and some trace of excitement, he demanded to know; "Is this, an order?" I told him that I did not have time for games. I told him that he smelled real bad, and that he had to be ready when I came back!

He was sure ready when I came back to pick him up. With a slight, half-hearted objection, he asked, "Do you know that this is kidnapping?" I did my best not to smile, and turned my head slightly to pretend that I was ignoring him. That was the last objection! Later on, I found that what had made him ready for being "Kidnapped" was that he had an evacuation order on his hands for a few weeks resulting from past due rent. We landed in San Francisco and had to stay in a nearby inexpensive motel. Interesting thing is that, while I was playing James Bond, my cancer had grudgingly given me a respite. He found a job after two months of unemployment. I continue to babysit for more than thirty hours a week. On top of that I am studying like crazy to get one of those guaranteed jobs in the cancer ward. Life is sure interesting. My grandmother still has a faded poster in her dining room. She has a picture of Golda Meyer, the first Prime Minster of Israel who was originally a schoolteacher in Milwaukee. My grandmother, who is very Jewish, liked to remind us about Golda with a thick German accent. I am convinced that she must have for ever wondered why none of her kids ever turned famous, or had Golda's guts. The caption in the bottom of the poster reads, "Can She Type?" Well she did not know how to type, but she became a Prime Minster. She had a goal, a mission, a passion, and she really wanted to make a difference. So do I, even more so with the cancer.

I had an interesting thought as I got back to my desk that day. I was thinking about what the first glimmer of hope might have looked for her. She probably could just get off her wheelchair one day and stand for a few seconds. Yet it was respecting of that baby step and eventually might even make her better and better in conquering her disease.

Copyright © 2008 - 2009 Razban Internet International, Inc. All rights reserved, File:20091022, P a g e | **155**

CHAPTER 64:   ABBA Musical Group

I am a big fan of ABBA, the musical group. ABBA is a group from Sweden. It was originally composed of two married couples as the singers. Their music was fantastic and they had several platinum records. As co-workers, they really made excellent music together that seemed to be perfect. Not one iota could be changed. It was that perfect. The definition for a masterpiece in management is that nothing can be taken and nothing could be added. The final work was just fine. They also seem to share a great deal of joy when they worked together. This is in spite many differences among them.

In July of 2008, I saw the movie, *Mama Mia*. This is an excellent movie that is based on ABBA music. It has a charming and interesting story about a wedding. It is filmed in a picturesque Mediterranean island in Greece. The acting is superb. The cinematography is excellent and so is the choice of the music.

In spite being an excellent movie, something was missing. It was not the original labor of love that was done by the original Swedish group. As such, the music did not really touch my soul. Please do not get me wrong, the movie is fantastic on its own. Unfortunately, it did not set my soul on fire that I felt when the original group sang. Nevertheless, the story of friends coming back to help their friend, who was a single Mom, to get her only daughter married was inspiring and heartwarming.

You may not be a composer, and you may not know anything about music. Just the same, you can create a masterpiece in your line of work each day and for that day. The freedom to do this in your own way is invigoratingly refreshing! If you are a toll collector on a bridge, and if you do not enjoy your job, why not make it interesting? Why not figure out some mental exercise or focus more and pay more attention on each customer? This will help you feel better about your job, and for customers to feel better too.

Another musical group that I used to love and admire was The Zasu Pitts Memorial Orchestra. The teamwork, harmony, and love that radiated from this group's performance was captivating. They did in fact set my soul on fire. They had a mega passion and creativity that flooded the TV screen during their New Year's performance. I could see the Mutual Trust and Loyalty that empowered and strengthened the team. They all seemed to rejoice in their perfect labor of love. This is the type of work we all love to have. This is what makes people creative and happy in the work place.

I forgot all my concerns and worries for this fantastic TV program.

Copyright © 2008 - 2009 Razban Internet International, Inc. All rights reserved,

***Section 3:

- Challenges to readers, government, and corporate executives to imagine a 107.8% employment as a way to not waste $2.4 Trillion each year in productivity loss and resulting human suffering.

- Hope, insight, and advice for those employees who are already affected by layoffs, or they are suffering from Fear of Sudden Job Loss (SJL) and associated Pink Shock.

- Challenge to ourselves to cope with the situation, recover, regroup, and even benefit from it. This truly is a major challenge, but *we can overcome this*.

- **Let's go do this!**

CHAPTER 65:   Productivity

Productivity generally holds the key to success in finding a job. It also spells success when you already have a job. More importantly, success is the direct result of accomplishments from productivity. Human unlimited potential is perfectly capable of producing masterpieces. Using productivity as the foundation, we can accomplish just about anything. Due diligence combined with intelligent hard work can make many things that we hope for actually happen.

When I have a contract or assignment and I am working, I usually had an office or a cubical. That place means work and productivity for me. I would bring my favorite books and pictures of my family. First thing each day, I make a list of action items. Then I will sort them based on priorities. Then I do these action items one by one. This will help me find additional energy that even I did not know that I had. I get things done the best and most efficient way for my employer.

Most places these days have cubicles. I think that cubicles are an HP invention. I have heard some bittersweet things about cubicles. This nicely organized area is what I usually miss first, even though I have a home office that occupies an entire room. PG&E was the most generous of all the places that I had worked. They gave me a real office. I decorated it with books, pictures, and two computers. As an indication of my appreciation, I always had a plate full of chocolate there. Co-workers loved to visit and enjoy those tiny chocolates. Some mornings, after a ninety-minute commute from Mountain View to San Francisco, I would be a bit tired. That would quickly go away as soon as I would sit in my chair in which meant productivity.

When I am unemployed, I would go from doing one unimportant thing to another and waste most of the day. For example, I started by cooking breakfast, and then I would take my car in for some minor repair. Distraction randomly set priorities most days for an unemployed person. I might notice there was a computer sale at the electronics store; I would end up spending an hours trying to save a few dollars. Before I know it, it is time for dinner and I wondering where the entire day had gone.

The truth is that when you are in between jobs, you are the CEO of your life and career. You definitely feel great if you did your humanly best in each day as you did for your previous employer. Remember that at this stage, you do have a full time job even with over time, and this job is to find a job!

The most fortunate people are those that use this time that they have on their hands to self-improve, get started on a new career, start new friendships and contacts, learn new things, and enjoy every minute of this life by observing all the beautiful things.

Let us get productive, effective, rejoice in our work, and even try to make a masterpiece.

Copyright © 2008 - 2009 Razban Internet International, Inc. All rights reserved, File:20091022 , P a g e | **158**

CHAPTER 66:   Forgiveness Seminar at Stanford University

I have lived about thirty years in an inexpensive house about fifteen minutes away from the Stanford University Campus in Palo Alto, California. At the time that I was buying this small townhouse, I could have bought a bigger and somewhat better house in San Jose or elsewhere for the same price. Nevertheless, I insisted on this one because of its proximity to Stanford.

Once or twice a year, as part of their continuing education courses, Stanford offers a course in forgiveness. Unfortunately, I could not afford to take this course, but I bought the textbook that was written by the professor who teaches the course. The book made a lot of sense to me. It basically says that when something bad happens to us, whether it is our fault or if we blame someone else for it, it hurts and we make a narrative. The narrative is a story of what has happened and the hurts as seen by us. Then, for years and years, we let this fester and it gets bigger and more real in our minds. Then we use this narrative either to convince others, or to develop hatred towards the person or persons that we think did something to us.

Amazingly, it is in forgiving that we can stop or greatly reduce the damage that such human reaction to things cause. We first have to forgive, if we want to be free of the ongoing hurt because of layoffs, firings, divorces, hatred, emotional and physical hurts, etc.

In the first glance, this does look like religious advice. Astonishing enough, this is not advice based on some religious teaching; it is practical and experiment-based scientific advice. There is proof that this helps people recover from setbacks, hurt, and to enable them to get back on their feet, survive, and sing again. Forgiveness helps them free themselves from bondage of hatred, resentment, and to live and plan for the future without the pain.

When I was about ten years old, my mother taught me a Persian proverb. It says something to the effect that, "the pleasure in forgiving is much bigger than that of revenge!" I have learned and re-learned this lesson many times, when I felt that I was unfairly treated at a job or taken advantage of by one of my own employees. While it is not widely known, their own employees can hurt managers sometimes as well.

I do not want to ignore the profound value of forgiveness in Christianity and many other religions.

Grace Slick of Jefferson Airplane, in Let it Go song lyrics puts this in context:

<
Some people say "Don't go away just stay right here"
Some say "If you stay at home you're gonna wind up alone"
>

This song from youTube.com has been playing, and playing, and playing on my computer to sooth my nerves as I personally was going through the job search ordeal. After all these years, it is still an ordeal. I could not forgive myself. I was bogged down in a bad case of self-damnation. This prevented me from doing an all out effective job search. I had to learn to forgive myself, and let it go, as the song says so beautifully. If I continue to stay in my anger and frustration, I will be alone. Another part of the lyrics that talks about staying at home also fits our discussion here. It is imperative that we leave the house, at least once each day. Otherwise, cabin fever, leads into the disease of isolation. Isolation is the mother of all addiction, depression, and chronic unemployment.

Copyright © 2008 - 2009 Razban Internet International, Inc. All rights reserved, File:20091022, P a g e | **159**

Do get out of the house each day to get fresh air. Fresh air can ignite our spiritual, emotional, and the hope that says, "Do not give up fifteen minutes before the miracle happens!" I firmly believe that a thirty-minute walk each day goes a long way for our physical and mental health. We do not have to go to the gym if we are not the gym going type.

One hot summer day after the dot-com bubble had burst; I found myself deeply in self-pity, depressed, and wanting to spend the day in my room. I was unemployed again. I was again wondering why and scratching my unshaved chin and face. Suddenly, I decided that I had to get out. I burst into shower, put my cloths and even splashed some aftershave and ran out of the house as if my life depended on it. In fact, this was not an "as if", it was a certain understanding that I might do something stupid if I isolated more. I got a steak lunch to compensate for semi starvation. Then, I came back home, put on my swimming trunk and slowly strolled towards the swimming pool. I first got a glimpse of Melina's perfect body and long legs while she was sitting on the edge of the swimming pool and dipping her feet in the water like a mermaid. Her olive skin tone, with the turquoise shimmering color of the swimming pool would accentuate each other to create an extremely sexy picture. Her legs were perfect and the Fire Engine itsy bitsy bikini was covering only a little. Soon, I noticed her flawless Bikini shave. Her beautiful blonde her were too good to even be wet by the swimming pool water. She looked as if she was twenty or thirty years old. Although, I had a notion she must be older.

As I was admiring her captivating appearance and trying to make sure that she did not notice, I realized that she moved her hips just slightly so the bikini bottom would reveal more than the bikini shave. I am positive that she had noticed my desire for her. Her bikini consisted of two triangles struggling to cover her most gorgeous breasts, and an upside down triangle as the third part. I was lucky because her table was right next to mine. She looked at me and realized that my physical appearance was no match for her breathtaking sexiness. In spite that, I was the only man was there. I quickly started a conversation and offered to get her something to drink. "Just a Perrier." She then added "Thanks." as she started to apply some sweet smelling suntan lotion. I must have flown the forty or so steps to the drink counter to get her drink. I brought her drink to give her and right at that moment, and with a superb precision, pretending to align her top bikini, she opened the top just enough so I could see her beautiful breast. I was quick to tell myself, Ah, this is either my imagination or just a coincidence. As I bent to put her drink on her table, she did the same with the second breast. I was mesmerized and uncontrollably hot.

In my opinion and experience, it is much easier and happier to forgive and go on with life that to hate and fight! I remember the words of an Oscar nominee who said, "I had a choice between love and hate, and I chose love. You can the results!" Then he lifts up his Oscar trophy as a proof.

CHAPTER 67:   Work is the Best Therapy

I think it is a good idea to team up with a good therapist whom we respect and like. In other words, there is chemistry and mutual understanding. In some cases, so many of the psychological problems can be rooted in chemical imbalances that a good psychiatrist (who is an MD as well as a psychologist and can prescribe medications) is crucial for well being.

This book might help like some sort of reading material supplement to antidepressant. The book became Amazon.com top 60 most popular in Psychology, Counseling, and Education. Please note that I do not mean that this can ever replace any medication that a qualified psychiatrist might have prescribed for you to help you get the chemical balance needed for normal day-to-day living. More importantly, I am not a psychologist or psychiatrist.

In fact, for many years, I greatly benefited from regular psychologist sessions. I was lucky to find one of the best of the best. I had an appointment every Thursday. During that time, I would talk things over with the psychologist. I got my frustrations, worries, and anger out and talked about them. This is not because I have any psychological disorders (except for the truckload of the ones that my wife says I have.) This is a proactive attempt on my side to diffuse what might later hit me like a tsunami. Talking about things is a great way of proactively preventing potential future disasters.

An outstanding trained professional has helped me cope with many years of workplace blues, unemployment periods, my father and mother's passing away, etc. These sessions have also helped me channel my anger and my frustration into positive, creative work such as writing of this book. When, I first saw the cover of this book displayed on Amazon.com, I could not believe my eyes. Since this book is indeed a labor of love, I usually felt good for doing this. I am also proud that I wrote this on a shoestring budget. Some days, I even spend some of my daily $5.80 budget on printing, or other costs related to writing a book. I have done the writing, editing, cover design, and I am doing the best I can to market it. Writing this book was such good therapy that I could not wait to get back and do my daily writing after work. You might be asking, "What work? You were unemployed!" Sure. I was not employed all the time, but I was working all the time. I had a full time job of finding a new job each day. I am not proud of saying this, but I also went into a mild depression after I completed writing this book. I missed my daily treat of pouring my feeling out into this computer.

In "What Color is Your Parachute?", Richard Boles, whom I respect highly, points out several places that it is not just work for the sake of work. We must have a mission. I did not really understand my mission until I took the eight years that it took to write this book. My mission is to try to convince the world that layoffs are not a solution, and that there is a better alternative. By far a holier mission for me is to help people to cope, recovers, and even thrives after job loss. I am of the firm belief that constant job loss, job search, and periods of unemployment will be the norm in the future.

This is my mission because my life-long mentor and career coach said "Bravo" to me in his five star review of this book in the Amazon.com. Writing this book made work and play to intermingle with each other and give me pure pride and joy! There is a documentary in a youTube.com clip. A group of fifteen who go through training to

Copyright © 2008 - 2009 Razban Internet International, Inc. All rights reserved, File:20091022, P a g e | **161**

become flight attendants. One moving and heart-felt observation is, "Learn by doing, and enjoy by learning!" This is a point well taken.

I also like to add passion to the concept that work does not have to be work alone! I was obsessed to writing this book. I could not wait until 8:00 PM each weekday and Weekends to continue writing. This made this book a labor of love. While you are looking for that next job, try to also listen to what is your career passion and respect that too if possible.

Love is the answer to all our hate, sorrow, anger, frustration, and unemployment. I have seen repeatedly that some career driven executive loses his or her job. Then they discover that they have loved ones, spouses, and children all along. Unfortunately, work place zombification and toxicity prevented them from seeing or feeling the love that was so freely given to them. More importantly, they hated themselves instead of love and forgiveness towards themselves.

In the words of my therapist, sometimes it takes a crisis for us to realize how much love is all around us, even by some perfect strangers. Love is the basis and foundation. Jobs come and go, but self-love and love of those who matter in our lives are forever!

Work is also very therapeutic. It can never replace what I have with my psychologist, but it can be a great help in addition to professional help. Psychologists have proven that work, especially creative artwork, helps heal psychological wounds as a supplement to medications and/or talk therapy.

Work brings a certain structure in life. This structure then replicates itself in all aspects of our lives as well. Instead of sitting there and worrying about things, we become a lot more productive. This productivity is the antidote to hatred resulting from joblessness. In a way, while we are working, we do not have time for self-pity, or just sitting there. The pride of accomplishment and the steady paycheck goes a long way to help us.

It also stands to reason that since work is not just work, it must be a mission too. A mission that involves love of our family and friends, then it becomes indeed a labor of love!

One summer, when I had worked very hard and I could not go on any vacations, I was a bit jealous of others in the office would take a week off and go to vacation. Most their vacations were to nearby places around New York City. One night I got a telegram from my Dad that he would send airline ticket for me to vacation with my family in Paris. That is Paris, France! As the Air France 747 was about one hour to land, a lovely flight attendant came to my seat, and quietly asked, "Are you Monsieur Razban from America?" "Yes" I replied. "Please be ready to disembark right after First Class passengers have disembarked, and before coach!" "Is there any problem?" I worriedly asked. She answered me with a lot of respect and admiration by saying, "No, not at all, Air France likes to give you the VIP courtesy!" As soon as I got off, I found my Dad waiting a few steps away. He was smiling, and almost crying from the excitement of seeing me. As for that generous Air France VIP treatment, it must have been my Dad's ability to sweet talk French into helping him.

We had dinner very close to the Orly Airport with four friends of my Dad from his student days. Then, my Dad, who was still quite excited, made a short speech. "I am not a rich person in Dollars or Franks, but I am very rich in having superb friends and family. I worked hard from when I was four years old, and will work hard until a week before I die! I love my work, and I have a mission." After drinking a bit more of his favorite

Copyright © 2008 - 2009 Razban Internet International, Inc. All rights reserved, File:20091022,

Bordeaux wine, as if it was liquid gold, he was at peace for having said what he loved to say. His mission in life had been to raise a 'good son' to at least eighteen, well educated intellectual, and not without father!" "This last part hit me, not without father, since he had to suffer for not having a father" However, the fact is that my grandmother, a pioneer single Mom in 1950s, was both a mother and a father to all her kids. Then, my mother could not wait to talk. My folks always kept a code of perfect equality in their marriage. "My American educated son is rich too. We made sure that he gets as much as international culture as possible. We had enough courage to love him and be his friends too. It takes courage to love in parenting!" Upon uttering these words, my Mom's best friend who was the wife of one of my father's best friends in Paris, stood up and gave my Mom a one-woman standing ovation! She then concluded in saying Bravo, Bravo, and Bravo!" Bravo is also the word that my career and life coach, Jerry Wiener used when he gave me a five star review of my book. His bravo, helped me feel that I had finally arrived, and I had achieved a life-long goal of doing whatever I could to make world better. I had succeeded in first part of my mission by writing this book.

Confidentially, I like to share with you my private ideal of perfect marriage. This works equally well for men and women. Here is my Senior Management Consultant advice; make sure to marry a flight attendant. I almost did. Here is my superior logic: They are intelligent, brave, attractive, sexy, and more importantly attentive. You want something to drink; you just press the call button. You want newspapers; you just press the call button. They attend to all your needs. Insist on living in First class or at least business class. I suppose if you are married to them, and want to have kids, then you can press the call button. Imagine that you are not just a member of the Mile High Club; you can live it every day by marrying a flight attendant! Of course, you have to prove to be worthy of their love and marriage since the flight attendant spouse position is highly competitive! On the average, flight attendants get several million marriage proposals and they even consider a few dozen! There was a book called "Coffee, Tea, or Me" that did a big disservice to flight attendants' profession. I like to re-emphasize that their primary function is safety. During emergency landing, etc, they become the commander in charge of evacuation, and that really takes courage and leadership.

Some thirty years later on our daily grind of commute, my best friend and BN struck a conversation. As parents, we were proud that we did everything we could for our kids. My tired friend, who could barely carry his backpack at the end of a hectic day, told me that his biggest achievement in life is that he has raised two good kids. This revived my found memories of my Dad and his speech when I joined them in Paris. BN and my Dad were saying the same thing about what is important in life.

A title, even a coveted Executive one, is just a few milligrams of ink on a tiny piece of paper. A paycheck is a piece of paper. A paycheck is nothing compared to courage, accomplishment, love, life, and Mokado (Honor and dignity) that come from having a mission in life!

Copyright © 2008 - 2009 Razban Internet International, Inc. All rights reserved, File:20091022.

CHAPTER 68:   A Mind is a Terrible Thing to Waste

This was an advertising motto of the United Black College Fund many years ago. Many people did not go to college due to lack of funds. This was a smart fund-raising tool to prevent that problem. With my 32 years of experience, I have found this to be true for all! A mind is indeed a terrible thing to waste. To start with, we only use three percent of our mental powers. Unfortunately, most of us, including I, turn into Zombies when we get to work. Please note that that eight working hours is potentially the time to be most inventive, creative, happy, and proud of our accomplishments. Evidenced with so many heart attacks that happen on Monday mornings, clearly, we are not as productive and happy as we can be! This is huge waste. The Zombie idea was planted in my mind first when I heard an old co-worker complaining that he was not a "Goylem". I learned later that goylem came from Psalm 139:16 and it is meant to be matter without shape, a robot, a simpleton, a fool, a clumsy man or woman. Please do not misunderstand me. Human beings are human beings, but toxic work environment, and fear of sudden job loss does lower us to the position of a goylem. This is so bad that it seems to me that there was a hostile takeover of Capitalism with Foolism. We stopped being inventive, courageous, and productive. In the Foolism one does or say anything just to keep their job for that day. In the Foolism, we have Foolsheviks (Bolsheviks) who blind-foldedly follow orders without thinking. Unfortunately, this has a $2.4 Trillion price tag.
Sadly, human potential that is wasted this way is mind bugling. This is a problem that management does not cultivate the growth of human potential. It is also the employees that are guilty of doing nothing about this. Yet, the end result is the same awful, shameful waste.
I have friends and relatives who live in London and Paris. They love to tell me how awful we Americans are in wasting paper and other things. They cite the statistics about how many kilograms of paper Americans waste per year and compare it with much lower statistics about Europe in general.
As unhappy I am to acknowledge this to them and to myself, I think there is a much bigger waste that is humongous in comparison. Layoffs and mismanagement of our most powerful resources, which is human potential, cause this awful waste.
If we put empty soda cans side-by-side and head to tail, my calculations indicate that we can pave a six-lane highway from coast to coast with this awful waste of human talent and innovation.
Most of us have worked almost all our adult life. Being told that we are no longer needed and sent away from our work place, is a waste of about $2.4 Trillion each year. This is in wasted Human Capital, Productivity, and Innovation, that causes so much pain and suffering for the humans in and out of the work place. Equally as bad is the fear of Sudden Job Loss (SJL) that forces people to play politics. This fear prevents employees of all ranks to say or do the right thing since they are trying to save their job for one more day at any price. The price at some companies has been so steep that company has had to go out of business. When the same mistakes are repeated, and when these mistakes are covered up routinely, even massive frequent layoffs cannot cover up the fundamental ingrained mistakes that eventually can destroy any company.
We already know that about 83% of workers (including executives) who are victims of a layoff get sick more often. They also have more chances of being victims of layoffs

Copyright © 2008 - 2009 Razban Internet International, Inc. All rights reserved, File:20091022. P a g e | **164**

again. Interestingly, ABC news in September of 2009, trumpeted that 20% of working population is so worried about their jobs, that they get sick. This is because of the undue stress. Having a "Revolving Door Hire, Fire" policy is the most wasteful management practice that a company can have.

Europeans can make fun of our wasteful ways. Unfortunately, when it comes to human potential, they too, are just as wasteful as we are.

Copyright © 2008 - 2009 Razban Internet International, Inc. All rights reserved, File:20091022, P a g e | **165**

CHAPTER 69:   Empowerment and Confidence are the Antidotes to Workplace or Unemployment Intimidation

In one of my jobs, I felt trapped. I could not see any way out of a dead-end job situation. The company was having one layoff after another, and I knew that, in addition to losing market share, they were also losing many of their top-notch employees. Many days I would go home totally frustrated and disappointed. Each day, I will do my humanly best effort to be just as good a zombie as the rest of them. Each day I will do and redo the assignments several ways to succeed in keeping my work. The organizational stench of work place toxicity there was overwhelming. Inflicted with severe cases of Sudden Job Loss disease, productivity was almost impossible. There was no Mutual Trust and Loyalty. Whatever you said would get to the upper management and they would be misinterpreted. One of the executives, who were stuck with me in an elevator that took centuries to reach our upper floor, asked me if I had seen Wall Street Journal. I said yes. Then he smilingly me if I remembered the quote that said, "Fear, for the lack of a better word is good?" His spies had told him about my book. In fact, one of them even had a copy of the early manuscript. His remark forced me to pretend that I was going to my desk. Then I just turned around, went downstairs, and had a cold glass of iced coffee to regroup and not publish an article in the local paper.
I was in a no-win situation. The job market was bad, and I was not ready to move. I had not updated my resume in many years. I had lost contact with many friends. The work frustration was so bad that I felt like a total failure.
With all the turmoil, I finally got the courage to call a friend and go for coffee a few hours later. As we were talking about the good old days, I was greatly encouraged by his suggestion that I needed to start somewhere. We do not really have to do the entire job search, but doing something small to get started. He was very fond of the term "baby step." He would say, "Bruce, just take the first baby step and you will feel so much better." I found an old copy of my resume that had suffered from rain damage while in storage, which did not look very good. That was my first baby step as a starting point, and it really worked. I had indeed been spoiled before. My reputation and a good job market had kept jobs coming to me and not the way around. I had mastered the art of networking and having updated, certified skill set that the market valued.
In a few days, I had a relatively presentable resume. I noticed that the intense fear and anxiety was much less than before. As with that baby step, I had encountered the giant and had defeated it. Each day, I refined it a bit more until it was impressive and complete. In this book, I talk a lot about the fear of Sudden Job Loss (SJL) which I am convinced is just as bad as the well known Fear of Flying. Somehow, as we take these baby steps, the fear starts to go away. In a serious financial crisis like this, the Sudden Job Loss might become an awful fact of life. Luckily, the beauty of being proactive and taking steps is a powerful antidote to these fears. After all, we will not be caught with no resume, no contact list and nowhere to go which is a bad place to be.
When I lived in Santa Cruz, CA and I had to travel on the winding Highway 17 to go all the way up the 3,700 feet mountain in a winding road, I would sometimes have near miss accidents. One day I decided to do what I humanly could do, and then let go of the fear. I made sure I had the spare tire that was in a good shape, flares, medical kit, flashlight,

Copyright © 2008 - 2009 Razban Internet International, Inc. All rights reserved, File:20091022, P a g e | **166**

blanket, a small fire extinguisher, and some water. I had done what I humanly could do. I also made sure I drove that road carefully. The rest, I did not have control over. I was still in the same dangers, but I was not as afraid as before.

So, start somewhere. Do the best you can as a human being. Take that first baby step and soon, you will be impressed with your own work and a lot less scared. Soon you will rejoice in a sense of accomplishment that will help fear and pain to go away!

Copyright © 2008 - 2009 Razban Internet International, Inc. All rights reserved, File:20091022, P a g e | **167**

CHAPTER 70:   Put a Song in Your Heart. Music Heals!

During my four hours of roundtrip commute from Mountain View to Oakland each day, it became absolutely clear that if I did not have some music to soothe the tension during those four hours, I could get depressed and angry. I had seen so many people during my commute with earphones listening to music or whatever. However, it took a long time before I realized that I too needed music. Unfortunately, I should have acted on it sooner. Finally, I purchased a nice CD player from Stanford Shopping Center in Palo Alto California. Interestingly, I did not have to buy any new CDs since I had quite a few in my house already. When I was listening to the first CD, which was one of the Petula Clark's early songs that had lyrics like "Trains and Boats and Planes..." immediately the pain of the commute was reduced. It was interesting since I was in a train and I was hearing an excellent song about trains.

Music has an international healing power. Music has been with us since our ancestors' right along with the invention of hammers and bows and arrows, had invented musical instruments. I have seen this work for others and me and as I might have mentioned again in this book, music and art in general is used as a sort of therapy even for children. The soothing power of music is here to help us. So, please pick up whatever music you like and listen to it at least twenty or thirty minutes a day. Maybe you combine your music time and its healing power with your walking exercise each day. This is a fascinating, refreshing, and powerful meditation.

We also know that music can be a means of torture in some prisons, and even living rooms. Loud music does induce sleep deprivation in prisons. If the music we hear is not what we like, or even resent, then forcing us to listen is a sort of punishment or even torture.

Please note that I actually meant more by the song in the title of this chapter. The song is some hope for the future with some plan for the future. This is something worth looking forward to doing. Something to keep us going when going becomes difficult.

I knew a woman who had ended up losing almost all of her financial possessions. A mansion on a hill overlooking what is one of the most distinctive parts of California was gone, and so was the most beautiful, elegant antique grade of exquisite furniture was gone. In addition, her grown children, equally devastated by this misfortune, had to do odd jobs, and some of them had to move to another state to find a job. In this case, we cannot be too meticulous, a survival job will do. I had a chance to visit with her and her husband, and I felt the pain and devastation. Yet, as if by magic, I started to talk about her daughter's wedding. She started to crawl out of her shell. "Oh yes, it will be a very small wedding with very few guests, but I have found the most elegant dress for her at almost eighty percent off." I cannot afford many things now, but this I can afford. She went on and on. It was as if someone had given her a million dollars.

I also know an executive chef who was doing relatively OK in France. He fell in love with the love of his life, who was an American woman living in California. They got married and he relocated to California only to find the market difficult. He spent most of his lifetime savings. He finally decided to start a business selling sandwiches in a big professional building. This got him out his shell, and he started to compose a new song. He started to bake fresh French bread on Fridays and some hot but simple dishes. Then he went from one day a week to several days a week of doing this. Feeling empowerment

Copyright © 2008 - 2009 Razban Internet International, Inc. All rights reserved, File:20091022, P a g e | **168**

and using his human potential, he was so successful that people would line up outside his shop.

I noticed that, sometimes, he was wearing a very nice shirt and tie. When I asked him why, he said that he lived for a certain type of music. He would find performances that both he and his wife loved. Then, once or twice a month, he would indulge in getting the musical healing. This was what kept him very happy and alive.

The most striking one is about one of the vice presidents in one of the most well known companies. He had figured out a new technology, and he was sure that it would be the best for his then employer to try to evaluate this new technology. People in that company, thinking that the world was flat, did their best to talk him out of this.

At some point, he went out to have his lunch, and when he came back, his card key would not open the door. I just happened to arrive then. He told me that there must be something wrong with his card key, and he asked if I could please open the door. I did, and he went to his office to find out that his personal properties had been put in a box. On his desk, he found a note asking him to go see the president. He was told he was fired and he had an hour to "leave the premises while being followed by security guards". This was after many years of service.

This not only did not break him, but also made him more determined to go for it! Rumor has it that, at the age sixty, he got an MBA and started a technology company to do exactly what he had proposed to do for the other company. His company became even more successful than the company that had fired him.

When I was an engineer, the song in my heart was that I wanted someday to be a manager. Actually, I did not just want to be a manager, I wanted to be a CEO. I had dreams of someday flying in executive jets, making big decisions, and showcasing to the world. I wanted to be the "Poster Child" of the fact that companies can succeed immensely if they treated their employees and customers well.

My dream of being a CEO of a corporation has not materialized, yet. However, at the age of almost sixty, I am still in my "mid-life" crisis. I am CEO of my own life and my small business, Razban Internet International, Incorporated.

The passion to be CEO of a major corporation is the song in my heart!

By the way, having a song in my heart has given me something to lift my spirits a great deal over my entire life. I would be depressed without music and this explains my obsession in this book with all these lyrics.

The expression "Put a Song in Your Heart" comes from Lawrence Welk show. The conductor, Mr. Welk, would say, "Good bye for now, and until next time, put a song in your heart" as his signature good bye. So, now you know it. I learned this expression from Mr. Welk.

It is interesting that, at first, one gets mesmerized by a song and in many cases, one does not have all the lyrics to rejoice and be further conscious of the deeper meanings. Sometimes, these deeper meanings are covered, overshadowed, or hidden by the music and rhythm of the song. A study of lyrics, as well as poems by fine poets, songwriters, and philosophers really deepens our thoughts. I love Longfellow's work just for this reason.

In addition, I have used my limited talent to make this book somewhat poetic as well since the good life is very beautiful. It is just like a majestic poem.

Make a song of love and hope just for you. You do not need to be a composer, a poet, or a musician to do this and produce a beautiful song that you can play just for you to give yourself hope! It does not even need to have lyrics or words. It does not have to have a rhythm so long as it can play in our heads and make hopeful and happy. When frustrated or tired, this is what you hum just like a humming bird to live, succeed, or even survive life's difficulties and challenges for that one hour, one day, one week, or more to plan and prepare for better things for yourself and your loved ones.

Remember that music has powerful healing power. On those days that I do not listen to music, I get more tired, I am less inventive, and I feel depressed.

You can too. This takes a lot less than you might think, and you will have control over your own destiny. The business of America is small business.

Copyright © 2008 - 2009 Razban Internet International, Inc. All rights reserved, File:20091022, P a g e | **170**

CHAPTER 71:   My Worst Job. Ever!

When I was working for a major company in San Francisco, I was very happy with my job. My co-workers were used to my work and management style. There was a great deal of good will and teamwork. In addition to being professionals, we had pure joy in getting the job done well, in fact extremely well.

Our managers had indicated that they were happy with our work. We had a great deal of Mutual Trust and Loyalty that made our team super productive. I would bring small, individually-wrapped chocolates to meetings and, later on, to my office every day. I had plastic plates and every day I would fill it to the rim with these tiny chocolates. My colleagues would stop in my office to say hello or discuss something, and they would take one or more of these chocolates. I was learning the latest technology in my field, which was very important. I was proud of my productivity, and my job satisfaction was high. I had even gotten a chance to discuss aviation and photography with several of my colleagues during our lunch breaks. Like me, they had these as hobbies. A three to five-minute exchange of ideas after or before meetings went a very long way to build on an extremely good teamwork relationship.

One day, I got a phone message and several e-mails from a reputable recruiting firm. They were extremely interested and assured me that the new job they had, was an excellent fit and that I would enjoy the work. I had worked for one of their subsidiaries before. That was not a good experience. Finally, after the second phone call, I gave in agreed to go for interview. The interview went well. They offered me an hourly rate that was about fifty percent more than I made. The hourly rate was too good to be true! I talked to several of my friends and colleagues. It seemed like this was an opportunity that I should take. The offer came few hours later. I told myself, they must really need me badly if they are moving so fast. And they did! My immediate manager talked to me about making a career at this new company and that someone like me could do extremely well in this new company. I was taken care of and literally pampered from the first day. I produced a lot of results in a very short period of time. I was sure that the management also felt the same way. All the indications were that they also felt good about my work. I was asked to become a permanent employee instead of a consultant and build a career in this new and famous company.

After six weeks, one afternoon around 4:00 PM, somebody told me that my manager was looking for me. I was very impressed with this manager. There was some small talk and then we looked for an empty conference room. The day before this, I had gotten a nice compliment from an important person saying thanks for the excellent job I had done for their group. I was thinking about bringing that e-mail up in our discussion since a copy had also gone to my manager. The manager started by saying, "Bruce, I am very sorry to tell you this…you know I have a high opinion of you. We have worked well together, but there has been a bad report, and I am forced to let you go!" I could see the sadness in my manager's face. "What?" I asked to my extreme surprise. "It is beyond this. Upper management, way higher than me, has decided this is your last day!" I asked "Who?" She said she could not answer that. I asked what the bad report said. As far as I was concerned, this must have been a mistake. If I knew the details, I was sure that I could have convinced them that there was a mistake. I could not believe that in one of the most advanced democracies, I was being treated the same way a kangaroo court operated in a banana republic! It was a shock to me and my immediate manager and it was the first time that I had banged my head against this "hire, fire, revolving door" management practice! American management crisis was in full swing that day.

I had carefully been thinking, using my inventive mind that had given me patent grant and several patents pending, that I will work my way up the corporate ladder in that company by showing them a better way. I had worked on my evenings on a potentially great idea that would have improved their operation and products. All of those ideas were totally crushed after the bad report hit me.

Who had given me a bad report? Why? When? How? There had been no indications or reasons. How could this happen? The consulting firm was equally confused and surprised. "Bruce, let me see if I can intervene? Maybe we can get you back there. You do not know what I went through to find you, and they had interviewed several people before they literally fell in love with you." I said NO! I will not go back there anymore! I had my Mokato, dignity, and frazzled nerves that were brutally treated for the second time. I can be stubborn. Not just stubborn, I can be damn stubborn! I said I would never work for that company again.

I took my family for a very badly needed vacation to Seattle, Washington. My wife went on the ferry to a picturesque island, while my daughter and I went on a day tour of the Boeing Aircraft factory. We enjoyed seeing some Boeing 777s getting ready for delivery to customers. Boeing just proudly announced delivery of their 777th brand new 777 airliner to an airline. We also saw Boeing's latest and most advanced technology aircraft, the Dream Liner, or the Boeing 787 going through manufacturing. The 787 is one of the greatest, most advanced US made aircraft. The Airbus 350 and 380 are close competitors. During the tour, I started a conversion with the tour guide. She had been a Boeing employee for more than twenty years. You could see the pride of being a Boeing employee in almost everything she said. She also had a sense of humor. She said the logo for her and her family and friends is that "If AINT a Boeing, we AINT Going!" This was the time when Boeing, an American company, was in a dogfight for its existence with the European company Airbus. In addition, the employees of the European company's answer to the above were, "Boeing, Boeing!"

In a separate discussion, while we were waiting for our buses to take us back to Seattle, she told me that most employees were loyal and long-term employees at Boeing. She added, Boeing takes good care of us, and we love to work here with the best and brightest. I mentioned Mutual Trust and Loyalty (MTL) and she agreed that that was what kept the company in a good shape even during the hardest times. I could see that. When she was making her presentation and showing pictures, she was as proud about her company as she would have been talking about her family and friends. The coworkers, after a long period of time become good friends and almost like family. Moreover, when that happens, people will care a lot more and make their company a lot more successful. I have witnessed this everywhere. When the company shows enough Mokato (Japanese for respect), the employees also show respect in the form of loyalty and higher productivity and superior quality.

After my return, I realized that one of my immediate manager's managers at the subsidiary was suddenly fired after only ten or twelve days. He told me that there had been a bad report on him too.

Copyright © 2008 - 2009 Razban Internet International, Inc. All rights reserved, File:20091022, P a g e | **172**

In spite having had that great vacation, I actually did go through all the steps that one goes through after a big loss like this. Denial, anger (even though I had been taught as a child that anger is stupid energy, and smart people can convert it to good energy and work on the good energy).

I tried to get my old job in San Francisco back, but due to some budgeting constraints, it was not possible. I had to wait. There was the nightmare of Sudden Job Loss (SJL) playing in my own life! I got so angry that I decided to start a company, so I would never have to work for anybody else or any company again. I got two provisional patent filings and started a real hard effort to start a company. I made a business plan. I found my old friends to help me with the patents or the business plans. I talked to more than ten venture capitalists to get the needed $2.4 million to start a company that, in many ways, was like a mini-micro Microsoft.

Yet, underneath it all, the anger was simmering and burning me. I developed insomnia. I would work until 3:00 AM, and then go to bed to wake up around 9:00 or 10:00 AM, then work as hard as I could in job searches as well as my own company, Razban Internet International, Inc.

By writing my thoughts, feelings, and experience here, I started to find a channel to release the angry energy in a good way. Most of this book was written at that time. I went either to more than twenty interviews, screening interviews or in person. None of these turned into a job! I had run out of money. In addition, venture capital was not coming in. However, why this was my worst job, is the bigger question?

To start with, there was a lot dysfunctional behavior that I had decided to overlook. Although I had a high opinion of my immediate manager, the job had been poorly formulated. It was an impossible job for anyone to do. I could not develop Mutual Trust and Loyalty with the subsidiary before and could not again develop it this time. Unfortunately, even as a fifty-seven-year-old senior manager with more than twenty years of experience, I too had managed to internalize it. This shows that in spite all my experience, this process so painful that even I had let grief take its course.

I started to develop doubts about my abilities and my superb skill set. I felt rejected, dejected, and unwanted. I had kept up with the latest technology, and I had always been told that I was an excellent people and results manager. People tell me that I was spoiled for many years since I had an excellent reputation, jobs usually came to me rather than the other way around.

One day, I got an e-mail from an excellent colleague who was also looking for work. She had interviewed in Oakland with one of the companies that I had worked for before, and she called me to tell me that they were hiring and they were desperate to find someone like me with my skill set. She had given me a job description before in this company, but in my anger and wishful thinking that I was close to getting venture money, I had not acted on that. This time it was different. I had to find a job and quickly. I applied for a job well below my qualifications at this company in Oakland. A recruiter called minutes after I had sent the e-mail. He told me that he had even better work in mind for me. Then he got into his car and drove almost an hour to come and have coffee with me.

I was working at that company again in Oakland. Just like my previous work, my colleagues would come to say hello to me and tell me how much they enjoyed working with me before and how much they liked to work with me again. My project at that

Copyright © 2008 - 2009 Razban Internet International, Inc. All rights reserved, File:20091022, P a g e | **173**

company had been very successful. In addition, we had a lot of fun doing that work. More importantly, however, we had done an excellent job for the company in almost record time, and three percent below the original budget (this was unheard of at the time). I have boasted about a multi-million dollar invention that I agreed to give the rights to HP and National, and I gave it with love.

The saddest thing is that an invention several times bigger than the one I had made for HP and National hit me between the eyes. I tried to get the attention of the company that had terminated or "at willed" me and failed. I could have done so much more for them, had there not been a bad report and a sudden parting of the ways.

The invention that came after I was working for a startup and almost a year later would have had a huge impact in the market place. I started to write it down and get a patent for it. However, getting patents cost a good deal of money that I did not have. This new invention would have had a global impact and would have helped that company a great deal.

In their thinking, they had hired me with the idea that they could let me go any time they wanted. This idea behind "At will employment contracts." The fact that this had serious financial consequences for both of us did not even come into their thinking.

What I find stupid is that some companies who have the dreaded "At will" clause, choose to subject the poor "At willed" employee to ridicule and verbal abuse and other unethical or even illegal behavior.

For God's sake, you are telling somebody that he or she lost the job because it is as per contract due to *at will*. Just say thanks and make it an amicable parting of the ways.

In one very bad case of this insanity, an employee was told that he had never fit in, he never figured out how things were done at that company, and that he would have problems finding jobs anywhere. He took this to heart and did not even look for a job for some time. Then, one day, he found out about a job just five minutes from his home. He applied and got the job. After a few months, his manager who was a decent and caring manager told him that he had done great and that they had decided to increase his salary. Sitting across the table from his manager and in a total disbelief he finally lifted his head and said, "Sorry, the same thing happened in my last job. I do not know why I cannot keep my jobs. I guess my old manager was right. When is the last day? Is there any severance pay?" The ten-minute praise had fallen upon his deaf ears. It turned out that the manager patiently explained things again, and this time he really heard it. However, the shock of that brutal experience in previous company had done serious damage that took the next manager who was caring and experienced several months to fix. He is now a happy man. He is very active in his church and he helps those unfortunate people who lose their jobs.

Toxic work environments do more damage than just layoffs and firings.

Copyright © 2008 - 2009 Razban Internet International, Inc. All rights reserved, File:20091022,

CHAPTER 72:   Fear of Sudden Loss and Music

We know that what makes music is the silence between the notes. In fact, in addition to the notes, the silence in between and the pauses, is what makes music, music! I have noticed that after repetitions, I wonder if the song is over. In addition, when a few next notes are played, then I am joyful that this song is not over yet, especially if it is one of my favorites.

Let us look at this in another way. Fear of sudden loss is a bad thing. Yet, when it is used in an anticipatory way, as in music, it can be great. This is very similar to my experience from childhood to take anger and make it into something good and productive. Do the best that you can do each day, and put the fear into good use as they do in music by the silence between the notes.

Let us build on this argument. Our lives are like a symphony. Sometimes, bad things happen. However, that symphony does not need to be lost. In fact, Barry Manilou has a song about this. The song says take a bad song and make it into a good one. So, what if you were fired, or were the "affected" one in a layoff, or you are in a dead-end job, or you are underemployed, or you work for an idiot (in fact, there is book with the title of *How to Work for an Idiot*), what matters is how to take this bad situation and make into a great one. We are not alone in this. Many of us are stuck and are slammed in the revolving door hire fire that has resulted from a deep and long-term management crisis. A book that really talked about this work place insanity has the title of "Working with You is Killing Me: Freeing Yourself from Emotional Traps at Work ". I had the privilege of talking to one of the authors of this book. She was most helpful and gracious. Ironically, it was a short time after that discussion that the SiPort violence took place. Think of this job situation as a sort of slavery. It was not your fault. A friend was fond of saying, "pain is not optional, since bad things do happen in life, but suffering is." I strongly agree with him. By planning and working on finding the next job, we can shed this chain of slavery and have a better work life. Remember that we are CEOs of our own life and our career. We can survive the toxic work place. I hope that executives and CEOs who hire us try do better in using Human Capital and Knowledge. America means better small and major businesses, happier work places, and win-win for all involved. We shall survive and succeed!

Let me share a sure fire secret. Being the best of the best company and/or employee takes a lot less effort and costs less and at the same time it saves a lot of grief and money. Let us think of an action plan out of this mess!

CHAPTER 73:   The Jewish Passover Holiday and Christian Easter

This is a Jewish and Christian Holliday that celebrates the passage of Jews from slavery in Egypt to freedom in the Land of Israel. In practice, there is a lot of preparation that takes place in advance to celebrate this. Seder, as the Celebration night is called, is very interesting. In fact, the meaning of the word "Seder" in Hebrew is "order." Therefore, things are good when things are in order.

We can use some of these ideas to get your career back in order! One day, I had to work very hard on a dead-end project. The project was a mistake from the beginning, but that day, I had to work very late to prove something that no one would believe. My own manager himself was also frustrated. He knew what I was thinking, and I am sure that is how he agreed with me to do this.

I slaved over this project all weekend. I was even given the help of one of the best business analysts. Moreover, we finished it some time on Monday. That Sunday, I literally passed out on the couch in front of my TV.

Just like the Jews in Egypt, it is sometimes easier for us to slave and even destroy ourselves in a job we have rather than get ready to move on. I felt desperate. My wife and daughter were away on a family visit and I was alone. I tried the best I could week after week. I felt stuck. In addition, each time I got a nasty e-mail or some undeserved criticism, I internalized it. Then one day, I started to plan my escape and freedom!

I made a list of my contacts. I started contacting them. I updated my resume. Shortly after the first resume was out, I started to feel empowered. My simple plan consisted of calling certain friends and companies and to send resumes. Each day, I would have things listed to do. At the end of day, I would check to make sure I had done what I had planned to do for that day. I still had to work like a slave, but now I felt a sort of freedom. The first interview went badly because I was out f practice. The second interview was not much better, either, but I was refining my interview skills. After the fifth interview, I had one job!

This is very similar to freedom from slavery so symbolic to Christians and Jews. In Islam, there are similar Eids (Festivals) that involve elaborate planning and preparations that results in celebration. The same is also true in Hindu Festivals such as Devali.

Of course, Easter is the most profound symbol of such celebrations in Christianity. It is just ironic that this book comes out very close to Persian New Year Festivities, Easter, and Passover. All of these very near the time when days and nights become of the same length at the beginning of the spring.

However, a closer look at these festivals shows that there first has to be some sort of preparation. This is exactly like the job and life situation. We need to plan and prepare for the celebration and freedom. We need to update our resumes. We need to keep looking to see what jobs are available there. We need to make many networking calls. We need to go to screening interviews, and then follow-up interviews. Then, there is the joyous celebration of freedom. In addition, it will not need to be an extravagant expense. One of the best celebrations I had was to enjoy eating a big Mac sandwich right after coming out of my last final exam for that semester. My brother was kind enough to go the nearest MacDonald's, get them, and bring them to Memorial Library. Alternatively, it was when my sister insisted that I had to take one day off and go enjoy a good movie or something since I had stayed in the hospital too much when our mother was ill. Or it was the going

Copyright © 2008 - 2009 Razban Internet International, Inc. All rights reserved, File:20091022, P a g e | **176**

away lunch that my PG&E colleagues gave me while I was leaving PG&E after completion of my contract with them. I have formed a life-long friendship. Or, it was the going away party orchestrated by one of the best Graphic Artists on my assignment with HP in the form a surprise party at a Starbucks across the street. I had planned my next gig very carefully and I had made sure that no bridges were burned in the process and they were more than glad to help me enjoy the transition. Companies come and go, but working relationships between co-workers is forever.

One last example will help to illustrate this idea. I am sure that you have had airline flights. I hope that you have noticed that before you board a flight, the flight crew on the ground and in the aircraft, have to follow a plan with many checklists to make sure you have a safe and enjoyable flight. The aircraft has to be fueled. The pilot has to do a walk around to make sure all is well with the aircraft structure, the supplies, and food has to be brought in. In addition, a lot of this might have taken place a day or so before, you even got ready to drive to the airport. Then the celebration of flight took place. That celebration of flight would have never happened, had it not been for the preparation that went on beforehand.

Let us take slavery chains off from your work, career, soul, and life and plan for the freedom flight celebration from the present mess.

CHAPTER 74:   Let's Start with a Work Inventory

Make a list of all the jobs you have had in the past. Start with summer jobs and try to make sure you make as a complete list as you can. Then, make two columns. Make one for the good things about those jobs, and the other the bad things. I owe this to my best friend and lifetime management and life coach, Jerry Wiener. He has also given ma a five star review of this book. To start this inventory, you could write something like this:

Acme Job:
- Good things:
    - A lot of on-the-job training.
    - Excellent salary.
    - Good location.
    - Worked for an excellent manager who helped me learn practical aspects of my job.
- Bad things:
    - The job was too demanding.
    - Promotions were difficult to get.

This does not have to be done in one day. This is an evolving list and the more details you add to this list will help you better understand. With better understanding, you can make much better decision on what you want to do with your job and career. Look for patterns. If you see that most jobs you had were boring, you might spend a bit of time discovering what your experience was with those jobs.

As you work on this, start working on your network. Some social-networking groups like LinkedIn.com, Twitter, and FaceBook.com make networking a lot easier. I am in Twitter as BehrouzR, and use my real name in LinkedIn.com. Plan to spend thirty minutes or one hour each day and just look at the list of your previous colleagues and friends. Remember to ask for help and advice and not for jobs. Ask them if they know of a company that is hiring people like you. Ask them if they know a good recruiter. Ask them if they want to meet for drinks after work.

After the inventory, start to "design" your perfect job. What should the title be? What should the responsibilities be? Who should your manager be, as if you have perfect control over everything. This is important. When I did mine, I started to realize that I had gone from one area of specialty to another based on what was available without regards for my own passion, and interest. A vicious cycle of dead-end job after another repeated itself. I accepted the first one that came along since I was desperate. Interestingly enough, after I had done my own inventory, I was getting better chances at the jobs that I liked.

Practice a mock interview with a colleague, friend, or even family members. Start pretending that you are the interviewer and the same time the candidate that is looking for a job. Ask tough questions, but make sure they are fair. Moreover, keep in mind that you can only ask questions that other interviewers had asked you in an interview.

You can practice this while you drive or while you are parked and waiting for the kids to get out of classroom. If something does not make sense, since you asked yourself a stupid question, or you gave yourself a stupid answer, ask a friend or colleague to help with advice. You will be surprised how helpful this can be.

Then, pretend for a few hours that you had gotten the job and that some major TV station

Copyright © 2008 - 2009 Razban Internet International, Inc. All rights reserved, File:20091022. P a g e | **178**

is interviewing you for your success in finding this job. Ask yourself questions as if you are on national TV and, in return, boast and have fun. It is amazing how powerful the mind's eye can be in seeing the success that might have been very elusive to you all these times. Pretend you are a big shot, boast, and rejoice! The more convincing the interview is, after you have gotten the pretend job offer, the more helpful it will be for you.

I had made a practice of making sure that I called five colleagues and friends each week. I had their names and phone numbers programmed into my Blackberry and it never failed me. Each call either teaches me something new about my kind of work or tells me about somebody who knows somebody who is offering. Even if they do not know anything that can help you, the time spent on a phone call helps a great deal in keeping you relaxed and prevents you from internalizing the impact of a layoff. These colleagues still see you as the good man or good woman that you used to be. Besides you are that very same good man or woman, whether you have a job or not! Some old colleagues become an excellent cheering section. They understand what you are going through and they encourage you. Never underestimate peer support and help which is just as powerful as peer pressure. Some of my colleagues have written excellent books on the process detailing every step of recovery or how to find a job. Many of those books are fine too. They help finding a better job or just the next job. However, in my opinion, there is just no magic bullet. Here is a summary of steps needed:

- Take inventory, as you are doing here.
- Set a plan of action that details how many phone calls a day you will make, how many resumes you will send out, and where to find former colleagues for that essential Networking.
- Network, network, network.
- Communicate, communicate, Communicate.
- Follow up, follow up, follow up.
- Check the progress as per your plan; get advice and then repeat as needed.

Let us go back to the inventory. Make a list of why you left each company. This helps you feel better. After all, most people have quit some companies, which had proven to be the right thing even after a long time working there. In addition to making you feel better, this inventory might very well help you find trends. Trends that you could not see them when you were there and then busy working. Now when you sit back and look at the entire work inventory some patterns pop up right in our faces.

In my case, I went from one bad job to another. The vicious cycle in my case was that I did not look for my next job while I was working to have some potential backup plans. When I finished a contract, or lost a job, I would panic and get the first job that came around. I would do this regardless of how awful I felt about the job. I had to get the first one that came by. Other people find out that they had repeated a 6-month worth of learning and experience for more than 20 years. In other word, in 6 months they could have learned everything there was about a job. Then, they repeated the cycle repeatedly limiting their total learning to a net six months. Sadly, most of these people have a hard time, even during good economic times, in finding a good job.

Go over the list with a caring friend, a colleague, or even your spouse. Make sure to tell them that you are looking for positive, constructive advice!

CHAPTER 75:   Networking can Cure Not Working!

Take a look at classified ads in newspapers or places such as Monster.com, jobs.com, hotjobs.com, and Dice.com on the Internet. The sheer number of jobs might overwhelm you. Yet it is a popular belief that only seven to ten percent of jobs are from classified ads or internet job boards. Networking finds the majority of jobs.

Make a list of all the people you know. Family, friends, colleagues, even people you bumped into at a seminar, or those who take their kids to the same school, or those who shop in the same stores as you, the taxi driver who took you to the airport. Look at FaceBook.com, LinkedIn.com, Dice.com, Monster.com, and other places to find the list. Then force yourself to make ten to twenty calls a day. Do not ask for a job or money!

How would you feel if you got a phone call from a friend who said that he does not have much money left and needs a job desperately, and he asks you if you can find him a job, or worse yet, lend him money? I have received, and I have made such calls to no avail. In fact, I have lost some really good friends this way. A networking call is like to trying to rekindle a friendship or just get advice.

For example, I got a call the other day from a colleague from some years ago. He said hello and talked about the good old days and the good old job we had. He asked how I was doing and where I was working. Then, very politely, he said that his current contract would be ending in a month, and he wondered if I could advise him about any openings in my company. Usually, they also might ask if I know a good recruiter that had helped me get my present job with that company.

By the way, most networking calls do not help in the first and only one call. Usually, it might be two or three before the other person can think of a job or a referral to somebody else. For example, someone might say, "sorry, I cannot help, but the company across the street seems to be hiring like crazy." Alternatively, the advice could be not to waste your time with such a company. They interview many people but they do not hire, etc.

Sometimes, during the course of the networking call, the other party might ask for something from you. This is an excellent opportunity to give you a segue way to the next networking opportunity. For example, you might be talking about the latest book you read, and they might ask for the author's name or the exact title. Promise to get it for them and call them the next time with this information.

I usually get a notebook and write a summary of each networking call, and create action items for the next call.

Copyright © 2008 - 2009 Razban Internet International, Inc. All rights reserved, File:20091022, P a g e | 180

CHAPTER 76:   The Right Resume for the Job

The job of a resume is to get your foot in the door, nothing more and nothing less. The average manager spends a minute and a half reading your resume. That is it! Find a job that you really like and then make a custom-made resume for it. Make sure that if someone looked only at your resume, he/she could write down in detail the job you had applied for. In my experience, it takes about two to four hours to do justice to a resume that is supposed to get you the job you like. I make sure that the important things are reflected and highlighted in the summary, in the body of experience and in the cover letter. You should answer the question why they should hire you, and then make it easy for them to find this in your resume. I have yet to find somebody who really likes writing resumes.

Over the years, I have learned that the best way is to look for three classes of job opportunities in parallel in your job search. Here are the classes:

- In the first class, I find the jobs that I really like to do, they are a good fit, and I am qualified for them. I customize my resume for this class. Spend the time needed to do a good, but not perfect, resume.
- The second class is jobs that are not as good as the first class, but they are still a kind of fit. I spend a half hour to an hour and prepare a good resume to send to them. Depending on the job, I might even spend less.
- The third class is the one that I just send my "vanilla resume." This is where I send my resume without spending more than a few minutes for just a sanity check.

Many hiring managers like me have learned to grab the most important parts of a resume in ten to twenty seconds, or at most two or three minutes. You would do the same if you had to review hundreds of resumes for a single job offer.

There is one common pitfall to be careful about. Only seven to ten percent of jobs are found by sending "blind" resumes via internet job sites like career.com, jobfox.com, dice.com, monster.com, and bajobs.com.

Two thirds of jobs were obtained by networking. This is why networking is vitally important.

Also, note that networking is a two-way street. When you network, others will network with you too. I have found many of my assignments when someone called to tell me that they were going for an interview with some specific company for a job that was different than what I was looking for. They wanted a reference. In return, they gave me the name of the recruiter. In addition, the recruiter was able to find me a job as well. Remember that a resume is just to get your foot in the door.

Please view my "Networking Beats Notworking!" in www.youtube.com in "Layoffs & Hope".

CHAPTER 77:   Sometimes You Can Create Your Own New Job!

Sometimes, the manager does not even know what they want and why they need to hire someone like you. This is what I have done several times, and I can testify that it works. On one occasion, I had taken my car for repair to the dealer. The service manager was called in as they discovered that the repair would have to be major and costly.

I noticed that he was very upset about the fact that their computers were down for about thirty minutes. I told him that I had experience with computers. I asked him if I could help. He explained the problem and mentioned that they used to have a computer person before. However, he had left and they had decided not to hire a new one because it would cost too much.

As I started to look at his problem, I realized that it was a relatively simple thing to solve. I advised him on how to fix the problem. He followed my advice and, bingo, the computers were up and working.

He asked me to go with him to see the general manager in that dealership. Service Manager made a case for needing another "Computer Person" liked they used to have. He made a list all the problems they have had in the last month with computers. Then he left the room and asked me to talk to the General Manager. He had a lot of experience and was well educated. He inherited a dealership that had serious problems and he had improved it immensely. He was a fatherly figure and a caring drill sergeant. He told me that he agreed with his service manager. Then he asked about my qualifications. His main concern was whether I will be happy with a job like this. My honest answer to him was that I was a car enthusiast and I could improve their computer operation. Then I gave my word to him that I will work there for as long as he wanted me. He offered to buy me a Coke from the vending machine. Then he asked me if I could sign a contract for a minimum of three months. I agreed. In return, he offered to teach me sales. I did not think as much about learning at the time since I was financially desperate. I started to work there, for forty percent less salary the next day. It was a survival job. It did not make me rich, but I had something. This is a lot better than so many of my good colleagues who were going without a job.

As I did more and more for them, my salary was increased. Soon, I could find another job in the mainstream with my usual salary. I stayed there about five months. Before I went to finalize my next job, I had a nice talk with the General Manager and the Service Manager and made sure that I had their blessings to leave. I did not burn any bridges when I left. I gave them enough time to find a replacement and made sure my replacement was well trained.

This was shortly after the dot-com bust of the year 2000. To this day, I am very proud of having created a job for myself. To validate this, I have a friend and colleague of many years who went through a tough time when he lost his job. He could not accept that he was let go in spite his outstanding contribution. I went to personally meet him. I told him about my book and the Fear of Sudden Job Loss. I explained all other pains that I have suffered myself, and have seen others suffer. Nevertheless, he needed some time to catch his breath, some time to re-charge his batteries.

Then he created his own job, by working literally free for a friend and colleague in some startup that desperately needed help but could not pay. Right after funding, he was hired as corporate executive! I am very happy for him! He had the song in his heart, kept

Copyright © 2008 - 2009 Razban Internet International, Inc. All rights reserved, File:20091022, P a g e | **182**

working at improving himself, and did networking to beat "notworking". He is elated now.

In fact, later on, I learned that I could even start a company for myself, and I did that too.

Copyright © 2008 - 2009 Razban Internet International, Inc. All rights reserved, File:20091022, P a g e | **183**

CHAPTER 78:   Always, Always, Give Everyone Hope

My father was the section chief for a children's hospital that treated the poorest of the poor in the most destitute section of Teheran, Iran. People did not have enough money to put food on their tables or clothes on the backs of their children. The hospital was a charity hospital, sort of like the Saint Jude Hospital that would provide free treatment for the needy.
I would go to my Dad's work place for a visit once in a while. In each visit, I could see the pride and joy in my father's face. My Dad, the "Jewish Doctor" as he was affectionately called there, would give about two hours of his day to the hospital and get paid almost minimum wages. The money he got was enough to pay for his taxi fare and uniforms. Yet, it seemed that his day was designed to revolve around these two hours. He seemed to reserve his energy especially for this part of his tiring day. In addition, he did indeed need to have lots of energy for this task. On my visits, or my "going to work with Dad days," we would enter the building from the rear door. We could not enter from the main entrance, as there would be crowds that had waited from four or five that morning. Since the rumor had gotten around that the "The Jewish doctor had a healing hand and a big heart," patients would flock to this hospital during his shift. Some would wait for hours just for my Dad.
He had his white doctor's uniform that was especially tailored by an Armenian (Greek Orthodox Christian Sect) especially for him and patterned after the uniform that French doctors would wear in Paris. They used a material that was not that elegant so they could keep the costs down. The tailor would take pride in saying that his "sewing skills had made even the most mundane material come to life in this uniform," the same way my father "brought his dying son back to life."
Iranians, sort of like Europeans, love formalities. Each time my dad would pick up his new uniform, there would be about fifteen minutes of formalities. The tailor would say that he did not need to get paid since the pleasure of making this uniform and competing with the best French tailors was enough. My Dad would chime in that indeed the uniform looked just like what they had in Paris. However, my Dad would add that he insisted on paying. In fact, my Dad's uniform looked a lot better than other Doctors in that hospital.
My dad was very sensitive to the fact that he had lost his own dad when he was four years old, and he would remember that he and his family could not afford to go to a doctor when they would get sick. This made him determined not to let this happen to others. In fact, this had given him a passion and a mission. He would tell me that in that hospital, he would feel like a king and he would not give that job up for all the gold in this world.
I would also hear that the patients especially liked him because, not only his medications were effective, but almost as importantly, he would give them hope. Of course, at the time of the first visit, those were just words, but when they came back and testified that, their kid was getting better and better each day, then that was worth a lot to him. He used to say that, unfortunately, many medicines are much too costly. However, hope, he would add, is always free and can be quite effective. Of course, you must take the medicine, but do not forget that the combination of the medicine is highly potent.
I also remember another story that I will never forget. One day, when we lived in the South of Iran, my Dad had to go to a village to treat a very sick and hopeless kid. He had

a driver and an American-made Jeep at his disposal. That "rugged and well-made Jeep that only Americans knew how to make" had served him well. Many villages around where we lived had treacherous and narrow mountain roads that made driving almost impossible. Yet that part of the country has mesmerizing views of valleys and meadows and little brooks and tiny waterfalls. We woke up at 4:00 AM sharp to muffled, cranky, an intermittent, mechanical alarm clock that my Dad had had for many years. It was a bit rusted, but it did the job. It was not too accurate and my Dad was the only who could tell what the exact time was by looking at the alarm clock. He could figure out the additional minutes that he had to add to get the accurate time.

We hopped on the Jeep and soon we were climbing rugged mountains to get to the village with the sick kid. The kid was so sick that he looked just like those Jewish kids who were in the Nazi concentration camps. His bones were protruding from his bare skin. He had stopped talking. In addition, his mother was holding this kid in her lap. After seeing this, my Dad asked me to leave the room since I was very sad and shaken to see this. Of course, even though his family was not so bad off, this kid had not been able to keep any food down for more than seventy-two hours. I could still hear what they were saying. In a very assuring voice, my Dad repeatedly emphasized to them that he had seen hundreds of kids in similar shape and they almost all recovered. They all had to take the medicine and, just as important, have faith and have hope. It had taken us two hours to go there, so we had to hurry back before dark. I still remember those breath-taking views near Khoram-Abad, Dezful, Lorrestan, and Kurdestan. However, more importantly, the kid did survive and get well.

I know that the following paragraphs will sound arrogant. So I ask for your forgiveness in advance. I too have found that I have super-natural healing powers! I have found that my words as a manager, or CEO, or just a nobody sitting next to someone at the lunch counter, or on the train, or the shuttle, or airplane, cause miracles. I feel uplifted and feel as heavenly as possible for a mortal human when this happens. This heavenly power is so potent that it amazes me every time.

Hope is crucial to our lives. One day, out of total frustration I went to have lunch with a friend. We are two totally different people. However, we respect each other. In addition, being so different, I thought that he might have some hint or advice that I have overlooked that might help me. At that time, I had just successfully completed one assignment and was looking for the next. He cared and did not like to see someone as frustrated as I was. Therefore, he told me that my ideas of starting a new company would not succeed since Venture Capitalists only give money to twenty to thirty year olds. In addition, with all my technical experience, I will not be able to get a job in a technical area either, since they only hire those younger than thirty. As for writing a book, he would not do it because there is no money in publishing a book besides it takes a lot of effort to write a book. He assured me that I would not be able to complete the book since he himself had not succeeded in the several times that he had tried.

He had closed every door that I might have considered a path to hope. He did not mean to hurt me, but telling me these things did indeed hurt a great deal. On the way home, the car in front of me had a bumper sticker that said, "My boss is a Jewish carpenter!" Somehow, I came back to life. I turned on the radio in my car to some good uplifting music and cherished this moment. I do not believe in coincidences. I believe that God who rules this universe does everything for a reason. This bumper sticker was exactly what I needed to see right at that time. I was inspired and full of hope again! This is another proof why hope is so important.

When my boss had been suddenly, and for no reason fired, and was putting his office stuff in a box and taking them to his car, my words that he would find something better soon was all he needed. Although they had taken all his power and authority away from him, just like having taken General Patten's uniform and stars away from him, his face started to glow with a smile, yet very angry. I told him how good he was and how much I enjoyed working for him. He told me that I need not be nice to him any more since he was not my boss any more. However, when I told him that I meant those words and I would guarantee them, he seemed to forget his rage and disbelief in what had happened to him after serving that company for twenty years. I offered to be his reference. I told him about another company that might hire him. I offered hope and that made this person's life better. Those who keep the hope alive can always expect a miracle. I have seen miracles in my working life as well as others happen, because we did not give up hope.

If we are in a dead-end job, we prepared the Seder for the Festival of freedom and liberation from the slavery and bondage of that miserable job. If we are unemployed, we planned for that Easter festival of finding a better job, with a better manager that better suited our talents. In all these cases, hope is the foundation.

Again, forgive me for my arrogance, but please read the next paragraphs carefully and agree to put them to an open-minded test.

You too have the same heavenly miraculous healing powers that I "uniquely" own, and even yours might be more powerful. The thing is that I have more practice, and I have strong faith in them. You can do even better than I can. Just make sure that you always give everyone you meet hope! Also, remember that right now the most important person to give hope to is indeed you.

Hope helps us resist disabling fears and helps us persist in our planning and work on finding success in anything we are trying to get. Hope is like oxygen that brings life to us each minute and second of the day.

Copyright © 2008 - 2009 Razban Internet International, Inc. All rights reserved, File:20091022, P a g e | **186**

Chapter 79:   Hawthorne effect

From Wikipedia, the free encyclopedia

The **Hawthorne effect** is a form of <u>reactivity</u>, and describes a temporary change of behavior or performance in response to a change in the environmental conditions, with the response being typically an improvement. The term was coined in 1955 by Henry A. Landsberger[1] when analyzing older experiments from 1924-1932 at the <u>Hawthorne Works</u> (outside Chicago). Landsberger defined the *Hawthorne effect* as:

- A short-term improvement caused by observing worker performance.

- Also, if the workers trust that they will succeed, they will succeed.

Earlier researchers had concluded the short-term improvement was caused by teamwork when workers saw themselves as part of a study group or team. Others have broadened the definition to mean that people's behavior and performance change following any new or increased attention. Hence, the term *Hawthorne effect* no longer has a specific definition.

The Hawthorne studies have had a dramatic effect on management in organizations and how people react to different situations. Although illumination research of workplace lighting formed the basis of the Hawthorne effect, other changes such as maintaining clean work stations, clearing floors of obstacles, and even relocating workstations resulted in increased productivity for short periods of time. Thus the term is used to identify any type of short-lived increase in productivity. In short, people will be more productive when appreciated or when watched.

Here are my additional notes:
- Please note that these experiments were done during the depression years. This adds even more credibility to their finds.
- This experiment which is taught as an important part of each Organization Behavior or management class also strongly establishes the important of Mutual Trust and Loyalty (MTL) that is discussed in this book. Workers Trusted Management and Management Trusted employees in this experiment. They were Mutually Loyal to each other to do common good. They wanted to make work place better for themselves and others.
- What is left out in this article is that they measured the results each day and they increased the lighting each day to observe higher productivity.
- Then some smart aleck management consultant like myself quietly told them that if your theory that more lighting creates more productivity, then the reverse should also be true. Let's reduce the lighting and see if the productivity will also go down proportionally!
- They did! But productivity continued to go up as it had gone up in the previous day!
- This proves the MTL power. If employees, management, and customers which are the Human Capital of the new Capitalism have MTL they produce more!

Copyright © 2008 - 2009 Razban Internet International, Inc. All rights reserved, File:20091022, P a g e | **187**

CHAPTER 80:   Jurassic Park and Corporate Dinosaurs

When the economy went sour in 1996, and I was left without a job, I realized that small and medium-size companies fuel the American economy. I started my one-person company, Razban Internet International, Inc. Estimates then indicated that some 80% of employment was done by small to medium sized companies. At that point, I started to think that major corporations were either on the path to extinction, of they really had to change their ways. The 2008 Global Financial Crisis is an indication that a change is needed. Strategy and operations of many big corporations had to change. Bank failures or airlines that are in trouble is based mainly on the fact that they are simply much too big to be manageable. Corporation bigness that builds customer confidence is now doing the opposite. Small community-based banks are sprouting up where major banks and corporations used to be. In fact, they are using the same buildings that major corporations had to vacate. Many of major corporations act and look like "Holdupniks" which is Yiddish for having a penchant for robbing – holding up – people. Unless a global corporation learns to act locally, customer centered, and responsible, they will go out of business with or without government bailout money.
United Airlines, the airline of my admired hero Bob Sampson, is one of those dinosaurs. Bob Sampson for many years brought in a big donation check for Jerry Lewis's Muscular Dystrophy (MD) charity TV program. Bob was on a wheelchair and a source of inspiration for viewers. I love this airline along with Southwest, Singapore Airlines, El Al, British Airways, Virgin Atlantic, and JetBlue.
I have had many, many trips on United Airlines and others listed above. Nevertheless, as of this writing, United is in trouble. It is much too big of an airline. These bigger corporations must do something to survive. Otherwise, we will continue to have problems. However, the more important thing is that smaller companies generate most of the jobs and income. In addition, you can start a small business much more easily than a bigger one.
Small companies are resilient and agile. They can change direction quickly. They can offer service that is more personal. By their nature, they are a lot closer to their customer base and community than dinosaurs of the industry. Mutual Trust and Loyalty (MTL) permeates and thrives in a small business. Customer complaints, for example, get a lot more attention in a small business than a huge company. A better one in a matter of days replaces a bad product. A small company has to be more loyal to their customers.
In the airline business, the smaller ones are companies that are more profitable. They more resemble small business mentality. Sir Richard Branson's Virgin Atlantic Airline and Southwest are excellent examples of this. I do admit that there are some successful bigger companies too. However, a bigger company does not provide a more stable or more secure job. These big companies sometimes lay off employees much more frequently than their smaller counterparts did. We have learned that the only job security is in our refined, marketable skill set.
There is a serious analogy here between these huge companies and computers. In the sixties, IBM had mainframes. These were gigantic computers, like the IBM 360, that would occupy the entire huge floor space. Then there were personal computers and now there are palmtop computing devices. Some of the present day palmtop devices are almost as powerful as that IBM 360. Those IBM 360s are no longer in much demand.

Copyright © 2000 - 2009 Razban Internet International, Inc. All rights reserved, File:20091022, P a g e | **188**

The same holds true for giant corporations that have not learned to decentralize, build communities, deliver empowerment, and cultivate Mutual Trust and Loyalty for a distributed powerful work force to succeed in these difficult times.

Along the same lines, the golden age of all-powerful, yet isolated CEOs, who did not have a clue about how their company operated, or what it did and why. That was the command and control era similar to the IBM 360. Now, Agile, decentralized, customer-centered, community-minded, small to medium companies are the winners. Exactly two months after the first printing of my book, GM decided to declare bankruptcy. I must admit that some of the things that I had written in this book starting eight years ago were just thoughts at the time. However, when my predictions came to life, I was sad and scared.

Ever since the Blackberry and iPhone mega revolution, a more flat organization that can decide and operate almost independently has arrived! The concept of information available everywhere anytime will put the former corporation power in the hands of small to medium companies. Small, knowledgeable, and human-potential-based, innovative businesses will be even more powerful in the future.

Cottage industries using the "Virtually-organized, viral marketing," which is freely given to them via the Internet, will continue to take market share away from those stodgy and Old-fashioned dinosaurs that refuse to re-invent, innovate, and empower employees.

CHAPTER 81:   Do Not be a Serial Unemployed Person

After my Sudden Job Loss (SJL) and not agreeing to go back, I was unemployed for almost a year. This was partially because I was serially unemployed!

Here is how this works, or more accurately described, does not work. Each time, I focused on one job or one opportunity at a time. I went to the interview for that one job, and I would be excited and happy that finally this one would work. I would think that there would be a new job soon. I would think that I was finally going to be employed again.

I found a job ad, I sent a resume, and got an interview for the next week. Well, this meant two weeks went by. Then they took a week after the interview to decide. Soon, I discovered a month has gone by and no job offers. In one case, it seemed that I had found the ideal job for me. I got all excited about it. I updated my resume and studied as hard as I could for that one job. In addition, to be safe, I decided to put all my attention on that one job. I went all out. I stopped to look at other jobs.

It took a few weeks to set up an interview with the very busy hiring manager. He then took two weeks to decide whether he would invite me to the next interview. I was elated when I was invited to the second and even third interviews. In addition, two weeks after the second interview, I was notified that they had decided to withdraw that job. A two-month effort went down the drain! That is why, in my job search now, I make sure that I am pursuing at least four or five jobs at the same time in parallel. In other words, I am pursuing several jobs all at the same time. Then a week hurries by before I find out about the next opportunity, and another two or three weeks to not get yet another job offer. I have learned from experts in this field that we have to apply for three to six different jobs at a time. This is where my notebook that I use to keep track of different job applications becomes so handy.

If you go to www.Google.com, you will find as many sites that have something to do with jobs. Just a few general web sites help you send your resume to a great many different places that are hiring. The main ones are www.dice.com, www.craigslist.org, www.monster.com, www.bajobs.com, www.usajobs.gov (with a listing of all government jobs), www.jobfox.com, and another handful. The important thing is that when you become a member by getting a user name and password, each time you post your new resume on that site that triggers the attention of the web site to you.

There is usually a few days of lull, unless some recruiter or a hiring manager got super interested about your resume and decided to call right away. In general, it takes a few days before you will hear anything. Then in the next two weeks after that, different parties with different interests will either contact you by e-mail or call you. As I mentioned before, it is OK to give your cell phone number. You want to appear professional and eager to start a new job.

You must be ready to give them an "Elevator Pitch." An Elevator pitch is a three to five-minute quick summary of who you are, what is the most important set of your skills, and how they relate to a specific job (if you are pitching for a specific job), or in general. It should always showcase some of the most important accomplishments that you have had. It should start by saying: "Hello, I am 'so and so.' I have been an accountant for five years, I specialize in Tax accounting" (if that is the specific job you are going after), otherwise just leave it general. "I have done 'such and such' and produced 'such'

Copyright © 2008 - 2009 Razban Internet International, Inc. All rights reserved, File:20091022,

results." I usually end by saying I am eager for a better and more challenging opportunity. During the dot-com bust, there was a rule that for each ten-thousand dollars of the annual income you had to, on average, expect to be out of job for one month. Therefore, if you were making $110,000 per year, then you had to expect to be looking for jobs for eleven months. That was close to a year. In my experience, I dismiss such gloomy statistics. It all depends on how serious and self-confident you are about doing what it takes to find your next job. Time does not matter, and it is not a good indicator. It is again worth saying that the majority of jobs are at small businesses. This is especially true in the down market we are experiencing towards the end of 2008.While I am not going to discourage you from applying to IBM, or Boeing, or the big five accounting firms, I would like to encourage you to apply to small ones too. I think you will be pleasantly surprised to see the results.

I made sure that I avoided those Doom and Gloom Sayers and that helped me focus on the full-time job of finding a full-time job. You just cannot afford this kind of superstition. Who knows and who cares how much time it will take for you? Just do it! Take it one day or one hour at a time if you have to, but do it. The ideal situation will be to land written offers for multiple jobs so you have a choice. However, during a down economy, one might have to grab the first job that comes around.

Hey, let us face it, nothing is permanent. You cannot afford to wait for that ideal job to show up. As Dr. Seuss encourages kids in *Green Eggs and Ham*, just try a new job and see how it will go. A friend of mine was somewhat unhappy with her job. Therefore, she looked around and found another one. Then she convinced her then employer to give her six weeks time off without pay. During these six weeks she worked at the new place and, to her utter dismay, she discovered that the new place was nothing like what they had promised her during the recruiting. In fact, they had given her a bunch of lies about the workplace harmony and leisurely pace of work. Remember that "At Will" employment, which is usually to the employer's advantage, can also help you. Resign and walk out. In addition, if enough people did this, some companies that treat their employees brutally would learn to treat them better. However, she was very smart, she had not burned any bridges with the old company, and all she had to do was to notify them that she was coming back from her leave of absence.

This is the unfortunate reality of workplaces today. However, in the old days, we had dedicated HR departments that made sure the job and the candidate matched. They were good at explaining things so there would not be any surprises for anyone, and indeed, with that extra effort, they were able to make a good match. Well, I am sorry to say that was then, and now is now. We do not have this kind of luxury any more. The hiring process has become random and impersonal. This is one reason why we have such a mess. This explains why so many of us are unhappy with our jobs. Just why it is that companies cannot produce as well as they can.

One of the people, who had purchased my book, told me that this chapter is the story of his life. Each time he applies for a job, and each time he goes to interview he thinks this is this time really it! He stops applying for other jobs and puts all his eggs in this one basket. Time ticks away, a few weeks go by, or a month of two and one way or the other he does not get this job. Then he has to start from square one again, and again, and again. This is a $2.4 Trillion loss to our economy that has been going on for many years. Let me put this in perspective. If you stacked $1,000 dollar bills one on top of another, a million dollars would be about six inches tall. If you did the same with $1,000 dollar bills of a stack 350 feet high, then you would have a billion dollars (which is a $1,000,000,000.) Notice that the Washington Monument is about 450 feet tall. This illustration comes from a book with the title *A Billion Dollar War*. Now, for one trillion dollars, you have to have a stack of $1,000 dollar bills that is sixty-five miles high. What a grief Charlie Brown! However, this shows the price we are paying for people being unhappy and not productive when the workplace is dysfunctional, or when they are under-employed, or not employed, a sixty-five mile-high stack of $1,000 bills!

So keep on looking and hope to find that job that is the best for you. Be OK with even one that is the semi-best job for you. This is OK just for now! Unfortunately, based on my experience, you always need to be looking for your next job! Time Magazine in September predicted the same thing I have been saying. The nature of the employment has already changed. Reading this book is an excellent step in your career modernization. Who knows, maybe you will be as proud and happy as Michael Wimbeley of BBC News on TV that comes directly via satellite from London to our house. Michael starts the program by saying "Hello this is Mike Wimbley of BBC World News for America…" and then with a very proud sparkle in his eyes, he proudly continues…"And the Rest of the GLOBE." With his enthusiasm, he might as well say the Universe. He is so proud and so happy. He is proud and happy because he feels like he is working for the best of the best, and that he is the best of the best! This sparkle is very similar the same fire that was present in Cousin Brucie's voice at the height of his career with WCBS in New York City that was capable of setting our soul on fire. In both cases, this sparkle is something that genuine and nothing can be done to fake it. I myself have felt like this several times. In addition, no amount of money, or enticement would ever force me to be really happy and proud if I indeed was not. This was when my manager, in addition to providing guidance, was well respected and trusted by me and vice versa. My colleagues were my friends, and we were accomplishing outstanding results. It was a win-win. Everyone did his or her jobs as well as it were expected, or even a little better. Trade journal reporters would come to visit and interview us to write articles and we usually impressed them. I was never afraid of saying what was needed to say. In addition, even those times that my argument was just plain wrong, my colleagues politely helped me see what the problem was and they came to help. The person next to me went on a vacation and he felt so good about things that he brought us souvenirs. I cannot help it but it really was as if I was going to a party with friends and colleagues each day. Each day the team created some innovative, new great result. Another thing is that in some companies people like me, contractors and consultants are not trusted and not considered part of the real workers. However, in those excellent work places, everyone was part of the team and a lot of teamwork was going on. We were respected, and trusted, and in return, we did the other side of Mutual Trust and Loyalty.

Maybe in our next job, we all will be just as proud and happy as Mike. We too will smile and have a proud sparkle in our eyes.

Copyright © 2008 - 2009 Razban Internet International, Inc. All rights reserved, File:20091022, P a g e | **192**

CHAPTER 82:   Let's Go Find a Job, Together!

I was told thanks for my good and hard work, but the present consulting assignment would end on 12/19/08. As of this writing on 10/12/09, I still do not have a job! My manager is a good man, and I worked on an important project. Nonetheless, due to budgeting restrictions, my project and some others will have to be cancelled. My project was supposed to be a Mega project. A Mega project means that it will have many people working on it and for a longer duration.

Admittedly, this is the name of the game these days. There is not much job security even for a permanent employee these days. I know of quite a few people who went to work for the government thinking that have more security than the private sector who are worried about their jobs. I think it is a disgrace that teacher are laid off at the rate they are. As Petula Clark song says, this is the sign of the time.

It took me a half a day to get over the shock, even though I knew that this might happen a few weeks ago. Then I got organized. I took my latest resume, spent thirty minutes to add the latest information on it and posted it on Dice.com. I have relied on Dice.com for many years. For you, it might be Monster.com, CareerBuilder.com, Craigslist.org, or other ones. It took me about an hour to "post" my resume on Dice.com.

Then, during the lunch hour, I started to call recruiters that I have worked with before, colleagues, and friends to let them know that I was finishing my project and that I would be open to new projects, contracts, and/or full-time work. You do not have time to analyze things in detail at this time. You have to act and act quickly.

Now that I had posted my resume, I was in circulation. It was not just my clock that was ticking. It was the recruiters' clocks and hiring companies as well. A few e-mails and phone calls came in. I was flabbergasted, since I thought that, in such bad times, nobody would call. Nevertheless, I was pleasantly surprised since recruiters were calling. In addition, it was fun to find out what my colleagues, friends, and network had been doing. One guy had managed to get a full-time job that would have been ideal for me. This is the miracle of networking. He promised to check around and see if something like that was available for me.

Then I made a list of companies that I liked to work for and looked at their web sites. Sure enough, there were a few that were somewhat a fit, and a few that would have been dream jobs for me. The ones that were somewhat of a fit, I applied to right away. In this process, I do more for dream jobs. These jobs are worthy of more work. I composed a nice cover letter that explained why the job was a good fit for me and my skill set, and then it pointed out that I am highly qualified and interested in this job. This took about one hour per job.

Once I got the ball rolling this way, I gave my family and myself a break. I used our Frequent Flyer Mileage and Gold Passport points with Hyatt Regency to get a one-night stay in Sacramento, which is a three-hour train ride from where I live. The Amtrak train that goes from San Jose to Sacramento is nice. Inside, it is like an airplane. Conductors tend to be kind and nice to passengers. Service is as good as service used to be in the fifties.

This taking a day or more off to regroup is always effective. Take some time off to rejuvenate. Take some time off to regroup. Take some time off to say good-bye to what used to be, and fresh hopes to what is to be. Open a new chapter in your life book. Let

Copyright © 2008 - 2009 Razban Internet International, Inc. All rights reserved, File:20091022, P a g e | **193**

bygones be bygones. Even if for a few hours, get out of familiar surroundings. Give yourself a change of scenery and some fresh air.

That next Monday, my batteries were charged and I continued my job search. I had gotten a few more responses. I followed up on them. I called whichever companies that had a name and a phone number. I sent e-mail to the rest. Even though I had semi-blindly applied to one job, their show of interest encourages me to send them a better resume or to call them. I spent a bit more time to refine my resume and fine-tune it to accentuate what they were looking. I added more details on the related part of my experience.

A few jobs were outside the Bay Area. Unfortunately, I do not have the luxury of relocating at this time. Unfortunately, they are out. Nevertheless, I put together a nice e-mail response telling them how much I liked their job, but I indicated that I was only interested in the Bay Area. One sent an e-mail back with the name of their branch manager who was within walking distance from where I worked. This is how it works. Never give up. Keep asking and asking, and asking.

As disinterested as I was when I first heard about that one should never, ever give up, this old overused cliché rings a lot of truth now. These words have motivated me for a long, long time. I have more irons in the fire. I am seeing more accomplishments and more results. I do not have a job offer yet, but the anxiety has diminished a great deal now. I feel comfortable and hopeful.

I started to write down what my dream job, should I ever come across it, should look like: I need Director level job, in a good company, a good match for my skill set, a people-oriented manager with a style similar to mine. As for travel, it should be no more than twenty-five percent of the time. Due to my experience and background, I need a management job in Information Technology or Software Development.

Survey after survey says, and it has been my experience as well, that at least seventy percent of job satisfaction is dependent on your immediate manager. Therefore, I first indicated whom I wanted to work for.

Then, I have a bribe for myself. The bribe is that I will take about two days off after having found the new job and signed the contract to relax. I am thinking about going to a football game, car races, or playing golf.

I have also taken an hour to think about how much money I have in savings and where I might be able to borrow if I had to. Are you ready? I have about 2.8 weeks of reserves. After that, I have to borrow. Then, I have a best friend who has been helping me when I need a bit of cash for a few days or weeks.

The next thing is that I have prepared my notebook for writing down that I have contacted and keep track of follow-ups. This is very helpful. The biggest career hazard you face during unemployment is to lose track of things and not to be focused on the job of finding a job. Distractions are easily the biggest culprit in this. In my notebook, just like the workbooks I had while I was working, I have a page per day with the date on the top. It is very impressive when you call someone and say, "Remember, we talked on November 12th…." This helps you deliver a professional and organized image.

Surprisingly, these simple steps help you launch a professional and effective job search. This advice coming from veteran of thirty years of experience such as me might be valuable to you. This is valuable advice since it shows that someone with thirty years of experience, senior management consultant, and an executive coach does not know much more than you. These are all common sense ideas. There is no such a thing as a silver

Copyright © 2008 - 2009 Razban Internet International, Inc. All rights reserved, File:20091022. P a g e | **194**

bullet!

In any case, the important thing to keep in mind is that we need to apply and practice these ideas when we are most disappointed and vulnerable. The truth is that if you even take a baby step, you will feel a lot better and be able to take giant steps.

In this notebook, I also write down my feelings. Years ago, as a manager, as a friend, and even as a parent, I learned that we could not tell anyone how to feel about something. Feelings are extremely important at this point. We must respect your own feelings. Writing down about them is a way of being better in touch with them. After all, we are human beings and human beings have feelings. We are not like computers that have no feelings and are logic fixated! If you were not given the professional respect that you deserve during an interview, make a note of it in the notebook. Who knows, you might have multiple offers and you decide to compare two or more job offers that are almost equal in all aspects. Then, reading your notes about your hurt feelings, you know which interviewer treated you with the most respect. Interviews are two-way events. You interview them as much they interview you.

In my notebook, I have action items. A list of what needs to happen by a set time to find the next job. In a professional working environment, action items need to be:

- Specific, as in who is to do what, when, and how. Remember that action items can also be what others are supposed to do for you.
- Have a clear and measureable end result, such as sending twenty resumes on 12/15/08.
- Clearly understand if they depend on someone else, or something else.
- Do not worry be happy is not an action item! It is not specific. It does not have a deadline. It is also difficult for someone else to check to see if we are happy or not.

I have my support system. I have an excellent therapist, an uncle in Los Angeles who has been great with advice, our family friend in New York City, my best friends in Milwaukee, Madison, and my life coach. There are also many, many others too.

One of my colleagues just called, telling me that her job in the Midwest that was supposed to last a year, ended after five months and she would be driving back. This is not good news since she had considered permanent relocation, which was part of her contract.

In addition, one big piece of advice I offer is that you should never burn a bridge with your present (or any previous) company and never think they will not help you. Therefore, taking my own advice, I went to say farewell to the group director. He was very kind and sad that the funding had stopped. He also pointed out that since I was in good standing with his company, he would try his best to get another assignment for me the first chance that he got. I also had lunch with a friend who had a hardware store, and the present bad economy was just about killing his revenue. He was using the same networking idea that I had to find new customers. He printed flyers, and was thinking about advertisement. Granted that, his career and mine are considerably different. Nonetheless, we are in the same boat when it came to finding a new job. He needs to find more customers, and I need to apply to jobs, try to sell my book, and get a financial infusion into my company. He needed encouragement just as badly as I needed it. He also went to different stores that might need his products. He talked to their managers to see if they would buy some of his inventory if he gave then a discount.

Copyright © 2008 - 2009 Razban Internet International, Inc. All rights reserved, File:20091022, P a g e | **195**

On 12/17/08, which was only two days before my last day. I fell after slipping on the wet floor that was caused by rain. That made me somewhat depressed. There was some pain, but I decided to do what I considered ethical. If there were a broken bone, or a visible brose, then I would go to a doctor. However, I would not go to a doctor, or even think of suing, for minor pains and aches. A coworker told me that I should sue the building owners since I could make a case for negligence and make some money. Maybe, but we do not do these things!

As my last day of 12/19/08 got closer, several colleagues tried to find me a home so I could stay with the company a bit longer. While I looked for a job, they wanted to stretch my existing contract. In fact, the last two days were hectic. I "interviewed" with three potential hiring managers, and sent at least ten resumes out.

Then, as I had promised Shauna of BookSurge.com, I called her at 8:15 AM Pacific time to do the final book contract sign up. Most of the time, I do the honorable, and somewhat heroic, things I promise! I had invested my last dollar that day on this book, which has been my passion and dream for a long, long time to write. Understanding that I signed the book contract on my last day at that consulting gig, did take considerable courage. My great grandfather used to say, "Dare to dream and dream big". He used to say, "Luck is good to have, but courage is more useful."

On that Friday, my manager and my team gave me a farewell party. Then they briskly took care of formalities when an employee leaves. Leaving, I have to do. I felt sad, disappointed, and grateful at the same time. I could barely walk the four blocks that it took to the BART station to take the ride home.

In the last few days, a familiar pattern had emerged. I was suffering from physical exhaustion and sleep deprivation. Yes, I might be an experienced champion in having had to find many jobs during the last ten years, but still I am a human being. More accurately, I am a human being with an eating disorder. As stress sat in, on top of a four-hour commute each day, and my own fear of yet another job Sudden Job Loss, I started to substitute fatty, starchy, and salty food for lack of sleep, shame, and anger.

I went to a Greek restaurant and ordered two Gyros. Each Gyros is so rich that it must have 1,500 calories. The cashier tried to hide her disapproval, but I could see it and felt shame for it. Then, it was time to go to the coffee shop and order several cookies and a slice of carrot cake to take to my office for the last time. I made a cup of tea and poured more than half a cup of sugar in it.

Sudden Job Loss (SJL) is sort of like a death or an ugly divorce. I was saying goodbye to colleagues that had helped and supported me all along in this assignment. An excellent colleague, a fisherman in his previous life, made the last a lot more bearable. He had to be in real-life perfect storms in the North Sea to put bread on the table. When I asked him about that movie, he told me that events consistent with his experience. There is part of the movie that drowning is inevitable, but the individual who is involved has not realized it yet.

I am like that guy in the perfect storm. I broke my back and worked very hard for thirty years. I have $250,000 equity in house, but no bank is getting me a loan. I had to struggle to make arrangements not to get my wife's car repossessed. I get warning from my bank that I am default and the house will be foreclosed next month. Credit card companies are using whatever unethical methods they can to push me into bankruptcy. Nevertheless, bankruptcy is what I will not do. I still have my Mokato! Food stamps are also out of

Copyright © 2008 - 2009 Razban Internet International, Inc. All rights reserved, File:20091022.

question right now for the same reason. We have accumulated so many things in this house that a foreclosure will financially and emotionally wipe us out. What about all those memories? I hear my mother's cries that she misses her house in Teheran that she spent twenty-two years to decorate just right with the best of Persian carpets. I hear my Dad sobbing about missing that hospital and his fellow Doctors. He had a best friend fought in a war with him. My Dad knew that he was killed. His cousin had sent my Dad a short telegram that he had said his final goodbyes to my Dad the Jewish Doctor. He was devout Muslim who in my opinion needed to be buried with twenty-one gun salute. He served his country, Iran well.

As these memories were creating an emotional perfect storm in my mind, my friend kindly insisted that he had to buy me lunch on that last day. The lunch was my most favorite fish and rice with a slice of fresh lemon. I had had this many times. However, this time, it seemed like blood was curling in my throat. The food would just not go down. I would drink my Coke to see if I can get my appetite back again up to no avail. I am very impressed with this guy. He always calls his wife and daughter during his lunch. He knows a lot about music, as he is a multidimensional person with many interests. He read one of the early manuscripts and been extremely helpful and encouraging. He told me that he would have said many of the same things that I said in this book. He would tell me to be strong, and he would tell me that I am telling a story that needs to be told. Another colleague offered to make sure to read and review my book. Another one told me that reading the manuscripts had given her some thoughts that she wanted to discuss with me.

Another colleague put two one hundred bills in an envelope with a birthday card and gave it to me a few days before my 6oth birthday. I love the birthday card. Then I tried to give back the money. She would not take it back. "I will get insulted if you did not take it!" Use it to pay for editing your book. This is a gift. You are telling my story of heartfelt pains of toxic work. Do it! You owe it to yourself and us. Be our hero!

I will keep myself so busy with doing what I can humanly do so that I will not have time for shame, blame, or anger and frustration. This is very important. Just keep busy. I also need to increase my follow up attempts. I have made the list on an index card. When I got on my digital scale, as it has become a habit by now as part of my Empowered Weight Management (EWM), I realized that, based on facts, that the total damage was and will somewhat continue to be around 1.1 lbs. I plan to go to Subway for lunch. I have had to have two additional holes put in my belt since I have lost a lot of weight. I had no choice my totally worn out Blue Jeans was falling down. I must pay my mortgage, and the almost $2,000 monthly health-insurance premium. In addition, I must be grateful that bill collectors did not call, and are not calling. This had taken heroic acts just so I can stay a few steps ahead of them. In addition, even though I have only a cushion of 2.8 weeks in money reserves, I am going to dream and dream big! My mother used to say, "If you dream, you must dream big. It costs the same."

Will I ever see my dream of being CEO of a major corporation? If somehow I got it, would I be happy with being a CEO? I doubt it. Zumbification will kill me after having been a free agent for the last few years off and on. All that relationship building and teamwork that was carefully crafted to build Mutual Trust and Loyalty is now gone. The fact is that no one, absolutely no one can give us a shelter if we lost our house.

I got an e-mail from a coworker who had gone to Minnesota for what she had been

Copyright © 2008 - 2009 Razban Internet International, Inc. All rights reserved, File:20091022, P a g e | **197**

promised was a full-time, permanent job. Instead, she found out that the contract only lasted six months.

OK, enough of this!

I rested all of Saturday, and charged my batteries for Sunday, which happens to be the first day of the Jewish Hanukah. Hanukah is the festival of lights and is based on a miracle that had happened. Moreover, Hanukah started only four days before Christmas this year. Of course, the Kwanza Festival is just around the corner. All faiths say have faith and live in the light and not in the dark.

I will be spending Sunday for one final review of this book and make a practical plan of action for Monday. As part of this action, I will be calling several car dealers and former colleagues and friends to ask for advice. I will also respond to any job openings in Dice.com, and Monster.com.

The biggest problem is that distractions such as telephone and TV are extremely difficult to cope with when you are looking for a job. Remember, looking for a job is a full-time job in itself. This the same way that you could not take a half day away from work to talk about non-job related subjects, or chat with friends. You must not do it while you are looking for a job.

On this Monday, I was able to make about five job-search-related phone calls and send out ten resumes, as well as three very fine-tuned and directed resumes and cover letters to the jobs that I would be glad to have. Once I had fulfilled my job search obligations, then I responded to the e-mail from my publishers, BookSurge.com. The latter part of the afternoon would go towards follow-ups. I need to just send e-mails and/or call some of the job ads that indicated they were interested in me.

Jim Carey's movie *The Yes Man* has come up. I needed to cheer myself up, so, I got a chance to go see this. It is a good comedy and is entertaining. I especially liked the plot of the movie. I specially loved one of the lines that say, "Let life happen!" I am all for life happening. I am really looking forward to the publication of this book. This has been a passion for me for the last two or more years. I had never thought that I could write a book, and more importantly finish it. Of course, Shauna's encouragement and many e-mails were a major factor in getting serious about sending this book for publication. We hope that this book helps you cope, recover, and even do well with the economic Armageddon that is consuming our lives at this point.

On Tuesday, as I was shaving and looking at my face in the mirror, I realized my own advice is very true. The person in the mirror was exactly the same human being on Tuesday after two days of being jobless as it was on Friday, while I was still employed. More refreshingly and encouraging, I felt somewhat freer. I had rested more. I did not have to get up at 4:30 AM, as I had to do all these years to commute to San Francisco or Oakland. I had more energy. I seemed to be more alive. It seems that I had gained a freedom in return for a paycheck. The clouds were vanishing from mind, and I was a thinking human being again. There was the light of clarity. Of course, the bill collectors would not let me forget that I must have that paycheck!

It is important to note that I fight for my rights. I will fight for the fact that I am taking Wednesday (Christmas Eve) and Friday (Christmas Day) as two days off from unemployment, as unpaid, unemployed, holiday time. I will do the same with New Year's Eve, and New Year's Day. I may not be rich, but I have rights! I saw a very heart-warming article in the *San Francisco Chronicle* today. "Helping the Dismissed Find

Copyright © 2008 - 2009 Razban Internet International, Inc. All rights reserved, File:20091022, P a g e | **198**

Jobs" on the front page talks about www.Search.com HR manager who goes out of her way to find jobs for those who lost their jobs at her company. This article is a testimonial to the fact that the HR manager could quickly find jobs via her contacts and industry colleagues. This continues to be the best and most important fact regarding job search. Just keep calling friends and colleagues. Keep asking them if they know of some jobs. Keep networking, which beats not working!

On Friday 12/26/2008, I will be making at least another five phone calls and send another ten resumes out. Today, I got the letter from my mortgage company that I am in breach of my contract, a legal way of telling me that they are planning to start the foreclosure process.

Some years ago, way before the 9/11 terrorist attacks that made airline travel a lot more strict, passengers could request to go to the cockpit for a few minutes. This was done as a courtesy and done very cautiously even then.

I would like to tell you about this since I learned a great deal. I was traveling with my wife from Toronto to San Francisco on an Air Canada flight. I politely asked the flight attendant if I could go to "visit the pilots, when and if possible, for a few minutes, since I love aviation." My wife, sitting next to me, chimed in that not only did I love aviation, I am crazy about it. The attendant came back in just a few minutes and said that I could go visit in the cockpit. I mentioned to the pilot and copilot that I knew about the AB320 type that they were flying and got them really impressed. I continued to tell them what each gadget was about, with a few mistakes. The senior pilot, the one sitting on the left seat, the captain, was just elated. We started to talk about many things including how it was to be a pilot. He mentioned he loved his job, but it was rather difficult. The airplanes had become a lot more automatic, and the captain and the co-pilot usually just sit there and make sure all is going right. Of course, there are occasional moments of pure horror, when the pilot has to suddenly take control. "Boredom is the most difficult part of my job," he said. He also added that his company "has treated me with a lot of respect and trust, and in return, I plan to continue to do a great job for them until my retirement."

Around the time he was saying "until my retirement," I looked beyond the nose of the airplane, since I was standing in the cockpit, and I looked down. The speed of movement and the purely unbelievable altitude scared me, and I took a half step back. The senior pilot, who must have seen a similar reaction many times before, assured me, "we advise people not to look directly down, because it could be scary if you are not used to it." "Also, we think that you should never look down when you are doing heroics!" I had a similar lesson in Vancouver, Canada, during Expo 86. There is a roped bridge in a national park way up in the air above a river that connects two halves of the park. I was doing fine until I looked down. I almost froze! The fact that my house, and those of many middle-class Americans is close to foreclosure can be devastating to any family just like just looking down from a high altitude. In my remaining 1.8 weeks of financial security, I just do not have the luxury of looking down. I must go on. Just like Howard Schultz of Starbucks who is one of my hero CEOs, who signs his e-mails, "Onwards!" if I ever became a big CEO, I will sign mine, "Onwards, and upwards!"

The process of writing this book, on top of the end of my last contract, has created a sort of isolation for me. I missed my old colleagues at the last place I worked, and I needed to finish up this book as I had promised the superb editorial team at BookSurge.com on time. Therefore, it sort of felt that I had put a gun to my head with the deadline, and the

Copyright © 2008 - 2009 Razban Internet International, Inc. All rights reserved, File:20091022, P a g e | **199**

miserable 2.8 weeks of financial cushion. I need some extensive dental work that has to wait, but I have no idea for how long. I need to get my car fixed. Well, that will be after I have found a job. I need to get new Blackberry since my old one has been badly damaged when it fell from my hand in the train.

Let us see how the twelve steps of Alcoholism Anonymous can help here:

- Step 1: We are powerless over this unemployment and near Depression economics situation.
- Step 2: There is a Higher Power (What you in your belief system think of this to be) that can and will help us.
- Step 3: We give our "will" to this Higher Power! Admitting our temporary and situational powerlessness is a strong concept. Of course, we must be empowered, and of course we human being can do anything when we put our minds to it. For example, you do not have enough power at this point to force a hiring manager pick your resume at this moment and give you a job!
- Step 4: We made a fearless inventory. This is what we have been doing as it applies to our previous jobs.
- Step 5: Reviewed this with someone we respected and trusted in confidence. This by the way helps break the painful cycle of isolation.
- In addition, it continues. Please refer to the AA Big Book listed in the Reference section of this book.

I need some entertainment. Well, that has to wait too. I need a vacation. Well, that has to wait. I had promised to call my relatives all around the world during the holidays, but that has to wait, too.

My overeating is showing its ugly head from time to time. I ended up having a big breakfast and two apple turnovers right after that. For today, I do hate myself for this. Then, right after the heavy breakfast and the two apple pie slices, and the self-hating that ensued, I went to the next door pizza shop and had a small pizza and now I hate myself even more. The critical committee in my head has gone into overdrive, "Hey fat man, why do you eat so much? Have self control, without self control, who do you think will even give you a job? Well, actually, you do not even deserve a job at 278 Lbs."

A sobering thought jolts me out of this awful self talk. It is Veronica's words. Veronica, who suddenly lost a multi-million dollar mansion in Los Gatos, and now, has a diabetic husband struggling with death in and out of frequent hospital stays. She told me, "Bruce, this is not Bruce telling you these things, it is the Devil!" Moreover, she would emphasize, "It is the devil that makes things so bad for everyone." "You are a smart and educated man, just order the Devil to go away and leave you alone!" On Shabbats, she would say, "this is a time when we need to enjoy life and not talk or think business!" "Shabbats are days that God created for us to rest!"

Many others and we were invited to that beautiful hill top mansion many times. They always had lavish parties with excellent food and interesting guests. I think that they were of the ethical belief that since God had been so good to them; they needed in return to be good with others. The last time we were invited in their house was a few weeks before the house was foreclosed. That night the beautiful furniture and the professional lighting had created an out of this world beauty. Brand new furniture, polished and in mint condition looked gorgeous. Veronica decided to give a little speech after the dinner was served. She told us about the first few weeks after they had arrived in US. They did not have that much money and their fluency in three languages including French was not helping them since English was not one of their languages. She told us that she went to a supermarket and bought one apple, an orange, one carefully selected banana, and a small box of tea bags. She had hand carried these groceries for more than several blocks to bring them home. She and her husband with a lot of work and after many years did finally generate a great deal of wealth. Nevertheless, she never forgot her modest origins. With here seriously ill husband, she had to move several times until finally she found a very reasonable apartment. A few months ago, I visited them. She was somewhat sad, yet very strong and proud that she is taking care of her husband the best she can. She seemed to me to be much richer than she ever was. Somehow, the fact that she was taking care of her husband in a tiny apartment, was making her feel like a hero. The prosperous mansion and all that belonged to that kind of life was no match for her pride now. She said, "I have enough Mokato to take of my dying husband for as long as I humanly can." Seeing people like her having hope even in the direst situations restores my faith in humanity.

OK, I am back to reality and life. I need to call the recruiter and send him some more information about the people who worked for me in the past, so he can have a better chance of finding them a new job. Then, I was supposed to make five phone calls before my binge eating. I tried quite a bit did not succeed. I could not even bring myself to dial their phone numbers. Hey, I am a human being! I have enough, I know enough, and I do enough. Let me see! Maybe, I work a bit more on the book. That always makes me feel better. On the other hand, maybe I will go home. No, there will be nobody there and I would get even more depressed.

I miss my colleagues at the last place. I miss Allen to tell me that it seems like it was just yesterday that he and his family came here from Latin America. I miss the BART driver who would wave to me as he entered the Millbrae station at 6:20 AM. No trouble for him to make his BART horn go "Too, Tootootoo, Too" as a way of saying Good Morning, since he had been wide-awake for a few hours already. I also miss the clean-shaven CalTrain conductor, with a shiny mirror shaved head, who would always refer to me as "Sir" as if I was somebody important. One day, when our train was stuck for a few hours due to an "accident," he and I had a long conversation about my book. I will never forget his strong encouragement that I should write this book and then market it! He said I had things to say, and people need to hear the upbeat story of a fellow man. He pointed out that, "who knows, maybe, just maybe, we will have one less of these damned accidents and you have made your point!" The "accident" that day had happened because an older man with a pickup truck had driven his car right in front of the train. This was one of the most difficult things for the passengers to stomach several times during the year. A life is extremely precious, yet there is a mixture of rage and sympathy about these "incidents." This is a sort of feeling of the other person's hurt feelings that people on the train feel personally too. This pain is real to many especially since a lot them know how close they are to going homeless. It takes six or seven paychecks. A friend of mine had to go back and live with his parents. Not a big deal, but he is 59 and his wife is 55. The other one had to pull his daughter out of college. The other one could not pay alimony, and her spouse was making it almost impossible for her to see their children.

I also miss saying hello to the foursome who plays Bridge all the way from San Jose to Millbrae. Usually, they step out of the train disappointed when they get to Millbrae. "I would have won, and won big, if the train had taken one additional minute!" It is interesting that I am living, again for the umpteenth time, the jobless-jobless ugly scenario. I am well marketable, I have done this many times before, I am mentally very strong, but I tell you, this thing is difficult! It is awful. You have a right to feel bad about joblessness or fear of Sudden Job Loss! I feel better after pouring out the last few sentences, now I am right back to finding a job! A job, any job will be fine. Not a perfect job! Just a job! Just a job for now!

I talked about how these layoffs and unemployment situations are like a $2.4 trillion loss! Moreover, again $2.4 trillion is like a stack of 256 miles high of $1,000 Bills! As a miserable example, I attest to this being so! It is so, if not worse. This $2.4 Trillion loss is for 4% unemployment. Imagine that it will be $7.2 Trillion for 12% unemployment. It is not just one group or entity's fault it is all of us. We have to change our ways! What worked in the fifties will not work now. There has been a Blackberry revolution that has injected the information age into our bloodstream. Shockingly, our wasteful ways regarding human power and potential, cannot work anymore. We need to re-invent Capitalism. They cannot work anymore while we are experiencing a financial tsunami and/or economy Armageddon!

Look at me, instead of feeling sort of secure about my job, and inventing things, like the $100 million patented invention and the loving gift I gave to National Semiconductor and HP, I am spending my days feeling miserable, semi-depressed, and enduring a job search ordeal! Do not blame yourself if you feel like us too. We are only humans. If we were any superior than human beings, we would turn into perfectly logical computers. I do not want to become a computer!

I revolted a few days ago and bought a technical book about the latest marketing techniques, and new computer-programming language that I had never known before, just to get my mind away from this crazy situation.

If you are reading this book and you have $2.4 million to invest, send me an e-mail to bruce@razban.com. Maybe we can become partners and create a multibillion-dollar company that manages people's work life, like a global employer. I have the road map, business plan, and I will work as hard as I can to make this a success. I am sick and tired of being sick and tired of this job search, of dysfunctional and toxic workplaces. I have a better way that is so obvious that it does not take a rocket scientist to understand!

If you have some friends who need this book and cannot afford to purchase it, please send me an email and I will be happy to send them one of the older manuscript files free of charge.

My empathy goes to those work-a-day commuters on the Paris Metro, or London Underground (Tube), or Lexington Avenue Train in New York City, or the Bullet Train commuters of Tokyo (Shingansan) or in France, Ligne à grande vitesse (LGV), TGV is the "**Train** Grande Vitesse," which is the Rapid or **Bullet Train.** It really does not matter which of these trains you use for your commute, you have my empathy for having your life go passed you while you try to take it easy with some long commute.

At any rate, yesterday was not a good day and I am glad it is gone. I did not make much progress! However, today, it is an entirely different and better story. I was able to make several calls, and one of the recruiters told me that he had just gotten the requirements for a job in Pleasanton. The job happens to be with my last employer, but this one is more probable to work since I am working with a contact and not just some e-mail address.

There is a triple advantage here:
- I know the recruiter who has been a contact for some time,
- I know the company and I have worked there before,
- I think the recruiter knows the hiring manager; this is a big plus.

Therefore, as you can see, contacts are critically important in finding a job!
I will also post my resume on dice.com before I go home tonight.

- At some point in a job search or attempts to get a better job, one reaches an abyss! This is a dark point, where nothing seems to work. Nothing works: phone calls, attempts in planning, attempts in attending classes to refine and strengthen our skill sets, resumes, and networking.

- This has happened and will happen each time I try to find a new job. I have seen this in many others as well. However, you cannot give up fifteen minutes before a miracle. In addition, as they say, the best time to get back on the horse is right after being kicked down!

- According to US constitution, there is separation of Church and State. I think that in the cases where you are the sole breadwinner and your spouse or better half is used to being at home, then staying at home might not work well during your working hours. This I refer to as Separation of Work and Home.

- Remember, each time you make a phone call or do something with resume, or personal application at the local car dealer for a car sales job, try to figure out what you can learn from this. In addition, make sure to consider that in your next move. Sometimes hiring managers will be willing to help by providing some advice.

- During the last twelve years of constant work search as a consultant and CEO of a tiny company that lived or died on the strength of contracts that I was able to get, I have managed to create a buddy system. This is a team of friends and colleagues who will be in the same field and we have MTL, who will help me with brushing up on a skill set that they have and I need more practice on, or leads about jobs that they did not get, or do not want. Remember that to keep the level of MTL; this is a one to one barter of self-help and support, and even encouragement.

- Try getting any type of job, full time, part time, local, other places, with travel, without travel, etc. This way you will get something, even though it is not what you really want to do. Remember this is temporary until you get something better.

I have done this so many times that it has become a routine for me. I have my home office, which is one complete room in a tiny townhouse. I also have the routine places that I go in order not to come down with cabin fever. Here are my favorites:

- Digital Guru Technical Book Store in Sunnyvale. The owner and Steve, who works there, recognize me after many, many years. For years, they have been able to tell me what is selling and what is not and that way I have gotten to stay on the "bleeding edge" of technology that my technology consulting needs. They also have a fish tank and several comfortable chairs. I buy on the average one or two textbooks each month. This is the level of commitment that is needed to stay abreast of the fast leading technology.

- Next places are the Barns and Nobles and Borders. I go there frequently. Take a few books and enjoy a nice hot cup of coffee while I decide which book to buy. Usually, I buy at least three or four books on management, and technology.

Copyright © 2008 - 2009 Razban Internet International, Inc. All rights reserved, File:20091022, P a g e | **203**

- The Barns and Nobel in Hillsdale has special meaning to me. During those years that I took the CalTrain Bullet train from Mountain View to San Francisco, I could see this particular store from the train. I could only imagine how much nicer it could be if was going there instead of going to a ten hour work instead. It must have taken several years before, I decided to get out of the train and go there one day on my return from work. I found the manager there, Jackie, to be an outstanding professional with a great deal of help, advice, and support for the first time book writer that I was. I think that I will go there for my very first book signing celebration.
- The information desk at Kepler's in Menlo Park is one of the best. Several people helped me with my questions during the research for the book. I have been going there for more than twenty years. One of those times, I got extremely helpful advice that changed the direction of the book dramatically.
- By the way, I am an example of a person who is creating his own new job. I dream of becoming a famous writer. I love books and writing this book has been a labor of love. This is creative, exciting, and it has been what has kept me alive in the full cultural sense of the word.

The point is that I have created a supportive stumping ground to make it enjoyable for me to have a familiar place for my social contacts each time a contract ends in a Sudden Job Loss. Moreover, it is still sudden even after all these 32 years. Still I am not used to it even after writing a book about it. I say this so you can see that it a painful process to lose a job. You have my absolute permission to tell you working spouse, friend, or better half, "Hey, look at this guy Bruce Razban! He has thirty-two years of experience and he has been jobless for almost a year!" Buy or download a copy and give it to him/her. If you cannot, send me an e-mail and I will back you up. I have done this a few times already and I have a pre-prepared e-mail message that I can send them on your behalf. Do not let anybody kid you. This is one of the toughest times in history.

Please note that there is dignity and honor in working hard at the full time job of finding a job! There is even great honor and dignity for helping another jobless person. Networking has worked for me even when I was trying to get into the best high school in Tehran. This was the most advanced school and to get there, I had to take an entrance test. A French man Called Jordan founded this school. Later Dr. Mojtahedi became the president and he hired the best of the best to teach. I was so well educated that I passed many of the freshman classes at the University of Wisconsin, by just taking the test. That high school was that strong. However, I would have not passed the entrance exam had it not been for my friend Shahram. He was already going to that school and I bumped into him in a sidewalk café. He encouraged me to not waste my time with the books that I was using to prepare and instead gave me some other books. That was instrumental in 1964 and it still is instrumental now. I just had coffee with a good friend who advised me on what is important for being hired or getting a contract at the FaceBook.com Company. Speaking of contacts, another good friend and colleague of many years told me about his company. It is a startup, and does not have a great deal of money, but it will be a great place for me to work. I have started to do my research about this company since my colleague thinks that he can get an interview. I will even go work for free for a while, and they always find a way to hire me.

I am walking the talk that was presented in this book. Keep tuned, there will be more.

Copyright © 2008 - 2009 Razban Internet International, Inc. All rights reserved, File:20091022, P a g e |

I might have shared this with you before, but I came to the US when I was seventeen in 1967. Back then, I could not wait to become eighteen so I could be of legal age to drive. Of course, the idea of buying a car was really distant at that time since I was struggling just to make ends meet at college. I had to work part time and have good grades to get financial aid. In fact, aside from the first three semesters, I was always on the Dean's Honor list and I graduated with Honors. I used to hear the slogan "Do not trust anyone over thirty" in the sixties. I did not care then, because it would be a very, very long time before I was thirty and, worse yet, become a part of "the establishment."

Well, one day I was thirty. Soon after that, I was thirty-four when I became one of the youngest directors in Zilog, Inc.'s history. In addition, since Zilog was a subsidiary of Exxon at that time, Zilog management had to get special permission for such young a director. I was told that they had to build a case to prove that I was the best of the best. They had to prove that I was technologically extremely knowledgeable and that my management skills were superb, and that on top of that, I had excellent people skills and interpersonal skills. Then the years seemed to pile up against me!

The age *thirty* gets totally different dimensions in Silicon Valley these days. It is rumored that many companies do not even invite a person who is more than thirty to interview. Rumor and some TV accounts indicate that Google, which in my mind is the most innovative company on earth, does not hire anyone over thirty. I am pushing sixty, and I see this practice every day. It is unethical and illegal. However, as Dr. Phil says, "It is what it is."

Earnest Hemingway, in his novel, *The Old Man and the Sea,* depicts an old man who has to face the sea every day to earn a living. A young man would have fun fighting with the sea, but an old man would find it more and more difficult. To an extent, this is my story. At the age of almost sixty, where I should be calmly thinking about retirement, I have to work as hard, if not harder than I ever have. I used to think that I was as old as my colleagues' fathers were. Now, it seems that I am just as old as their grandparents are. Interestingly enough, I see some respect from some and some frustration from others. Yet every day, this old man has to go to sea! I think this, in turn, keeps me younger than my actual age and keeps my intellect sharp as opposed to vegetating in retirement playing golf from 9:00 AM to 5:00 PM. Come to think of it, golf eight hours a day, may not be bad at all. Here is Summary of the story of *The Old Man and the Sea* as found on Google.com:

The Old Man and the Sea recounts an epic battle between an old, experienced fisherman and a giant marlin said to be the largest catch of his life. It opens by explaining that the fisherman, who is named Santiago, has gone 84 days without catching any fish at all. He is apparently so <u>unlucky</u> that his young <u>apprentice</u>, Manolin, has been forbidden by his parents to sail with the old man and been ordered to fish with more successful fishermen. Still dedicated to the old man, however, the boy visits Santiago's shack each night, hauling back his fishing gear, feeding him and discussing American <u>baseball</u> — most notably Santiago's idol, <u>Joe DiMaggio</u>. Santiago tells Manolin that on the next day, he will venture far out into the Gulf to fish, confident that his unlucky streak is near its end.

Copyright © 2008 - 2009 Razban Internet International, Inc. All rights reserved, File:20091022, P a g e | **205**

Thus on the eighty-fifth day, Santiago sets out alone, taking his skiff far into the Gulf. He sets his lines and, by noon of the first day, a big fish that he is sure is a marlin takes his bait. Unable to pull in the great marlin, Santiago instead finds the fish pulling his skiff. Two days and two nights pass in this manner, during which the old man bears the tension of the line with his body. Though he is wounded by the struggle and in pain, Santiago expresses a compassionate appreciation for his adversary, often referring to him as a brother. He also determines that because of the fish's great dignity, no one will be worthy of eating the marlin.

On the third day of the ordeal, the fish begins to circle the skiff, indicating his tiredness to the old man. Santiago, now completely worn out and almost in delirium, uses all the strength he has left in him to pull the fish onto its side and stab the marlin with a harpoon, thereby ending the long battle between the old man and the tenacious fish.

Santiago straps the marlin to his skiff and heads home, thinking about the high price the fish will bring him at the market and how many people he will feed.

While Santiago continues his journey back to the shore, sharks are attracted to the trail of blood left by the marlin in the water. The first, a great mako shark, Santiago kills with his harpoon and then he loses that weapon in the process. He makes a new harpoon by strapping his knife to the end of an oar to help ward off the next line of sharks; in total, five sharks are slain and many others are driven away. But by night, the sharks have almost devoured the marlin's entire carcass, leaving a skeleton consisting mostly of its backbone, its tail and its head, the latter still bearing the giant spear. The old man castigates himself for sacrificing the marlin. Finally reaching the shore before dawn on the next day, he struggles on the way to his shack, carrying the heavy mast on his shoulder. Once home, he slumps onto his bed and enters a very deep sleep.

A group of fishermen gather the next day around the boat where the fish's skeleton is still attached. One of the fishermen measures it to be eighteen feet from nose to tail. Tourists at the nearby café mistakenly take it for a shark. Manolin, worried during the old man's endeavor, cries upon finding him safe asleep. The boy brings him newspapers and coffee. When the old man wakes, they promise to fish together once again. Upon his return to sleep, Santiago dreams of lions on the African beach.

However, who can afford retirement? More importantly, it is boring being retired. I think that I will retire about a week before I am totally dead. Until that day, I will work, and work, and work. According to 60 Minutes, we Americans are brainwashed to be workaholics. This was even before 401K IRAs become Zero1Ks (like my IRA that has Zero balance.)

CHAPTER 84:   Voulez-Vous in CalTrain Parking Lot at 5:41 AM

The CalTrain parking lot is right in Mountain View Downtown, at the intersection of the Central Expressway and Castro Street. This parking lot gets full around 6:45 AM. Therefore as the day progresses, finding a slot to park gets more and more difficult. In that dark of the morning, people have short fuses. Some of these people are even at their worst behavior. There are those who try to back into a parking spot and this takes so much time that some of the waiting drivers who are waiting for their turn to park miss their train. CalTrain is excellent in being on time. Frequently, at that early-morning time, I would rush to park, and then run to catch my train by crossing the rails, only to find that the train was closing its doors and getting ready to leave.

Since I had to do this commute and not go out of my mind, I decided on an excellent way to start my day. I have some fast beat music like the Voulez-Vous of ABBA playing as loud as possible in my car. Then I would really enjoy about four minutes of this uplifting music to prepare for the rat race. However, I have had to set my alarm clock to go off at 4:23 instead of 4:30 AM. This way, I do not have to rush to the parking lot and to also arrive in style! I figured that pain may not be optional, but suffering is. Therefore, I do not want to be suffering any more than I have to. Listening to this kind of rhythmic music is particularly effective in soothing nerves during the early hour during cold winters and drizzle. I used also to make a hot thermos of coffee, and that really added class to my style. However, that was taking another seven to ten minutes, and I was not about to wake up at 4:14 AM.

Listen to this upbeat and sexy music with a hot cup of hot chocolate on a cold and dreary morning and you will understand what I am talking about. Of course, we know that what goes up must come down. Sometimes, when I get back to the CalTrain parking lot at about 7:00 PM, I am so hungry that I cannot wait the fifteen minutes it takes to drive home. Therefore, I go to the kiosk that my friends Aki-San and Shawn-San have in the station. They have been very kind to me and they have helped me remember some of the business Japanese that I learned while I worked at National. I had learned some Japanese because of my admiration for Japan as a country, as well as their culture. This one or two minutes practice also helped me to remember those nostalgic times where I would go to Japan with all expenses paid on a business trip.

Anyway, when I get back twelve or thirteen hours after I had left the station, I treat myself to a sort of make shift picnic in the parking lot pretending it is a nice park. It does not matter. I can do this on a cold winter (day or night) or in the summertime with full sunshine. I buy a hotdog and a soda; put my briefcase in the car as if to forget the business world. Then I make a mini tailgate party for one! That hotdog just tastes heavenly, and it makes me decompress so as not to go home hungry and tired and fed up after a full day of work.

CHAPTER 85:   One Picture is Worth…

In my career, I have found the following relationship between things to be true for me. In your career and in your profession, it probably will be different. At any rate let me paint a picture for you of what it takes to get one job offer:
- To get one job offer, it takes about five to ten job interviews.
- To get one interview, it takes fifty to one-hundred resumes, or
- To get one interview it takes twenty to thirty networking calls.
Yes, it takes about 250 to 1000 resumes to get a good job, or it takes 100 to 300 networking calls. It seems to me that many resumes that are sent via the Internet end up in some black hole somewhere and never amount to anything.
Keep track of the phone calls and interviews since that is a good indicator of your rate of progress.
Sometimes, a little dumb luck can go a very long way. A friend was out of a job for less than three weeks. He and his wife were playing golf on a hot day. His wife went to buy a cold drink from a vending machine. She did not have change. She noticed there was someone nearby. She asked for change, started a conversation about golf, and somehow told the other person that her husband had a jacket similar to his. It turned out that the jacket was part of the "uniform" for that company. The other person continued by saying that, even though he still wore the jacket, there was a layoff there and he was now happily working for the competition. In addition, the competition was looking for people like her husband. They got together the same day and went for dinner. In less than two weeks, my friend was working for the same company, and happily too. So maybe, one dumb-luck encounter is better than sending and submitting 1,000 resumes. But you must be looking with your eyes open. Who knows, maybe the school janitor where your kid goes to school might know of a great job for you.
Ask. Ask. Ask!
This is a plan and a motivational tool to be used to cheer you up. This one I learned from a good friend who, like me, is also a consultant. He used some pictures of good things that he was dreaming about having, for example, going to a vacation to Hawaii. Then he went to Google.com, clicked on images, and used "Hawaii vacation" as a search word. Then he picked one or more of the pictures that looked interesting to him. Then he pasted that picture all over his plans, etc. Another friend was all excited about his daughter's wedding. Therefore, he had pasted pictures of brides pasted to his plans.
There is something very powerful in the eyes seeing a picture. Then the eyes convince the mind's eye to also believe that we will succeed and go on that vacation we always wanted. So, let us work hard and be motivated by what is sort of a "self-bribe." This is the only type of bribe that works and is legal as long as the bribe giver and the bribe taker are one and the same, namely ourselves! This concept of pictures is so powerful that management consultants who were teaching Leading Change to National Semiconductor Management Employees used it. One of their handouts had a cover of Time or Newsweek printed on a shinny, mirror-like paper. The Title was "Man of the Year" and there was another as the "Woman of the Year." Therefore, when you were looking at this picture and your face was reflected in the shiny paper, it would sort of look like that; you were that man or woman of the year.

Copyright © 2008 - 2009 Razban Internet International, Inc. All rights reserved, File:20091022, P a g e | 208

Then we were told to write an article explaining why we had been given this award of being the man/woman of the year. This article was supposed to be as realistic as it could be, and have as much detail as was possible to put in a 3,000-word article. In our team, our challenge was to show that we had implemented the Activity Based Cost (ABC) Accounting and pretend that we had been able to develop several products in parallel in a record time. We were to pretend, the same way they pretend in Hollywood. After all, in Hollywood everything is make belief. I know I was a movie star for one whole week at "Good Bye Columbus." We were to do the high-level long-term strategic plan, and then day-to-day tactical plan and the budget for it.

One more thing, we were to develop Success Criterion, and plan a celebration party in some details. I was thinking that "My God, we fooling ourselves with these elaborate make believe things" when a colleague started to tell me "No. This is not making believe, this is positive thinking." Seemed like he had had read my mind. Our presentation of individual success speeches completely had convinced our mind eye that we had done it, and since we had done it successfully, then it could be done!

One reason, why I keep talking about soothing music and lyrics in this book is to emphasize the song that we need to have in our hearts. If there is anything I know for sure is that with the song in our hearts we will always been alive and capable of doing anything sine empowered human beings can soar and the blue sky is the limit. Do not let clouds get in your way! You can see this on the front cover with a seagull flying above the clouds and in the "Sky is the limit" beautiful clear skies. You can also see this in the imagery in the back cover.

In Joni Mitchell's Song "Both Sides Now", she describes clouds as:

<
But now they only block the sun
They rain and snow on everyone
So many things I would have done
But clouds got in my way
I've looked at clouds from both sides now
>

Copyright © 2008 - 2009 Razban Internet International, Inc. All rights reserved, File:20091022, P a g e | **209**

CHAPTER 86:   ProMatch and Nova, and Forty-Plus in California

These organizations are there to help people get back into jobs and jumpstart their careers. Either President Clinton started the idea, or he was the power behind it.

- ProMatch is a self-help organization that helps with resume writing, interviews, and job selections. However, it does a lot more of that. It is a community for people to belong to and benefit from each other's help and support.
- Nova, on the other hand, has resources to help pay educational classes so people can update their skill sets. Nova also helps with the same job finding efforts too. I have seen many careers revive by Nova paying for some badly needed courses.
- Forty-Plus was located in Oakland and their focused was helping older job hunters. I saw some people in their late sixties, and mid seventies attend or even run the sessions. Forty-Plus was located very hear Oakland Airport and I could not help but remember all those flights that I had from Oakland.

These great organizations introduced me to "What Color is Your Parachute?" as being the bible for job seekers. That was some twenty years ago. Ever since then, these books, which are re-written each year, remain the gold standard. Many of my colleagues and I are very grateful to these organizations. They helped us immensely. As a self-help organization, they do a great job of helping people affected by layoffs or unemployed to get their resumes re-written. They have up to the minute advice about who is hiring and who is not. They do a great job of getting people ready for interviews, and all aspects of job search.

On Thursdays, we would go to the amphitheater and people who had found jobs the prior week would talk. They would explain explaining what worked for them and what did not. More importantly, they would encourage others on continuing their job search efforts. I have found some great friends and colleagues because of these wonderful programs. The most powerful that has persisted all these years is the colleagues and friends that have become my network. We keep in touch whether we are working or not. We keep each other in terms of skill sets and latest information about different companies. I have found that it is true as "What Color is Your Parachute?" describes that it increases chances. This book over the years has discovered that chances of finding a job in internet is somewhere between seven and ten percent, while chances of finding a job via contacts is around seventy or more percent.

Some "graduate" members of Nova and ProMatch formed sub-groups that were for special disciplines. One that was helpful to me was for IT members. I joined a couple and the results were amazing. Not only we would challenge each other each day to apply to certain number of places, or follow up on others, we also had social time when we would have lunch or coffee together. This is a powerful tool to get people out of their isolation and back into circulation.

Nova assigned me a counselor who would meet with me on a weekly basis. She had the latest information about the different jobs that were available, and she helped me overcome some of my frustration. She also helped me re-learn some of my interviewing skills.

One of the seminars they offered had to do with an effective coping mechanism for age discrimination. People, who knew what they were talking about, wrote helpful handouts in their expertise. For example, it suggested that a resume should not go back more than

Copyright © 2008 - 2009 Razban Internet International, Inc. All rights reserved, File:20091022.

fifteen years. Try not to say things like "In the good old days…" try to gap the age difference as much as you can. For example, try to have clothes that are more of the style that a younger person prefers. Instead of my usual navy blue Nordstrom suit, I had some sports jackets and Khaki pants when I was interviewing for an IT job.

One day, I was upset about an interview. The interviewer obviously did not like me. I was a lot more experienced, I was smarter, I had graduated from a major university with honors, and I knew their business inside out.

He kept asking questions that were designed to make me look bad. He asked about the year I had graduated. It is not as illegal as asking the person's age, but is just as unethical. In frustration, towards the end of the interview, he asked what I do for fun. My answer that I love to play amateur golf seemed to be somewhat insulting to him. I quickly asked what he did. His answer was "I skate board and clean up after an old dude who does not get it!" I was supposed to report to this "Dude." I prayed that he would not select me. If he did, this would have been the job from hell. Luckily, I got a terse e-mail from the recruiter that they had more qualified candidates, and they selected one of them. Upon seeing this e-mail from that Dude, I had a deep sigh of relief!

I discussed this with the Nova Counselor, and she told me that that company had had many issues, and in fact, there was an age discrimination suit against them. Then with a very respectful voice, she asked me if I really wanted to work for that company. I said yes, because they were in the leading edge of technology. Her thoughtful follow-up question was extremely helpful to me. She said that she knew at least three people who work there. They work more than sixty hours a week and they can do this only because they do not have a family and they practically live on the campus. They have and know of no other life. Well, I have a family that I dearly love, and I think that I have already paid my dues with working for five startups with sixty-hour weeks.

I guess that I am no longer the right "dude" for this "Nerdy Job"!

CHAPTER 87:   Work and Play, One and the Same

In the summer of 2008, there was an interview with an author. He had written a book about running. The book had become very successful and he was on a world book tour. He mentioned that he did have a different career before this. In addition, at that time, his running was his hobby. He ran every day and said that running was excellent for his good health. It also cleared his mind. Running was a kind of meditation for him. I feel the same about my won thirty-minute daily walk.

It also turned out that the work that he had was highly frustrating, depressing, and stressful for him. At some point, he realized that his regular job, the job that he went to college for, and the job that was his specialty, was killing him. A little bit of him died every day on that job. He thought about becoming a world champion in running and tried to earn a living that way. However, he was too old for that. He did something very smart that I encourage all those who are frustrated with their jobs do. He put together a plan. His plan included coaching others, writing and lecturing, and learning from other professionals. There was a meager revenue stream and his wife was gracious enough to support and help him. As the word got around that he was an excellent coach, he started to build a client list. Eventually, he was so much in demand that there was a waiting list. He also made sure that he wrote regularly until he finished his book. Gradually, he was able to get a sufficient income from his running job that was able to curtail and stop the other job. His income was not anywhere as high as his previous profession provided, but he was much happier. People tell him that he has even lost some weight and looks years younger and happier. This is an example of having work and play be the one and the same.

The opposite is a medical Doctor that I know who hates his job. He does not communicate. He frequently prescribes a medicine before really understanding all the symptoms. He looks a lot older than his age. His son was my classmate and my good friend. This Doctor never even tried something else. His belief was work is a sort of punishment. He had convinced himself that almost nobody liked his or her jobs. This also had an adverse effect on their kids, especially my friend. In a French movie, a famous actor in defending himself in front of his children said this. "I am a writer, and only know how to write! Nothing more. My parents never spent time with me when I was child because they too were just farmers. What do you want from me?"

Writing this book has indeed been work and play at the same time for me. I could not wait to go to the FedEx Office in San Jose to write down what I had been thinking. The four hours each week would pass by in the blink of an eye. I could spend ten hours instead of the two. I do not get tired because this has been a labor of love. This is work and play the same. It is my passion and my mission!

Ever since my good friend Lior told me that everyone has a book in them, I have been seriously thinking about sharing my good and bad, happy and sad experiences with others. The great hope here is that this will help them to understand the dynamics of what a dysfunctional workplace is and not to internalize a layoff or a firing, as it is not their fault. I want to motivate those who are affected by a layoff to search, improve, and have hope to find a better job. I like to encourage them to look at this job search as a journey of getting better and not just to find a job! I want everyone to live the good life, in spite of job loss. I have found this work, as most work in general, is an extremely

therapeutically important and joyous for me. I hope this will be the same for you too.

Today is 5/21/09. It is a few days more than five months that I have been unemployed. I have sold a number of the first edition of this book and I am now starting to write the "Second Extended Edition." Each day, I spend at least four hours of sending resumes and making network calls. However, after eight PM it is time for me to write. For me this is work and play at the same time. Writing this book has been indeed a labor of love. I do live with the "Ordeal" of finding a job during a day, just to do this "Work and Play, One and the same" from eight PM to eleven PM. During the job search ordeal it seems the hands on the clock move so ever slowly. In contrast, right after eight, they seem to move at the speed of light. I have gotten some $12,000 loan from a friend to work on the second edition while I am looking for the next job. At the same time, I am pitching to Venture Capitalists about my latest business adventure. In the mean time, I am brushing up on my PHP5 programming skills to qualify for a number of available jobs in this area. I have a team of about nine super qualified people doing some work now for free. The hope is that as soon as I get the funding, I will start to compensate them. In addition, if there is no money, well, we move right on to the next project, and the one after that.

CHAPTER 88:   Jean Sibelius and Finlandia

Many people think of classical music as that starchy music that old and elite rich people like. Finlandia is the first classical music I fell in love with, and it is very special to others and me.

Jean (or John) Sibelius is a Norwegian nationalist. When he was born, Russia and Sweden had territorial claims over Norway, and Norway was not considered an independent country. In fact, the intellectual community in what is now Norway had to go to Sweden to study, using the Swedish language. The place he lived had a rather dark-looking and depressing lake with a floating island. In fact, one of his first compositions had almost no rhythm at all. This, intentionally or unintentionally, was his way of accentuating the darkness and disappointments he had in his life. His father was an alcoholic who either died or left the family when he was four. Jean had a younger brother and his mother was expecting another child. I identify with him because my own Dad lost his loving and caring father he was four too. This happened in some forgotten war. Unfortunately, this made my Dad and my Grandmother's life miserable. My Dad, at the age of four, would help my Grandmother clean homes. However, my father was an optimist. He and I enjoyed attending Optimist International Meetings.

Unfortunately, Sibelius's difficult childhood made him a pessimist. Nevertheless, he went to study in a good school that in fact used Norwegian as the instructional language. He was studying music and something else. That something else quickly faded away since Jean found that his passion in life was music. He wrote several pieces. For some reason or other, the German and Swedish critics did not like his work. This was partially because his work was different. He had refused to take old folklore and make it sound like a new composition. The extreme and harsh critics started to result in self-criticism and this got him down.

However, as his mother explained later, his Symphony Number 8 was what he used to "burn all that criticism" and channel his energies in a positive way. That symphony is now loved around the world as an uplifting and beautiful piece of art.

Music and life have a lot in common. There are highs and lows, and there is joy and sadness in life as it is in the music. In this book, we first focus on the lows in life that were induced by most difficult financial situations. However, we can build a future for our careers and lives. We are CEOs of our work and lives. We are in charge.

I would like to share with you another story. In a BBC news broadcast, in late May of 2009, there was a stunning interview with some Icelandic bank executives. The CEO was asked, "In view of the fact that most of your banking institutions, and for that matter the entire Iceland economy has failed, how is it that your bank has been one of the exceptions that has succeeded?" I clearly remember headlines about how bad the banking collapse in Iceland had been. In fact, they were so badly off that they were asking the Russians to help.

The CEO proudly said that she had a better alternative. She mentioned that her bank did not solely rely on what I have termed things capital in this book. Her bank considered human capital just as importantly in any decisions they made. She pointed out that before giving a loan to a company, they would consider the usual assets such as building, capital equipment, real estate, etc. At the same time, they would also evaluate the people who worked in the company. In fact, this is measuring the Mutual Trust and Loyalty (MTL)

Copyright © 2008 - 2009 Razban Internet International, Inc. All rights reserved, File:20091022, P a g e | **214**

position of a company. They would look into whether employees seem to be genuinely happy, did they really knew what they were doing, was the company direction, mission, and standing clearly understood by them. The BBC reporter somewhat impatiently tried to say, "These things are called touchy feely things and they are not that important." The CEO strongly disagreed and pointed out that these factors have been one prime reason for them doping so well.

In fact, the same Mutual Trust and Loyalty (MTL) is also a major success factor in the success of Micro Lending in some of the poorest countries in the world. The bankers would give a tiny business was a loan of $100 or $200 based on trust. Trust that was based on the dignity (Mokato) and people did their humanly best to not let their Mokato be diminished by foolish mistakes. They delivered what they promised.

This is music of symphony proportions to my business ear. People were trusted with respect; there was MTL, and they it became a win-win for all! The women executives of the Iceland Bank and all of the tiny business owners must have been frustrated. Nevertheless, they figured a way out to succeed. They burned their frustration by producing a beautiful symphony not unlike the Finlandia. Let us burn our work related frustrations and pains by making a new song, in fact a new symphony for better work life!

Another extremely important fact about Finland is that it was the first European country to emancipate women and give them same exact rights as men. And, this was in 1920s!

CHAPTER 89:   Our Accomplishments are the Best Reward of Our Work to Ourselves

Years and years of experience tell me that the happiest employees are those who have accomplished the most. It is as if they were working for themselves even though it was their job. The pride in a job well done is by far more rewarding than that of just squeezing through, or barely making it. My work with Lexus and HP and other fine companies indicates that being the best of the best might even be easier than just trying to do minimum work to get by. This way, there will not be too much aggravation, worries, and hassles. I have noticed that some people tend to always get the job done well; they always show up for meetings a few minutes early; they do their work with a smile; they are optimistic about the future; and they are not that worried about things. These people always do a bit more. Moreover, they do it well in the first place.
I guess here is where I might be able to put closure to the hurt and pain that I felt in my worst job ever. Beyond that, I will also discuss the joy that I had in my best job ever. Then a few words about humdrum jobs that were not particularly good or bad.
A few weeks after my contract were suddenly stopped and I experienced the awful loss and disappointment. After my vacation trip to Seattle, I decided to not just sit there and be a Chippie. I decided to rekindle the song in my heart. Thirty years of experience in my field made it possible for me to invent a new computer technology. I had invented things before. But my first invention that must have saved and/or created more than $100M for National and HP took a great deal of effort by intellectual-property experts and attorneys to help me get a patent grant. It was a long and difficult process. This time I was on my own. I used the money that I had, and the time in between when the telephone was ringing about some potential interviews, I decided that I would whatever I could to make the latest two patent-pending products. Then I created a company, called Razban Internet International around these patent-pending products, and incorporated it. Do not get me wrong, I am not rich. In addition, Razban Internet International is a tiny company fighting for its survival. However, I am so proud that I had the guts to make inventions and create a company. Maybe, you are into inventing things or starting a corporation. You might be able to start a small company in the form of "Doing Business As" or create a Limited Liability Corporation as a start. It will cost less than incorporation and it is easier to keep.
I take great of pride in this.
I am sure that you might have interpreted some of this book as a criticism of the workplace or even American business and economy. Let me tell you that even though my country, America, has and will make many mistakes and, even though I might be the first to admit to bad things, still, America is one of the most powerful industrial forces in the universe. Before my colleagues in Europe or the former Soviet Union make fun of my country, let me point out that America is still the best with its freedom. The unlimited resources and human intellectual potential in America is still the best there is. Small business makes this country a powerful, industrial, and even social power. Therefore, we all have a potential part in this huge and unlimited power.
Other countries also have things we can learn and copy here is America. Maybe we can relearn from the Asians, what family values and respect for elders used to be here in America. Maybe, we can relearn from Europeans the art of good living. So, as an American, I encourage you not to be a Chippie and to not just sit there letting the chain of

Copyright © 2008 - 2009 Razban Internet International, Inc. All rights reserved, File:20091022. Page | **216**

foolishness in the workplace stop your singing.
As it is in the *Phantom of Opera*, "Sing, Sing, Sing!"

***Section 4:

- Blueprint for future success for all of us, particularly:

  - Government
  - Small Business Managers and Leaders
  - Corporate Managers and Leaders
  - Everyday workers

CHAPTER 90:   The Human and Knowledge-Management Era

While most management education and practices are based on asset management, a new era, especially with the advent of the Internet, started in the mid 1990s. In the 1980s, we as managers had a hard time assigning the right capital equipment Dollar value for the ever more important software. I recall clearly that the design-automation software we developed at Zilog would reduce the labor required by 100 times, and it had to have a dollar value in the inventory system.

Some of our senior managers would give a token value of $1.00 to their entire packages. This would at least get the accountants off their backs. Some would take one year's worth of savings resulting from software, and make that the Dollar value. The truth was back in those days, we knew how to assign a Dollar value for a truck or a chair. However, when it came to software that was beginning to run our entire sections, we were clueless.

For example, we had absolutely no problem assigning Dollar value to our raw silicon, chips, packaging, or chemicals that were needed to produce the products. Shortly thereafter, many companies either paid lip service, or actually presented a new idea: "Our employees are our most important asset!" It became fashionable to not only boast that a company is "People-Oriented" but to even try to show that. In was in that time that any attention was paid on intellectual property and its value.

Today it is all about knowledge!

I will use an awfully insensitive idea to convey the idea. Let us say that we could connect probes to our employees' heads and read the alpha, beta, and other waves. Then, use our supercomputers to analyze it and convert it to knowledge. Then we could package and sell knowledge. Knowledge will be a commodity of extremely high value. We have already started on it. Think of knowledge the same way as the running water that comes out of your tap. Knowledge is just as critical to our financial life as water is to our life. Therefore, we must learn to respect, understand, and work with it.

Unfortunately, a lot of companies are well prepared to manage the things capital and not the human capital. The human capital of a company is the employees of all ranks and standings in the organization. It is the customers who buy the company products and services at some price point. Of course, it is also other things capital that consists of real estate, buildings, trucks, computer, etc.

It turns out that even in June of 2009; our management is capable of working with things capital a lot more than they can work with the human capital. However, the balance has shifted from things capital to people capital in terms of what is the most important asset of a company. Human capital is the number of employees, their skill sets, how up to date these skill sets are, and when last they were used. The crash of 2008-2009 has proven how critically more important humans are to a company success than the things capital especially the Real Estate.

Some of the early readers of this book took me to task about my claim that big corporations are like danseurs. Look at United Airlines, one of my most favorite airlines. I go back to be their fan when Bob Samson would represent them in Jerry Lewis's charity MDA show. I was a big fan of them, when I had many pleasant trips on business and for vacation. I even loved their anthem, which was George Gershwin's "Rhapsody in Blue". However, the airline of the future might be highly reliant on the internet. It might take the shape of regional airline with smaller jets like Boeing DreamLiner 787, or Airbus 310

Copyright © 2008 - 2009 Razban Internet International, Inc. All rights reserved, File:20091022, P a g e | **219**

that will offer you the best schedule, the best rates, and the best everything on line. It might very well also by using the Knowledge power, make all the cab or limousine car rentals, hotel stays, show tickets and give you the best GPS information all with a few clicks and seamlessly. Instead of charging you a lumped payment, it will offer a few dollars each week or month. Affinity groups will spring up that will give you a free ticket if you purchase this and that. All with no gimmicks, and no hidden charges. In addition to being regional airlines, a lot of airlines might also become charters. I really mean very frequent charters. Flight on demand concept.

Remember the two amendments to Capitalism that I suggested? Human Capital, and Information. These two work well here. What if you got a round trip San Francisco to Paris Business Class ticket from United Airlines? To pay for this, you as an accountant, worked ten hours in one evening for a company in Zurich. Then you worked another 24 hours for a local company and another 40 hours were used to make a business plan for a startup. All arranged well based on Mutual Trust and Loyalty. Nobody was shortchanging anybody else. Everybody benefitted from this. As much as I like internet and computers, I strongly suggest a human connection in all of these to make sure all is fine. Customers cannot be treated with cold awful internet driven support.

I worked for a California startup that was pioneering Knowledge Management in early 2000. The company had many Stanford MBAs and many top-talent engineering professionals from top-notch schools, somewhat similar to Zilog. The business plan and business model, in my interpretation, was like making and selling a knowledge bottling company, nothing more, and nothing less. Here is how it was supposed to work. A set of certified experts on general and specific expertise, could be hired by a potential customer who was willing to pay (by direct charge of his telephone account) a per-minute fee. Just to build confidence, there would be a set of three questions that a potential customer could ask a number of experts, and based on their answer and rates, he could decide to hire one.

Copyright © 2008 - 2009 Razban Internet International, Inc. All rights reserved, File:20091022, P a g e | **220**

CHAPTER 91:   Knowledge Bottling Enterprise (KBE)

You have a right at this point, with my crude bottling company example to throw this book against the wall and then on the ground and step on it. You could say, "This dude who claims to be a people-oriented senior manager is comparing people to bottles." How could he? Does he mean that soon we will all get layoff notices and be replaced by bottles? I hope not. Nevertheless, just do look around you next time you go to Starbucks, or an airport, or anywhere else. So many people are working with their iPhones or Blackberries sending and receiving text and e-mail. Palmtops have replaced laptops as the primary computer. This trend will accelerate and increase exponentially.

In fact personal computers (PCs) and the Internet created massive freedom and empowerment for business. This had never existed in the entire industrial world or even world history. Information available instantly everywhere, is the iPhone or Blackberry revolution that is by for more powerful than Industrial Revolution ever was. This in turn has created a serious dilemma for Capitalism. Capitalism must respond by re-inventing itself. Companies in Silicon Valley and elsewhere re-invent themselves regularly to recover, regroup, and thrive. Why not the old form of Capitalism? A single PC is all it takes for a student in India or China to compete with mega corporation IBM! In addition, the Internet and e-commerce makes a tiny company such as mine able to freely compete in the same market as IBM.

In the fourth grade, my daughter is using the Internet to send e-mails around the world. In addition, students in the fourth grade have learned to use the Internet as a part of their homework. In my career, which is technology and management consulting, the Internet has played a vital role. I could not survive without it. Many companies could not survive without internet either. It has helped me stay knowledgeable on the latest technologies. It has also helped me immensely in finding new jobs and opportunities. I have kept my skill set current only because I can do extensive research on the Internet, using my Blackberry. When Dr. Gil Amelio was the CEO of Apple, I sent him and the Board of Directors a letter telling them that they need to jump on the Internet bandwagon. I even suggested that they change the name of the company to Cyber1! My letter that was circulated in the Board of Directors was sent long time before the iPhones, iPods, and when Apple was happy just making Macs.

For many years I have used the "What Color is Your Parachute" as the bible for finding a job, writing resume, and everything else. These are fantastic books. These books have kept pace with the times. For example, the one that is for 2009 is somewhat focused on the Global Financial Crisis at hand. This is a fantastic book, or more correctly series of books that has always helped me for many years.

In the 2009 edition, the book goes into details about what is our mission in life and work. I have known that my mission is to formulate a viable management alternative to layoffs and unemployment so that this is not such a painful process for those who lose their jobs, and for the companies that I estimate lose $2.4 Trillion each year in wasted productivity. This $2.4 Trillion loss is only if the unemployment is 4%. In summer of 2009, unemployment rate was at 11%. The 11% unemployment rate makes the total productivity loss add up to $6.1 Trillion for US only. This does not even try to attach a Dollar figure to horrors of people losing their houses due to foreclosures. It does not comprehend the human pain and suffering that results from a job loss. It cannot possibly

Copyright © 2008 - 2009 Razban Internet International, Inc. All rights reserved, File:20091022, P a g e | **221**

include the unacceptable services, and inferior products that were produced by companies whose scared employees said and did anything each day just to keep their job for that day.

I am sorry that I got distracted. Distractions are a job hazard for the job of finding jobs, which is a full time job in itself. This is fancy writing, thanks to my mentor at Stanford University Professor Tobias Wolff. I have read many of his writings and he has had a profound impact on me. He is also my role model. Unfortunately, he does not personally know me. However, he has helped mold my writing greatly. OK, I got distracted again. Let us go back to that Knowledge Bottling Company. The only job security that any of us could have is to have outstanding skill set that is highly in demand. Then, the employers will come after you, instead of you going after them. You will have a job even during financial down time.

Figure out what this skills can be for you. Develop them. Refine them and you will be fine in the work place of the future.

CHAPTER 92:   Human and Knowledge-Based Capitalism (HKC)

I am not an economist, and I am not into politics. Nevertheless, it is clear that Capitalism has used human greed, which in excess can be a terrible thing, and channeled it into something positive. Unfortunately, Capitalism continues to be based on some old ideas. Many years later after their invention, the knowledge and Internet revolutions need to be updated. Remember that asset management is turning into knowledge management. The awful problem and the serious shortcoming of the Internet, and industry for that matter, is that it needs to be humanized! Capitalism needs to be re-invented so it pays a lot more attention to humans than things.

In the Jewish religion (Hebrew), when you count things, you use numbers. However, when you are counting humans, you use the word blessings. For example, you have five prayer books and six blessings (Bracha) of people. This is a strong concept in Judaism that emphasizes human aspects. As of this writing, Capitalism seems to have done OK, in spite all its terrible shortcomings. Unfortunately, what was good in the 1920s, cannot possibly still be good in now. Information has changed everything. It is no longer the raw materials, or the labor. It is the information content. It is our ability to capture information real time, process it mightily, and turn it into power. The most power is inherently and ultimately in our people. Our people, that is our employees, customers, and management can make information come to life.

Instead of some sixty years that the computer industry has tried to make people act like computers, it is time to have computers act more like humans. By this, I do not mean robots. I mean software that has to be a far more powerful human interface. I mean HKC that thinks, plans, and designs with human beings in mind, and implements human-oriented devices.

In one recent TV program, we learned that as we depend more and more on the software, it turns out that software is not working as well as it is supposed to. Many corporations are allowing customer abuse to go on instead of fixing the software. The same also holds for management and Capitalism. We need to re-invent both so the bigger emphasis is on people.

If you take care of the human aspect of your business, money and plenty of it, will be yours. It will accrue almost effortlessly.

Copyright © 2008 - 2009 Razban Internet International, Inc. All rights reserved, File:20091022, P a g e | **223**

CHAPTER 93:   Paperless Workplace

When I joined CISCO for a consulting assignment, I discovered that many cubicles were totally devoid of paper of any kind. On neither the employee's desks nor bookshelves was there was any sign of paper. There was no piles of computer print outs, nor were there any memos printed out and stacked on desks, nor on the chairs, or even on the floor as is the case in many places. There were no magazine or newspaper articles cut out and pinned to some bulletin board, or anything else like it. In fact, they would remove bookshelves from their offices to create more space in their cubicles.

Then I remembered the big talk in the sixties about "paperless offices of the future," which many big companies were promising would happen around the seventies but did not. Well, now it had finally happened, at least at CISCO. When I went to meetings, people would bring their laptops, connect them to power that was at any desk in any conference room, and connect to the Internet. Instead of writing on some note pad, they would type the information into their computers right there and then. They were also able to communicate via text messages all the time during the meetings to help each other better with input to help the meeting be more and more effective.

Slowly, I was able to adapt this new idea in practice. I kept my information on my laptop and I would send e-mails instead of printing handouts. I must have saved many trees during the time that I worked for CISCO. Moreover, having only a laptop to carry around and have all the information that was needed was a fantastic blessing. Founders of Google told an interviewer that their original motivation was to put "All the information in the world into one suitcase." It is interesting to note that information is more and more considered super perishable and fluid. Therefore, knowledge is even more critical now than it ever was in the history.

Back to CISCO, employees and management had also learned to attend a meeting and at the same time check their email in parallel and convey a chat with another colleague half way around the world. This made sure that most recent information was available everywhere instantly. Processes were in place that kept track of work follow that would route the product or service under development from one workstation to another. This way, information, test, and quality were an integrated, closely controlled, and automatic part of the process. I am positive that, within the next five to ten years, we will all have to be part of the paperless revolution.

This brings me to a critical point here. We all need computers even more than ever before. Computer literacy, which used to be an additional skill set, is now required and basic.

In fact, I am a bit ahead of that in that I use my blackberry eighty to ninety percent of the time instead of the laptop or the desktop to check my e-mails, etc.

CHAPTER 94:   Virtual Global Teams

At CISCO, I was supposed to work with a huge team in Australia, Israel, Canada, Germany, Belgium, several time zones on the US continent, and some other places. At that time, CISCO had a company directory internal to the employees that had pictures of the people. Some pictures were professional pictures taken at a studio, and some were just a two Mega-pixel pictures that did not really look that good. However, aside from those pictures, you had no way of knowing anything about the people you exchanged hundreds of e-mails with, or spent hours talking to on conference calls. Sometimes, you called someone at 9:00 AM Pacific, and they said they were having their dinner in Israel, and then, you called somebody at Midnight Pacific, and they had just started their breakfast. Or, in some difficult negotiations, in order to be able to have everybody on the call, you needed to be in your office at 4:00 AM Pacific, and then you caught people having lunch and dinner and breakfast all at the same time, and some were even into the next business day. I found this to be very interesting.

However, it also meant that, no matter what hour of day or night in California, somebody somewhere else in the world was working during their natural working day. Somebody described this as GIT (Global Insomnia Time), similar to PDT Pacific Daylight Savings Time. However, in spite all the distance, we were able to get things done almost as rapidly as if we were in the same building.

One interesting advantage of this Global Virtual Team is that things can be done quickly. For example, at the end of a normal workday in California, I prepared what needed to be worked on in another time zone. Usually, I would send it to Israel or India. Then, first thing the next day, they had the result of their work at my desk when I showed up for work. Interestingly enough, this was the time when they were getting ready to go home for the day.

CHAPTER 95:   Permanent, Perpetual, Consulting Jobs

As we go from asset-based industries to knowledge-based industry, then it will be the case that companies will be interested in hiring people with narrowly defined skill set for a very detailed, defined task for a certain period. For example, you might work for a company that will hire you for your set of skills inventory that includes x, y, and z, and for a certain period. You might be working with a French company that only needs skill set x for three weeks, and then right after that, you will work for a British company that needs your skills y and z and wants to use your services for seven and a half weeks afterwards. Therefore, instead of being a technical writer, your "consulting firm" will present you as the person with the following skills sets:

- Detailed proof reader, intermediate, level 3, English   Available June 3rd
- Copyeditor, advanced, level 8, English   Available July 5th
- Book Reviewer, Entry Level, English   Available August 8th
- Coversheet design, intermediate, English and French   Available August 2nd

You will have a set of refined, certified, and marketable skill set and expertise. The consulting firm will try to provide you with full-time work based on your expertise and availability. As you might have noticed, in the future you will not work some place full time as a Software Engineer. Your talents will be rented at different times and in different places. This is extreme consulting. In fact, they might have certification levels and performance levels that will be helpful for companies to decide who to hire for which project. In addition, employee owned track record and customer satisfaction history could be helpful here. In fact, I am all for taking an on line test so they know I am qualified. In one of the start-ups, we were totally stuck in one technical area. Our research and asking around indicated that there was one and only one internationally known and respected expert in this high-tech area with many years of experience who worked and lived in Austin, Texas. We invited him to come to our company and guide us. He took a look at our elaborate presentation and told us that he only needed ten percent of that. Then, he carefully and patiently listened to everything we had to say on that ten percent that he had specified. After this, he excused himself, went back to his rental car, and came back with several notebooks and data sheets.
To make a long story short, he was able to guide us in the right direction. We had the solution a week after his visit. Even the loudest critiques of the high consulting fees that he charged, could not argue with the results. Although, I am not anywhere as famous as he is, I have found the same thing. Companies bring me in as an organizational, or Project Manager, or Technologist "Heavy Hitter" and pay me well. In addition, they get what they pay for. In addition, I also try to cross-train their permanent employees as an ethical practice.
This reminds me of a story about a man who spent several days to fix the pluming in the house. Finally, he got smart and listened to his wife. The Plummer was done in ten minutes. The man questioned him why it only took ten minutes. The Plummer's answer was that it took actually two years and ten minutes. He explained that the two years was for him to become an expert and stay on top of the latest in that field. We must focus on one, two, or three diversified skill sets that are highly in demand in the market place even during the difficult times. Remember, the only job security that we have is in our refined and marketable skill set; our track record and work history, and our ability to continue to

Copyright © 2008 - 2009 Ruzbun Internet International, Inc. All rights reserved, File:20091022.

be the best of the best in those diversified areas.

Another one that is as important is a good network that is kept alive even when we have jobs. We can actually keep track. If we found a job for someone in this record, then he or someone else in the network will also be able to find us a job at our hour of need. This is critically important. I have a friend and colleague whom I call when I am upset about something at work. As a friend he always listens to what I have to say patiently and without any judgment. Then gently as a colleague, he helps me find the right solution. He remains fair, productive, and supportive. On one occasion, he helped me to learn to delegate. As a manager, I had a hard time with this. As individual contributors, we learn to do things and get them done. If we do a good job, it is our credit and if we do a bad job it is ourselves to blame. However, a manager has to rely on others to do things that he or she is responsible for being done. He asked me to pretend that he is my employee and I will do exactly what I did when I was delegating that assignment. As a trusted outsider, he had no trouble finding what was wrong, and he gently helped me understand. Then we did a role-play making sure I had understood. The next day, I was elated to find out how much easier life can be with having a network. Interesting thing enough is that I was not the only person that was happy. The poor person who had had to put up with me and my inadequate delegation skills was on cloud nine!

In a re-run of a Sixty Minutes program on CBS tonight (May of 2009), the reporter asked an interesting question. He asked whether it was even fair to give all tax Dollars to Mega (Very Big) banking institutions. The answer from an NDIC official was that she was not sure since repeated bailouts of these huge banks have not completely solved the problem. Also, note that GM finally went bankrupt. Some few years ago, I had written that these dinosaurs or imitations are just too big to be manageable. We need smaller, community-based ones, that are more efficient and more in tune with their local community customers.

CHAPTER 96:   "You've got to be very careful if you don't know where you are going, because you might not get there."

I love Yogi Berra!
He is an American hero, and icon, and he is one of those that are the best in his job. This is something that you might consider. For example, in several areas, I can be considered one of the best. My resumes that focus on these skills usually get me some results. Yogi Berra, perhaps by being great in what he did never had serious problems in finding jobs. Jobs came to him rather the other way around. He had a great career that is admired and coveted by many people, fans or not. Maybe you and I will never become famous. However, if we make a plan and work on it each day, we will succeed. We must know where we are going, as per Yogi's advice. We do not want to waste our time and not get there either!
One of the best managers I know, who used to work at HP, was the first to tell me that people do not fail, they fail to plan. Unemployment, or underemployment, or a dead-end job, or the effect of Zombification in a job, makes it difficult for us to plan. You do not have to be an expert in making Microsoft project plans to do this. Take a piece of paper and write the names of ten of your colleagues to call. Go online and look at jobs. However, your plan has to be specific. It always helps your plan to be written down. Make a list of everything you found. Follow up on those names and jobs that you liked. Write down the results. Invest in a notebook especially for this. Mark your calendar. Ask for help. We can do it! We need only one job. To get that one job, we need to make fifty calls (let us say), and send one hundred resumes. Do it. You deserve better than this. Get yourself a good or better job. Many people just love to blame a dysfunctional workplace on bad management. Yet they are not willing to take a few hours to start a journal and to write in it for a few minutes every day, a sort of the captain's log!
In my journal, I usually write about daily activities on the job, and the job search. One can write goals and what makes a future job ideal. It is amazing what you can find out in this type of effort. We do not want twenty years to go by without us making a plan and acting on it. We do not want to be stuck in one dead end, awful job and have no way out!

Copyright © 2008 - 2009 Razban Internet International, Inc. All rights reserved, File:20091022. P a g e | **228**

CHAPTER 97:   You are Your Own Job Security

In the old times, companies used to take pride in that they provided job security for their employees. In addition, this was respected and it was common practice. In addition, many established companies carefully monitored their employees' job satisfaction. Neither of these two exists any more.

Disappointedly now, the trend is more and more towards hiring a special talent/skill set for a certain amount of time and specific expected output. Therefore, it is critical for employees to develop, refine, and constantly update their skill sets.

I have lived with this fact of life and career that if I did not keep up with the latest and greatest in the high-tech industry, my skill set would become completely obsolete after two or three years. Of course, those who are not in high-tech might have less pressure on them to keep updating their skill set.

Even major corporations, who used to boast about having abundant opportunities, have stopped bragging about job security. It just does not exist. They do know within their hearts that there is no such thing anymore. The only job security comes in our ability to keep our skill set in great shape and to keep networking.

One great place to network professionally is LinkedIn.com. This Mountain View Company has grown a great deal. FaceBook.com and MySpace.com can also be great assets in marketing yourself. We have to constantly make sure our skill set is in demand and that it is as sharp as possible. I owe a great deal of gratitude to many local colleges and Stanford that have helped me keep my skill set sharp. Yet there will still always be immense pressure for employees to be computer literate and to be comfortable with computers and the Internet.

Instead of panicking about Sudden Job Loss (SJL) happening to you, please consider doing these things:

- Re-write and update your resume(s),
- Sign up for some community college classes to fortify your skill set,
- Make networking calls and keep a list of companies that are hiring in your area,
- Take good care of your health, spirits, and respect yourself.

After all, we can only do our humanly best for one hour, one day, or even one minute at a time.

Then make sure you enjoy a life lived well. Remember one of the heroes in the book saying that it seemed like it was only yesterday when her little two-year-old girl would ask for ice cream and she is now all of a sudden 24!

CHAPTER 98:   Employment is the Foundation of the American Economy

Employment is extremely critical to the American economy. The US government keeps track of the percentage of people that are employed. This unemployment statistics is published each and every month. As an indicator, this is considered in most economic analyses. Unfortunately, by its definition this is not as good as it could be. It does not include those who used up their unemployment or those who just gave looking. Estimates are that a more accurate unemployment figure is 1.5 to 8 times this. The 8 times figure, also includes the underemployed. Maybe we in US become so advanced that we also gather and track the employee satisfaction figures too. Maybe Gallop or other statistics gathering companies might want to privatize this.

Since I believe that Global Financial Crisis could and should have been predicted, we could use a more reflective employment statistics as an indicator or alarm. We do not have the luxury of looking at the world financial system the same way we look at weather. Weather, that we think that we do not have any control over. Even in case of weather, we can "seed" the clouds. A financial crisis is just like the 1902 San Francisco earthquake. It was not the earthquake that devastated San Francisco then, it was the fire. Although earthquakes are unpredictable, we have learned to do much better job of the aftermath.

Just for us in US, imagine that we have an economic equivalent of US Coast Guard. US Coast Guard does a great job of rescuing ships before they sink. In addition, some of its rules and regulations proactively prevent future disaster. I love to go to Pier 9 in San Francisco. There are many nice restaurants that overlook the beautiful San Francisco Bay. I always see at least one and perhaps more US Coast Guard ships.

I know, some of you reading this are thinking that this violates "Free Markets!" No, it does not. Just like freedom itself, we are free to whatever we want except violating somebody else's freedom.

Employment creates money, and money runs the world. This is so important that during a recession, government has to create "works projects" just to make sure people are working. Some of our highways and infrastructure were created this way. This is more like an afterthought put in place after the damage has been done. We need proactive preventive business models.

Joblessness is not just the loss of a paycheck or a title. There is also the dehumanizing and devastating psychological side of unemployment. In this case, the money needed to run the economy does not circulate and percolate among different people and industries. Despair and misery seem to quickly replace hope and slow down even the most productive people and organizations.

Misery is so serious that economists have a measurement for it called the misery index! On September 26, 2008, Washington Mutual collapsed. This collapsed was really bad and we had reached a dangerous point. Both Presidential hopefuls stopped their campaigns and went to Washington to sit down with President Bush. All three tried to come up with a solution. A $700 Billion Bailout proposal was being considered. Moreover, right then, as I was watching CNN, a very good friend called me and said, "You have been giving me hope and encouragement to keep searching for a job. As you can see, the situation is grim. I plan to give up looking for a job and give up in my

Copyright © 2008   2009 Ra..bun Internet International, Inc. All rights reserved, File:20091022, P a g e | **230**

career." My answer to him was that I agreed that the situation was very grim in view of what was happening. However, I told him that, for his own sanity and his family, he just could not give up. I even hit him with the worn out cliché that says, "Do not give up hope fifteen minutes before the miracle." Never give up fifteen minutes before a miracle and/or breakthrough actually happens. We never know. I gave up on a job after the third interview, thinking that they would never give me that job. Sure enough, two weeks after I had started a new contract, the recruiter called me with the "good news" that I could start the very next Monday, and, that job was a lot better than what I had at the time. However, I had given up and had signed a new contract that I could not break. However, I did apologize to my friend for hitting him with a cliché.

- Remember, there are a lot of options.
- There are many alternatives to sending a resume for an existing job.
- You can literally create a job for yourself by proposing something that will bring a company additional income.
- You can downshift. If you were a senior manager, now you might even accept a manager's job and do your best to do justice to that job.
- You can go for a survival job. This is a job you get that is way below what you were used to get. Importantly, this will restore the income stream and helps you stay in shape and be on your toes for the next job. This gives you agility and hope. You will not be making as much money, but you will be doing something and earning something. Something is always better than nothing!
- As President Sarcozy of France is encouraging his countrymen to do, you can become an entrepreneur and do what is your passion.
- You can go back to college and get the badly needed education to improve your career or create a new career.
- If you can afford it, take a Sabbatical.
- If you can afford it, spend more time with family and friends and enjoy this most important thing in life.
- If you can afford it, travel all around the world.
- Do the things that you always wanted to do but work Zumbification prevented you by draining your energy, desire, and mood after a hard day's work.
- Learn a new hobby.
- Get married, engaged, move in, move out, fall in love, fall out of love, or get unmarried if you absolutely, positively had to.
- Lose weight, or gain weight depending on your needs and desire. However, please be reasonable and safe.
- Give your health spa or sports club the run for their money. You them as much as they said you can use them. You might have already paid for it.
- Get excited about home improvement, only if you are the type! This option is definitely not for me. It is not for me in million years!
- Etc., Etc., Etc.

Let us look at our present unemployment situation intelligently. We do not get paycheck. Nevertheless, we time. We are free. We are alive and there is so much to enjoy and do. I assure you that almost all our working colleagues are jealous about our freedom. I also assure you that it was not our fault to be unemployed now. We might as well enjoy life.

CHAPTER 99:   Adam Smith's Contract with Capitalism

Capitalism has a good and a bad image. Adam Smith to my understanding, says that businesses do whatever they have to do to make money. After all this is supposed to be a free market. This in itself implies no rules either. He adds that this pursuit of money by Capitalism might even hurt human beings, such as customers, employees, and competition.

However, based on my thirty-two years of experience I strongly disagree. I argue that, if you are in the business to make money, and make a lot of it, there is only one way to do this. It is looking for the human side of things. At the beginning of the dot-com revolution, there was an excellent book titled *Customer.com*. This book rightly argued that the most important thing in any business is the customer, employees, and the humans that are involved. Unfortunately, this concept is so badly violated that there are companies that do not give you a phone number to call for customer service. Some computer at their end scans your email and decides to send some totally irrelevant pre-composed email in response. Computers are meant to automate things and not to replace humans.

In Archie Bunker's sitcom *All in the Family*, in the 1960s there was an episode when a prune company was sending Archie a full box of prunes. He spent the entire sitcom calling many different people and companies to finally get hold of the company that was sending him the unwanted and almost hated box of prunes. After a long discussion, the company representative explained, "This is caused by our computer that has a mind of its own and we cannot control our computer, so sorry." What is sad is that Archie accepts this and says, "Well, if it is your stupid computer, then I understand THAT!"

Today with gigantic progress in the computer industry, the same excuse is given. I propose that we should not accept it. Computers are tools. Tools are only as intelligent as the idiot who uses them.

Capitalism, hand in hand with humanitarian processes and procedures instilled in a company daily operation, will make the most profitable companies. Maybe, I as a nobody or just a work a day stiff should strongly propose that instead of measuring human misery as part of capitalism, we measure humanitarian index for each company.

This old Adam Smith concept is based on win-lose concept. For someone to win, others must lose. However, it is a fact that companies with their win-win culture like HP have proven that you can have a win-win operating and strategic plans. Nobody needs to lose if it is possible for all to win.

The basis for this is to put people first. This is practicing Human Oriented Capitalism. This is to use the latest technology for the benefit of your employees and customers and not as a means of isolating or enforcing a customer abusing policy.

The best way to make the Capitalism greed to work is to take good care of people. A cup of coffee served in any other place might just taste and look as good as Starbucks. But the monumental Starbucks success was mainly, in my opinion, because they treated their customers with a lot more care and respect than others.

CHAPTER 100:   Charlie Chaplin and Modern Times Movie

Charlie Chaplin, in my opinion, was not just a movie star. He was one of the greatest geniuses we have ever seen. In his movie, *Modern Time*, he shows machines and operators like himself who work with these machines, and even at some point, they become just like a part of the machine. His behavior is perfect example of what I have described as Zombification. In this role, he starts to lose his humanness and become a mechanized human doing. I have seen executives act this way, I have seen individual contributors act this way, and I have myself done my share of this.

In my thinking, what the Global Financial Crisis has established is that there has been a hostile takeover of Capitalism by Foolishism. All of us acted so much like Zombies that we did not even realize what this hostile takeover has done to our work and life. We were too busy being workaholics.

Let us say that you are a professional with ten years of experience in editing newspapers and you live in Texas. Suppose, there is a company trying to make a label for their wine in English in South Africa. The ad campaign for selling this wine claims something like it is the type of wine that Egyptian Pharos used to drink and offer to high priests of the time. An Egyptian history professional has already spent time and was compensated for some potential wording for the label. Then, an artist living in Tokyo, Japan, has prepared a few sketches. Some sophisticated Enterprise Company, which had hired you many times before to benefit from your expertise, has defined details, and will hire you to do your magic on this to finalize the wording. Then someone else will check to make sure the entire artwork fits what the company needs.

Now, let us assume that people need to only work four or eight hours a week to earn a very comfortable living. You work with a virtual global team that gets the best possible job done with the absolute least cost. The next day, suppose you need to change the oil in your car. You order the oil online, along with finding that someone in your neighborhood is a professional oil change in his/her spare time. In addition, you pay for his knowledge (which is in a bottle just like the oil.) Then, either you do it yourself or give it to the neighbor on a negotiated fee and agreed on by the company to do the work.

In "What Color is your Parachute", the point is strongly made that we are constantly learning, unlearning, and then learning again to keep up with the latest and greatest in our careers.

The funny silent era Charlie Chaplin movie is now becoming more and more true to life. Instead of spending a lot of time and learning something, and then forgetting it, we can now hire that expertise and get things done better and cheaper. I personally have to learn this better to unlearn some of my old believes as far as my career is and to replace them with new learning. Just like the Modern Times movie, we become the best in several marketable skill sets as the workers. Then the employers will need to learn to rent our skills to complete a project. Then we go to the next project, and the next, and the next. This is the wave of the future.

CHAPTER 101:   You are the CEO of Your Life and Career

Nobody can be as good and caring as you are with your life and career. You are the captain of the ship. You are the CEO, Chairman of the Board, Board of Directors, and the only employee!

It used to be that managers and HR departments helped employees take training courses, get better in their fields, learn management, and have a short-term and long-term career plan. Those days are gone. Take an on-going inventory of your skill sets and accomplishments. Check to see which skill sets are in demand. Compare yours with those that are indicated in job descriptions. If you see any gaps, make sure to fix that by going to college, taking evening classes, engaging in self-teaching, or even better, hiring a tutor. Over the years, I have greatly benefited from this advice. I have attended technical colleges to make sure that my technical skills were on the "Bleeding Edge" of technology. For example, I took a Java programming course in Foothill College well before most technical people knew what Java was. I paid a small tuition for this and it really helped me for many years. Recently, I have been teaching myself Ruby. Ruby is the next generation programming language that will have a profound impact on the computer industry. During my commute, I listen to Steven Covey and others in making sure that I have mastered the latest management concepts, which I will put into practice. This keeping on keeping on also has another fantastic benefit. In addition to keeping me employable, it also keeps me alive! By constantly learning, my brain and my self-respect and confidence will keep thriving.

So many people waste their talents in dead-end and non-productive jobs. Then they complain about their awful jobs. However, they have to realize that they have the power, and they do have to take this bad situation. They can get out. Since America is the land of opportunities, there are a lot of opportunities that can be yours. Nevertheless, you must plan try, and try a bit harder.

People do not fail! They fail to plan and then act on it. So many people do not know what they would like to do next month or next year. So many people cannot tell you what the next promotion for them is. They have no clue. They go into a job review and come out disappointed. However, they are quick to tell you that they are unhappy and that their jobs have been a waste of their lives.

One of my best friends told me that career planning was not his job. This really baffled me. What does he mean? It is his job! He needs to work at it. He needs to decide what his next step is and what he needs to do to achieve it. He cannot leave his destiny in the hands of others. This is no criticism of HR departments. They do the best they can. However, in my opinion, they cannot possibly figure out what makes you tick. They cannot predict what the most desired next step for you can be like. Sadly, many of the HR departments were decimated as results of the repeated and frequent layoffs, off shoring, and shortsighted "Cost savings." This leaves you, and you alone, as the CEO and Captain of your life and career.

I have been convinced for a long time that there is no such a thing as job security any more. Many companies are doing the best that they can providing some sort of job security. Nevertheless, nothing can be as powerful as you taking your job security in your own hands.

One prime indicator of job security, these days, is that the company that hired you must

Copyright © 2008 - 2009 Razban Internet International, Inc. All rights reserved, File:20091022, P a g e | 234

need you more than you need the company. Here are some tell-tell signs:

- Does the work pile up and wait for you to come back from a vacation or sick leave?
- Do you hear people say that you do a great job?
- Does your manager listen when you talk in a meeting?
- Do your colleagues come to you for help and advice?
- Do you usually deliver about five to ten percent more than what is expected of you?

Starting a small business is much easier than you might think. It also gives you freedom that you could never have imagined before as you were slaving to work for others. Please read the reference section. I have listed several helpful books on this subject. In addition, who knows, you might be one of those who succeeds and even succeeds big. Being your own boss makes things a lot more meaningful and you get your own dignity and sanity back. You have the control over your business and your money. Please let me put it this way, with your own small business, you have control over your own life! It has also been my experience that the entire American business world will try to encourage you and lend you a hand. They literally tried to cheer me up to start my small business and to continue once I had started.

Remember that if you have done everything humanly in your power to prepare for that eventual Sudden Job Loss, then your self-confidence will improve and you are more immune to anxiety attacks and stress. In the old days in San Francisco Airport, there was a vending machine that sold you flight insurance. Of course, those days air travel was a lot more dangerous than it is today. As the single breadwinner, I would be encouraged by my family to buy these flight insurances. This was good for them, and was good for me too. I remember the feeling that I would have when I would take my seat knowing that I have done everything humanly possible for any eventuality and I have even purchased the flight insurance. A powerful job insurance in addition to doing the best job we humanly can do each and every day is to do what I have formulated in another chapter. We need to have an updated resume at all times, and an active and live network.

I just do not sit there doing nothing. I keep learning, unlearning, and relearning. In spite all the hardships life is sweet. In 2009, some nights I would go to bed hungry. I have a pile of rejections. I have many colleagues who have been jobless for a year or more that it makes me wanting to cry. I put ¾ Gallon of Gasoline in my each time and carefully calculate how far I can go. I, the big shot Senior Management and Technology Consultant am in constant fear of foreclosure. My old car is on its last leg. We are several months behind in paying my daughter's tuition. Several time, I have found out that the money in my pocket is not enough for the bare essential groceries, we are damned if we go for food stamps, not yet! I have been rejected in interviews because I am sixty years old, or overweight, I have offered to work for free as a volunteer only to be rejected. It hurts when you are rejected when you offer to work for free. Is there such a thing as being overpriced even if the price is free?

But, I have a mission! I have unconditional love! I have long ego forgiven all those who harmed me. I have done my humanly best to help all those whom I can. I do not have money to give them, I wish I did. Nevertheless, I have tried to give them hope. I have tried to be their friend even as a fellow blogger to another.

I am proud. I might financially poor, but I am spiritually, mentally, rich and blessed with lots of love, understanding and care. A total stranger jumped to the front of line and offered to pay for my groceries when I was $2.80 too short. Can you imagine that I used to get $150.00 per hour? My friends have lent me all they could.

The astonishing thing is that I am not defeated! I do my humanly best each day. Some days this can be only two hours of work. The superhuman side of this is that I have a mission, I have a passion.

As Veronica had told me, the mansion in Los Gatos hills was nothing compared to her sense of self-respect and happiness for taking care of his dying husband in an apartment that is smaller than their garage area in the mansion. There is proverb in Persian that says money is just like the dirt that makes our hands dirty. It comes and goes, but love, respect, and our humanity is by far more important. Our Mokato is what no amount of money can ever buy! My Aunt, who lost her young son, and is now taking care of her dying husband in a nursing home, told me that we only have this instant. Nobody knows what tomorrow will bring.

I believe that we all have lived forever and will live forever more. I believe that love is what it is all about. Try to help someone today. It does not take too much. Until tomorrow, let us let go and let God (of your understanding and your belief system!) In Hebrew, we say L'Chiam as a salute for drinking wine. L'Chiam loosely translates to, "To Life!"

This too shall pass!

Copyright © 2008 - 2009 Razban Internet International, Inc. All rights reserved, File:20091022, P a g e | **236**

CHAPTER 102:   Work as the Expression of Career Love and Passion

In general, people love to express their interests, ideas, feelings, and experiences. I miss those old days that my Grandmother would tell us about things that had happened in her life. Some of those were funny and some serious. She was one of the best storytellers I have ever seen. My mother and father were also good at telling stories.

I remember my mother telling me about her first trip to Paris. She would describe the French as one of the most cultured and civilized people in the world. I had heard about the Louvre Museum when I was three or four years old. She had described it as a city where children had better hold their parents' hands so that they would not get lost. She would add that, if you get lost there, it would be very difficult to find you. Then she will try to describe different paintings and artwork that they had there. We will go to different museums in Teheran, she would compare those with Louvre, and hope someday there will be a museum as huge as Louvre in Tehran.

My father loved to be able to speak French fluently. He took pleasure in reading the latest medical books in French. Being an MD with special training in France, he had fallen in love with their medical technology, language, and culture. He would spend days writing papers that he would present to other MDs at conventions. He would not get tired of doing this. He would come home after a long day at work, and then he would clean up, have dinner with us, and go to his study to continue working on his presentations.

In fact, his "real" job was his passion. He had lost his Dad when he was only four years old. My mother would proudly tell me that my Dad would follow his mother to work as early as four years old. One time when he got sick, they did not have the money to buy the needed medicine. Therefore, his minor sickness lingered, until an MD agreed to treat him and be paid in four installments.

His career passion was that this should not happen to kids. He worked for a charity hospital for children and he eventually became the section medical chief.

Unfortunately, working at a charity hospital did not pay too well. When we would encourage him that he had paid his dues and that he needed to join one of those richer clinics, he would say that not everything in this world could be measured with money. His job satisfaction each time he treated a poor kid was worth millions to him.

By the way, he wanted me to also become an MD and serve my community. However, after a great deal of effort on his part and mine, we finally decided that the medical profession was not for me. My passion was in electronics, and later, management. When I am confronted with the pain of layoffs for employees, managers, and the workplace, I cannot help but think of better ways to handle cutbacks. When layoffs happened to me, I decided that this is not a good thing and nobody should experience this pain.

One of these better ways was what HP practiced for many years. HP would not lay off anyone. Instead, they would give all employees the option of working either four-day weeks and/or nine days out of ten. This was ethically, morally, and practically a win-win for all involved. Everybody was paid a bit less. This was capitalism at its best!

Since this chapter has the title of career love and passion, I feel that I have shared a lot of my life passion, including the Mile High Club, Red Light District, etc. in this book. This shows that I am a human being just like all others. Paradoxically, my passion for beauty and glamour, re-invented itself into love after I was married. Some Yiddish proverb, or other type of proverb says that, "You are nothing until you get married. After that your marriage is nothing until you have children". My love for my family is by far stronger than the passion I felt when I was free and single during the height of sexual revolution of the sixties. I have seen this love take different forms and shapes in my wife and other members of family. As my unemployment and dedication to this publishing of this book lingered into its tenth month, I saw my wife go without food, or new cloths. I saw my wife's family send a loan for us from Israel, which was way beyond their means. This is the most passionate type of love and the most beautiful. This love, lasts a lot more than that five minutes of pleasure in becoming a member of Mile High Club. My mother in law's chicken soup and chocolate cake, my wife's elaborate Shabbat preparation of meals including hard-boiled eggs and Yemenite Jachnoon (Bread), or my daughter bringing a home work assignment from school home. On my sixtieth birthday, my daughter made a picture for, and took all of us out for dinner. She used part of her college funds to pay for a lavish dinner at Shalizar Restaurant in Belmont. Shalizar, Chelokababi in Sunnyvale, and Maykeadeh in San Francisco, are the best Persian restaurants in the bay area.

I bumped into one of my old flames. In 1968, she was one of the best dressed, beautiful, and most romantic women I had ever met. When I saw her after some forty years, I noticed that she had not been taking good care of her health or her appearance. She was a totally different person. As much as e wanted to talk about those fun years, we both quickly realized that we were so much older that those days seemed like they happened in another planet. As I recall she is about one month younger than me. She has been living on disability and she felt lonely. "Bruce, you have not aged as much as I have. Is it your wife's cooking?" I responded, "Being married does help a great deal. However, I always kept busy. I did not just sat there!" A Yiddish proverb says it best, "An old man should have never been born!"

A dedicated employee who knows that a company cares for him or her produces more and better results. Of course, HP also had profit sharing, and it was one the first to offer employee stock plans. Employees knew that bad times would end, eventually. They also knew that good times then would create a profit-sharing check that more than compensated for those four out of five or nine out of ten days. Intel Corporation has also tried to minimize the impact of layoffs by avoiding them.

HP is one of the few companies that have had a consistently good stock rating even in most difficult financial times.

CHAPTER 103:   Imagine!

The word "imagine" has a very special importance to me. Aside from being the title of one of the most profound Beatles songs, it has a great significance to what we are discussing here.

Imagine that you started your career working for the very same company until you retired from there. Imagine the company started working with you while you were in high school or even before.

- Imagine that the company worked with you, and for you, while you were getting ready to get your first job.
- Imagine that they knew you so far ahead of time that they had actually one, or several, alternative jobs waiting for you after high school, college, or technical training.
- Imagine that this company helped you get your first credit cards, a good and dependable insurance, loaned you money, and made time for on-the-job training, was constantly in touch with you, and helped you manage your career.
- Imagine that they provided outstanding childcare (similar to Kibbutz establishments in Israel.)
- Imagine that this company was constantly in touch with hiring companies and helped them plan their needs, including immediate needs, near future needs, and even long-term needs.
- Imagine that your time was so well organized that you had the flexibility of taking time out for vacations, family gatherings, emergencies, sick times, leisure and vacation times, time to go to college or special training, time to plan your life and career, etc.
- Imagine that you could resign from one company, or one gig, and start in a new one in a matter of days, or even hours.
- Imagine that your dedication, accomplishment, and loyalty to companies was never lost or ignored.
- Imagine that you could plan for your promotions, salary increases, and as a part of a win-win team get them on time as expected. No surprises.

Then consider some of these what if questions:

- What if just like college, employers could have a WPA (Work Point Average), something similar to GPA (Grade Point Average) that colleges have?
- What if there was a Central Registry that could keep track of the WPAs and, just like in college where a 3.5 GPA from the University of Michigan, Ann Arbor, could be used as one of the admission standards for a manager, an executive, iron worker, pilot, and engineer to be evaluated and hired at a new company?
- What if there was an Achievement Point Average (APA) for outstanding achievements standards for different companies?
- What if there was an Experience Point Average (EPA, or ExPA) to account for useful experience one has had in one specialty area in different companies?

My experience with resumes, both from hiring and being hired, points of view have been dismal. I have learned to be very cautious about resumes. I worry when a resume is too poorly made and when it is too good. I have hired some very poor candidates who had excellent resumes, and some excellent ones whose resumes were not particularly good.

Next time you start blaming yourself or getting angry with yourself, or internalizing why you have not been able to get a job to that point, consider the next few paragraphs. If you feel sick of being sick about finding a job, remember you are right. This is because the entire process is extremely foolish. Again, I want to emphasize that it is not your fault. Just the same, you still need to get one job and be productive again. You have to soar like an eagle even if turkeys surround you. I must confess that I have had to ask professional resume writers to write my resumes. Moreover, for the most part, I have been lucky (or cursed) by not really having to have an excellent resume. People who knew of my experience and accomplishments hired me. For many years, I had a set of resumes that were a poor reflection of my experience. Finally, I did the right thing. I asked two or three colleagues to review and comment on my resume. Finally, it took a very experienced resume writer/recruiter to put together an excellent one for me.

On the other hand, many job descriptions are a total hit and miss as far as really describing the job. The terrible side of this is that people do not apply for a job, even though they might very well be the best for it. They take the job description and its requirements list too literally. Even if the job description is correct, in our workplace, many jobs change as time goes by. Therefore, the job description that was marginal at the time of employment is now totally irrelevant.

My experience tells me that if I feel like I have sixty to seventy percent of the requirements, I should apply for it. I have also at times, sent resumes for jobs where I only satisfied twenty to thirty percent of the job requirements. Nevertheless, the manager was so impressed with that thirty percent that she called me in for an interview. Thus, the resume had done what it is supposed to do, which is to just get your foot in the door. In several cases, I had a verbal offer before I even did an interview.

Interviews can also be very foolish. For example, questions asked are usually the same mundane and meaningless ones. In one interview, they asked me if I was good in handling stress. Well, what do you answer? Should I say, "No, I am a human being, and I generally do not like stress." Alternatively, should I say, "For what you are paying for this job, you can only attract people who like low stress." Most candidates say, "I like Stress. It makes me be on my toes at all times." They say this and do not mean it. Unfortunately, if they do not say this, they will not get the job!
Other equally stupid questions are:
- What do you really want to be doing five years from now?
- Why do you plan to leave your present job?
- What are your strengths and weaknesses?
- What was your last salary?

As you can see, the entire process is *Meshugga* ("crazy" in Yiddish). On the other hand, as they say it in Dutch slang, these people have windmills in their heads! In Persian, there is the expression that "with their wisdom, they can lift rocks!"

The most important thing to do when you get a rejection, just laugh it off and go on to the next interview. Remember it is not you, it is the entire setup. Do not take it to heart. It is not your fault. Nevertheless, do talk this interview with your friends and colleagues and see if they can provide any insight. The fact is that with each interview you are getting closer and closer to your next job! This is so funny that I would have laughed if the subject was not so painful. Consider the fact that being a slave to a dead-end work in a

Copyright © 2008 - 2009 Razban Internet International, Inc. All rights reserved, File:20091022, P a g e | **240**

dysfunctional workplace, with toxic working relationships with other workers, can be much worse than not having that job! What if you got the stupid job and then dropped dead from a heart attack? I almost did. There is also another book that my best colleagues have written. The title says it all: Working with you is killing me!

In 1976, when I got my first job in California, I used Management Recruiters. The recruiter had previously talked to the hiring manager and he knew exactly what the job was all about. He had asked many questions to determine what the job really was. He had figured out what was not written that was critical to job. The recruiter, Richard Van Dorn, started his interview with some small talk, since he had noticed that I was too nervous about this being my first real job. His ancestors were from Holland, and he was very impressed to hear that I had a friend at Utrecht near Amsterdam. I spent a few minutes telling him about my visit with my friend and his wife in their beautiful house. We also talked about a distant relative of mine that had lived and worked in Rotterdam. He discussed several jobs, and then he told me that he had the ideal job for me. Moreover, indeed he was right he had the ideal job at Plantronics. He then picked up the phone and called the hiring manager, made arrangements for the interview, and I went to Santa Cruz for the interview. Most things were as he had predicted, including an offer on the spot! I would have never thought that I would take an offer on the spot. Looking back at that experience some thirty years ago, I still think that the recruiter was fantastic. I wish there were more people like that as opposed to the anonymous Internet recruiting of these days. Let us imagine and dream some more:

- Imagine that you were never fired!
- Imagine that, instead of being fired, you were offered new opportunities along with paid training time and mentors to help you get productive and excel at your new job that you love and cherish, a job that is a good fit for your skill set, likes, and interests.

Am I daydreaming? No! As The *Bionic Man* said, we have the technology. In addition, we can save and make a lot of money with this while improving the awful situation we now have. Imagine that I had stayed in the very first company I joined. Of course, as part of the chain of foolishness that goes everywhere in the workplace and work life, it was my decision to leave. However, let us say that I was encouraged to stay. Then, what they had invested in me would have paid off handsomely. They might have benefited from my inventiveness and created a new product line. My good will towards them would have permeated to all other employees.

Unfortunately, after my contract suddenly ended with that company, I realized later how much my conflict resolution skills could have helped them with their subsidiary. How much my inventiveness could have made them the one and only company that would pioneer a new concept way ahead of others. I really had my mind set on building a career there. In fact, my manager had told me that she would help me make a career with this company. I loved to go to my desk that was near a beautiful window looking outside. I had immensely enjoyed working with some of the best brains in the industry. That teamwork would have created outstanding results for that company. Instead, we both lost.

I have a friend who is less than half my age. His way of coping is to say that he will do the least that he can get away with for the company. As soon as a better job comes along, he is all set to pack his things and leave his present company. Nevertheless, unlike me and a lot better than me, he has learned all too important survival methods in a workplace

Copyright © 2008 - 2009 Razban Internet International, Inc. All rights reserved, File:20091022, P a g e | **241**

that has chains. He has learned to quickly recognize wolf packs, and he has learned how to "navigate" in shark-infested waters of back stabbers, politicians, and "play the game" politicians that might not have produced and "value-add" to company sales in months or even years. He has learned where the power base is and his behavior and actions are always consistent with that power base. He told me that first question that he always asks is "What is the political side of the problem?" When I asked him if he was happy with his work life, his answer was "you do not go to work to be happy, you go there to make money." He added, "You want to be happy, go to Lake Tahoe for skiing. Buy a new supercharger car. Buy the latest gadget for your laptop." To him work meant suffering. How about creativity above and beyond work requirements? How about learning new skills? How about creating a good circle of friends? "Well I do not have time for them. I learn as little as I absolutely need to. Moreover, I have learned that the workplace is a bad place to make friends. In fact, I do not even have time for a minimum social life." Look at the loss that this creates. A high potential mind and career is put in a holding pattern the same way airplanes sometimes have to circle the destination airport and wait. The discouraged employee cannot contribute as much as she wants to the company. The company gets into trouble because it is not competitive enough, and this creates a lose-lose instead of a win-win situation for all involved. This is another of those vicious cycles. This chain of fools really breaks my heart.

Fortunately, there still is room for hope. As the citizens of the most powerful industrial power in the universe, we can do many things here to improve this. If you happen to be the manager of such an employee, you might want to help this individual understand that we owe it to ourselves to constantly improve our skill set to be employable. You can find a mentor for this individual or be the coach that he might need to help him get over the rout. You, as a manager, are ethically responsible for his future and his career. If you see yourself as this individual, try to understand how fulfilling it is to be needed by companies more than you need them. The only way you could do this is by being a person that has excellent skills and who can do "value-add" to a company's bottom Line." Be the "go to person" rather than the "go for" person. On another painful subject, I like to say that the American acceptance of 4% unemployment as ideal, it is not a good thing. This is a faulty assumption that has persisted for a long time and it is just plain wrong. Let us say that the economic conditions in US, or even on the global basis gets worse and worse. I do not think either small businesses or the governments are able to fix the bad economic situation. Therefore, let us declare war on this bad economic situation. Let us do what countries do when they are attached. In that case, they will create the reserves in addition to the regular army. I would like to claim that it is my theoretical prediction that we can have a 107.8% employment, and that this figure should be considered as full employment and not the 96%.

Here are my reasons:

- Each company, at each given time, will have a set of additional part time employees, or potential future employees to job-share with existing employees.
- These people will be getting on the job training as well as help the company in the case regular employees are on vacation or need to take time off.
- Instead of unemployment, the government will create incentives for companies to practice what the additional work force will need.
- Each employee might have several of these jobs to even create a full time for

Copyright © 2008 - 2009 Razban Internet International, Inc. All rights reserved, File:20091022. P a g e | **242**

herself.

Unfortunately, workplace Zombification drains our brains and motivational power a little bit each day and makes it difficult to look at the future. As a result, many of our corporations, and small businesses act like shlock-houses that sell cheap, distressed, defective products and services in a most unproductive way. Then the future comes sooner than we thought when an employee has to go through the pain of layoffs and a manager has to go without the help of that employee that makes all others' work so much more difficult. Then, just like Chippie, he sits there without a song, and corporations go bankrupt because they cannot compete! Ironically, as sad as the down times are, they are the time to start a new business.

Copyright © 2008 - 2009 Razban Internet International, Inc. All rights reserved, File:20091022, P a g e | **243**

CHAPTER 104:   What and Who Can Do This?

HIPAA stands for Health Insurance Privacy and Protection Accountability, which is a regulatory requirement for health insurance companies. This is mandated by the US Government and is in effect now. I know that a lot of you do not like government to do things for you. And, in fact, this is perhaps one of those things that the government, US or EU, will not be able to do. I am also positive that the huge magnitude of this economic downturn during these times will require the government to make work and generate new jobs. This tsunami is huge!

It is just as easy and as important for a company to become the global employer of everyone who wants to join this company in a free membership. This global company has members who will do what the HR departments were supposed to do in cultivating and improving skill sets of the employees. This can be done by:

- Creating a career path for each employee
- Creating a reserve workforce of the 107.8% of the working force to act as a hybrid mechanism to proactively prevent layoffs
- Create ongoing Statements of Work (SOWs) for the employees
- Create a buffer list of potential employees for a company to satisfy a higher work force forecast
- Create a buffer potential employers for the employees

But aside from the government regulations or make-work plans, it is just you and I at the end of the day. That is all there is!

My tiny company, Razban Internet International, Inc., is gearing up to be to careers and workplace blues, what Amazon.com is to books. We have grandiose plans to be the global employer of choice. This is a great dream for such a tiny company. My ambition is to publish this book and then base on this book make a business plan and present it to several movers and shakers of the industry. I have put every ounce of training I got at Stanford University Continuing Education Seminar, "How to Start a Successful Startup" to work. I have generated a powerful business plan and have shared it with many venture capitalists.

My company has survived the difficult seed phase, and we are hoping to get the first round of $2.8M funding.

Copyright © 2008 - 2009 Razban Internet International, Inc. All rights reserved, File:20091022, P a g e | **244**

CHAPTER 105:   1929 Déjà vu all over again

Yogi Berra is a well-known American baseball hero. He has many quotes, and one of them is the title of this chapter.

In 1929, the Great Depression started. It was the beginning of a lot of financial problems for America. When a play repeated his mistake again in the baseball game, Yogi Berra would scream or complain that this was the same thing all over again, meaning we did not learn from it and we should not do it again.

On October 5, 2008, there was a major news report on the French television channel that the American banking collapse might have spread to Europe. However, France will not let it damage the French economy. Nicholas Sarcozy, who is my favorite French President, standing united with seven other European leaders. Together, they will do the best for Europe.

In a Public Radio program last night, there was finally admission that things are "very bad" from an American banking executive. On TV, there seemed to be a picture showing that the historical $700 Billion was ready for signing and will go into effect soon. Soon, of course, means tomorrow, Monday October 6, 2008. Obviously, by the time you get to read this book much time will have elapsed.

I am no economy expert. However, the fact remains I did research into what actually happened to families like yours and mine during the depression. They just did the best they could to live their lives. It was a huge crisis, but we need not let it consume us.

During the 1929 Depression, to survive meant to take joy in little and unimportant things in life. They did not need to drive a luxury car, or go to fancy restaurants, or spend lavishly on what they did not absolutely needed.

In addition, it meant taking joy in things that did not cost much or anything, but were very important, like family and loved ones and other human beings.

This reminds me of that Big Mac sandwich that my brother and I got to celebrate our successful completion of the semester at the University of Wisconsin-Madison.

We must have had Big Macs hundreds of times before then, but taking joy in having that after the exams and enjoying almost each and every sesame seed that was on the bun brought a great deal of joy to us. Thirty years later, I still remember that Big Mac and that occasion.

Our financial systems should function, even when they are damaged. Nevertheless, we need to do our humanly best to Survive each day, each hour and each minute of the day. All we can do is "our humanly best for that hour or day."

I Will Survive!

CHAPTER 106:   I Will Survive!

Donna Sommer sang this beautiful song. The lyrics are:
<
"Oh no not I.
I will survive.
Oh as long as I know how to love
I know I'll stay alive.
I got all my life to live
and I got all my love to give.
and I'll survive. I will survive.
I WILL SURVIVE"
>
You have every right to tell me "This is a love song. What does this have to do with layoffs and dysfunctional workplace blues?" You are right it does not have much. The fact is that it is upbeat, and it has captured the essence of being let down and then getting stronger and surviving or even succeeding. It builds on the idea of not just sitting there, but singing, I WILL SURVIVE! Life is very sweet, in spite all that goes wrong every day. In spite all the world hunger, incurable diseases, human cruelty to other humans, natural and human-made disasters, layoffs, and dead-end jobs. Yet, there is a moment in each day that one needs to sit still and enjoy in realizing the immenseness of the universe, love, and the humanity. A moment to cherish human beings that sometimes blossom. The love of a mother for her children, even though she has to use food stamps, is love in its purest form. The love of father who does not buy a car, just to send his son or daughter to college is golden. These joys in life cannot be replaced by millions or billions of dollars. We human beings can do anything if we put our minds and hearts into it! Human potential and creativity is unlimited and will always remain unlimited.
You too have this potential. Job loss, or even a foreclosure or bankruptcy, is only a financial problem. As an under-employed executive who was making a dire living from working in some college told me, "I looked at the entire American prison system and did not find a debtor's jail anywhere." In other words, in the US they cannot put you in jail just because you do not have money. Therefore, unless you internalize it and put chains on yourself, you are free to make the best of your life as you can.
Right before the 1967 war between the state of Israel and the Arab states, and when a lot of newspapers had predicted the devastation and destruction of Israel, right at the time where I noticed a magazine article comparing Israeli resources, and its number of soldiers compared to the humongous Arab armies that were determined to destroy it, I was convinced that Israel would not survive. Then the Israeli airline had an advertisement that said something like this: For thousands of years flowers have grown in our gardens, and children have played. It was this way yesterday, and it will be this way tomorrow too.
In the face of an impending inhalation and being pushed to the sea, this was a message of hope and defiance in a face-to-face situation with adversity and defeat! I have experienced the miracle of hope with regards to agony and despair of joblessness and hopelessness.
On one of my visits to Israel, I met a distant relative in Dizengoff Center. Dizengoff Center is one of the modern Tel Aviv Shopping Centers on the corner of Dizengoff and King George St. What I remembered of them during my childhood and now were a study in extreme contrast. They lived in the poor Jewish section of Tehran called Mahaleh (A

small place). As Jews in this overwhelming Moslem country, we had learned to be modest about our Jewish heritage and especially not boast. They were not oppressed, but they did not want to stand out, make political noise, and they knew that their chances of becoming a General in the army were Zero. Unfortunately, Jews had internalized and accepted this. This was a way of not letting antiemetic zealots to be provoked. It was an unwritten agreement. The first thing I noticed was the younger children were just as proud and alive as any European or American. In fact, too much so since, Israelis are typically blunt and outspoken. Their mother who had immigrated to Israel in 1947 explained, "My kids are real Sabras!" Sabra is a native born Israeli. One more thing about Israel is that long ego, they decided to have only happy songs to help their morale. One of the younger generation relatives told me that there were millions of light years between the "less than thinking" of Mahaleh and blue-sky freedom of Israeli pride. I hope that there be hope and peace for all parties and soon.

One day, everything looks gloomy and doomed. Moreover, the next day, if something positive like happens a recruiter calling, and then everything looks nice.

However, as a human being, I cannot help but realize that there is a very sweet time right after a job offer is signed and delivered and accepted. I usually celebrate by doing something nice for myself. It does not have to be something elaborate or expensive. Once I have a job lined up and my mind is at ease, I use that time to rest and prepare myself and family for the next job. I also celebrate each day of surviving the stupid job search. As it says in Psalm 100, I do my best to rejoice in each day. This outlook helps me to do my humanly best for each day. In addition, as they say in the Twelve Step Programs of AA and others, "One Day at a Time."

However, I am the same person. Nothing has changed from yesterday to today. Similarly, I am the same person I was before the layoff, and I will be the same person after the layoff. The layoff is just too insignificant to take away my pride and my humanity.

Why not have that same optimism when I am looking for a job? Why not use that energy and power in finding a better career and life?

We can and will survive!

CHAPTER 107:   I Have a Dream

Again, in that very same ABBA Gold Album, there is a song called "I have a Dream."
Dr. Martin Luther King's, speech, "I have a Dream", of course might have inspired this
song Yet, its sweet lyrics, have been a great source of inspiration for me.
<
"I have a dream, a song to sing
To help me cope with anything
If you see the wonder of a fairy tale
You can take the future even if you fail
I believe in angels
Something good in everything I see"
>
Further in the song,
<
"I believe in angels
When I know the time is right for me
I'll cross the stream - I have a dream
I'll cross the stream - I have a dream"
>
It talks about angels. I have had several earth angels in my life.
One, when I was near death in the University of Wisconsin hospital and in a comma. This
angel was in the form of my cousin Mike who sat by my side for hours and hours even
though he had a very important test to take. He was studying and yet he did not let go of
my side.
The other angel is Al. As a friend, he saved my life and helped me during some of the
most difficult periods of my life; he was and will always be like a brother to me.
When I had just about had it with college and was getting ready to quit, Al told me that I
should not be stupid and give up my dream. My dream was to go back to my family after
completing my degree, a family that was extremely proud of me. Al's voice has always
been in my ear.
My other angel is John. He is a devoted Christian. Unfortunately, diabetes has made him
almost blind. He spends a lot of his time reading books (he unfortunately cannot afford to
buy them) at Barnes and Noble. In addition, with his dim eyesight, he was telling me that
it takes forever to read a chapter of a book. Nevertheless, according to him, a chapter here
and a chapter there keeps him occupied and prevents him from going crazy. Of course,
his wife, a wonderful woman who has had to become the sole bread winner these days,
would correct him and say, "this prevents John from becoming crazier" as if he was crazy
before.
Wives and husbands, and other better halves have interesting ways of laughing together
even if it looks like they are laughing at each other. My wife likes to remind me that I
promised her a much better house in Palo Alto "two years after we got married," and that
was fourteen years ago. At least I think it was fourteen years ago! I am beginning to
panic! Have I been married fourteen or fifteen years? Well if it was fifteen, then it makes
it thirteen years ago. Math is an awful thing!
In difficult times, and especially in a sudden job loss situation, we need to believe in
something bigger than ourselves. For example, as something to rely on, we could use our
religion, value system, friends, or family, or whatever makes sense for us. Of course, you
might have different source or types of angles. Of course what I just mentioned, may not

Copyright © 2008 - 2009 Razban Internet International, Inc. All rights reserved, File:20091022. P a g e | **248**

work for you all together. At any rate, it has been my experience that there are angles in this world. These angles appear in a so-called coincidence. These angles and coincidences happen at the right time and spot saying and doing the exact right "intervention" that can save a day or a life! These angles are real and I have seen them at least in mind's eye. I have seen them in my life and in other people's lives.

One of the most painful things that can happen in a Pink Shock situation is to try to go it alone! After all, the Western Culture over-emphasizes self-sufficiency. A heavy dose of shame falls on us like a ton of breaks, when we finally admit that we need help.

Yet, these angles are waiting and at the ready to help. Sometimes we just do everything we can to keep them away. Angles are patient; they can wait, and wait. They try and try again.

I have long realized that a man or a woman without a dream is just as good as someone who has no soul, no purpose. He or she is like a boat without a rudder, which drifts around.

In many years of management, I have learned that a dream for an ordinary person is just as critical as a blue print for a manager of multibillion-dollar construction project! There has to be a carefully written description of requirements too.

My friends John and Veronica had dreams of raising their kids and seeing them married. A new college graduate that I have been working with as a management coach has the modest dream of just hanging on to his job, even though he is working for a company with a corporate policy of hire, fire at will, revolving door practice.

I had heard the expression that "Not even a drop of water is wasted in this universe" many times before. One day, I came across an angry friend who was bitter about being pushed out of a lucrative job in a major corporation. That was the first time that I used this drop of water analogy. To his angry cry that he and his career were wasted, I was able to parrot, "Not even a drop of water is wasted in this universe". I am sure that he hated my guts for saying this to him then. I do not think he hates me any more since he did find a better job working for the competition.

CHAPTER 108:   It is Jobs, Jobs, and More Jobs, Stupid!

On October 11, 2008, the Democratic Vice President Candidate, Joe Biden was talking about jobs.
As I have mentioned before, jobs are the foundation of America business, and, for that matter, the world economy. Jobs create income. Income creates money to spend to live. In return, spending creates more opportunity for jobs. This is not rocket science.
In reality, income is not all that jobs do. For many people who have worked from the age twelve or thirteen, going without a job is punishment. This makes them depressed and they feel that they are no good and unwanted.
My father, having been an MD who had several times tried to get the certification to work in US as an MD, was beginning to get depressed. He worked on the garden in their house. He repaired the windows in his house and mine. He planted those beautiful Texas Yellow Roses that still bloom in my garden so many years after he is gone. My mother was getting really worried about his well-being.
Therefore, I created a job for him. He would carefully study the stock market listing for five or six stocks that I had, and every day he would call me and tell me where they ended that day. Based on that, I got my start in trading in the market. I never became rich. Yet, this kept my dad excited, and he was helping his friends invest in the market.
After a year or two, he was making two and three-dimensional graphs that were excellent decision analysis tools for stock market investment. Of course, these days, these tools are not that important since we have computers and the Internet. Back then, these were great and innovative things.
Let us look at California. Our mass transit system, of course aside from BART that you have read about in this book and a few others ones, stinks. We are way behind France and Japan and Germany and other countries. Sadly, our highways have aged so much that it is time to build the best and leap frog all the countries that I mentioned.
This will create enough jobs in so many sectors, that the economy will have to get better. I was elated to see that President Elect Obama is talking about job creation as his first order of business.
I also saw the $700,000,000,000 bailout headline that corporations may get in an Oakland newspaper. Sadly enough, right next to it, I saw that Oakland would be losing 320 jobs.
We have a long and tedious way to go. I have trust in our next president elect, and faith in American institutions.
We can do this!

Copyright © 2008 - 2009 Razban Internet International, Inc. All rights reserved, File:20091022, Page | **250**

CHAPTER 109:   Rejoice Each Day!

Psalms 100, 112, and 113 actually point out that we need to rejoice in each day. Each day is a new day, a new beginning and we owe it to ourselves to each day to treat this brand new freshly minted new day as a chance to do our humanly possible for this one day. The cliché of one day at a time applies here. If that is not possible one hour at a time, or even one minute at a time should do.

Each day, I like to take pride in what I had done, as little as they might be. However, I do not kick myself for the fact that I am an American, Middle Class, and Unemployed (AMU).

When others talk down to me, or when it just gets to be too much to handle, I give myself a short break, and in some occasions, I take a day off here and there.

The past is behind us. That is just like the rearview mirror in our cars. We need to look forward. Forward to our own next birthday, our loved ones, friends, family, associates.

We might be an AMU, but we are all decent people who are doing the best we can during this crisis. Being an AMU is not a crime and it is nothing to cause us shame.

This Global Financial Crisis (GFC), which is one the worst in the history, will be in our rear view mirror, and good things will wait us in our journey in the future.

In one discussion among great minds, somebody asked a scholar, "What is the most important time in history?" The scholar said, "Right now, because we can do something about this here and now!"

At the time of writing this chapter, summer of 2007, a new management technology had become the craze for employees, management, and corporations.

We call this management technology "Agile Management." The older technology, called "Water Fall" was effective for big projects, which had set goals that did not change much, and a big effort eventually produced results. Also sometimes, as the project got bigger and bigger, the entire effort caused a minor obstacle, and the work done for months and months by lots of people had to be re-done.

In some cases, companies went under because they could not provide the next generation product on time and within budget.

There is a great enthusiasm about Agile Management. Agile helps one decide goals for one week at a time. It has a daily quick review of what everybody did. It has a set of tasks that team members need to be accomplishing each week, and these tasks are well defined. Agile Management also has a monthly meeting with all parties to demonstrate right there and then, their accomplishments.

During each week, the manager has to decide what the next iteration of this iterative process needs to produce in that week. Is it just to improve quality and not change or add any features? Alternatively, is it adding one or more features? On the other hand, is it just fixing documented problems that we have documented with the solution? The other important aspect of this methodology is that decisions made here are fact-based! Each week, you see on the computer screen what has developed and, each week, you see the results of the completed work.

In "Today" song by Jefferson Airplane that was angelically song by Juice Slick in Monterey Festival, we hear:

<

To be anymore than all I am would be a lie

Copyright © 2008 - 2009 Razban Internet International, Inc. All rights reserved, File:20091022, P a g e | **251**

>

Today, we can do our humanly best and proactively create a change for the better for the others or ourselves.

You may not have a job today, but you are the same carpenter, surgeon, airline pilot, hairdresser, teacher, fire fighter, or shop keeper that you used to be before you lost your job. You have not changed. The job, the companies that gave you that job, the management who was supposed to plan and budget and organize you to keep your job, they have failed not us. So, we need to day for today, our humanly best. In Yiddish, there is a proverb that says, "Don't worry about tomorrow; who knows what will befall you today!"

Here are some practical suggestions:

- Place an ad in Craigslist.org in your area and in your field. The ad would say, "Beginner in programming, or advanced accountant, or experienced teacher will work for free between 8 to 12 Hours a week" or whatever terms. I did this and got no less than fifteen responses.

- Go Door to Door! Go downtown, or go where there are people working (remember even 12% unemployment means 78% working) and with a nice smile introduce yourself and say that you wonder if you could volunteer to work there. No strings attached.

- My wife's friend came to visit us from another country. She had loved to be a chef. She had lost her job and decided to switch her career to something that was her dream as a girl. When visiting us for a few hours, she went to kitchen and cooked us a wonderful meal. The next I called everyone I knew to find her a job. I could not get her a job, but few weeks later, she was working in a good restaurant downtown.

- Make phone calls. After a while, they become fun. Calling a colleague or sending an update e-mail always is the right first step. Share something interesting. Tell them you are looking and ask them if they have any suggestion. Then, add something like, I will keep you posted on my adventures in the job hunt!

- The new Social Networking has improved things a great deal. You can benefit from this a great deal.

- Look at Google for example. You can do a search for "Tutorials sales basic" or whatever, and get the most up to date information about sales.

- Then still in Google go to videos and do the same. You will be highly impressed with so much information about any subject that helps you bring your marketable skills to latest and current. I watch these videos the first as if I am watching a movie. Many things in these videos sound difficult at first. Then on the successive times, it becomes more and more clear. Then, I try to see if I have learned enough by watching one last time and trying to understand everything.

- There are many groups now called "Communities" that you can join or use as a means of advertising your skill set. For example, I joined a PHP Programming community online. They are good in helping me with my questions and they were instrumental in getting me started. Later, when I had some ideas to offer I did that too. It is good to be connected!

Networking does indeed beat not working and keeps the day goes faster. Networking creates a bound. Americans and many Europeans that I know love to help and give

Copyright © 2008 - 2009 Razban Internet International, Inc. All rights reserved, File:20091022, P a g e | **252**

advice. Networking caters to our most human needs, since we do not like to be isolated. I kept in touch with the first person who sold me my Lexus ES 250 and the service manager along with the part manager for many years. Our common interest of cars made it always interesting to get a call or exchange an e-mail or "Do Lunch" occasionally. Sure enough, I got one job through them.

In 1981, I bought a tiny "starter" town house from a married couple who worked together, Robert and Myrna. This, is, the same house that I had planned to sell in two years and move up to something better. Some thirty-eight years later, I called Robert and told him that I was worried about losing this townhouse. His reaction was, "The house that I bought for you some thirty years ago?" and then after a long pause on the phone he said he would do the best he can to save me from foreclosure. I spent two and a half hours in his office. He tried his network to the limit. He called many people that he knew who specialized in "Hard Loans". Hard loans are loans with higher interest rates for those who would otherwise not qualify for a conventional loan.

I was not working with some realtor trying to get me a loan. I was visiting and connecting with a friend of more than thirty years. It was fun and it was work.

In Richard Bolles' book, "What Color is Your Parachute?" he goes beyond finding a job. He helps us reflect on our career, and our potential, and think of a Mission. This had been very important in my career and life. With my meager resources, I tried to help others. That was my mission. In fact, after reading his fantastic book, I realized that my mission now was to come up with a better vision for the work life to reduce, or minimize layoffs and resolve the management crisis that results in toxic work place.

Let us say, your goal in three months is to get a promotion. Try to find someone who has had the same or similar promotion. Finding that person is step one. Then, on a fact-based decision, you can tell whether you have done this or not. Meet with him or her. Discuss how you too can get the promotion they have already achieved. Remember, Americans, in general, are very proud of giving good advice that helps others.

One inch at a time is a synch.

CHAPTER 110:   Soda Cans for Unemployment Misery

November 07, 2008
Nonfarm payroll employment fell by 240,000 in October. Job losses over the last 3 months totaled 651,000. In October, the unemployment rate rose from 6.1 to 6.5 percent, and the number of unemployed persons increased to 10.1 million.

The above quote is directly from Google. It proves one of the most important points that this book is trying to make. Let's say that 10.1 million Americans are unemployed at this time. This is based on the next direct quote:

From Wikipedia, the free encyclopedia

"The term **Average Joe** or **Average Jane** also **Joe Shmoe** is used in the United States to refer to the <u>average American</u>. Today statistics by the <u>United States Department of Commerce</u> provide information regarding the societal attributes of those who may be referred to as being "average." While some individual attributes are easily identified as being average, such as the median income, other characteristics, such as family arrangements may not be identified as being average. In 2000 for example no single household arrangement constituted more than 30% of total households. Married couples with no children were the most common constituting 28.7% of households. It would nonetheless be inaccurate to state that the average American lives in a childless couple arrangement as 71.3% do not.[1] Other "average" characteristics are easier to identify. In terms of <u>social class</u>, the average American may be described as either being <u>middle</u>[2] or <u>working class</u>.[3][4] As social classes lack distinct boundaries the average American may have a status in the area where the lower middle and working class overlap.[5] Overall the average American, age 25 or older, <u>made roughly $32,000</u> per year,[6] does not have a <u>college degree</u>, has been, is, or will be married as well as divorced at least once during his or her lifetime, lives in his or her own home in a suburban setting, and holds a white collar office job."

So, let's do the math. There are 10.1 million Americans unemployed. Each was making $32,000 per year. So this adds up to about .323 trillion Dollars. This amounts to a waste pile of $6.46 trillion empty soda cans! This is not to mention that we are sticking dollar amounts on human misery and suffering! As a senior manager, I have many times had to "dollarize" the impact of something so people could put it into perspective.

What would happen if American corporations and other businesses dumped those many soda cans?

We are trying to become a "green" nation that reuses, recycles, and saves. We do this with paper. But we have not considered doing this with our people's careers, and lives. American ingenuity and our limitless natural and intellectual resources will make this possible.

We can do this!

Copyright © 2008 - 2009 Razban Internet International, Inc. All rights reserved, File:20091022,

CHAPTER 111:   A serenade to Sir Richard Branson

Sir Richard Branson is the founder of Virgin Atlantic Airline, Chairman of Virgin Group, and many other enterprises. He has done extremely courageous things including pioneering InterGalactic, which is a company that will send tourists to space.
There is a story about his management practice and sense of humor at the same time. When he was trying to hire some top-notch executives, he himself did a "live" case study with these candidates. In addition to interviews, he arranged for them to arrive at the same time, and he disguised himself as an unkempt old and slow bus driver for the bus that they had expected to pick them up from the airport.
These candidates for an executive job had no idea who this scruffy old bus driver was. Some of them got angry with him since he was not moving fast enough for them. Some tried to push him to drive faster. Yet, some were understanding and tried to help this old man.
Sir Richard Branson later informed them that this was part of their screening and points were lost for those who were not nice, and points gained for those who were nice. I perfectly understand and admire his decision to do this screening this way. Unless a person as a person is not kind and nice, he or she will not succeed as a top-notch leader, or even a manager. This same point is also reflected strongly in Debra Benton's book "CEO Material". Debra is an internationally known author of New York Times Best Seller books. In addition, I have greatly benefitted from her advice and guidance. In "CEO Material", she gives list after list of requirements for an excellent CEO. These lists were prepared with a lot of research and many CEOs participated in defining these requirements. The fundamental and essential ingredient in all of these lists is that a leader or manager has to be a good human being first. Otherwise, no training in the world will compensate for the lack of humanity!
After carefully studying Sir Richard Branson's many youTube.com videos, I have concluded that he is one the very few executives in this world, or galaxy, capable of helping the world fix the Global Financial Crisis (GFC) mess! The world needs his kind leadership to recover from GFC!
In my opinion, the GFC will not go away until and unless we realize that this crisis has been in the making for at least two decades. To start with, there has been a serious management crisis in the management ranks all over the world. Another factor is that a mega revolution in the shape of Internet has made data available instantly everywhere. Our financial and legal systems are decades away from integrating this mega revolution in the business and economic systems. For example, there is a SOX regulatory criterion in US that tries to make company financial transactions more transparent and more honest. This is an excellent start, but we need to put a Razban amendment in it (i.e. take SOX, and make it SOaR) that ingrates other metrics (Such as Mutual Trust and Loyalty) into the business of companies. Moreover, many other innovative ideas such as 107.8% employment and Free Market Governance to preserve Free Market to operate the way Capitalism has intended it to operate, but not go again into a Free Fall like the one it did in 2008.
I will make sure to send a copy of this book, along with a business plan for starting the universal actually galactic system that will be instrumental in proactively preventing

another GFC. Who knows, they might decide to found another mega success. Here is an excerpt from Sir Richard Branson's blog:

"Find good people and set them free

Posted by <u>Richard</u> on September 30, 2008

You will find the 'Virgin type' of person all over the world. I bump into them frequently in bars, cafes, hotels and small businesses, in libraries, post offices, in hospitals, at the jetty in the Caribbean, even in government offices and the civil service. Virgin types pop up everywhere, and in every nation. These people don't know they're special, but they are; they are out there, and you can spot them. If you're in charge of a company, or a human resources department (I hate this description – I call them 'people' departments!), you should be searching for them, too. These people, by their nature and their outlook on life, enjoy working with people. They're attentive. They smile freely. They're often lively, and fun to be with. I don't underestimate qualifications – I just don't assume they're going to tell me anything about a person's character. Having savvy is much more important than having a formal education. The things you learn can only complement who you are – and in my book, who you are counts for a whole lot.

Across the whole Virgin Group, we encourage people to take ownership of the issues that they confront in their working lives. In a service-led industry especially, this kind of attitude pays huge dividends. I think if people are properly and regularly recognized for their initiative, then the business has to flourish. Why is this so? Because, this is their business and it is an extension of their personality. They have a stake in its success."

How right this is. Sir Richard Bronson's companies set their employees free (I understand this to mean that they are trusted and empowered), they choose them carefully to begin with, and then do not lay them off in the first sign of financial difficulties. So many American CEOs lay off top talent and dedicated employees as a knee jerk reaction the first time there was a sign of potential market loss. This clearly tells me that Virgin Group is indeed practices MTL! Their employees care for the customer, because their company cares for them. Besides, if you are a good Capitalist, then you are greedy. AS Michael Douglas said it in the Wall Street movie, "Greed, for the lack of a better word is good!" Therefore, if you are greedy, you want to make money and lots of it. So, put your bets on people, as in your employees and customers, and not things such as buildings, desks and computers. Kevin Covey said that the era of asset management is gone and we are in the era of knowledge management, and people, as in HP Way are the most important capital we have. Remember in Hebrew, we count one building, two buildings, etc. However, when we are counting people, then it becomes one blessing, two blessings, etc. Some 5,000 or more years ago, Bible told us this. Somehow, we forgot to practice this concept of humanity in management.

In addition, asset capital has serious limitations as seen in the real estate market during the financial recession of 2008 and 2009. On the other hand, human capital and its potential are indeed unlimited. In other word, human capital and intellectual properties cultivated by it have sky as their limit!

In an article in Daily News, the headline said:

"Hero of the Hudson: Pilot of US Airways Flight 1549 saved every passenger with miracle landing." This refers to heroic and outstanding job that this one in a million

Copyright © 2008 - 2009 Razban Internet International, Inc. All rights reserved, File:20091022,

airline pilot did. Here is some more from CBS official website:

The captain of Flight 1549 told CBS News anchor Katie Couric that he's concerned the industry will soon have trouble attracting experienced pilots. Low salaries offered for new employees are the main reason for this.

"One way of looking at this might be that, for 42 years, I've been making small regular deposits in this bank of experience: education and training," said US Airways Capt. Chesley "Sully" Sullenberger. "And on January 15, the balance was sufficient so that I could make a very large withdrawal." Yet, Sullenberger is uncharacteristically worried. He's worried that when it comes to the bank of experience for airline pilots, there may someday be a significant shortage.

"I don't know a single professional pilot who would recommend that their children follow in their footsteps," he said.

There was a time when airline pilot was a coveted job - glamorous, respected, with plenty of benefits. However, now "The airline employees have been hit by an economic tsunami. Pay cuts, loss of pensions, increased hours every day, days per week, days per month," Sullenberger said. "It's a heavy burden." Last year alone, more than 6,000 commercial pilots were either furloughed or permanently laid off. Unfortunately, so many companies are so poorly lead that Airline industry is not unique in this area of poor management practices.

Couric said: "What effect do you think that is having on the industry itself and on the people's it's attracting?" The answer to this from Captain Sully was: "I know some of our pilots, who have been laid off, have chosen not to return". "I can speak personally, for me and my family, that my decision to remain in this profession that I love has come at a cost to me and my family."

I, as a senior management admire and even worship this greater than life hero and professional. Moreover, I echo what he is saying. He is pointing out that about 40% or more of the employees (which even includes executives) in the Western World are unhappy with their jobs! Layoffs have destroyed MTL by a constant fear of sudden job loss and the "Pink Shock" associated with it. Remember, when people are scared, they can not invent, they cannot produce, or produce high quality. Companies that rely on regular layoffs and revolving door hire, fire lose in the long term. They never get to their full potential, or just disappear. Sometimes they disappear because the chain of fools broke the MTL and only one single employee did not go that one extra step needed to get the company succeed again. It takes one disgruntled employee, and one call to mess up a multimillion dollar deal when nobody cares.

I think that Captain Sully will not be surprised to hear that I know architects and directors who quit. They now work in the airport security, or as a supervisor in a hardware store. One outstanding and experienced senior manager decided to write children's book out of his "downsized" studio apartment. His company after many years of excellent service "downsized and out sourced" him." In one case, one "downshifter employee" refused to go back to his glamorous work even though the company was offering him bigger salary, better benefits, and even a "sign on" bonus.

In an interview with American Express, Sir Richard Branson pointed out that this GFC is much bigger that other crisis, and small business which is the backbone of economy alone will not be able to solve this huge problem. Governments, along cannot solve this either. In fact as of this writing, I am impressed with President Obama's decision regarding his efforts to revive the economy. They were heroic. Yet the third part that is needed are the innovative ideas that are presented in this book!

In the eight years that it took me to write this book, and my talks with many people, I came across this painful question that is frequently asked by those affected by layoffs: "If the company does not care about me, why should I care about the company?" Imagine, building the most respected and profitable on-line career management company on earth and making a lot of money. Imagine making 107.8% employment a reality and having millions of thankful employees. Imagine making a company that is the outmost in

Copyright © 2008 - 2009 Razban Internet International, Inc. All rights reserved, File:20091022, P a g e | **257**

capitalism and is powered by the unlimited human potential and is empowered by knowledge and the mega Internet revolution.

We are at a historical point in the history of the world. This monumental occasion that has been jolting our entire economy can be either a global disaster. It can also be a wakeup call that forces us to beat the Global Financial Crisis (GFC) into Global Humanitarian Economy (GHE). The 2008-2009 GFC proves that an earthquake has occurred in our free market, western freedom culture, and our ways of doing things. The same way that collision of two tectonic plates creates an earthquake, collision of old Capitalism with Humanitarian has produced the GFC. This is just like transition from prop planes to the jet age. We have been shocked and jolted into a new era a century or two before we would have been comfortably ready.

The battle cry of this new era will be jobs, jobs, and more jobs! Either corporations will learn to integrate, honor, and operate with new age of philanthropist capitalism, or like dinosaurs, they will disappear. Social unrest, as seen in Korea, France, Japan, and other countries will spread. The humanitarian and instant information based new capitalism, will not allow us to hide it under carpet since it has a fire-like nature. It will burn our house of economy down.

Let us harness this superbly profitable epoch! We harnessed atomic energy into peaceful and useful technologies and economies; we can and must do the same with this new era. Imagine that we channel advertising and marketing budgets into humanitarian uses. Humanitarian uses create jobs and viral trusted human-to-human communication via more smart consumption created gigantic profits for new Global Distributed Companies (GDCs).

Imagine that we treat each child as a corporation. Imagine that on a voluntary and free basis, we take stock in that child's health, well-being, education, and invest in his or her evolution. With each accomplishment, and with each marketable skill set, the individual's "Stock Value" increases. Imagine companies will invest in thousands of Yoyo Ma's as they start playing. Imagine we expand the Micro Loans into Micro Global Investments (MGIs). Imagine each company then becomes a holding company for all of these human capital knowledge-workers. I am working on a serious business plan for this. This cannot go wrong!

This is the flipside of what good companies practice. In every action and every word, they say that they care for employees and customers. This builds MTL that will manifest in high-quality products and services that make a company successful.

Copyright © 2008 - 2009 Razban Internet International, Inc. All rights reserved, File:20091022.

CHAPTER 112:   An Open Business Plan for Paul Allen

Similar to Sir Richard Bronson, Paul Allen of Microsoft has captured my attention and admiration for many years. He has successfully done brave new initiatives in technology and other fields. Therefore, I thought maybe this might be an interesting new business plan for him.

Let us say you form a company that becomes the biggest employer on the planet. Millions and millions of employees will love, admire, and cherish by this would be company. This company that invents and refines the revolutionary concept of work by actually implementing Human Potential; Knowledge based Capitalist (HKC). This is nothing more than re-invention of Capitalism as we know it.

Betting on people and integrating the latest technology, this company can do what the government could not do. Again, remember the US Post Office. It took FedEx to do it right. In addition, by doing the mail delivery correctly, it made a lot of money in the process. Therefore, it takes a pioneer like Paul Allen to see the immense potential in such an undertaking that has a potential Return on Revenue (ROI) of 1,000 percent!

Let us get rid of the inefficiencies in the workplace that create the awful feelings and less-than-excellent work results. That huge performance enhancement and human empowerment will then more than pay for the costs and produce astronomical profits.

In my thirty-two years of experience, I have discovered that the work place of the future will depend on a "Tripod". To re-invent Capitalism, we need to work on all three legs. No matter how hard we work on one or two of these legs, we still will not be able succeed. We might clean up after the latest Global Financial Crisis this time or this year, only to be hit with another one in a year or two. In fact the awful situation in 2008 and 2009 with all the hardships, might have actually brought out with it the best in us! We just cannot continue what we did before, and the way we did them before. The tripod is:

- US Government
- American Business
- American Consumers

As of October of 2009, the US Government had done all they could. American Consumers are doing OK. However, the most important part it is the American Business to create jobs and efficiencies so we proactively prevent future crisis. We need to stop this roller coaster of feast and famine cycles. We need to privatize the Employment Development Department. People should not go unemployment for as long as they have been going all these times. We need to make the process of hiring faster and more efficient. We need to have companies that specialize in helping other companies run better and not have to do these massive and frequent layoffs.

It is easy and practical, and it will deliver outstanding results.

CHAPTER 113:   In the End, The World Expects America to be America and Lead!

In 1929, it looked like it was the end of American business know-how. America that takes pride in its know-how was in a recession. The recession had brought Americans to their knees. Soup kitchens and unemployment was rampant. It was a depressing scene and experience for millions of Americans. Capitalism seemed to be dead. The depression that followed was devastating. There were soup kitchens, bankruptcies, and more. Yet, Americans are resourceful. They found a way to cope and not let this economic Armageddon destroy them. They went to more basic things in life, cherished family life, and did things for each other that they themselves could not afford.

The Wall Street Journal of October 11, 2008 says, "…market is probably wrong in its obsession over whether this decline will turn into cataclysmic collapse…" and this article quotes a passage from Emily Dickinson's poem "After Great Pain a Formal Feeling Comes." *The Financial Times* of London on the same day quoted Christine Lagarde, the French Finance Minster as saying, "Moral hazard has to be dealt with later….Maintaining the functioning of our markets is the top priority."

In the 1940s, Nazi Germany seemed to be on the verge of world dominance. This of course meant the destruction of American ideals of democracy and freedom.

Some 61 years later, on September 11, 2001, as the World Trade Center was going up in smoke and crumbling down, it seemed that it could be the end of America being the leader of the financial world.

As proud as I am of my Judeo-Christian, Persian heritage and the strong influence of European and Eastern philosophies, I am even more proud of being an American.

I remember once, when my mother was very ill. My youngest aunt was attending to her around the clock. She was telling my mother that she had to get well soon, because everybody needed her. My mother was the pillar of the family. She helped my uncle with his difficulties. She helped another aunt buy a house and start a rental shop. She helped her youngest sister a great deal. Now, my mother, one of the strongest women in the world, at least our world, was ill and could not function. Years later, my mother told me that, although she was herself ill, it was the strong plea from my youngest aunt for help that inspired her to get well soon. My mother, who was in excruciating pain, decided that she was not going to let down her young sister who needed her.

America helped rebuild Europe after the world war. Now, America is economically ill and needs to get well. It needs to get well, if not just for America's sake, then for the sake of the rest of the world. There is a strong analogy between my mother's illness and America's economic illness at present. We just cannot afford to give up our leadership! We Americans, as General Patton said, "Do not like losers." We stand united and face adversity.

America is country of vast resources. Human Capital and Knowledge are the most important type of potential that can help us get out of this mess. Dr. Martin Luther King, Jr., said, "We shall overcome."Overcome we shall, hand in hand with our European, Asian, African, Australian, and global human and knowledge power.

Do you remember Chippie's story? We do not just sit there!

CHAPTER 114:   Executive Summary

The main message in this book is one of hope and faith for those affected by layoffs and an economic tsunami in a business Armageddon that started in 2008. This in a depressing recession (and even an economic depression by the time this book comes out), full of bank failures, home foreclosures, unemployment, and painful fear of Sudden Job Loss (SJL) and Pink Shock which can be just as real and just as disabling as the well known fear of flying is. Unfortunately, even though most people know of fear of flying, not too many people know SJL, at least not yet. It might very well be that this book is a first to introduce fear of SJL!

With 40% or more of the workers (including executives) in the Western World unhappy with their work life, productivity, inventiveness, creativity, and even American know-how is fast eroding. I have concluded that psychological depression resulting from toxic work place unhappiness combined with the pink shock of frequent layoffs, can and will produce economic depression.

I strongly argue that the serious management crisis that causes some of these business failures has been there for many, many years. These business failures have a magnitude of $2.4 trillion total impact resulting from the productivity loss, waste of human talent, potential, and a lack of leadership management to harness the Blackberry revolution and to amend capitalism to include knowledge and human potential as a foundation of the new Human Power and Knowledge-based capitalism. Let me put the Trillion-dollar waste in perspective. This waste is like a stack of $1,000 bills 153.6 miles high! Again, let me give credit to the writers of the "Trillion Dollar War" book for teaching me this analogy to emphasize the magnitude of trillion-dollar waist. Based on the facts presented in this book, the total waste resulting from a workplace that is dysfunctional, in a management crisis, and causing frequent layoffs to balance budgets on a quarterly basis, etc, amounts to a $2.4 trillion waste. Management crisis in many companies resulting in repeated layoffs, which gets its roots from "hire, fire revolving door employment policies", causes immense human pain and suffering as well. This book shows that there are better ways to make profitable big and small companies and happy employees. Not only this does not cost more, it saves too.

A $2.4 trillion waste is a stack of $1,000 bills that can go from Wall Street in New York City to US Capitol in Washington, DC. This is that bad! We can proactively prevent, or at least minimize this shameful, massive waste.

This analogy is powerful message to our financial systems and its nerve center in Wall Street in NYC and to our legislative home in Washington DC. Wall Street needs to be looking at longer term and human capital and realize that the era of asset based capitalism is gone. In addition, our legislative systems need to realize the importance of Knowledge Revolution and its impact on our lives and society. This is a by far bigger revolution that the industrial revolution and we need to adapt our laws to it! So far, we have failed on a global basis. Based on my own experience, and that of many colleagues, also as a manager and employee who has had to live this turbulent rollercoaster of layoffs, firings, dysfunctional workplace-related depression and recession for more than a decade, I try to cultivate hope and make this book a motivational element to cope and recover in such difficult times. I have tried to accomplish this, first, by showing that there is a chain, like

Copyright © 2008 - 2009 Razban Internet International, Inc. All rights reserved, File:20091022, P a g e | **261**

what is referred to Aretha Franklin's song "Chain of Fools" without blaming any one group. Someday that something is going to break, as this has been too painful.

A cold-blooded murder in a startup triggers some of the delayed painful reactions in myself and resonates with several management books published by Stanford University and reminds me of my own experience of looking into a loaded gun's barrel from the wrong end and the horror that it can permanently leave. Sometimes even the expression Pink Shock cannot describe the intensity of the damage that layoffs cause in human beings. This, doubled by life loss and stress that I and my colleagues and friends have experienced, has jolted us into the conclusion that there is a management crisis. We all as employers, employees, customers, and stakeholders need to change our ways.

Layoffs are inherently a result of American management crisis. The delays in recognizing BlackBerry knowledge revolution or ignoring the Human Capital are causing a lot of present economic Armageddon. A hire fire revolving door implemented in the form of frequent layoffs shatters Mutual Trust and Loyalty (MTL). The ensuing fear of Sudden Job Loss, then robs corporations and employees of benefits of a better work life and results in massive losses for everyone. The MTL extends itself and propagates from a well run company into products and services that sell well and happier work life for all. Once we deal with this fear, creativity and innovation will blossom again.

America cannot compete without its small business and innovation backbone! We make excellent leaders and awful followers!

Actually, it costs less and it is easier for employees to be the best of the best, and companies to be the best of the best for their employees and customers. The lyrics in this book will cheer up the reader and encourage him or her to put a song in their hearts and go on with the full time jobs of finding a full time job. Can we not live the good life that this world can still offer us even after a layoff? We can do this even without that paycheck. We can do this while we are obsessively looking for the next job or career move! As government's most appreciated make, work projects are established, and as the small and big businesses in America and around the world do their share, then most everything will have changed by the time we come out of this economic Tsunami mess. In addition, I argue that we can and should change everything for the better.

My admiration goes to outstanding heroes like Captain Sully that saves 154 lives (and perhaps even more) and says that he was just doing his job. It also goes to those everyday heroes listed that worked and sent their kids to college.

In addition, by writing this book I like to send a serenade to our enterprise heroes like Paul Allen, Sir Richard Bronson, Fredrick Smith, and others. The message is that we are in a serious economic tsunami as Greenspan called it. America, UK, France, and all of the Western World governments are in this mess together. Governments cannot fix this disaster alone. The small business, even though it is the backbone of our economy, cannot alone fix this. Yet combination of us working together, we can do this! Moreover, we can even make a better world for humanity while we make more and more money.

This book is meant to be a blueprint for successful workers and workplaces of the future, and it provides practical alternatives to layoffs such as Intel's one-hundred-and-ten-percent productivity, HP's reduced working hours for all employees that enabled that company to avoided layoff of even a single employee for more than fifty years.

As a proud American, I applaud America as the leader of free-market economy and continue to have faith in America to be the world's expected leader in the economy that it

Copyright © 2008 - 2009 Razban Internet International, Inc. All rights reserved, File:20091022, Page | **262**

has been forever. I am highly confident that a combination of small businesses like my tiny company, Razban Internet International, Inc., will use that American ingenuity and know how will re-invent us and our business to create win-win solutions again.

ABOUT THE AUTHOR:

The Author, Bruce B. Razban, has over 32 years of management and technology experience and considers himself a technologist and a people-oriented senior manager. In his management practice, he himself has suffered from a constant fear of Sudden Job Loss (SJL) "syndrome" and related phrase of Pink Shock. He strongly believes SJL can be just as real and painful as the well-known fear of flying syndrome.

He has had first-hand experience as a manager who had to lay off employees, and as an employee who himself was fired for no reason, laid off, down-sized and sent out, out sourced, forced into semi-retirement, down-shifted, whose career was derailed, etc.

As a manager, he has felt emotional pains that any manager goes through to lay off employees. In addition, as an employee he has also felt the emotional and financial pains of layoffs including, but not limited to depression, rejection, humiliation, fighting an uphill struggle to get back on his knees, the anger, the lack of productivity, and so on.

Without blaming management, employees, companies, and even customers, this book establishes that layoffs are dysfunctional, ineffective, and in general, they harm all parties involved, including community.

While the author's empathy and sympathy, even as an experienced senior manager, goes to the affected employees, the second half of this book offers time-tested management, employee, organizational, business, and management solutions to prevent, or at least minimize the devastating impact. In addition, we hope that we use this experience for future success.

We have no intention, directly or implied to blame any group of people such as managers, employees, or companies in this book.

Yet the author's dream and passion is that, by mutual understanding of the layoffs, we can invent a better way, even though, until now, the record is abysmal for an invention of a better way to avoid such practices.

However, this book insists that there is a better and easier way than layoffs and firings to prevent the $2.4 Trillion waste each year in the American workplace alone!

DISCLAIMER:

Mr. Razban refers to many companies, people, and situations in this book.
Please take into consideration that what he describes here is his own opinion. There is no intended or implied blame for any company, people, or situations. In addition, this book does not endorse any company, person, or situation unconditionally.
In fact, the main focus of this book is for those affected by layoffs (as the managers who have had to administer it or the individuals who were at the receiving end) to:

- Understand the inner workings and reasons for layoffs as a way to make the pain and impact less on all involved,
- Give hope to all involved that it is really not their fault,
- Propose a better solution as an alternative to layoffs.

In addition, please note that we did not consult any of the companies or people mentioned in this book in advance about this book. Mr. Razban did this to make sure that the book is not influenced by anything else except Mr. Razban's deep and heartfelt ideas, interpretations, and experience.
As such, the ideas presented in this book are Mr. Razban's understanding and interpretation.
In addition, this book and the author are meant to be respectful to all people, all nations, all religions, or entities, all cultures, all governments, and all ideas.
The main purpose for this book was to help others who are having a hard time with unemployment, underemployment, and unhappy employments and Mr. Razban admits that these ideas reflect mainly American and European points of view and experience. This can be right or wrong.
Please contact him at bruce@Razban.com if you have a feedback, question, comment, or correction. It is greatly appreciated in advance. You can also find the author in Twitter as BehrouzR.
In addition, Google.com was heavily used in many finding many quotations, pictures, and facts. Mr. Razban sincerely thanks Google.com.

COVER DESIGN:

The following people helped the design of the cover of this book:
Dana Razban created the idea and the initial concept.
Hannah Razban reviewed and critiqued many different initial designs and created an original design of her own. My portrait on the back cover is also Hannah's photographic work. Hannah took my portrait picture in a restaurant that is inside the old Delta King Paddle ship of Mark Twain era. The ship has become a hotel, restaurant, and theater tourist site. The restaurant serves excellent fresh food. In addition, we can go upstairs, sit on the deck of the ship, and enjoy a nice drink from the bar. The service is also superb. Taking the Amtrak from San Jose for a day trip to Sacramento and enjoying lunch at this restaurant has been an excellent way to avoid cabin fever when I am in between jobs!
Larry Larsen from www.lorenzonet.com was the graphic artist and technologist that created the final cover design used for this book.
I also like to thank several people from Barnes and Nobel in Hillsdale, and Kepler's Bookstore in Menlo Park, for their review and comments regarding improvements to the cover design.
In addition, I want to say thanks to the family whom I met in a Sunnyvale, CA McDonald who cheerfully gave me the permission to take a picture of their family stick figures on the rear window of their SUV.
In several photography books and classes, I have learned that we can actually read a photograph as much as you can look at it.
The cover of this book uses the one-third rule. This means that we have divided the cover picture into three distinct parts:

- The top one third with clear skies and seagull, attempts to depict the mental image of freedom. Something like, we are free and the sky is the limit idea. This is graphical rendition of hope in the title.
- The middle one third with cloudy skies and a barely visible seagull in the lower left corner, braving an overwhelming amount of clouds, depicts our struggle with the unhappy work place or unemployment.
- The bottom one third is the empty parking lot of a workplace. We show the typical non-distinct work place in the upper right side of this part. The empty parking lot is a sad reminder, symbol, and after effect of layoffs. Yet the most important thing here is the stick figure of a family. Family, especially in a single income family, is usually the one that feels the pain of layoffs the worst.
- The shadow in the lowest right side of the picture seems to be one of someone praying. When, I took this picture, I was not aware of this shadow. However, I did not notice its particular shape that does have a strong resemblance to someone, who might be even beyond hope and is praying.
- Finally, the red flower in the lower right corner is a college tradition of mine. Then I could not afford to buy flowers from stores. Therefore, I would pick just one and only one flower from my dorm's garden, put it in a paper cup with water, and admire life and nature's beauty and goodness. As we added that to the cover, it became clear to me that unconsciously, I was trying to tell the recent college graduates who have graduated in one of the worst economical times that there is hope and we will survive! Some of these college graduates have $90,000 student

Copyright © 2008 - 2009 Razban Internet International, Inc. All rights reserved, File:20091022, P a g e | **266**

loans and in can feel their pain. Like them, I graduated in one of the worst times. Yet, 32 years later, I am still OK. I am not rich! Nevertheless, I did OK. In addition, I am proud to have a message of hope to give.

ADDITIONAL RECOMMENDED READINGS:

Lair, Jess Ph.D. *I Ain't Much, Baby—But I'm All I've Got.* (Paperback - Mar 1, 1995)
Kubler-Ross, Elizabeth. *On Death & Dying* (Paperback)
Ziglar, Zig. *See You at the Top: 25th Anniversary Edition.* by (Hardcover - Aug 30, 2000)
Drucker, Peter F. *Management: Tasks, Responsibilities, Practices* (April 14, 1993)
Management Challenges for the 21st Century (Jun 26, 2001) by Peter F. Drucker
The Practice of Management (Oct 3, 2006) by Peter F. Drucker
Out of the Shadows: Understanding Sexual Addiction by Patrick J. Carnes (Paperback - May 1, 2001)
The Three Trillion Dollar War: The True Cost of the Iraq Conflict (Sep 17, 2008) by Linda J. Bilmes and Joseph E. Stiglitz
Of Dreams and Deeds: The Story of Optimist International (Hardcover - 1983)
How to Stop Worrying and Start Living (Oct 5, 2004) by Dale Carnegie
How to Win Friends & Influence People (Oct 1, 1998) by Dale Carnegie
How to Develop Self-Confidence And Influence People By Public Speaking (May 31, 1991) by Dale Carnegie
Rubaiyat of Omar Khayyam (Dec 2002) by Edward Fitzgerald
The Quatrains of Omar Khayyam: Three translations of the Rubaiyat (Jul 2, 2005) by Omar Khayyam, Justin, Huntley McCarthy, and Richard Le Gallienne
The Book of Psalms: A Translation with Commentary by Robert Alter (Hardcover - Sep 10, 2007)
The Book of Psalms: In the Authorized Version by David Fordham (Hardcover - Oct 1986)
The Book of Psalms: The New Translation According to the Traditional Hebrew Text by Jewish Publication Society of America (Hardcover - April 1997)
The Book of Miracles: The Healing Work of Joao de Deus by Josie Ravenwing (Paperback - Mar 1, 2002)
A Course in Miracles by Dr. Helen Schucman and Foundation for Inner Peace (Paperback - Sep 30, 2007)
Bible Code II: The Countdown
Paperback by Michael Drosnin
JPS TANAKH/ The Jewish Bible by Jewish Publication Society (Hardcover - Mar 8, 2007)
The Essential Kabbalah: The Heart of Jewish Mysticism by Daniel C. Matt (Paperback - May 10, 1996)
The Power of Kabbalah: Technology for the Soul by Yehuda Berg (Hardcover - Jul 26, 2004)
The Lion and the Throne: Stories from the Shahnameh of Ferdowsi, Vol. 1 by Abolqasem Ferdowsi and Dick Davis (Hardcover - Jan 1998)
Fathers and Sons: Stories from the Shahnameh of Ferdowsi, Vol. 2 (v. 2) by Abolqasem Ferdowsi and Dick Davis (Hardcover - Jul 2000)
The Legend of Seyavash (Persian Classics) by Abolqasem Ferdowsi and Dick Davis (Paperback - Mar 2004)
Night Flight by Antoine de Saint-Exupéry and Stuart Gilbert (Paperback - Mar 20, 1974)
Wind, Sand and Stars by Antoine de Saint-Exupery (Paperback - Dec 9, 2002)
Night Flight: Charles Lindbergh's Incredible Adventure: Charles Lindbergh's Incredible Adventure (All Aboard Reading) by S. A. Kramer and Dan Andreasen (Paperback - Feb 18, 2002)
Life After Layoff: Six Proven Courses of Action by Richard J Van Ness Phd and Edith M Donohue Phd (Paperback - Sep 2, 2004
Healing the Wounds: Overcoming the Trauma of Layoffs and Revitalizing Downsized Organizations (Jossey Bass Business and Management Series) by David M. Noer (Paperback - Mar 16, 1995
The Disposable American: Layoffs and Their Consequences by Louis Uchitelle (Paperback -

Copyright © 2008 - 2009 Razban Internet International, Inc. All rights reserved, File:20091022.

April 10, 2007
Surviving A Layoff by Theresa Banks (Perfect Paperback - Jun 7, 2008
Since the Layoffs by Iain Levison (Paperback - May 1, 2004
Surviving a Layoff: A Week-by-Week Guide to Getting Your Life Back Together by Lita Epstein (Paperback - Jan 17, 2009)
Industrial Inefficiency and Downsizing: A Study of Layoffs and Plant Closures (Garland Studies on Industrial Productivity) by Matthew Krepps (Hardcover - Sep 1, 1997
Practical Money Making-Surviving Recession, Layoffs, Credit Problems, Generating Passive Income Streams, Working Full Time or Part Time and Retirement by Kim Isaac Greenblatt (Paperback - Aug 23, 2008)
Responsible Restructuring: Creative and Profitable Alternatives to Layoffs by Wayne F Cascio (Hardcover - Aug 2002) – Illustrated
Maintaining morale by handling layoffs humanely. (Issues@work).: An article from: Fairfield County Business Journal by Rose Redding Mersky (Digital - Jul 30, 2005) - HTML
Reinventing Your Career: Surviving a Layoff and Creating New Opportunities by Stephen P. Adams (Paperback - Oct 1996
Layoffs by D.M. Read (Paperback - Dec 20, 2004
No-layoff policies and corporate financial performance.: An article from: SAM Advanced Management Journal by Peter Allan and Peter H. Loseby (Digital - Jul 28, 2005) -
Electric Railways Around San Francisco Bay: Bay Area Rapid Transit-East Bay Transit Interurban Electric (Sp)-Key System (Electric Railways Around San Francisco Bay) by Donald Duke (Paperback - Sep 1999)
Transit Maps of the World by Mark Ovenden and Mike Ashworth (Paperback - Oct 30, 2007)
Guerrilla Marketing for Job Hunters: 400 Unconventional Tips, Tricks, and Tactics for Landing Your Dream Job by Jay Conrad Levinson and David Perry (Paperback - Sep 29, 2005
The Unwritten Rules of the Highly Effective Job Search: The Proven Program Used by the Worlds Leading Career Services Company by Orville Pierson (Hardcover - Dec 16, 2005)
The Job Search Solution: The Ultimate System for Finding a Great Job Now! by Tony Beshara (Paperback - Jan 2, 2006)
Job Hunting for Dummies by Max Messmer, Robert Half, and Max Messmer Jr. (Hardcover - Feb 1, 2001)
Job Hunting Online: A Guide to Using Job Listings, Message Boards, Research Sites, the Underweb, Counseling, Networking Self-Assessment Tools, Niche Sties (Job Hunting on the Internet (Online)) by Mark Emery Bolles and Richard Nelson Bolles (Paperback - May 2008)
What Does Somebody Have to Do to Get a Job Around Here?: 44 Insider Secrets That Will Get You Hired by Cynthia Shapiro (Paperback - April 1, 2008)
Job Hunting Online: A Guide to Using Job Listings, Message Boards, Research Sites, the Underweb, Counseling, Networking Self-Assessment Tools, Niche Sties (Job Hunting on the Internet (Online)) by Mark Emery Bolles and Richard Nelson Bolles (Paperback - May 2008)
Knock 'em Dead 2009: The Ultimate Job Search Guide (Knock 'em Dead) by Martin Yate (Paperback - Oct 17, 2008)
Job Hunting Tips for People With Not-So-Hot Backgrounds: 101 Smart Tips That Can Change Your Life (Career Savvy) by Ron Krannich (Paperback - Feb 25, 2005)
10 Insider Secrets to a Winning Job Search by Todd Bermont (Paperback - Mar 15, 2004)
What Color Is Your Parachute? 2008: A Practical Manual for Job-hunters and Career-Changers by Richard Nelson Bolles (Hardcover - Oct 2007)
What Color Is Your Parachute? 2009: A Practical Manual for Job-Hunters and Career-Changers by Richard Nelson Bolles (Paperback - Oct 2008)
301 Smart Answers to Tough Interview Questions by Vicky Oliver (Paperback - May 1, 2005)
Job-hunting and Career Change All-in-one for Dummies by Rob Yeung (Paperback - Dec 14, 2007)

Copyright © 2008 - 2009 Razban Internet International, Inc. All rights reserved, File:20091022, P a g e | **269**

The AMA Guide to Management Development by Daniel R. Tobin and Margaret Pettingell (Hardcover - May 27, 2008)

Up the Organization: How to Stop the Corporation from Stifling People and Strangling Profits (J-B Warren Bennis Series) by Robert C. Townsend and Warren Bennis (Paperback - May 25, 2007)

Further Up the Organization: How Groups of People Working Together for a Common Purpose Ought to Conduct Themselves for Fun and Profit by Robert Townsend (Paperback - Jan 1988)

Power Up: Transforming Organizations Through Shared Leadership by David L. Bradford and Allan R. Cohen (Hardcover - Feb 1998)

Working With You is Killing Me: Freeing Yourself from Emotional Traps at Work by Katherine Crowley and Kathi Elster (Paperback - Mar 14, 2007

Coping with Toxic Managers, Subordinates ... and Other Difficult People: Using Emotional Intelligence to Survive and Prosper (Financial Times Prentice Hall Books) by Roy H. Lubit (Paperback - Nov 27, 2003)

The No Asshole Rule: Building a Civilized Workplace and Surviving One That Isn't by Robert I. Sutton (Hardcover - Feb 22, 2007)

You Want Me to Work with Who?: Eleven Keys to a Stress-Free, Satisfying, and Successful Work Life . . . No Matter Who You Work With by Julie Jansen (Paperback - Feb 28, 2006)

Dealing with People You Can't Stand: How to Bring Out the Best in People at Their Worst by Dr. Rick Brinkman and Dr. Rick Kirschner (Paperback - Feb 27, 2002)

Toxic Coworkers: How to Deal with Dysfunctional People on the Job by Alan A., Ph.D. Cavaiola and Neil J., Ph.D. Lavender (Paperback - Jan 15, 2000)

I Don't Know What I Want, But I Know It's Not This: A Step-by-Step Guide to Finding Gratifying Work by Julie Jansen (Paperback - Jan 28, 2003)

A Survival Guide for Working With Bad Bosses: Dealing With Bullies, Idiots, Back-stabbers, And Other Managers from Hell by Gini Graham Scott (Paperback - Nov 25, 2005)

When Bad Things Happen to Good People by Harold S. Kushner (Paperback - Aug 24, 2004)

Living a Life that Matters by Harold S. Kushner (Paperback - Aug 20, 2002)

I Wasn't Ready to Say Goodbye: Surviving, Coping and Healing After the Sudden Death of a Loved One by Pamela D. Blair Ph.D. (Paperback - May 1, 2003)

How Good Do We Have to Be? A New Understanding of Guilt and Forgiveness by Harold S. Kushner (Paperback - Sep 1, 1997)

Why Good People Do Bad Things: How to Stop Being Your Own Worst Enemy by Debbie Ford (Hardcover - Mar 11, 2008)

Overcoming Life's Disappointments by Harold S. Kushner (Paperback - Aug 21, 2007

The HP Way: How Bill Hewlett and I Built Our Company (Collins Business Essentials) by David Packard (Paperback - Jan 3, 2006)

1001 Ways to Energize Employees by Bob Nelson, Ken Blanchard, and Barton Morris (Paperback - May 1, 1997)

ABBA - Gold: Greatest Hits for Easy Piano by ABBA (Paperback - Sep 1, 2006)

The Very Best of Abba by Dannhauser, A. L., and A. l. Dannhauser (Paperback - Mar 1, 1985)

ABBA Thank You For The Music by Robert Scott (Paperback - Jul 1, 2003)

The Little Book of Abba by Claire Welch (Hardcover - Oct 23, 2007)

The New York Times Great Songs of ABBA. (Words and music [mainly] by Benny Andersson & Björn Ulvaeus.) Arranged and edited by Milton Okun. (Associate music editor-Dan Fox.) by Abba, Milton Okun, and Dan Fox (Paperback - 1980) – Import

PETULA CLARK Une Baladine by Francoise Piazza (Paperback – 2008)

Pet Clark Hits [Songbook] by Petula Clark (Paperback – 1966)

On the Firing Line: My 500 Days at Apple by Gil Amelio and William Simon (Paperback - April 7, 1999)

Profit from Experience: The National Semiconductor Story of Transformation Management by Gil Amelio and William L. Simon (Paperback - Nov 1995)

Amelio defines Apple's product roadmap for Next's Web Objects tool.(Apple Computer Inc. CEO Gil Amelio; NeXT Software Inc.; World Wide Wen development ... An article from: Software Industry Report (Digital - Jun 1, 2005) – HTML

A Survival Guide for Working With Bad Bosses: Dealing With Bullies, Idiots, Back-stabbers, And Other Managers from Hell by Gini Graham Scott (Paperback - Nov 25, 2005)

How to Work for an Idiot: Survive & Thrive— Without Killing Your Boss by John Hoover (Paperback - Nov 2003)

Bad Bosses, Crazy Coworkers & Other Office Idiots: 201 Smart Ways to Handle the Toughest People Issues by Vicky Oliver (Paperback - Sep 1, 2008)

Defective Bosses: Working for the "Dysfunctional Dozen" (Haworth Marketing Resources : Innovations in Practice & Professional Services) by William Winston, Kerry D Carson, and Paula P Carson (Hardcover - Oct 1, 1998)

I Think There's A Terrorist In My Soup: How to Survive Personal and World Problems with Laughter - Seriously by David Brenner (Paperback - Sep 1, 2003)

Hitotsubashi on Knowledge Management (Feb 9, 2004) by Hirotaka Takeuchi and Ikujiro Nonaka

Lexus Story by Johnathan Mahler, Maximillian Potter, and Denny Clements (Hardcover - 2004)

NO MARGIN FOR ERROR: The Making of the Israeli Air Force by Ehud Yonay (Hardcover - April 13, 1993)

On Eagles' Wings: The Personal Story of the Leading Commander of the Israeli Air Force by Ezer Weizman (Hardcover - Jun 1977)

El Al: Star in the Sky by Marvin G. Goldman (Hardcover - Sep 1990)

Ernest Hemingway's The Old Man and the Sea (Bloom's Modern Critical Interpretations) by Harold Bloom (Hardcover - Jul 30, 2008)

The Old Man and the Sea by Ernest Hemingway (Paperback - Mar 1981)

Old Man and the Sea by Ernest Hemingway (Hardcover - 1952)

Real Change Leaders: How You Can Create Growth and High Performance at Your Company by Jon R. Katzenbach (Paperback - Jun 10, 1997)

Technology Blueprints: Technology Foundations for High Performance Companies by James M. Butler (Paperback - Sep 2003)

High Performance with High Integrity (Memo to the CEO) by Ben W. and Jr. Heineman (Hardcover - May 28, 2008)

High Performance Nonprofit Organizations: Managing Upstream for Greater Impact by Christine W. Letts, William P. Ryan, and Allen Grossman (Hardcover - Oct 16, 1998)

Revitalize Your Corporate Culture: Powerful Ways to Transform Your Company into a High-Performance Organization by PH.D., FRANKLIN C. ASHBY (Hardcover - Aug 27, 1999)

Product Strategy for High Technology Companies by Michael E. McGrath (Hardcover - Oct 12, 2000)

The Paradox Principles: How High Performance Companies Manage Chaos Complexity and Contradiction to Achieve Superior Results by Price Waterhouse LLP (Hardcover - Sep 1, 1995)

The Knowledge Dividend: Creating high-performance companies through value-based knowledge management by Rene Tissen, Daniel Andriessen, and Frank Lekanne Deprez (Paperback - Dec 22, 2000)

Shared Purpose: Working Together to Build Strong Families and High-Performance Companies by Maria G. Mackavey, Richard J. Levin, and American Management association (Hardcover - Dec 17, 1997)

Business Without Bosses: How Self-Managing Teams Are Building High-Performance Companies by Henry P. Sims (Hardcover - Jan 1, 1993)

Who Moved My Cheese?: An Amazing Way to Deal with Change in Your Work and in Your Life by Spencer Johnson and Kenneth Blanchard (Hardcover - Sep 8, 1998)

Who Stole My Cheese? by Ilene Hochberg (Hardcover - Jul 13, 2003)

The Five Temptations of a CEO: A Leadership Fable by Patrick M. Lencioni (Hardcover - Jun 23, 2008) - Special Edition

Jesus, CEO: Using Ancient Wisdom for Visionary Leadership by Laurie Beth Jones (Paperback - April 18, 1996)

What the CEO Wants You to Know : How Your Company Really Works by Ram Charan (Hardcover - Feb 13, 2001)

Speak Like a CEO: Secrets for Commanding Attention and Getting Results: Secrets for Communicating Attention and Getting Results by Suzanne Bates (Hardcover - Mar 31, 2005)

How to Become CEO: The Rules for Rising to the Top of Any Organization by Jeffrey J. Fox (Hardcover - Sep 30, 1998)

CEO Tools: The Nuts-n-Bolts of Business for every Manager's Success by Kraig Kramers (Paperback - Dec 2002)

CEO Logic : How to Think and Act Like a Chief Executive by C. Ray Johnson (Paperback - May 15, 1999)

Why CEO's Fail: The 11 Behaviors That Can Derail Your Climb to the Top and How to Manage Them by David L., PhD Dotlich, Peter C., PhD Cairo, PhD, David L. Dotlich, and PhD, Peter C. Cairo (Hardcover - April 15, 2003)

New Ideas from Dead CEOs: Lasting Lessons from the Corner Office by Todd G. Buchholz (Hardcover - May 8, 2007)

Campus CEO: The Student Entrepreneur's Guide to Launching a Multi-Million-Dollar Business by Randal Pinkett (Paperback - Feb 1, 2007)

Secrets of a CEO Coach: Your Personal Training Guide to Thinking Like a Leader and Acting Like a CEO by D. A. Benton (Paperback - May 23, 2000)

The Big Book of Small Business: You Don't Have to Run Your Business by the Seat of Your Pants by Tom Gegax and Phil Bolsta (Hardcover - Feb 6, 2007)

Small Business For Dummies (For Dummies (Business & Personal Finance)) by Eric Tyson and Jim Schell (Paperback - Mar 4, 2008)

Small Business Start-Up Kit by Peri H. Pakroo and Catherine Caputo (Paperback - Jan 30, 2008)

The Small Business Owner's Manual: Everything You Need To Know To Start Up And Run Your Business by Joe Kennedy (Paperback - Jun 2005)

How to Succeed as a Small Business Owner ... and Still Have a Life by Bill Collier (Paperback - Jun 30, 2006)

Start Your Own Business by Rieva Lesonsky (Paperback - Mar 7, 2007)

The Small Business Bible: Everything You Need to Know to Succeed in Your Small Business by Steven D. Strauss (Paperback - Sep 16, 2008)

The 4-Hour Workweek: Escape 9-5, Live Anywhere, and...

Hardcover by Timothy Ferriss

The Paris Metro: A Ticket to French History by Susan L. Plotkin (Paperback - April 18, 2001)

BAA Ltd: a report on the economic regulation of the London airports companies (Heathrow Airport Ltd and Gatwick Airport Ltd) by Competition Commission (Paperback - Oct 16, 2007) – Import

Air Traveller's Guide to London Heathrow International Airport (Jetset Air Travellers Guides) (Paperback - May 12, 1997)

London Heathrow: The World's Busiest International Airport by Freddy Bullock (Paperback - Oct 12, 1999)

Pour Your Heart Into It: How Starbucks Built a Company One Cup at a Time by Howard Schultz and Dori Jones Yang (Paperback - Jan 6, 1999)

It's Not About the Coffee: Leadership Principles from a Life at Starbucks by Howard Behar (Hardcover - Dec 27, 2007)

The Starbucks Experience: 5 Principles for Turning Ordinary Into Extraordinary by Joseph Michelli (Hardcover - Sep 14, 2006)

Starbucks' Schultz reveals how firm keeps perking. (Starbucks Coffee Corp. Chmn and CEO Howard Schultz): An article from: San Diego Business Journal by Liz Harman (Digital - Jul 28, 2005)

The Unemployment Survival Guide by Jim Stringham and David R Workman (Hardcover - Mar 8, 2004)

Fired, Laid Off or Forced Out: A Complete Guide to Severance, Benefits and Your Rights When You're Starting Over by Richard C. Busse (Paperback - Feb 1, 2005)

Hardest Times: The Trauma of Long-Term Unemployment by Thomas J. Cottle (Paperback - Dec 2003)

The Joys of Unemployment by Jim Hayes (Paperback - Jul 15, 1998)

The Job Loss Recovery Guide: A Proven Program for Getting Back to Work — Fast! by Lynn Joseph (Paperback - Jun 2003)

Surviving Unemployment: Staying Centered While Your World Turns Upside Down by Valerie Pederson (Paperback - Aug 4, 2005)

Career Comeback: Eight steps to getting back on your feet when you're fired, laid off, or your business ventures has failed—and finding more job satisfaction than ever before by Bradley Richardson (Paperback - Jan 6, 2004)

The Leader in Me: How Schools and Parents Around the World Are Inspiring Greatness, One Child At a Time by Stephen R. Covey (Hardcover - Nov 18, 2008)

The 7 Habits of Highly Effective People by Stephen R. Covey (Paperback - Nov 9, 2004)

The SPEED of Trust: The One Thing That Changes Everything by Stephen M.R. Covey, Stephen R. Covey, and Rebecca R. Merrill (Paperback - Feb 5, 2008)

Living the 7 Habits : The Courage to Change by Stephen R. Covey (Paperback - Mar 14, 2000)

Quest: Discovering Your Human Potential (Quest (Simon & Schuster)) by Deepak Chopra, Steven Covey, Thomas Moore, and Bernie Siegel (Audio Cassette - Dec 1, 1996)

The 8th Habit: From Effectiveness to Greatness: Miniature Edition by Stephen R. Covey (Hardcover - May 29, 2006)

Principle Centered Leadership by Stephen R. Covey (Paperback - Oct 1, 1992)

The 7 Habits for Managers: Managing Yourself, Leading Others, Unleashing Potential by Stephen R. Covey (Audio CD - Mar 20, 2007)

The Human Side of High Performance: Empowering Yourself for the Future by Steven B. Wiley (Hardcover - Jan 1998)

Alcoholics Anonymous: The Story of How Many Thousands of Men and Women Have Recovered from Alcoholism/Third Edition by Anonymous

Alcoholics Anonymous: Big Book, Original Edition (Hardcover - Jul 26, 2007)

Compulsive Overeater: The Basic Text for Compulsive Overeaters by Bill B (Hardcover - Jan 1, 1988)

Twelve Steps For Overeaters Anonymous: An Interpretation Of The Twelve Steps Of Overeaters Anonymous by Elisabeth L.

Forgive for Good by Frederic Luskin (Paperback - Jan 21, 2003)

Forgiveness Is a Choice: A Step-By-Step Process for Resolving Anger and Restoring Hope (Apa Lifetools) by Robert D. Enright (Hardcover - May 2001)

How to Forgive Ourselves — Totally: Begin Again by Breaking Free from Past Mistakes by R. T. Kendall (Paperback - Sep 4, 2007)

Focus on the Good Stuff: The Power of Appreciation by Mike Robbins and Richard Carlson (Hardcover - Aug 24, 2007)

Van Gogh: The Complete Paintings (Klotz) by Ingo F Walther and Rainer Metzger (Paperback - Jun 1, 2006) – Illustrated

Vincent Van Gogh: A Self-Portrait in Art and Letters by H. Anna Suh (Hardcover - Oct 30, 2006)

Van Gogh Paintings: The Masterpieces by Belinda Thomson (Hardcover - Sep 15, 2007)

The Van Gogh Blues: The Creative Person's Path through Depression by Eric Maisel (Paperback

- Dec 28, 2007)
Vincent Van Gogh: The potato eaters, in the collection of V. W. Van Gogh, Amsterdam (The Gallery books) by Jan Gerrit van Gelder (Unknown Binding - 1947)
Stranger On The Earth: A Psychological Biography Of Vincent Van Gogh by Albert J. Lubin (Paperback - Aug 21, 1996)
Van Gogh : La Lumière du midi by Sylvie Gaché-Patin and serge Briez (Paperback - May 20, 1997)
Vincent Van Gogh Paintings,Watercolors And Drawings The Washington Gallery Of Modern Art(2 February 1964-19 March 1964) The Solomon R. Gugenheim Museum(2 April 1962-28 June 1964(Exhibition Catalog) by Washington Gallery of Modern Art and Solomon R. Gugenheim Museum (Paperback - 1964)
Management Skills for New Managers by Carol W. Ellis (Paperback - Jul 30, 2004)
Innovation: The Five Disciplines for Creating What Customers Want by Curtis R. Carlson and William W. Wilmot (Hardcover - Aug 8, 2006)
The Ten Faces of Innovation: IDEO's Strategies for Defeating the Devil's Advocate and Driving Creativity Throughout Your Organization by Thomas Kelley and Jonathan Littman (Hardcover - Oct 18, 2005)
Diffusion of Innovations, 5th Edition by Everett M. Rogers and Everett Rogers (Paperback - Aug 16, 2003)
The Myths of Innovation by Scott Berkun (Hardcover - May 15, 2007)
The New Age of Innovation: Driving Cocreated Value Through Global Networks by C.K. Prahalad and M.S. Krishnan (Hardcover - April 8, 2008)
The Art of Innovation: Lessons in Creativity from IDEO, America's Leading Design Firm by Tom Kelley, Jonathan Littman, Tom Peters, and Tom Peters
Disrupting Class: How Disruptive Innovation Will Change the Way the World Learn Making Innovation Work: How to Manage It, Measure It, and Profit from It by Tony Davila, Marc J. Epstein, and Robert Sheltons by Clayton Christensen, Curtis W. Johnson, and Michael B. Horn
Innovation and Entrepreneurship by Peter F. Drucker (Paperback - May 9, 2006)
Inc. Yourself: How to Profit by Setting up Your Own Corporation (Inc Yourself) by Judith H. McQuown (Paperback - Jun 2004)
How to Incorporate: A Handbook for Entrepreneurs and Professionals by Michael R. Diamond (Paperback - Jun 29, 2007)
Nuts! Southwest Airlines' Crazy Recipe for Business and Personal Success by Kevin Freiberg and Jackie Freiberg (Paperback - Feb 17, 1998)
Lessons in Loyalty: How Southwest Airlines Does It - An Insider's View by Lorraine Grubbs-West (Paperback - Aug 1, 2005)
Do the Right Thing: How Dedicated Employees Create Loyal Customers and Large Profits by James F. Parker (Hardcover - Nov 30, 2007)
Nuts!: Southwest Airlines' Crazy Recipe for Business and Personal Success by Jackie Freiberg and Kevin Freiberg (Paperback - Aug 2, 2001)
LUV is in the Air at Southwest Airlines by Bob, Ph.D. Nelson (Digital - Oct 1,
The Southwest Airlines Way by Jody Hoffer Gittell (Paperback - April 14, 2005
The Nordstrom Way to Customer Service Excellence: A Handbook For Implementing Great Service in Your Organization by Robert Spector (Paperback - Mar 8, 2005)
JAPANESE PROVERBS AND SAYINGS by Daniel, Crump Buchanan (**Paperback** - Mar 15, 1973)
Between Jobs: Keeping Faith and Hope Alive by Daniel J. Welte (Pamphlet – Liguori Publications)

Copyright © 2008 - 2009 Razban Internet International, Inc. All rights reserved, File:20091022, P a g e | **274**

It is hoped that this book will do and be the following for you:

- A Mild Over-the-Counter Anti-Depressant supplement in paper form for work-life blues in the age of economic Armageddon and Recession. Of course, this is not a prescription.
- To help you with toxic work place, this book is like Dale Carnegie's Book on *How to Enjoy Your Work and Your Life*.
- It is also similar to Steinbeck's book on life in California, which a sort of entertaining and site seeing tone to make the subject of layoffs more palatable. It even has a sense of humor.
- In spite the subject, this is an inspirational book to give you hope and advice in a very difficult time. We can survive exactly as this book says we can!
- It can help us 'not to just sit there' after my awful and unexpected layoff and sing all the way to finding a better career.
- This is a practical 'how to' advice from a seasoned manager. Written in an entertaining and interesting language that is easy to understand and put to use.
- It will help you realize that you are not alone in this mess and that it was not all your fault.
- This book will help you forgive your manager for your layoff and move on to better things.
- A must read for every 'work a day' people like you and me, or even executives, to better understand that there is a better way than stupid layoffs to break the chain of foolish things ruining people's work and even their lives.

I think that after twelve years, I have nailed the subject of layoffs, unemployment, underemployment, and unhappy employment down in this book.

www.ingramcontent.com/pod-product-compliance
Lightning Source LLC
Chambersburg PA
CBHW072032190526
45165CB00017B/169

* 9 7 8 1 4 3 9 2 2 7 4 0 4 *